BLACK PERFORMANCE AND CULTURAL CRITICISM

VALERIE LEE AND E. PATRICK JOHNSON, SERIES EDITORS

BEYOND LIFT EVERY VOICE AND SING

The Culture of Uplift, Identity, and Politics in Black Musical Theater

~

Paula Marie Seniors

THE OHIO STATE UNIVERSITY PRESS
COLUMBUS

Library of Congress Cataloging-in-Publication Data
Seniors, Paula Marie.
   Beyond lift every voice and sing : the culture of uplift, identity, and politics in black musical theater / Paula Marie Seniors.
      p. cm. — (Black performance and cultural criticism)
   Includes bibliographical references and index.
   ISBN-13: 978-0-8142-1100-7 (cloth : alk. paper)
   ISBN-10: 0-8142-1100-3 (cloth : alk. paper)
   1. African Americans in musical theater—History. 2. Musical theater—United States—History. 3. Johnson, James Weldon, 1871–1938. 4. Johnson, J. Rosamond (John Rosamond), 1873–1954. 5. Cole, Bob, 1868–1911. I. Title.
   ML1711.S46 2009
   792.6089'96073—dc22
                                    2008048102

This book is available in the following editions:

Cloth (ISBN 978-0-8142-1100-7)
CD-ROM (ISBN 978-0-8142-9198-6)

Cover design by Laurence Nozik.
Type set in Adobe Sabon.
Text design by Jennifer Shoffey Forsythe.
Printed by Thomson-Shore, Inc.

∞ The paper used in this publication meets the minimum requirements of the American National Standard for Information Sciences—Permanence of Paper for Printed Library Materials. ANSI Z39.48-1992.

9 8 7 6 5 4 3 2 1

This book is dedicated to my scholar activist parents

AUDREY PROCTOR SENIORS

CLARENCE HENRY SENIORS

AND TO MISS PARK SENIORS

Their life lessons and love nurtured me.
My parents modeled their activism after
the quintessential
African American scholar activist

PAUL ROBESON

gave me his name, and educated me by example about
the importance of African American and ethnic studies,
history, culture, learning, knowledge, and scholarship.
I dedicate this book to my parents and Park
with the sincerest and purest love and admiration.

CONTENTS

ILLUSTRATIONS

~

ACKNOWLEDGMENTS

I WOULD LIKE TO thank the New York City opera diva Dr. Linda Elliott and Dr. Susan Hayes of New York University for encouraging me to pursue the master's degree and the PhD at a incredibly difficult turning point in my life, when I was grieving for the death of my cherished mommy and struggling with the transition from dancer and singer and wrestling with moving beyond a performance career. They provided comfort, unbending support and guidance, and compelled me to take the leap into academia. Miss Kharen Fulton, Director of Graduate Admissions at Emory University, steered me through this transition and I count her as a true friend. I cannot express how much these women mean to me, how much I cherish their friendship, or how grateful I am to them for guiding me at that sorrowful juncture in my life. The Department of Ethnic Studies at University of California, San Diego provided a rich environment for scholarship. They also gave me travel grants, a research grant, and a dissertation fellowship. I thank the department wholeheartedly for helping me to make a smooth transition from dancer and singer to scholar, no small feat indeed.

I must express my gratitude to Sandy Crooms, Senior Editor at Ohio State University Press, who proved one of the most supportive, understanding, patient, and kind persons in this whole process, and she is a dog person! What else can you ask for in an editor? I am so thankful that I met her and that she accepted *Beyond Lift Every Voice and Sing,* although by the time I finished with the corrections, I had written two books.

Thank you, Valerie Lee and E. Patrick Johnson, editors of Black Performance and Cultural Criticism Series, for including my book in their series. I also must thank Eugene O'Connor, the in-house editor, and Benjamin Shriver, the copy editor for The Ohio State University Press. I must express my appreciation to Dr. Jenny Greene, who through a casual conversation let me know she knew Dr. Jewel Plummer Cobb, the niece of Bob Cole. She graciously introduced me to her, thus making this a richer study. I am indebted to Dr. Jewel Plummer Cobb for her munificence of spirit and candor, for inviting me into her home, sitting for interviews, and allowing me access to her priceless archives on Bob Cole. I am ever grateful to the two anonymous readers who recommended *Beyond Lift Every Voice and Sing* for publication. They offered a critical, thoughtful, and erudite analysis of the manuscript that led to its transformation. Heath Renfroe proved invaluable as a friend, scholar, and editor as he read the manuscript, gave me thoughtful intellectual critiques, and helped me to craft the book.

Beyond Lift Every Voice and Sing began as a dissertation, and my committee remained an extraordinary one that included Dr. George Lipsitz, Dr. Ramon Gutierrez, Dr. Ross Frank, Professor George Lewis, Dr. Benetta Jules Rosette, and Dr. Jane Rhodes. After reading *Telling Histories: Black Women Historians in the Ivory Tower,* a must read for all African American scholars and graduates students, I realize how truly amazing they are, for they gave me boundless support for my research and the dissertation. My mentors, Dr. Ramon Gutierrez, Dr. Ross Frank, Dr. George Lipsitz, and Professor George Lewis, provided kindness and constant guidance over the years and I am truly grateful to them. Ramon and Ross read the book proposal, gave me comments, and aided me in my pursuit of the coveted book contract. I am thankful to Dr. Benetta Jules Rosette, who mentored me and whose Arts, Culture, and Knowledge group, including my friends and colleagues Dr. Ricardo Guthrie, Dr. Cristin McVey, J. R. Osborn, Dr. Jonathan Markovitz, Lea Marie Ruiz, Dr. Francesca Castaldi, and Mylene Ribadeniera, offered an intellectual environment that sustained me as we met weekly, ate pizza and cookies, and assessed the manuscript. I am also grateful to Dr. Jack Allison, Dr. John Gilbert, and Dr. Pina Mozzanni of New York University, whom I met while pursuing the master's degree in vocal performance. Drs. Allison and Gilbert encouraged me to pursue my subject, black composers of musical theater. I am ever indebted to Dr. Kelly Wyatt for introducing me to a wide array of African American composers.

Dr. Michael Truong of the University of California, Merced, Ivonne Avila, Dr. Katrina Bledsoe, the talented filmmaker Adriene Hughes of UC San Diego, actress Verna Hampton, Dr. Charlotte Houston, Ray Zenick, Kharen Fulton, Sharon McFarland, Angelo Adkins, Paul Crutchfield, Pat Garruba, Nadine Saxton, and my aunt Doris Proctor proved to be a great and supportive family, and I love them all for bringing brilliance into my life and sustaining me through graduate school and beyond. Their love and support made this book possible.

Dr. Carole Boyce Davies of Cornell University took on the role of my mentor after graduate school. She remains an outstanding mentor, as she has been kind, giving, and supportive of my research. In my first year of graduate school I met Dr. Claudia Tate in the archives at Yale University, and she remained a supportive force. I would also like to thank my friend and colleague Dr. Rose Thevenin of Florida Memorial University for impelling me to join two of the most fantastic academic organizations, The Association for the Study of African American Life and History and The Association for Black Women Historians. Dr. Thevenin and the colleagues I met in these associations offered intellectual sustenance, camaraderie, and friendship. I must thank in particular Dr. Stefan Bradley of Saint Louis University, Dr. Elizabeth Clark Lewis, Dr. Ida Jones, A'Lelia Bundles, Dr. Sharon Harley, and Dr. Ula Taylor. I must thank Dr. V. P. Franklin, Professor of History, UC Riverside, member of ASALH, and the editor of the *Journal of African American History,* for his mentorship and his careful analysis of "Cole and Johnson's *The Red Moon* (1908–1910): Reimagining African American and Native American Female Education at Hampton Institute," which appeared as the cover article of the Winter 2008 issue of the journal, and appears as a section of chapter 5 of this book. The erudite scholar, mentor, and my dear, dear friend Dr. Gloria Louise Harper Dickinson of ASALH and ABWH remained a driving force in advancing my academic career as she introduced me to editors, scholars, and the National Council of Black Studies. She insisted that I try to publish within *The International Journal of Africana Studies.* Her not so gentle prodding led to the publication of "Ada Overton Walker, Abbie Mitchell and the Gibson Girl: Reconstructing African American Womanhood" in the Fall 2007 issue of this journal, which is part of chapter 6. It is with heartfelt gratitude, admiration, and love that I thank Gloria for all she has done for me as my friend and as my mentor. Gloria, Heaven is brighter because you now emblazon the skies and shine there.

I would like to thank my undergraduate research assistants Berline Altidor, Desiree, and Patrice, whose namesake is Patrice Lumumba, all former students of Florida Memorial University, who proved invaluable to me. I also would like to acknowledge all the smart and inspirational students of Florida Memorial University. I want to express my appreciation to Amy Sorenson, my graduate research assistant in the Department of Sociology at Virginia Tech, whose work remained essential for the last stages of the book.

It is with deep gratitude that I acknowledge Dr. Terry Kershaw, former chair of the Africana Studies Department, and Dr. John Ryan, the chair of xiv ~ Acknowledgments

the Sociology Department at Virginia Tech, for granting me a one-year post-doctoral fellowship which allowed me to complete the revisions of the book manuscript. I would also like to thank all my colleagues in the Africana Studies and Sociology Department at Virginia Tech, most specifically Dr. Carol Bailey for offering advice concerning the revisions of the manuscript, and Dr. Kwame Harrison for his careful evaluation of certain texts. I must also extend thanks to Dr. Paolo Polanah, Dr. Ellington Graves, Dr. Mike Hughes, Dr. Woody Farrar, Dr. Fred D'Aguiar, Dr. Jill Kiecolt, Dr. Ted Fuller, and Dr. Dale Wimberley for their kindness. Of course I must acknowledge the Africana Studies and Sociology Department's Brenda Husser, Joyce Moser, and Diane Marshall.

Growing up in Brooklyn, New York means that I cannot remember a time when I was not at the Schomburg Center for Research in Black Culture or the Lincoln Center Library for the Performing Arts mining the archives. The curator Diana Lachatenere, Andre Elizee, Steven G. Fullwood, Berlina Robinson, Anthony Toussaint, Deborah Willis, Nurah Jeter, and James Huffman of the Schomburg Center always remained incredibly supportive of my research from elementary to graduate school. Diana always extended herself and offered her knowledge by calling and introducing me to descendants related to my research. At the Schomburg the librarians and the archivists gave me advice and pulled materials that they thought I should look at. Like a cheering section over the years, they pushed me on to victory.

I must also thank Suzanne Eggleston Lovejoy, assistant music librarian at the Irving S. Gilmore Music Library at Yale University, for her help in the archives and the raspberry teas and lunches; Karen L. Jefferson Head, Archives and Special Collections, Stacy R. Swazy, and Catherine Lynn Mundale of the Robert F. Woodruff Library at Atlanta University Center; Mrs. Joellen El Bashir, curator, Donna M. Wells, Ida B. Jones, Miss Simms, and the staff at the Moorland-Spingarn Research Center at Howard University; Beth Madison Howse, the reference librarian of the Special Collections at Fisk University, Anne Marie Menta, Ngodi Kpouno, who graciously let me stay in her home, and the librarians at the Beinecke Rare Book and Manuscript Library, Yale University; Randall K. Burkett, Kathy Shoemaker, associate reference archivist, Kathleen Carroll, Ginger Cain, Nancy Watkins, and Tien Tran of the Special Collections & Archives Division at the Robert W. Woodruff Library at Emory University, Atlanta; Donzella Maupin, director Vernan Courtney, Andreese Scott, and Cynthia Poston of Hampton University Museum and Archives; Anne Lewellen of the United States Department of the Interior, National Park Service, Fort Caroline National Memorial, Timucuan Ecological and Historic Preserve, Jacksonville, Florida; the archivist and guidance counselor Grace Galvin at the Stanton School in Jacksonville Florida; and Rhonda James, Victoria Williamson, Norma Karram, Jock Oubichon, and Laura Galvan Estrada at the Theodore Geisel Library at the University of California, San Diego.

Finally, I would like to pay homage to my dance mentors Miss Denise Jefferson and Mr. Walter Raines. Their elegance and style touched my life in such a unique and wonderful way. I must also pay tribute to the dancers Darryl Sneed, Leni Williams, and Cedric Mickels, who lived magnificently, but died too young. On the first day of ballet class at the City College of New York Mr. Raines told us to live today as if it were the last day on earth and to dance as if there were no tomorrow. We are.

BEYOND LIFT EVERY VOICE AND SING

~

Figure 1. J. Rosamond Johnson, James Weldon Johnson, and Bob Cole.
Manuscripts, Archives and Rare Books Division, The Schomburg Center for Research in Black Culture

INTRODUCTION

~

LIFT EVERY VOICE AND SING
[THE BLACK NATIONAL ANTHEM]
WORDS BY JAMES WELDON JOHNSON, MUSIC BY J. ROSAMOND JOHNSON, 1896

LIFT EV'RY VOICE AND SING, TILL EARTH AND HEAVEN RING, RING WITH THE
HARMONIES OF LIBERTY; LET OUR REJOICING RISE, HIGH AS THE LIST'NING
SKIES, LET IT RESOUND LOUD AS THE ROLLING SEA.

SING A SONG FULL OF THE FAITH THAT THE DARK PAST HAS TAUGHT US,
SING A SONG FULL OF THE HOPE THAT THE PRESENT HAS BROUGHT US;
FACING THE RISING SUN OF OUR NEW DAY BEGUN, LET US MARCH ON TILL
VICTORY IS WON.

STONY THE ROAD WE TROD, BITTER THE CHAST'NING ROD, FELT IN THE DAYS
WHEN HOPE UNBORN HAD DIED; YET WITH A STEADY BEAT, HAVE NOT OUR
WEARY FEET COME TO THE PLACE FOR WHICH OUR FATHERS SIGHED?

WE HAVE COME OVER A WAY THAT WITH TEARS HAS BEEN WATERED,
WE HAVE COME TREADING OUR PATH THRO' THE BLOOD OF THE SLAUGH-
TERED,
OUT FROM THE GLOOMY PAST, TILL NOW WE STAND AT LAST
WHERE THE WHITE GLEAM OF OUR BRIGHT STAR IS CAST.

GOD OF OUR WEARY YEARS, GOD OF OUR SILENT TEARS, THOU WHO HAST
BROUGHT US THUS FAR ON THE WAY; THOU WHO HAST BY THY MIGHT, LED
US INTO THE LIGHT, KEEP US FOREVER IN THE PATH, WE PRAY.

LEST OUR FEET STRAY FROM THE PLACES, OUR GOD, WHERE WE MET THEE,
LEST OUR HEARTS, DRUNK WITH THE WINE OF THE WORLD, WE FORGET
THEE;
SHADOWED BENEATH THY HAND, MAY WE FOREVER STAND, TRUE TO OUR GOD,
TRUE TO OUR NATIVE LAND.

(ATLANTA UNIVERSITY EDITION, 1900)

ROM 1898 TO 1911, Bob Cole, James Weldon Johnson, and J. Rosamond Johnson were one of the most prolific song writing teams of
their era. In their all-black musicals *Shoo Fly Regiment* (1906–1908)
and *The Red Moon* (1908–1910), theater, uplift, and politics collided.
With these two musicals, Cole and the Johnson brothers (designated in this
text and in their day as the show business team Cole and Johnson) made
their mark on musical theater. Following Booker T. Washington's lead, W. E.
B. Du Bois's ideology, the tenets of Atlanta University, and Cole's "Colored
Actor's Declaration of Independence," and informed by their own brushes
with United States racism and subjugation, the team actively worked to
"become leaders and helpers of their race" through music and theater.[1] Their
careers as producers of black musical theater lasted approximately four
years, but these years proved pivotal to black musical theater and politics.

Lizabeth Cohen argues in *Making a New Deal* that in the 1930s a culture
of unity existed in Chicago through the Congress of Industrial Organizations, which allowed workers of all races nationwide to unite as "political
participants."[2] She states that while this culture collapsed after the 1930s, it
is important to understand what that unity meant to the people who participated during that historical moment. Cohen maintains that during this period
significant changes occurred in the political lives of the workers involved with
the Congress of Industrial Organizations. They accomplished their goals by
participating in a political movement for the *common* worker and taking part
in eradicating racism in the workplace.[3] These activists felt that they made a
difference. Correspondingly, even though whites gained control of the black
theatrical product after Cole and Johnson's career ended in 1911 and though
structural racism ultimately prevented African Americans from gaining control, Cole and Johnson believed at their historical apex that they had contributed fully to the uplift and education of African Americans through theater.

The advances that Cole and Johnson made during the four years they produced *Shoo Fly Regiment* and *The Red Moon* might, to many, seem inconse-
quential, but their innovations proved enormously progressive for their time.
While many scholars dismiss Bob Cole, J. Rosamond Johnson, and James
Weldon Johnson as conformists who bought into hegemony, the contention
of this study is that they used the very tools of hegemony to create a distinctly
black theater informed by black politics, history, and culture. It is important
to understand that the historical epoch in which they lived differed greatly
from our times and that, as products of their era, they made progressive
political statements through their musicals. They argued for inclusion in the
political fabric of American society, and, as followers of the African American boxer Jack Johnson, Theodore Roosevelt, and the manliness movement,

they envisioned black male inclusion within U.S. society. While it appears that they ignored Roosevelt's overt racism, in *Shoo Fly Regiment* Cole and Johnson included a commentary on United States racism and Roosevelt's refusal to acknowledge the accomplishments of black soldiers during the Spanish-American War by portraying black soldiers as the heroes of the war. They worked within the limits of their time and, like Booker T. Washington and W. E. B. Du Bois, felt that they had served their community.

Cole and Johnson believed that blacks deserved respect in U.S. culture, and they used tropes of masculinity, femininity, and education to advance their beliefs. Their musicals also reflected the relationship between what happens off and on stage, and the playwrights utilized key historical events in African American life to flesh out their musicals. The life of Booker T. Washington, as well as their experiences at Atlanta University, served as background for *Shoo Fly Regiment* and *The Red Moon*. The settings for both productions included industrial institutions patterned after Tuskegee Institute and Hampton Institute. In addition, the team conceivably patterned characters in *Shoo Fly Regiment,* such as the Lady Principal, Rose, and Professor Maxwell, after people they had known at the schools and in their lives. They used Booker T. Washington's experiences as a teacher of Native Americans in *The Red Moon*. Their productions also reappropriated African American history and reflected historical realities, such as the African American soldiers in the Spanish-American War and the black and Native American education program at Hampton Institute. In the case of the biracial educational program at Hampton Institute, Cole and Johnson reimagined the actual program, which attempted to position blacks and Native Americans as adversaries, by portraying alliances between the two races on stage.

James Weldon Johnson's commitment to politics, the death of Bob Cole, and J. Rosamond Johnson's move to London to forge a career as a performer and educator marked the end of the attempt of these three to create a distinctly black theater. Cole and Johnson created theater productions in part to educate audience members about the history of African Americans, to champion the race, and of course, to entertain. Because of his experiences with the theft of his sketch "At Jolly Cooney Island" and his music by the producers of The Black Patti's Troubadours and the appropriation of "La Hoola Boola" by Allen Hirsh and Yale University, Bob Cole made it his life's mission to control his theatrical product; for the most part he accomplished this goal. The team adhered to Bob Cole's "Colored Actor's Declaration of Independence" and accomplished many of the objectives mapped out in the declaration by writing, directing, and producing their own shows; hiring their own orchestra leaders and composers, such as James Reese Europe;

hiring their own stage managers, such as Charles A. Hunter; and controlling their publicity. But the very real fact that they lived in a society in which structural racism prevented them from owning their own theaters thwarted complete fulfillment of their aspirations.

While we cannot deny that Cole and Johnson in some ways conformed to hegemony and an ideology that embraced patriarchy and color caste, in many respects they moved away from hegemony and committed themselves to an inclusionary form of uplift. Their theatrical productions reflected their attempt to dismiss color-caste casting: while many in their cast were in fact light skinned, blacks of every hue appeared in their productions, including the dark-skinned performers Ada Overton Walker, Anna Cook Pankey, Henry Gant, and Andrew Tribble.[4]

Like Booker T. Washington, they included black women in their project by hiring Ada Overton Walker, Siren Nevarro, who choreographed *The Red Moon* and *Shoo Fly Regiment,* and Elizabeth Williams, who taught drama classes in addition to performing. Cole and Johnson's ideology for black women included elevating their status off stage through the newspaper series "*The Red Moon* Rays." Ada Overton Walker also participated in changing the representative image of black stage women through a series of articles she wrote about show business and black female respectability. The use of the print media by Cole and Johnson and the actress proved truly revolutionary. Additionally, their wives, mothers, and sisters played active roles in their careers and most certainly informed their decisions to include women in their endeavors. Both James Weldon Johnson's and J. Rosamond Johnson's wives tended to their business while the husbands worked overseas. Bob Cole's mother, sisters, and wife Stella Wiley all played instrumental roles in his life.

Abbie Mitchell's life offered an object lesson in the relationship between the world of the theater and daily life. Indeed, her life mirrored the character Minnehaha in *The Red Moon* as she liberated herself from societal constraints placed on her as a performer and as a person of mixed-race heritage. She reconfigured her place in society by dismissing the notion that the stage was a place of debasement. Mitchell imagined the theater as a place of dignity and respect for black women. Bob Cole, James Weldon Johnson, and J. Rosamond Johnson also dismissed societal restrictions. Because the team drew the character of Minnehaha as a lady of repute, they departed from stereotypical renderings of the mixed-race Native American and African American. Abbie Mitchell used education and marriage as a form of uplift to position herself as decent, upright, and dignified. Through the character of Minnehaha, Cole and Johnson used marriage as a marker of repute and social standing and rejected the prohibitions placed on black and Native American women at Hampton Institute by portraying romance and marriage between Minnehaha and the African American Plunk Green.

Cole and the Johnsons' family lives also impacted their musical theater careers. Bob Cole's experience with white supremacy, the threat of lynching at the age of fifteen, his family's slave and Native American heritage, and his fight with the white producers of The Black Patti's Troubadours all informed how he would run his theatrical business and how he would attempt to change the representative images of blacks, Native Americans, and Filipinos on stage. The Johnson's family heritage also influenced their lives and their theatrical products. The Johnson brothers' family background reflected a more international view because of their mother's Haitian and white heritage. The threat of enslavement propelled their free-born mother and father to leave New York for the Bahamas and to eventually relocate in Florida. These incidents surely influenced the Johnson brothers and proved essential to their commitment to the uplift of the black race globally as well as nationally. Despite their parents' status as freeborn blacks, slavery still touched the family. James Weldon Johnson's experience with racism, his writings on the lynch laws, his education at Atlanta University, and his commitment to serving others all pointed to his dedication to the welfare and interests of African Americans.

Placing their shows within a black center, Cole and Johnson made significant advances by crafting black musical theater as a form of protest, breaking the love scene taboo, incorporating romantic songs in their shows, and promoting interracial solidarity between blacks, Native Americans, and Filipinos on stage. Knowledgeable about the negative impact of U.S. politics on the minds and bodies of these racial minorities, the team offered audiences new forms of representations of educated blacks and Native Americans, blacks as soldiers, teachers, doctors, and lawyers.

While we might look at the attempt of Bob Cole and the Johnsons to create a distinctly black theater as a failure, for a brief moment in time they accomplished their goals. Their productions proved so innovative that black and white musicians, writers, composers, and audience members spoke of their accomplishments for years after their deaths. In the *Crisis of the Negro Intellectual,* Harold Cruse argued that African American history reflects the conflict between whether blacks should fight for inclusion through integration or fight for a nationalist project that would exclude whites. He argues that nationalism remains the only solution for African Americans. Cole and Johnson's attempt to create a distinctly black theater incorporated both the nationalist agenda and integrationist agenda and, for a fleeting moment, they succeeded.

Overview

The main objective of this book is to explore how roles and representations in black musical theater both reflected and challenged the dominant social order and to examine how Cole and Johnson worked as part of a collective culture of uplift that combined conservative and progressive ideas in a complex and historically specific strategy for overcoming racism and its effects.

Chapter 1 discusses significant events in the lives of Cole and the Johnsons that helped to shape their political and social thought. It looks at how these events instilled in the team a strong commitment to uplift. This chapter includes the biographical background of Bob Cole, his business networks, and his resistance to hegemony through musical theater. It also examines the life story of James Weldon Johnson and how key incidents in his life instilled in him a sense of racial responsibility. I detail how Johnson's forays into politics acted as an outgrowth of these events and influenced *Shoo Fly Regiment* and *The Red Moon*. The chapter also offers the reader biographical information on John Rosamond Johnson, including his commitment to all facets of the theater and his full participation in performance, acting as director of music schools in London and in Harlem. It also details how he incorporated this commitment to the theater into the musicals written with Bob Cole and James Weldon Johnson. It investigates the trio's influences in the public and private spheres and how these forces led them to reject minstrelsy and black stereotypes on stage. I also investigate the ideologies of Booker T. Washington and W. E. B. Du Bois and shake up the common notion that they remained totally dissimilar. In doing so I examine how Cole and Johnson as well as other African Americans adopted both ideologies to advance their agenda by successfully combining the two seemingly discordant philosophies.

I also look into how their business skills informed their attempt to secure financial control of their theatrical products and publicity. I investigate their use of the stage as a tool of uplift to educate both black and white theatergoers about the historical accomplishments of African Americans and examine the ways in which black entertainers worked to change the image of the stage.

Chapter 2 investigates how Cole and Johnson changed the projected images of African American men and women in *Shoo Fly Regiment*. This chapter looks at how the two coupled the ideologies of Booker T. Washington and W. E. B. Du Bois and reigning notions of African American womanhood in shaping the musical. I also consider how Booker T. Washington's and the trio's experiences as teachers and students further informed *Shoo Fly Regiment*. This chapter examines the restoration of the black male body through sports, the boxer Jack Johnson, and what I term the African American hypermasculine übermensch, the authoritative ideal for black male power, black masculinity, bodily strength, and the conquering of hegemony and how the team adopted these tropes. Chapter 3 delves into how the playwrights modeled the characters within the production after real people from their lives. I survey the stereotypical characters in *Shoo Fly Regiment* and audience responses to the production.

The fourth chapter considers the case of Cole and Johnson's *The Red Moon*. This chapter includes a summary of *The Red Moon* and exemplifies how history informed the production. In this vein I explicate the relationship between the Civil War and industrial institutions and how the Civil War served as a training ground for white soldiers placed in charge of creating and running black industrial institutions. Furthermore I describe how their understanding of Booker T. Washington's experiences teaching Native Americans students fleshed out Cole and Johnson's *The Red Moon*. This chapter discusses the romance and educational hierarchies set in place at Hampton Institute by the white administrators and instructors and how Cole and Johnson reimagined these hierarchies by presenting on stage interracial unity, solidarity, and romance. It also chronicles the real-life experiences and relationships between the black female teachers at Hampton Institute and the Native American students and how Cole and Johnson imagined these interactions. I look at how Cole and Johnson eliminated the problematic white presence in the production and envisioned the amalgamation of black and Native Americans on stage. This chapter also examines the stereotypes of Native Americans in U.S. culture and looks at the affirmative representations in *The Red Moon*. It grapples with identity issues through an analysis of the black and Native American character Minnehaha and how this character reflected the life of Abbie Mitchell, the actress who played the role.

In the fifth chapter I consider the female artists of *The Red Moon* and Cole and Johnson's efforts to transform the image of African American women on and off the stage through the popular cultural icon "The Gibson Girl" and the newspaper column "*The Red Moon* Rays." I also look at how the stars of *The Red Moon*, Ada Overton Walker and Abbie Mitchell, changed preexisting perceptions of black women through their attempts to dignify stage life.

Cole and the Johnsons' musicals and their political activism refracted the variegated, multilayered reality of African American life. Emblazoned with African American agency, politics, and art, Cole and Johnson changed the theatrical and social landscape of the United States by fusing their aesthetic agenda with their political goals and, in doing so, unremittingly and unapologetically challenged the cultural and racial hegemony of the day.

Figure 2. Bob Cole, James Weldon Johnson, and J. Rosamond Johnson. James Weldon Johnson Papers, Yale Collection of American Literature, Beinecke Rare Book and Manuscript Library.

CHAPTER ONE

THE ORIGINS OF
THE COLE AND JOHNSON MUSICAL
THEATER TEAM

~

COMEDIAN, PLAYWRIGHT AND COMPOSER, HE WAS THE MOST VERSA-
TILE AND GIFTED COLORED ARTIST ON THE STAGE, AND HIS DOMINANT
THOUGHT WAS TO ELEVATE THE RACE TO WHICH HE BELONGED.[1]

ROBERT ALLEN COLE, known professionally as Bob Cole, was born in
Athens, Georgia, in July 1868 to Isabella Thomas Weldon and Robert
Allen Cole, Sr. His birth occurred five years after the emancipation
of the slaves and during the height of the gains made during Reconstruction. Both of Cole's parents were former slaves who lived and worked
in Athens. According to his descendent, Dr. Jewell Plummer Cobb, Robert
Allen Cole, Sr., was part Seminole Indian and part African, and Isabella was
an octoroon.[2] Bob Cole's father worked both in politics and as a carpenter,
and his mother tended to the children and home[3] (figure 3 on next page).

Cole's parents exhibited musical talents: Robert Allen played the drums
occasionally in a band led by George Davis that performed on showboats,
while Isabella Cole led square dances.[4] Cole's parents instilled in their children a love of music. Bob Cole played the banjo, guitar, piano, and cello.[5]

At the age of fifteen, Cole was spirited out of Athens by his parents after
a bloody fight with the son of the city's former mayor.[6] The fight occurred
at a drinking pump where Cole and the mayor's son stood with members of
their respective baseball teams, according to Cole's sister Carriebel Plummer.
An argument erupted concerning which team should drink first. Neither team
would defer to the other.

11

Figure 3. Bob Cole and family. Dr. Jewel Plummer Cobb Collection

[S]o a fight resulted when a knife was drawn and Bob drew his. His middle finger was severely cut which resulted in a stiff finger thru life. The ex-mayor's boy received many slashes. Being when, and where it was, my father concealed him in a clothesbasket until night and then smuggled him in a wagon down to the railroad. He rode into Florida where my mother's sister was.[7]

During Reconstruction, African Americans in the South faced widespread racialized violence at the hands of the white citizenry, which resulted in murder, lynchings, and live burnings. This form of mob violence continued for decades in the United States, sanctioned both covertly and overtly by the government.[8] If Bob Cole had remained in Athens after the altercation he most certainly would have faced the lynch mob. The near lynching of Cole became so deeply ingrained in the Cole family history that his sister recounted the incident in her (unpublished) autobiographical play about Bob

Figure 4. Bob Cole, perhaps in his early twenties.
James Weldon Johnson Papers, Yale Collection of American
Literature, Beinecke Rare Book and Manuscript Library

Cole called "What's in a Song." She wrote that even though the mayor's son remained relatively unscathed, the "Crowd of Crackers [left] for Buddie's [Cole's] home anyway," to enact the lynch law.[9] After escaping the threat of lynching, he moved to Jacksonville, Florida, where he lived with relatives. Cole eventually reunited with his family in Atlanta, where he completed elementary school.[10] According to Carriebel Plummer, her family was one of the first to leave "in an exodus from Georgia."[11]

After completing his education at Atlanta University, Cole worked as a bellboy in Jacksonville, Florida, and then in New York City, and later in Asbury Park, New Jersey, where he found employment as a singing bellboy.[12] Cole moved to Chicago, where he gained notoriety as a singer and guitar player. While in Chicago he worked in vaudeville with Lew Henry and Pete Staples and joined Sam T. Jack's *Creole Show* in 1891. He developed the white-faced character of Willie Wayside, a tramp. While working in Sam T. Jack's show, Cole married the soubrette Stella Wiley and published the songs

"Parthenia Takes A Likin' to a Coon" and "In Shinbone Alley."[13] A year before Cole's successful production of *A Trip to Coontown* hit Broadway, he moved to New York and relocated his parents and sisters to a brownstone on West 53rd Street. It appears at this juncture in his career Cole used the pejorative "coon" quite liberally. Henry T. Sampson maintains that African Americans did not protest the coon song genre until the 1900s, due in part to their former slave status and the use of the term on the plantations by whites and blacks. He suggests that the high illiteracy rate among African Americans might also account for the lack of remonstration and that blacks began protesting coon songs in the early 1900s due to the growth of the black middle class and pressure from the black press. Cole used the term early in his career, unaware of the longterm and negative repercussions to the black community. His ideology matured over time and he took a stand.[14]

In 1894, Bob Cole formed the All Stock Theatre Company to train black actors in a building at Sixth Avenue and Thirtieth Street.[15] African American composer Will Marion Cook recalled that

> on this corner was a small theatre where the best performers Benn Hunn, Tom Brown and Bob Cole often put on afterpieces and shared in the proceeds with the proprietor. I lived on Thirty-second Street near there. When Bob Cole told me he was to run the show for a week and asked me to be musical director, I jumped at the chance.[16]

James Weldon Johnson later recalled in *Black Manhattan* that the All Stock Theatre Company was the first school for blacks that offered dramatic training and a professional theatrical experience.[17] While working with the company, Cole formed his first successful songwriting partnership with Billy Johnson (1858–1916), whom he met while performing in the *Creole Show*.[18] In 1896, both Cole and Billy Johnson joined the Black Patti's Troubadour Company, headed by the African American opera diva Sissieretta Jones. Cole worked with the company as a writer, performer, and stage manager.

With this company he performed in whiteface as the character Willie Wayside and wrote the sketch and music for *At Jolly Cooney Island*. Will Marion Cook lauded Cole as the co-composer (along with his partner Billy Johnson) of the dialogue and songs and identified Cole's "bright sayings and catchy, humorous songs" and his "wit, humor, and sarcasm" as evidence of "talent of the highest order."[19]

Yet the white manager of the Black Patti's Troubadour Company, Rudolph Voelckel, became incensed when Cole claimed authorship of the sketch and demanded better working conditions and a salary increase for all the members of the company. Voelckel instigated Cole's arrest on the stage of the theater. He charged Cole with stealing the music performed in the show. Bob Cole adamantly protested and charged that "[t]hey have amassed a fortune from the product of my brain and now they call me a thief." He asserted, "It's mine [the music] and I won't give it up."[20]

The judge in Manhattan's Yorkville section ordered Cole to give up his claim to the music and, when he refused, sentenced him to jail. Upon his release, Cole soon discovered that the management of the Black Patti's Troubadours had conspired to blacklist him and his supporters in an effort to prevent them from performing on the stage.[21] The blacklist attempt reflected a conscious effort on the part of white producers and writers to suppress African American performers through the control of their finances. Insisting on his innocence, Bob Cole eventually created his own show with his collaborator Billy Johnson, *A Trip to Coontown,* which they wrote, produced, and directed. This was the first all-black musical theater production in the United States. Because of the blacklist, Bob Cole and Billy Johnson took the show to Canada, where theater owners and producers remained unaware of their blacklisted status in New York. Due to the success of the show in Canada, white theater owners and producers lifted the racial boycott in the United States.

Cole rose above the oppressive environment to create a highly successful all-black musical, which toured between 1897 and 1899, and culminated in a triumphant run on Broadway despite the fact that Rudolph Voelckel attempted to derail the show. Voelckel spread the word that if any New York entertainers joined the cast they would face a boycott for life.[22] In addition, he made sure that theater managers passed on the production by warning that if they booked *A Trip to Coontown,* no other black show would play in that theater. This greatly limited the venues where the show could play, thereby closing the significant theaters in the country to the production.

However, the fact that in Canada the show had proved extremely popular, receiving rave reviews, captured the attention of U.S. theater managers, who began to bid for the show. Ultimately, Marcus Klaw and A. L. Erlanger resisted the boycott and booked the musical for a New York opening at Jacob's Third Avenue Theater, where its success led to bookings throughout the United States.[23] Despite the efforts by the Black Patti's Troubadour Company to limit Cole's creativity and compensation, *A Trip to Coontown* proved both popular and profitable.

The incident with the Troubadours exposes racism as a powerful and corrosive tool for controlling the life chances of African Americans. The use of structural racism against Cole and his followers was an attempt to destroy any and all opportunities for economic advancement. Crafted to isolate Cole from the larger theatrical community and fashioned to alienate him from his theatrical colleagues, who feared being blacklisted, we learn how people such as Rudolph Voelckel could use racism to control people of color. As a fighter, Cole abnegated racism and refused to allow it to dictate his life opportunities. Cole combined Booker T. Washington's ideology of black economic nationalism and a politics of black survival with W. E. B. Du Bois's radical ideological practices of public protest, activism, and cultural resistance to conquer hegemony and racism.[24] He took on structural racism, not only by publicly challenging the producers of the Black Patti's Troubadours but also by producing *A Trip To Coontown,* which offered some economic stability for those who joined him in this endeavor.

Bob Cole wrote the "Colored Actor's Declaration of Independence" in 1898 in response to the blacklist. He stated, "We are going to have our own shows," declaring, "We are going to write them ourselves, we are going to have our own stage manager, our own orchestra leader and our own manager out front to count up. No divided houses—our race must be seated from the boxes back."[25] *A Trip To Coontown* became a direct product of this declaration. Cole came to conceive of uplift as retaining full ownership and control of the theatrical product. Following the model of W. E. B. Du Bois, Bob Cole also refused to allow the performance of his shows in segregated theatrical spaces.[26] The importance of the production lies in the fact that it was the first musical written, produced, and acted entirely by black performers. Cole also achieved his goal by hiring an all-black behind-the-scenes staff with manager Samuel L. Corker Jr., stage manager Jesse A. Shipp, business manager Ed W. Cook, and musical director William Carle.[27]

Cole's ultimate achievement included founding a highly trained and skilled repertory company. These performers worked with him between 1897 and 1911, the majority of his performing career. These entertainers worked with Cole in *A Trip to Coontown, Shoo Fly Regiment,* and *The Red Moon.* Their ranks included Ada Overton Walker, the star of *The Red Moon,* whom Cole met during his tenure at the All Star Stock Theatre Company and while performing with the Black Patti's Troubadours. Abbie Mitchell also starred in *The Red Moon* and most likely met Bob Cole when she appeared briefly with Black Patti's Troubadours or when she appeared in the operetta *The Cannibal King* (1901), a collaboration of her husband, Will Marion Cook, and Cole and the Johnsons.[28]

A Trip to Coontown offered audiences the first black theatrical production with a fully integrated plot. Cole also discarded the use of blackface and cork. The plot revolved around the efforts of Jim Flimflammer's (Billy Johnson) attempt to con Silas Green "an old Negro" out of a five-thousand-dollar pension before Willie Wayside (Bob Cole) saves the day. In June 1901 the *Colored American Magazine* reported, "More people will remember Mr. Cole as the funny tramp, who says so many striking funny things and performs so many grotesque and nimble dance steps in that funny play, 'A Trip to Coontown.'"[29] The show introduced Lloyd G. Gibbs as "The Greatest Living Black Tenor"; Juvia Roan, "The Cuban Nightingale"; and twenty-two songs, including "Sweet Savannah." The show also included variety acts such as "consortional dancers" the Freeman Sisters, and "equilibrist" Jim Wilson.[30]

A Trip to Coontown served as a means of cultural resistance for Cole, especially through the character of Willie Wayside. The nineteenth century saw the appearance of abhorrent stereotypes of African Americans created by white entertainers, which proved much worse than parodies.[31] Through Cole's creation of the white tramp Willie Wayside he inverted the stereotypes of Jim Crow, the dumb plantation Negro in ill fitting, tattered old clothing, and Zip Coon, the outlandishly dressed, effeminate, city dandy, and contested the racial discourse of the times. [32] While the stereotypes created in blackface minstrelsy remain well known to this day, few people know of Bob Cole and the whiteface character of Willie Wayside. Cole's obscurity and his absence from the history of musical theater is based on the industry's backlash against him as a result of his efforts to control his own productions and his attempts to convert blackface into whiteface.

Carriebel Plummer gives us insight into the production of *A Trip to Coontown,* Bob Cole's portrayal of Willie Wayside, and his comedic style. She relates:

The year passed and my brother's show, *A Trip to Coontown* was booked for an opening at the Bijou Theatre on Broadway. My mother and sisters dressed in dimities, frills and rosettes, reached the theatre at the long waited hour. Scene after scene, the curtain rose on gaily singing and dancing choruses, lyrics, and comedy skits. Finally, out of a large dog house came my brother, dressed as a tramp with red whiskers and his tongue hanging out, and giving evidence of being infested with fleas, fleas, fleas. Billy Johnson his stage partner, a passerby, was asked where one might find some water, he replied to the tramp: "The nearest well is three miles from here." A very bewildered expression spread over the tramp's red whiskered face.[33]

How I cried, when I first went to see *A Trip to Coontown* because his partner Billy Johnson demanded of him to go to a well miles away for water, and my brother the red whiskered tramp, who had been sleeping in the dog Bow's house was so tired. As I reflect, my tears and chatter from the box seat in the theatre must have added more comedy to his emerging from the dog's house infested with fleas for the audience simply howled at this point of the production. This stunt of his was worth the price of admission to any show.[34]

While Cole dispensed with most of the minstrel show format in *A Trip To Coontown*, coon songs remained a prevalent aspect of his show, although he would later confess that the "so called coon songs are rough, coarse, and often vulgar."[35] These songs consisted of dialect lyrics set to sorrow songs/slave songs or ragtime music, with derisive lyrics that characterized blacks as lazy, violent, lascivious people with voracious appetites. J. Rosamond Johnson stated that "[m]any of the coon love songs carried a double meaning, decidedly vulgar at times. Their treatment was rough, unpolished and cleverly constructed as [with] the songs today that juggle on the edge of wholesome morals."[36] Coon songs became incredibly popular with both black and white songwriters who popularized the words "darky," "coon," and "nigger" in their songs. White male and female performers gained popularity by performing coon songs in blackface and with black juveniles.[37] The stereotypes in the coon song worked in conjunction with the minstrel show to produce negative representations of "blackness." While coon songs popularized black music both in the United States and overseas, they also perpetuated stereotypes of African Americans.[38]

Because few options existed for the black performer, many of Cole's African American contemporaries, such as Bert Williams, George Walker, Billy Kersands, Ernest Hogan, and numerous other performers, donned blackface and sang coon songs to gain access to the stage.[39] Cole would eventually dismiss the coon song genre and try for a more refined image of African Americans on stage, incorporating "the finer feelings of the colored race." He later wrote "the Negro has his sentimental side just as the white man has." The campaign against coon songs actually coincides with Cole's rejection of the genre in the 1900s. On October 7, 1905, Cole gave a lecture at the Marshall Hotel and argued "the word is very insinuating and must be eliminated." He noted that Lester Walton successfully rallied against the use of "nigger," "and now I am going to crusade against the word 'coon.'" Cole saw nothing wrong with the use of "Afro-American," "colored," or "darky," which indicates that his understanding of the damaging effects of words did not extend to "darky." He asserted that elite white Americans and the British detested the term "coon," and that like the Irish who rejected "mick," or "shenee," and the Italians who protested "dago," African Americans should follow suit. With the question posed by Walton of how he could name his show *A Trip To Coontown* and still protest the term, Cole asserted "[t]hat day has passed with the softly flowing tide of revelation." [40] He used the term "coon" early in his career, unaware of the longterm and negative repercussions to the black community, but his ideology matured over time and he took a stand. Later in his career, he and the Johnsons would humanize African Americans in their music by writing romantic ballads and lyrics that reflected black life.[41] Cole's insistence on ultimate control of his cultural product and finances, while influenced by the appropriation of his theatrical pieces by the Black Patti's Troubadours producers, was also influenced by his rejection of blackface and the coon song genre.

Another incident, which certainly reinforced Cole's insistence on controlling his cultural product, included the appropriation by Yale University of one of the more popular songs from *A Trip to Coontown,* "La Hoola Boola," which became the university's football cheer. Howley Haviland and Company published Cole's song in 1897, but in 1901 Allen "Pop" Hirsh claimed he wrote the song and published it with different lyrics under the name "Yale Boola." Jay Gitlin asserts that the "melody is pretty much an outright steal," Carriebel Plummer confirms this, and Thomas L. Riis diplomatically notes that Cole's tune "inspired" the Yale song.[42]

After the completion of the run of *A Trip to Coontown,* Cole's partnership with Billy Johnson dissolved because of Johnson's heavy drinking.[43] To fill his partnership void Cole joined J. Rosamond Johnson and James Weldon Johnson to form one of the most productive black theatrical teams, Cole and Johnson.

James Weldon Johnson and J. Rosamond Johnson

James Weldon Johnson was born on June 17, 1871, and his brother J. Rosamond was born on August 11, 1873, both in Jacksonville, Florida. Their mother, Helen Louise Dillet, was a free woman born in Nassau, the Bahamas, on August 4, 1842, the descendant of a Haitian woman and white man. Their father was James Johnson, a freeman from Virginia, who was born in 1830. He met Dillet in New York City, where she attended public school.[44] When the Civil War broke out, the couple feared that it would mark the enslavement of northern blacks, which compelled them to move to Nassau, the Bahamas, where they married. The Johnsons eventually settled in Florida, where they established themselves as part of the black bourgeoisie. Helen Dillet, a trained singer, worked as the assistant principal of the Stanton Public

School for African American children, while their father held many jobs, including head waiter, owner of a Bahamian sponge fishing fleet, and finally a minister in Jacksonville.[45]

E. Franklin Frazier notes that educated free blacks of mixed ancestry (like Dillet) and Caribbean immigrants dominated the black upper class in the postbellum period.[46] Although for the most part employed in less prestigious jobs than their white counterparts, educated freedmen held jobs as doctors, ministers, teachers, and small business entrepreneurs.[47] Frazier doubted the political judgment of this group because he believed that "they have accepted unconditionally the values of the white bourgeois world: its morals and its canons of respectability, its standards of beauty and consumption. In fact, they have tended to overemphasize their conformity to white ideals."[48] The Johnson brothers belonged to this black elite by birth; however, they did not fully conform to Frazier's diagnosis. In *Aristocrats of Color,* Willard B. Gatewood maintains that some of the black privileged class committed themselves to serving African Americans in need.[49] The Johnson brothers exhibited a strong commitment to serving and helping the black community, the foundation of which perhaps lay in the very real threat of enslavement their parents faced. Their parents encouraged their interests in education, writing, and music. *The Colored American* periodical of Washington, D.C., stated that the brothers lived at home with their parents and their grandmother and that the family owned "a comfortable dwelling on a quiet street in La Villa, one of the residence portions of the city. The home atmosphere is refined and gentle, interest naturally centering in the music room and library; both are simple in appointment but each bears the unmistakable individuality of its presiding genius."[50]

James Weldon Johnson

Several incidents prompted a sense of racial responsibility in James Weldon Johnson. Soon after the *Plessy vs. Ferguson* case of 1896 in which the Supreme Court ruled in favor of segregation, Johnson traveled first class with a Cuban classmate by rail to Atlanta to attend Atlanta University. On the train the conductor asked Johnson and his friend to leave the first-class section. Johnson's classmate asked in Spanish what the conductor wanted and Johnson answered him in Spanish, "As soon as the conductor heard us speaking in a foreign language, his attitude changed; he punched our tickets and gave them back, and treated us just as he did the other passengers."[51] At this time the formation of racial codes for African Americans to keep them

Figure 5. James A. Weldon Johnson, Atlanta, n.d. Possibly 1887–1889. George A. Towns Collection, Box 7 Folder 18. Atlanta University Center, Robert W. Woodruff Library

in place remained malleable and not fully formed, so if one spoke in Spanish or showed other signs of not being "black," he or she might avoid being discriminated against as an African American. In the 1900s African American clubwoman Fannie Barrier Williams traveled the Southwest by railway on a speaking engagement for the National Association of Colored Women. When asked by the conductor while seated in first class if she was black. she replied "Je suis française," and received deferential treatment.[52] Unlike Johnson, she consciously used white racist practices of Jim Crow to maintain her first-class seat by passing as white. African American political activist Louise Thompson Patterson's family discovered that they received respectful treatment from whites during their frequent moves in the West in the late 1920s and 1930s whenever they passed as Mexican, Native American, or white in the respective towns in which they landed. Nathan Irvin Huggins illuminates the psychic affect of racial passing in his discussion of Patterson when he wrote: "What kind of ego could survive such effacement? Masks always, the constant denial of self. And, of course, one had to remember to forget Negro friends in public when it was necessary. But humiliation only fed a longing for race identity within Louise Thompson [Patterson]."[53] These instances of white racism and the strategies African Americans use to deal with them tells us more about the complexity of race relations in the United States and the psychic affects of passing.

Another incident of overt racism occurred when Johnson took the exam for his law degree. After proving his knowledge of the law to a panel of white lawyers, one of the men on the panel agreed that Johnson proved himself qualified, but Johnson recalls that he "commented—I quote him precisely; for his words blurted out in my face, made their sizzling imprint on my brain: 'Well I can't forget he's a nigger; and I'll be damned if I'll stay here to see him admitted.' With that he stalked from the courtroom."[54] Johnson gained admittance to the bar that day, but he never forgot those humiliating words.

James Weldon Johnson expressed a strong sense of morality in his willingness to fight for social justice. While a student at Atlanta University, he wrote about lynching and kept a scrapbook of news clippings about such incidents. In a letter addressed to the editor of the *Lutheran Courier,* Johnson condemned lynching as a practice in which men were "taken from jail and even taken from their beds" and murdered. He argued against the practice and asserted that the lynch mobs went unpunished.[55]

James Weldon Johnson spent seven years at Atlanta University. He attended the preparatory school and the university, graduating in 1894. At the university, his commitment to political activism, social justice, and his strong sense of duty to the black community became fully galvanized. One of the school's main tenets included a commitment for service to others. In an article entitled "What Atlanta University Has Done for Me" that appeared in The *Bulletin of Atlanta University* in April 1894, Johnson wrote that not only did the university engage in offering education to a "poor and needy people," but that his education enabled him "to become a leader and a helper to my race which so much needs leadership of well trained men and women, and to give that aid which I could not otherwise have given."[56]

In 1894, Johnson performed and toured with the Atlanta University Glee Club for the purpose of raising money for the university.[57] Two years after his graduation, Johnson and his college colleague, George A. Towns, contributed to a scholarship fund for Atlanta University students. In a letter to Towns, dated December 30, 1896, Johnson wrote that he believed that he and his classmates could raise money for the fund. "If we can raise $500 and invest it at say 6% and give the interest each year as a prize for oratory or something such it will be a very creditable thing to do."[58]

While in New York, Johnson wrote to Towns on May 14, 1914, about contributing to the scholarship fund. "If it comes to pass that I cannot possibly get to Atlanta, you may pledge me for my [part] of the $1000 class fund, and I shall forward the amount at commencement time, or as soon after as is possible."[59] Johnson also participated in the graduation ceremonies at the university and, after he and his brother joined in partnership with Bob Cole, they contributed money to the school in the name of Cole and Johnson.

As a student, James Weldon Johnson cultivated his oratorical as well as his musical skills. He participated in elocution contests at the university, placing first in 1892 and second in 1894.[60] Johnson also participated in sports and intramural contests.[61] His oratorical skills, musical skills, and his interest in sports would all play a role in his musical career with Cole and Johnson.

Upon graduation from Atlanta University, James Weldon Johnson returned to Jacksonville and became the principal of the Stanton School, a normal school for blacks, where his mother worked as the assistant principal. Johnson maintained a strong commitment to education and to imparting knowledge to African Americans, so it is not surprising that he took the prestigious position at the Stanton School. He also maintained an incredible amount of admiration and respect for his mother, and by becoming the principal of the school Johnson in effect honored her. As the principal, Johnson supervised a student body of eleven hundred students. He "developed [The Stanton School into] the largest colored high school in the state, at a time when there were only three high schools in the South for Negroes." He initiated a high school curriculum, adding three grades and raising the standard of education by instituting a more rigorous course load so that a certificate from Stanton held prestige in academia.[62]

He participated in several activities while serving as principal, such as writing the lyrics to his brother's musical compositions; founding a black newspaper, *The Daily American;* writing articles condemning lynching; and ultimately passing the bar in 1897.[63]

In 1896 Johnson wrote the lyrics and his brother J. Rosamond Johnson wrote the music to "Lift Every Voice and Sing," for a celebration honoring Abraham Lincoln's birthday.[64] The Johnsons dedicated the song to Booker T. Washington and extolled the hopes and resilience of blacks through the uplift discourse.[65] The song also reflected Washington's life as a slave and as a freeman. Johnson recalled in his autobiography that at its inception five hundred school children sang the song and that, because of its popularity, "Lift Every Voice and Sing" became an anthem for black public school children across the country. Due to the widespread popularity of the song, several editions were published, including an Atlanta University edition, with a cover that read "words and music by James Weldon Johnson, Class 94."[66] Because the song gained such renown in the African American community, the National Association for the Advancement of Colored People adopted the Negro National Anthem, now referred to as the Black National Anthem, in the 1920s.[67] The anthem offered hope and faith to African Americans in the face of a degraded slave past and argued that, despite the horrific conditions of slavery, blacks remained victorious in their survival.

The song illustrated the perseverance of African Americans during and after slavery and asserted that because of their survival blacks emerged as "bright star[s]."[68] The foundation for the Johnsons' use of music and lyrics as an instructional tool of education for African Americans lay in the song. The ideals of the uplift ideology embedded in "Lift Every Voice and Sing" reflected the message that Cole and Johnson included in *The Shoo Fly Regiment* (1906) and *The Red Moon* (1908), an unwavering commitment to hope, freedom, social progress, and the affirmation of African American accomplishments in U.S. history.

J. Rosamond Johnson

J. Rosamond Johnson opted for a musical education and attended the New England Conservatory of Music, graduating after six years.[69] In about 1895, he toured the country with John Isham's *Oriental America*.[70] Rosamond returned to Florida in 1896, where he opened his own music school, held the position of supervisor of music for the Jacksonville public schools, and taught at the Florida Baptist Academy. A contemporary journalist reported that "Pro. Rosamond Johnson is not without honor in this his native city. The people are justly proud of him as a composer. If he had done no more than produce the music of "Lift Every Voice and Sing" he would have endeared himself to us all."[71] In 1899 Johnson moved to New York, where he and Bob Cole began their long association as songwriters and performers.

The Stage as a Political and Educational Tool

Cole and Johnson used the stage as a political and educational tool of uplift. Their theatrical productions worked simultaneously to comment on American injustice and to teach audiences about the achievements of African Americans in the United States. *Shoo Fly Regiment* offered audiences a story in which the characters attended a fictional black southern educational and industrial institution patterned after Booker T. Washington's Tuskegee Institute. In this play, the characters prove they "deserve" full rights and responsibilities of citizenship by participating in the Spanish-American war, (fought in Cuba in 1898 and the Philippines between 1898 and 1914).[72]

Shoo Fly Regiment presented an overt commentary on the United States government's refusal to commission African American officers during the war. *Shoo Fly Regiment* was a protest play, which followed W. E. B. Du Bois's strategy of public protest; Cole and Johnson's later *The Red Moon's* message of racial pride, interracial solidarity, and uplift proceeded through more covert mechanisms. Based on the actual project of biracial education at Hampton Institute in which blacks and Native Americans confronted social prohibitions, which forbade them to date, live in the same dormitories, or attend classes together, *The Red Moon* reimagined the Hampton project of biracial education as that of an amalgamation of the black and Native American races as a means of apotheosizing both groups. The team placed on stage the very forms of interethnic solidarity and romance forbidden at Hampton Institute. Ultimately the team made a progressive and political statement for their time, that African Americans and Native Americans could unite. Both productions presented revolutionary messages for their times: educational attainment for African Americans and Native Americans; the importance of multiracial alliance building between African Americans, Filipinos, and Native Americans; and Washington's specific agenda of the inclusion of black women in the project of uplift. Cole and Johnson envisioned theatrical uplift much in the same way that Booker T. Washington foresaw social uplift, as an effort to carve out a space for African Americans in U.S. society. This connection between Washington and Du Bois and Cole and Johnson illustrates the links between politics and culture.

From 1906 to 1910 *Shoo Fly Regiment* and *The Red Moon* gave African Americans a respite from the brutality of the times and the adverse conditions that they faced by giving them affirmative black characters on the stage. These musicals also placed African American history at center stage at a time when the attempt to erase the accomplishments of African Americans in United States history was markedly widespread. By advertising the shows as "Presenting Real Negro Plays of Real Negro Life" Cole and Johnson contested the hardships that blacks faced and argued that victory and hopefulness will prevail. Uplift, dignity, and respect win out. Blacks in these musicals emerge triumphant.[73]

James Weldon Johnson wrote the opera *Tolosa* with J. Rosamond Johnson, which culminated in a trip to New York City in the summer of 1899 to try to get it produced. Although unsuccessful in their effort, the Johnson brothers made significant strides within the music industry, most importantly meeting Bob Cole and joining him in partnership. During that summer they collaborated with Cole writing popular Broadway songs. Johnson returned to Florida to continue his position at the Stanton School, but eventually joined his brother and Bob Cole in 1901 after resigning as principal.[74]

Cole and Johnson

From 1899 to 1911, Bob Cole, J. Rosamond Johnson, and James Weldon Johnson worked as successful musical collaborators in the realm of theater. They held two lucrative songwriting contracts in 1901, and they maintained careers as writers of popular songs. Their most famous compositions included "Maiden with the Dreamy Eyes" and "Congo Love Song." In 1901 Cole and Johnson joined in partnership with Marcus Klaw and A. L. Erlanger, who produced large-scale Broadway musicals and controlled the majority of Broadway theaters. In 1898 they broke the blacklist of Bob Cole and Billy Johnson by booking *A Trip to Coontown* in their theaters. Klaw and Erlanger subsequently contracted Cole and the Johnson brothers to contribute to musicals such as *The Sleeping Beauty and the Beast* (1901), *Humpty Dumpty* (1904), and several other productions.

To capitalize on their acclaim as writers of popular songs, Cole and Johnson formed a vaudeville team in which they presented themselves as cosmopolitan by dressing elegantly in tuxedos. White audiences as well as black were not accustomed to seeing stylishly dressed black men. While by today's standards dressing sophisticatedly may not seem like a form of resistance, in 1901 the most common representations of blackness in the minstrel show and in the minds of most Americans included that of the Jim Dandy/Zip Coon or Jim Crow. One of the first things that newly freed slaves did to distance themselves from their slave past included dressing handsomely to command respect and citizenship rights. The black bourgeoisie also used dress to connote their repute. Cole and Johnson followed this ideology and made a concerted effort to dress stylishly and behave in a manner that countered common discourses on black masculinity.

Racial Terror, Stereotypes, and Cole and Johnson

Long before Bob Cole and Billy Johnson produced *A Trip to Coontown*, distorted representational images of African Americans within the minstrel show tradition worked to keep exploited blacks in place and remind white Americans of African Americans' slave past. Several stereotypes to justify slavery emerged, including the Uncle Tom, Mammy, the Pickaninny, and Jim Crow. These caricatures made their way into the minstrel show, coon songs, popular entertainment, mass culture, and advertisements for anything from cereal to pancake mix and they remained so entrenched within society that they exist to this day. Ella Shohat and Robert Stam contend that stereotypes exist as more than picturesque lies; they embody distinct ideological and social goals. Thus these representations worked to remind the public of the black slave past and keep stereotypes at the forefront of American minds.[75]

Degrading stereotypical images of blacks in white minstrelsy materialized in American popular entertainment as early as 1767 and became widespread and tremendously popular from the 1840s to the 1890s. Jacqui Malone asserts that by the nineteenth century these images "shifted from tragic or pitiful to comic." With this shift came another representative male stereotype, the hypersexual and violent Brute. Two images emerged as extremely popular, that of Zip Coon the city dandy, and Jim Crow the plantation slave, immortalized and popularized by Thomas Rice. Rice's interpretation of the movements of a crippled black man became the representative model for characterizations of the black male.[76]

African American female stereotypes also made their appearance within popular culture. These stereotypes included the asexual Mammy, the oversexed Jezebel, and the Tragic Mulatto.[77] Peter Stallybrass and Allon White fully articulate the nature of black female stereotypes in their discussion of "the low other." They characterize the "low other" as "something that is reviled by and excluded from the dominant social order as debased, dirty, unworthy, but that is simultaneously the object of desire and/or fascination."[78] Stallybrass and White argue that due to the "low others" position in society, these persons face exclusion from political and social power. The perception of white Americans that African American women fit the "low other" model of low, ignoble, and base types found its way into these caricatures. This "low other" continues as a fascination within the media, surviving to this day through stereotypical and denigrating images of African American women pervasive in theater, cinema, music, and television.[79]

In *With His Pistol in His Hand,* Americo Paredes illuminates the direct relationship to social power, domination, and white control of the black image. Paredes notes that negative racial representations often grow out of projection and inversion. White slave owners raped and subjugated black women and then invented the image of the black male as a "sex fiend."[80] Similarly, Hazel Carby asserts that "the objective of the stereotype is not to reflect or represent a reality but to function as a disguise, or mystification, of objective relations."[81]

Stanley Lemons argues that African American people emerged as comic figures in popular culture due to bad race relations in the United States. He maintains that the minstrel show came into existence during the 1840s at a time when "slavery was a serious political question." Lemons adds that during the 1880s and 1890s, a time marked by extreme violence against blacks, "the comic black man became the most common figure in America's new popular entertainment vaudeville and the musical revue."[82] He suggests that African American stereotypes continue as familiar models, so familiar in fact that few Americans realize that they degrade black people.[83]

The Victorian mores of the nineteenth century revolved around hard work, self-sacrifice, self-control, cleanliness, good manners, good morals, and sexual restraint. This created an atmosphere of repression for white people. With the creation of the minstrel show stereotype, the antithesis of the work ethic appeared on stage as a means of release for white viewers from the repressive work ethic. George Lipsitz argues that through theater, white audiences escaped their sexually oppressive environment and lived vicariously through the events they witnessed on the stage. The theater "offered audiences an opportunity to view the forbidden and to contemplate the unthinkable."[84] The minstrel show through its debased characterizations offered audiences an opportunity to not only view "the other" but become him/her, by donning blackface.

White men who purported to emulate blacks created the minstrel show in the nineteenth century. It bore no resemblance to real slave life or to the lives of African American freedmen. There was no mention of the whip, the chain, or the horrific conditions of slavery, but rather, as William J. Mahar aptly notes in *Behind the Burnt Cork Mask,* it presented "the escapist notion that forced labor differed little from supervised play."[85] The minstrel show offered the audience images that ridiculed blackness.

Based on European, African, and African American styles of music and dance, the minstrel show for the most part did not reflect purely African styles; thus it remained inauthentically African. Both Jim Crow, the plantation slave in ragged costume, and Jim Dandy (Zip Coon), the city Negro, exhibited vulgar behavior. These characters sang sexualized songs; told "broad and gross jokes"; appeared lazy, slow, and childlike; and exhibited insatiable appetites. Food proved so paramount that the representative images on stage included actors with makeup that made their mouths appear "cavernous," and the stage Negro responded orgasmically and grotesquely to food.[86] This representation continues into the twenty-first century in the

Broadway musical *Grey Gardens* (2007), and the films *The Nutty Professor* (1996), where the engorged Klump family eats monstrously at the dinner table, and *Hairspray* (2007) which features Motormouth Maybelle (Queen Latifah) singing "scoop me up a mess of that chocolate swirl, don't be stingy I'm a growing girl," in front of a mountain of gastronomic delights, reinforcing the infantilization of African American women as Maybelle refers to herself as a girl.[87]

On stage these characters exhibited extremely undisciplined behavior and acted without decorum. The stage Negro moved with exaggerated wild uncoordinated body movements and sat with his legs wide open. They distorted their faces grotesquely and scowled monstrously. The stage Negro dismissed cultured and articulated English in favor of dialect made up of crude speech patterns, which denoted ignorance.[88]

According to Nathan Irvin Huggins, when white men donned the black mask on stage, they experienced more freedom than without the mask. They expressed lust, passion, and uninhibited freedom as a stage Negro, behavior that proved taboo to Victorian mores and in "white civilization." For the most part blacks responded to these stage representations by adopting the uplift ideology and accepting the Protestant work ethic. They emulated their white counterparts by working to achieve success in life, superiority over the underclass, and they rejected self-indulgence by practicing restraint.[89]

African American theater emerged as a form of reappropriation of black representation, and as a response to blackfaced minstrelsy and negative imagery. Several strategies came into existence to fight this form of representation; the most notable one was the "New Negro" movement, which reflected the uplift ideology. David Krasner states that the New Negro movement stressed solidarity within the race, self-dependence, and race pride, and attempted to counter "scientific racism." Bob Cole, a veteran of the theater, was at the forefront of the movement.[90]

Rejection of Stereotypes

Through a calculated campaign to advance the race, W. E. B. Du Bois called for the creation of artistic productions that edified and resisted the common stereotypes of the nineteenth century.[91] This call to action took many forms in literature and theater. James Weldon Johnson echoed this call in *The Auto-biography of an Ex-Colored Man* (1912). In the book the protagonist passes for white, marries a white woman, and fathers mixed children. The narrator writes of his shame and selfishness for not contributing to the uplifting of the race through action and resistance. He concludes that praise should go to the "earnest and faithful" leader Booker T. Washington and others (W. E. B. Du Bois), who through renitence fought publicly for the race and contributed to history.[92] Johnson most certainly included Du Bois in this argument and highlighted and alluded to the dual strategies of Booker T. Washington and W. E. B. Du Bois that many African Americans adopted and molded together to resist hegemony.

In their studio Cole and Johnson displayed a photograph of Washington and the Harvard University flag, which represented Du Bois and his alma mater.[93] The homage given to Washington and Du Bois in *The Autobiography of An Ex-Colored Man* and in Cole and Johnson's studio elucidates the linkages between the two strategies of uplift, and reflects the commitment of Cole and Johnson to the ideologies and the goals of the two leaders. In 1895, while giving a lecture at Fisk University, Washington underscored his ideology: "We went into slavery with slave chains clanking about our wrists; we came out with the American ballot in our hands."[94] Washington made this statement in 1895, stressing his belief in the importance of the right to vote for African Americans and reinforcing his commitment to higher education by his presence on the campus of Fisk. This occurred the same year as his famous speech in Atlanta.[95] For most of his career Washington pushed for African American civil rights secretly, for he did not want to alienate the white patronage of the North or the South who funded his school in Tuskegee and funneled money through him for other schools. But in some instances Washington publicly voiced his convictions. In a letter written to Francis J. Garrison on August 31, 1903, Washington protested the loss of the vote and the reversals of Abolition Democracy in Mississippi, by arguing against "the reduction of the race to a system of industrial slavery, or peonage."[96] Washington wrote to Garrison and the Southern Education Board concerning the state's move toward African Americans' educational disenfranchisement and insisted that the board speak out against the loss of African American educational rights.[97] Du Bois openly argued for black political, civil, and social rights and to end segregation. In 1899 Du Bois wrote "Memorial" in protest of a proposed Georgia bill designed to disenfranchise blacks through property restrictions and literary tests, while Washington wrote a private and confidential letter to Wilford H. Smith on March 3, 1904, suggesting a legal case to fight the poll tax in Monroe, North Carolina.[98]

Du Bois's Niagara Movement was founded in 1904, the National Association for the Advancement of Colored People in 1909; those who belonged to both groups offer examples of the bridges built across both ideologies. The Niagara Movement, the precursor to the NAACP, formed as a radical organization to actively participate in protests for voting rights, desegregation, equitable educational and employment opportunities, and to advocate for the rights of freedom of speech.[99] People such as African American Episcopal clergyman George F. Bragg from Baltimore, Maryland, belonged to the Niagara Movement but maintained "cordial relations with Booker T. Washington by claiming that the difference between him and Du Bois was one of methods, not ultimate objectives." Others, such as Mary Church Terrell, the first president of the National Association of Colored Women's Clubs, Kelly Miller, a scholar at Howard University, and George Dereef, an attorney who lived in Wisconsin, subscribed to both ideologies. Terrell was on the steering committee for the National Negro Committee, which became the NAACP, and Miller and Dereef belonged to the NAACP and Booker T. Washington's Negro Business League. Terrell noted that many blacks did not join the NAACP for fear of losing their jobs or their position in the community.[100]

Washington's public stance against the NAACP proved threatening to those who joined the organization. Because he wielded incredible political and social power, Washington easily found ways to punish those who he felt abandoned his ideology for the NAACP, namely by withdrawing support and calling in favors, causing his adversaries to lose jobs or political office. Despite the threat, many African Americans negotiated both Washington's and Du Bois's camps and utilized both philosophies, because the goals of both remained the same: *full* African American enfranchisement. In 1905 Du Bois invited Cole and Johnson to join the Niagara Movement; according to James Weldon Johnson, Du Bois suggested that the team organize "the colored musical and theatrical talent in New York, in connection with the Niagara Movement." Johnson promised to talk with J. Rosamond and Bob Cole about the proposition when they returned from a tour of the West.[101] James Weldon Johnson's 1906 appointment as consul to Cabello, Venezuela, a political appointment brokered by Booker T. Washington on Johnson's behalf a year after his amenable correspondence with Du Bois concerning the Niagara Movement, illuminates how African Americans built bridges across the ideologies and worked together for the common good. James Weldon Johnson also held the position of president of the Colored Republican Club, an organization strongly associated with Washington, and went on to join the NAACP as field secretary in 1916.[102]

In *The Crisis of the Negro Intellectual* Harold Cruse identifies Washington as one of the founders and key proponents for black economic nationalism and what Cedric Robinson calls a "politics of black survival." At the Seventeenth Annual Session of the Tuskegee Negro Conference, Washington proposed several strategies: "We urge our people to seize upon every oppor-

Figure 6. Cole and Johnson, *Shoo Fly Regiment* postcard, April 15, 1907. Photograph Department. Moorland-Springarn Research Center, Howard University

tunity to get possession of land, to the end that they may have homes of their own and become permanently settled," and "[b]usiness opportunities that present themselves should not be allowed to pass by unimproved."[103] Cole and Johnson and many African Americans drew allegiance with Washington and Du Bois and molded their philosophies together for the common goal: full citizenship rights of African Americans in the United States. Cole and Johnson adopted Washington's black economic nationalism as a model for their theatrical endeavors.

Cole and Johnson's Business Practices

By adopting Washington's ideology of black economic nationalism and W. E. B. Du Bois's cultural resistance, Bob Cole and the Johnson brothers proved themselves extremely shrewd businessmen in theatrical endeavors, capital accumulation, and property ownership. The Johnson family business of land ownership and leasing in both Jacksonville and New York, along with Bob Cole's property ownership, serve as excellent cases in point. James Weldon

Johnson leased his family's land holdings in Florida and, in times of financial uncertainty, family members such as J. Rosamond Johnson lived off the interest accrued from these properties.[104] Bob Cole acquired property in New York City, including his family home, and helped buy the building that housed the Frogs, the black theatrical union.

As a team, Cole and Johnson made a rigorous effort to protect their musical property. They held contracts with music publishers that bound the music companies to pay them royalties. These contracts greatly benefited Cole and Johnson during their lifetime, and their heirs reaped the benefits well into the 1950s.[105] Cole and Johnson borrowed $1,223.47 in 1907 from A. M. Edwards to produce *The Shoo Fly Regiment*.[106] Their business perspicacity worked its way into their theatrical endeavors and informed their promotion of *The Shoo Fly Regiment*. As sagacious businessmen, the Cole and Johnson team cultivated audiences through an intensive effort to control the publicity for their shows. While performing in *The Shoo Fly Regiment* in 1907, Cole and Johnson sent out postcards advertising the production. On the front of the postcard they included portrait photographs of themselves (figure 6).

On the back of the postcards the team included their best reviews from January 1907 to March 1907. These postcards offer us a clear understanding of Cole and Johnson's agenda of self-promotion and self-representation. Another postcard that they distributed included the caption "Cole & Johnson in 'The Shoo-Fly Regiment.' What the City Newspapers Say About Us."[107] Determined to protect their product, the team made a strenuous effort to promote their show and to control it financially.

Theatrical critic Lester A. Walton viewed the stage as an educational institution and envisioned black theatrical representation as a key tool for advancing the race. He noted that Cole and Johnson made a concerted effort to change the image of African Americans on stage in *The Red Moon*. In discussing the production Walton noted that, "[i]f you believe in the advancement of the colored performer on the stage and you desire to see the colored member of the theatrical profession accomplish much then you will like Cole and Johnson's new show."[108] Like Walton, Bob Cole and the Johnson brothers envisioned the stage as an educational tool for uplift. They used actual historical events in black life as themes for their musicals. Because they saw African American life as worthy of being dramatized, they rejected minstrel forms of representation in favor of portrayals that dignified and celebrated their culture. In a letter to Walton printed in the *New York Age* in 1908, Cole argued that dramatists should farm black culture for dramatic plays due to its fertility and richness.[109] He identified African slavery as the basis for the greatest social and political problems within the United States and offered the black experience in and after slavery as a worthy subject for dramatization. Cole offered the fact that no other group overcame the obstacle of slavery as did the African in America and asked both black and white dramatists the following questions.

> Do they cease to hold in holy reverence the millions of souls sacrificed in order that the slave might become a man? Is it that they do not know that the progress of the ex-slave in religious education and accumulation of property is the most [magnificent], under like conditions of any race in the history of the world? Do they not know that this creature loves, hates, cries and laughs like other mortals do? Are they not aware of all these facts?[110]

Cole also noted that African Americans played a major role in United States political life and that leaders from George Washington to Theodore Roosevelt attempted to form alliances and friendship bonds with blacks. He maintained that dramatists should look to African American culture for ideas for theatrical representation as opposed to Rome or Germany, echoing Booker T. Washington that playwrights should "cast [their] buckets below."

> Anywhere you see a Negro there's a drama. The dandy darky in the street, the mulatto elevator boy in your fashionable apartment, the Negro criminal in the prison docks. You don't have to go to the "Black Belt" for atmosphere of color. As to your unifies—say: Locale, America. Time, now.
>
> The drama is that the Negro is in your midst, the comedy is that he survives, the tragedy is that he is black. For no such fertile field exists anywhere in the civilized world as does here for dramatic material and a dramatic poet should want for no more a divine inspiration than the spectacle of the great American spirit.[111]

Ada Overton Walker, the star of *The Red Moon,* held a view that mirrored Cole's. In 1905 she suggested that black life presented a far richer study for the stage than any other culture, including the English as represented in the Shakespearean repertory. She pointed to "characteristics and natural tendencies in our people which make just as beautiful studies for the Stage as to be found in the make-up of any other race, and perhaps far better."[112] She suggested that instead of trying to imitate others, black artists should study "our own graces" and "learn to appreciate the noble and beautiful within us." Walker ultimately argued that black artists must learn "self appreciation and practice it."[113] Walker unequivocally argued that African American actors should strive for originality and create African American characters reflective of African Americans' culture and integrity.

Cole and Johnson and their company actively worked to change popular perceptions of the stage and its performers from disreputable to respectable. In an article entitled "How to Make Good," Theodore Pankey, a cast member of *The Shoo Fly Regiment* and *The Red Moon,* asserted that the stage offered a worthy profession for African Americans and that it abounded with opportunities for advancement. Pankey identified Cole and Johnson as role models due to their success at the vocation and proposed that other performers should try to emulate them because of their strong business skills. Pankey warned potential performers that they should study hard and avoid drinking and gambling because "[t]he infatuation for a good time has ruined many an aspirant, who failed to realize he had little money and less knowledge of the profession in which he wished to shine." Pankey stressed hard work throughout the article, stating that aspirants should avoid becoming enamored with the "beautiful scenery," and that they should not expect "social favor[s]."[114] He recounted the story of a young man whose talent could have propelled him to that of a musical director with a good salary if he had only forgone the allure of good times.[115] Pankey stated that this man complained "There's no chance for the Negro!" to which Pankey responded:

> I will admit that our opportunities for development are few, but we must so strive that our place in the dramatic world shall be appreciated. Let us portray and preserve traditions, humor and racial traits in so commendable a way that Negro plays, thrilling with past records of loyalty under adverse conditions, interwoven with traditions, weird and entrancing, and with a romance peculiarly our own shall teach objectively that we can build nobly and well.[116]

Although they initially contributed to the coon song and the dialect genre, Cole and Johnson eventually spurned these forms after 1900.[117] Several reasons point to why Cole and Johnson moved away from this genre. James Weldon Johnson notes that around 1900 he began to grapple with the viability of Negro dialect in poetry due to its "artificiality" and its adherence to caricatures of African Americans, while Bob Cole began his militant stance with what Johnson calls "pro Negro propaganda" for raising the status of the African American artist. James Weldon Johnson wrote that the team decided to reform black music by writing Negro love songs in "a conscious effort to raise the level of Negro songs, especially the level of the words, which at that time was pretty low. And our work did actually have that effect."[118] Booker T. Washington endorsed Bob Cole as early as 1898 perhaps because of Cole's use of the stage as a site of uplift with *A Trip to Coontown*.[119] With racial uplift at the forefront, Cole and Johnson then wrote two Broadway musicals for African American performers, *The Shoo Fly Regiment* (1906) and *The Red Moon* (1908), both of which, quite originally for the genre, incorporated a storyline.[120] Innovative in their delineations, both these productions presented black men and women as college students. *Shoo Fly Regiment* also offered to audiences black men as heroic patriotic soldiers.[121]

The Red Moon also presented positive and uplifting representations. This show offered a plot in which blacks and Native Americans intermarried and formed interracial solidarity. *The Shoo Fly Regiment* and *The Red Moon* gave audiences the first serious love scenes between a black man and woman on the musical theater stage, breaking the "love scene taboo."[122] According-ing to James Weldon Johnson, previous love scenes between black men and women could only be portrayed on stage as buffoonery in "deference to the superiority stereotype that Negroes can not be supposed to mate romanti-cally, but do so in some sort of minstrel fashion or in some more primeval manner than white people."[123] Ada Overton Walker asserted in 1906 that a "prejudice [existed] against love scenes enacted by Negroes" and this ulti-mately prevented the Williams and Walker company from placing love scenes on stage.[124] Cole and Johnson fully resisted these stereotypes and proscrip-tions.

The appearance of Cole and the Johnson brothers' musical productions proved an anomaly during a time when the minstrel show was the most popular form of entertainment. A love scene between a black man and woman would not appear in the theater again until 1921 with Sissle and Blake's *Shuffle Along*. Love scenes would remain just as elusive after that. After 1924, revues with black casts but written, choreographed, and directed by whites dominated the stage. African American shows became white-pro-duced commodities, which stifled black creative talent, suppressed the black cultural product, and purged the theatrical stage of black romantic love.[125]

Cole's and the Johnson brothers' contribution to the eradication of stereotypes and their new representations of blackness proved important to African American theatrical representation. The team rejected the coon genre after 1900; the full transition from the coon genre to racial pride took full form with *The Shoo Fly Regiment* (1906–1908) and *The Red Moon* (1908–1910) and coincided with the protest of the term "coon" by African Americans. Despite corrosive and repressive U.S. racism at the turn of the century, Cole and Johnson rose above intolerance and, for a moment, created new and innovative ways for representing African Americans.

Figure 7. *Shoo Fly Regiment* sheet music. Manuscript and Rare Books Collection. Schomburg Center for Research in Black Culture.

CHAPTER TWO

COLE AND JOHNSON'S SOCIAL AND POLITICAL THOUGHT

The Case of *Shoo Fly Regiment* and the Spanish-American War

∽

BOB COLE WAS ONE OF THE REAL GENIUSES OF OUR RACE AS A WRITER, PRO-
DUCER, AND ACTOR. . . .

(WILL MARION COOK)[1]

BOB COLE WAS ASSOCIATED WITH JAMES WELDON JOHNSON AND HIS BROTHER
J. ROSAMOND JOHNSON IN THE WRITING OF SOME OF HIS GREATEST SONGS;
BUT THEIR HELP WAS SIMPLY OF THE MECHANICAL SORT—BOB WAS THE
GENIUS.

(WILL MARION COOK)[2]

A S EARLY AS 1893, Bob Cole began collecting data on U.S. imperialistic projects, which enlightened the production of *The Shoo Fly Regiment,* set during the Spanish-American War. Cole placed an illustration of the sinking of the battleship *Maine* in the water near Havana in his scrapbook with the heading "We Have to Remember."[3] Cole also kept clippings on African American soldiers who played an integral role in fighting the Spanish-American War. From these clippings, we can conclude that Cole maintained an acute awareness of the heroism of black soldiers and of the destructive nature of war.

Cole most certainly knew what was at stake in the United States, Cuba, and the Philippines: that blacks faced white lynch mobs here while Filipinos faced U.S. armies; that black soldiers fought against the Filipinos, another aggrieved group; and that black and mulatto Cubans had achieved civil rights through their insurgent war against Spain while the United States denied

African Americans rights in their own country while still expecting them to fight to free the Cubans from Spanish rule.

The setting of *The Shoo Fly Regiment* in Cuba and the Philippines within the Spanish-American War proved a subversive and political act. Cole attempted to educate both black and white audiences through *The Shoo Fly Regiment,* by including black men as soldiers who ultimately win the war. Additionally, by creating sympathetic Filipino characters within the production, Cole not only humanized the Filipinos, but also presented them as allies to African Americans, and replicated some of the real-life relations that developed between the Filipinos and the African American soldiers. By placing African American men within the context of a war fought against other people of color, Cole and Johnson found themselves stuck within the framework of structural racism. This framework denied blacks and other people of color overseas basic human rights while at the same time it promised African Americans citizenship and inclusion by fighting against these very people of color. *The Shoo Fly Regiment* also appeared during a time when the fear of black insurrection weighed heavily on the white imagination; the black, mulatto, and white Cuban insurrection against Spain acted as a reminder of the black "threat" in the United States.

James Weldon Johnson and J. Rosamond Johnson's political thought coincided with Bob Cole's in relation to the war. Before the formation of their partnership, Cole was preserving newspaper articles on the Spanish-American War while on tour with *A Trip to Coontown,* while the Johnsons made their foray into the New York musical theater scene with a musical based on the war. Johnson noted in his 1931 farewell speech to the NAACP that he and J. Rosamond Johnson moved to New York in 1899 to pursue a career in the theater. He recalled that they wrote a satiric musical about the Spanish-American War and upon their arrival in New York shopped the show around to theatrical people in the hopes of getting it produced. Johnson recalled that Oscar Hammerstein and many others rejected the show's premise. Johnson asserted that although his show was well written, he felt the reason for its rejection lay in the fact that "producers feared it was unpatriotic. [He recalled that] The Spanish-American War had just closed, and the opera, first called *Tolosa* and afterwards *The Czar of Zam,* attempted to satirize the new American imperialism."[4]

The Shoo Fly Regiment epitomized Cole and Johnson's effort to educate blacks and whites about the achievements of African Americans. The March 2, 1907, issue of the *Indianapolis Freeman* proposed, "The play covers very thoroughly, and teaches most useful lessons concerning American Negro life."[5] *The Shoo Fly Regiment* performed this service by offering audiences a fully integrated plot in three acts, a departure from the previous forms of musical theater, which failed to use interconnected story lines. Cole and Johnson advertised the show as "The First American Negro Play," and *The New York Age* reported, "all the songs of the piece are written to fit the character that will render them," which indicates that the storyline and the music remained interrelated.[6] The music offered a unique innovation for the time period with the use of ragtime, grand opera, and plantation-style melodies.[7]

Shoo Fly Regiment Summary

The story revolves around the romance of Ned Jackson, a Tuskegee graduate, and Rose Maxwell, the daughter of the principal of Lincolnville Institute. The conflict in the story surfaces when Professor Maxwell refuses to give his consent to their marriage. Because of this turn of events, Ned Jackson joins the army to fight the Spanish-American War in the Philippines. In the military battle scenes, which included a chorus of black soldiers, he emerges as a hero because of "acts of personal bravery" which garnered him military honors. The emergence of Jackson as the hero in the Spanish-American War in the Philippines replicated the actual accomplishments of the black military. *The Cincinnati Enquirer* underscored the fact that "the chorus of men look quite convincing as soldiers."[8]

The secondary plot of the show centered on Cole's character Hunter Wilson, the janitor of Lincolnville Institute. Hunter Wilson marries Ophelia, the Village Pride, a widow with ten children. *The Wheeling Daily News* described Cole's character as somewhat of a social climber, a man who is "ambitious to shine in society."[9] This review identified Cole as the comedian of the production, as the "chief fun maker" who offered the viewers "violent laughter running through the show." In Carriebel Cole Plummer's fictional rendering of Cole's life "What's in a Song," the character who represented Plummer, Mrs. Kingston, states, "Yes he was a funny soldier in his 'Shoo Fly Regiment.' A brave soldier in the thickest of the battle where the bullets were thickest, he would say, 'In the ammunition wagon.' A natural Negro comedian and never used cork to add to his comedy."[10] Comedic female impersonator Andrew Tribble portrayed Ophelia, the Village Pride, which reflected the trend in African American cultural productions. African Americans incorporated female impersonation into minstrelsy and vaudeville, but, according to Ann Marie Bean, female impersonation remained minor in these forms of entertainment.[11] One of the sequences in the play revolved around a scene in the Philippines with Grizelle the Filipino dancer, played by Siren Nevarro, and African American Lieutenant Dixon, played by Theodore Pankey.

The resolution of the show presented Ned Jackson as the hero of the war, heralded and celebrated by those at the school and in the town. With this turn of events, Professor Maxwell grants Ned Jackson permission to marry his daughter.[12] The last act also included Cole and Johnson in a "singing sketch" reminiscent of their "old days in vaudeville."[13]

Cole and Johnson included settings and situations that replicated actual events in African American life, as the *Indianapolis Freeman* aptly noted: "the old plantation home filled with fidelity to the traditions of the past," the Lincolnville Institute reception hall with the male student "wooing the dusky maid in classic English," and in the performances of "the cultured song, or piano rhapsodies, in all these various phases reality appears, the eloquence of truth speaks."[14]

Uplift and Shoo Fly Regiment

While Cole and Johnson utilized some minstrel modes and stereotypes, including a female impersonator, Pickaninnies, and songs with Southern-themed titles such as "Southland," and "I Will Always Love Old Dixie," they made progressive changes in African American theater. One of the most important and significant advances offered by the team included a change in the representation of African American characters. They discarded the stereotypical images of Zip Coon, Jim Crow, and Mammy and replaced them with black men as heroic, patriotic, educated, and loving, and black women as literate, virtuous, and romantic.[15]

Cole and Johnson incorporated three important uplift strategies within *The Shoo Fly Regiment:* education as an important tool of uplift for the black community, the depiction of black men as masculine through their participation in the Spanish-American War, and the use of a serious love scene.[16] Their inclusion of African American women within the uplift agenda, while perhaps appearing to communicate heteronormative patriarchal ideology, actually rearticulated Booker T. Washington's progressive approach to gender equality at Tuskegee Institute.[17] As for why the inclusion of a serious love scene and African American men as stouthearted is so significant in African American characterizations, we must look at why proscriptions existed.

The prohibition against the portrayal of realistic love scenes between African Americans existed to consign them to a marginal place in society, to control African Americans, and, most significantly, to mask the humanity of African Americans. In 1906 Ada Overton Walker asserted that African Americans wanted to present theatrical productions just as "beautiful and as artistic in every way as do the white actors," but that African American performers confronted racist barriers, including the love scene taboo and "ten thousand" other obstacles, which limited the ways in which they could craft their shows due to white hegemony.[18] The interdiction existed to dehumanize African Americans and to argue that they did not experience the full spectrum of human emotions as whites, thus justifying their oppression. The taboo against portrayals of African American men as manly and heroes of war existed for several reasons. First, the African American male posed a threat to white male hegemony by contesting their consigned position as slaves and marginal workers. Their masculinity also proved dangerous to white power because the African American male body became unmanageable and difficult to control. The risk of their demanding equality in the United States loomed large given their show of patriotism through their male power. African American men as warriors fighting U.S. wars might expose the weakness of the white male body and threaten white supreme power if African American men proved the victors of the war. Finally, the image of African American males with weapons brought into the forefront of white supremacists minds the risk of an African American uprising in the United States. By white supremacists I am talking about ordinary white men and women in the North and South, as well as those belonging to organizations such as the Ku Klux Klan who believe in white domination and the subjugation of nonwhites. The use of the Spanish-American War offers one of the most interesting aspects of the plot given the role that black men played within this war.

The Spanish-American War and Black Masculinity

The concept of manliness developed significantly between the Civil War and World War I. The prevailing definition of manliness in the late 1800s placed white men at the center as noble, worthy, strong, brave, independent in spirit, and magnanimous. Gail Bederman argues that the subjugation of the "lower races" through white masculine power and racial and gender dominance proved necessary in order to assert the myth of the ideal man as white and to maintain the power structure. Davarion L. Baldwin argues that both Booker T. Washington's and W. E. B. Du Bois's ideologies regarding African American masculinity revolved around edifying African American men, raising their rank in U.S. society, and, most importantly, "the repression or at least disciplining of the body toward 'higher' moral ideals."[19] Booker T. Washington employed the Spanish-American War to locate African American men at the core of masculinity through Victorian morals, education, and battle. Washington contended that education provided an avenue in which African American men could assert their manliness. Washington also incorporated war into his discourse on black masculinity in *A New Negro for a New Century,* where he tendered a not so veiled response to Roosevelt's demeaning remarks concerning the stoutheartedness of the black soldiers of the Spanish-American War. Washington dedicated several chapters to the heroism of the black soldier beginning with the Revolutionary War and included the writings of many of the African American soldiers who contested Roosevelt's depiction of them. Washington asserted that Roosevelt's account "makes very nice reading, but it is not history, in which it is always hazardous to sacrifice truth to make a period round."[20] In response to the new ideologies concerning masculinity, Cole and Johnson created new perceptions of black manliness by incorporating some of the ideas from the white manliness movement, including proving one's masculinity through war, prizefighting, the conquest of the West, and education. They defined black masculinity by reference to the Spanish-American War, just as Theodore Roosevelt used the conflict as a test of white manhood. Cole and Johnson attempted to redefine black masculinity by proving the black male manly and civil, thus deserving of full citizenship.

Bob Cole, J. Rosamond Johnson, and James Weldon Johnson propounded that scholarship and education proved key qualities for their ideal, masculinized, black man. They succeeded in projecting this image through publicity in the media about their college careers. Books by Shakespeare and Balzac, as well as music and other literary volumes, characterized Cole and Johnson's studio as a place of erudition, all of which added to the narrative of the team as both educated and refined.[21] As part of their strategy of redefining black masculinity, Cole and Johnson used the manly sport of boxing and the career of Jack Johnson to aggrandize African American men.

Jack Johnson: The Hypermasculine African American Übermensch

WE ARE IN THE MIDST OF A GROWING MENACE. THE BLACK MAN IS RAPIDLY FORGING

TO THE FRONT RANKS IN ATHLETICS, ESPECIALLY IN THE FIELD OF FISTICUFFS. WE
ARE IN THE MIDST OF A BLACK RISE AGAINST WHITE SUPREMACY. . . .
(CHARLES A. DANA ON THE BLACK BOXER PETER JACKSON, 1895)[22]

In 1895 Dana likened black superiority in boxing to the loss of white supremacy, which foreshadowed the rise of the ultimate representation of black male power, Jack Johnson. Before Johnson, whites dominated the sport and used boxing to prove their masculinity and physical prowess. When Johnson asserted his manliness by defeating whites and flaunting his middle-class status, he proved that black men were a force to be reckoned with. He challenged the discourse of black male inferiority, proved that the black male body symbolized a source of supreme power, incited fear by displaying the vulnerability of the white male body, and raised the hopes of the African American community.[23]

Frederick Douglass typified the power of the black male body in his physical resistance to slavery through his triumphant battle against the slave breaker Covey. Douglass realized the full potency of his body—"I was nothing before; I was a man now."[24] Douglass's victory marked how the black male slave body came to represent a commination to hegemony and led to the invention of the black male as an irrepressible sexual threat to white womanhood, what James Baldwin referred to as a "walking phallic symbol."[25] White supremacists participated in violence to control the black male body, like the 1899 "race war" in Blossburg, Alabama, where whites accused African American Johnson Shepard of sexual assault and attacked armed blacks, murdering four.[26] The black male child's body also proved dangerous, as the October 1958 "Kissing Case" of Monroe, North Carolina demonstrated with the arrest of nine-year-old Hanover Thompson and seven-year-old David Simpson, both charged with rape punishable by death, because a white girl kissed Thompson."[27] All learned that the black male body remains sinister. A strategy used to dominate the black male body included theorizing that it was inherently different and foreign from whites, in need of containment through enslavement, lynching, stereotypes, laws, incarceration, military training, and rendering it impotent.[28]

Many of the theories surrounding the black male body appeared to be crystallized in the body of Jack Johnson, the hypermasculine African American übermensch, the New Negro, prepotent in body and regnant over hegemony, a menace to white male dominion while at the same time personifying the authoritative ideal of masculinity and power. Johnson promoted racial superiority, exhibited pride in his African heritage, and physically fought white power and anyone who offended him.[29] Johnson fashioned a public persona as a super-confident, erudite sophisticate, a sportsman who graced the cover of *Les Sports Illustrés* and attended the Grand Prix; a world traveler; a master of many languages, including French and Latin; and a wealthy connoisseur of fine things such as fast, expensive cars and luxurious clothing.[30] As part of his persona he publicly paraded and courted the forbidden and dangerous—white women. He squired them around the world, married them, and brashly taunted white men and their lynch laws through these associations. These actions added to his celebrity and the perception that he was one all-powerful black man who unequivocally refused the designation of degraded black male.

In 1908 a bellicose Johnson sought the heavyweight title from Tommy Burns, who repeatedly rebuffed him for fear that it would dishonor the white race.[31] The cartoon "The Man They All Dodge," illustrates this. It depicts a well-muscled Johnson in a checkered suit and reads "Jack Johnson in street togs." He holds a cigar in his right hand and sports a diamond ring on his left. His face is drawn beautifully, with a shaven head, prominent forehead and nose, smooth lips, and expressive eyes gazing right. In the background are "coons" with large eyes and lips. One peeks from behind a door and states, "Mistah Johnson is still waiting for Tommy Burns."[32] They do not detract from Johnson's powerful image; rather they advance Johnson as the hypermasculine African American übermensch. Omitted are the boxers who "all dodge" Johnson, which exposes their hypocrisy.

White racists calling for the preservation of the white man's honor dragged Jim Jeffries out of retirement, away from his farm, off the vaudeville circuit, and into the ring, where in July 1910 Johnson annihilated him, further exposing the white male body as impotent, which resulted in lynchings and pandemonium.[33] To preserve white power, white newsmen painted Johnson as beastlike and comedic. In 1925 they reported, "'Mr. Jeffries,' said Jack, his lips parting in a big grin, 'ain't no use in talking. Dis is one time you'se met yo Waterloo! Jes' go an tell em I said so. Yas sir—Waterloo is right!'"[34] This exemplifies the tactics used to depose him. Johnson utilized the media to counter misrepresentation and carefully shaped a public persona as a master of English. On July 5, 1910, Johnson avowed "I won from Mr. Jeffries because I outclassed him in every department of the fighting game. Before I entered the ring I was certain I would be the victor. I never changed my mind at anytime."[35] Johnson cleverly used "outclass" as a double entendre and asserted that he outclassed Jeffries in the ring, and he outclassed Jeffries, a farm boy out of the ring, as a refined, stylishly dressed black man with a "beautiful" white wife. Johnson incensed racists, for they could not control him, and he taunted their lynch laws by flaunting his white wives. Johnson's vaingloriousness drew the admiration of some in the black community, such as W. E. B. Du Bois, and the ire of others, such as Booker T. Washington.

In 1913 Dubois cleverly used Johnson's interracial marriages to promote the protection of African American women so that "that white men shall let our sisters alone," while also exposing the degenerate behavior of white southern men toward African American women.[36] Conversely Washington felt Johnson disgraced the race by marrying white, violating the Mann Act, and living a flamboyant lifestyle, which did not fit his uplift ideology.[37] Many African Americans like Cole and Johnson idolized Johnson for his prowess, his kindly demeanor, and his ascendance as the hypermasculine superman, while not giving weight to his choice in women.

Cole and Johnson befriended Jack Johnson around 1905; James Weldon Johnson described him as the most interesting person he had ever met, a very likeable, affable, gentle person with his soft-spoken "Southern speech and laughter" and a sad face "until he smiled."[38] At this early juncture in Jack Johnson's career his physical strength and expertise remained praiseworthy, ever present, and something that many, including Cole and Johnson, wanted to emulate. James Weldon Johnson immersed himself in Jack Johnson's masculine power through the "'manly art of self-defense." Johnson states that "Jack often boxed with me playfully, like a good-natured big dog warding off the earnest attacks of a small one, but I could never get him to give me any serious instruction."[39] Although Jack Johnson did not take their lessons seriously, James Weldon Johnson admired Johnson greatly and felt that he represented African American male power. Johnson wrote that Jack Johnson symbolized all African American men and their masculinity, and that when faced with the myth of Anglo-Saxon physical and intellectual superiority "the black man did not wilt." With this statement James Weldon Johnson fused together all African American men with Jack Johnson and put forth that the African American male communally claimed his power over white hegemony as their own.[40] James Weldon Johnson noted that Frederick Douglass hung a photograph of the Virgin Island–born, Australian-raised black boxer Peter Jackson in his office as an example of an athlete "doing his part to solve the race question," and "solv[ing] the race problem."[41] By offering Douglass's endorsement of Jackson as a race man James Weldon Johnson merged Jack Johnson and Peter Jackson together to argue that Jack Johnson also ennobled the race.[42] James Weldon Johnson followed Douglass's ideology concerning sports and uplift and linked Jack Johnson with masculinity and the physical joy of sports, as an approach to apotheosizing black men.

Cole and Johnson and the Hypermasculine
African American Übermensch

For a portion of the African American community, Jack Johnson represented the restoration of the African American male body from slavery and oppression to redemption, potency, and power. So it is no wonder that Cole and Johnson would use their bodies and their manliness to redeem the African American male in U.S. society. Like Jack Johnson, the Cole and Johnson team showed their masculinity through their bodies. Newspaper articles described Cole and Johnson's physical prowess in athletics (especially boxing), thus helping to redefine black masculinity and encouraging the belief that black males deserved full rights and privileges of citizenship. A newspaper article in *The World* described Rosamond as "best developed about the chest, arms and hands. His chest expansion is six inches. Cole is best developed in the legs, back and muscles of the stomach."[43]

The *New York Age* reported that Cole and the Johnsons' daily physical regimen began at seven-thirty in the morning with "systematic exercise," including a little boxing. Accomplished at golf, swimming, football, and baseball, the trio competed in these sports as they did at Atlanta University.[44] Their studio resembled a gym, complete with rowing machines, parallel bars, punching bags, dumbbells, "Indian Clubs," "African weapons of warfare" including the flail of a Zulu Chieftain, assegais, boomerangs, and bolos.[45] The Cleveland *Plain Dealer* stated that while Bob Cole and James Weldon boxed regularly every morning, Rosamond "does not indulge in boxing on account of his piano playing."[46]

Sports played a significant role in the uplift agenda and ideology of Cole and Johnson and the *New York Age*. By using the print media to redefine blackness as respectable and masculine, the team worked to educate blacks as well as whites by positioning themselves and the members of the company as role models in the quest for black racial uplift. During the tour of *The Red Moon*, a series of articles on the physical prowess of the company ran in the papers. In one, Lester Walton reported that Theodore Pankey "is doping out all the theatrical baseball teams. He can tell you about baseball away back in the '70's."[47] On January 10, 1910, Walton reported that *The Red Moon* company organized a baseball team named The Cole and Johnson Giants. Henry Gant, who played Bill Gibson in the show, used his expertise as a former member of the professional team the Cuban Giants to captain the Cole and Johnson Giants. According to Walton, Gant "carefully arrang[ed] a system of signals for use this coming year."[48] *The Red Moon* company participated in charity games, including one against Howard University on the campus, and a charity event played for the benefit of the Washington, D.C., Y.M.C.A. building fund.[49]

While performing in Toronto, Canada, the company entered a championship skating match at the Crystal Palace on February 4, 1910. The Cole and Johnson Giants learned and played ice hockey, with Sam Lucas as the goalie.[50] Walton described Cole as "a baseball fan of the thirty-third degree," who, when in Washington D.C., watched a baseball game between the Ridgewood-Royal Giants and the Royal Giants-Philadelphia at Melrose Park.[51] Walton reported that Cole remained in ill humor at a game because his favorite team, the New York Giants, displayed an embarrassing losing streak.[52] Carriebel Plummer described his longstanding affinity with baseball as originating in his boyhood when he excelled at sports and belonged to a baseball team in Athens, and eventually pitched on the Atlanta University baseball team with Johnson.[53] Cole's dedication to sports proved a lifelong passion and offered an avenue in which Cole and Johnson could create an African American masculinity infused with veneration and uplift.

Just as Theodore Roosevelt connected white masculinity with expansion to the West and the Indian Wars, Cole and Johnson also chose the West to define their masculinity. *The World* maintained that the team lived in the West for several years after college, where they showed off their athletic skills. In an article for the *New York Age* the author described James Johnson's expertise as a runner and a sheepherder as almost superhuman. J. Rosamond Johnson recounted that while driving sheep to flock without his bronco, James Weldon ran faster than four jackrabbits.[54]

Cole and Johnson's efforts to positively affect the hegemonic discourse on the black male proved daunting given that the print media found ways to stereotype and demean them. For example, the *World* newspaper article entitled "Athletics Evidently Help Cole and Johnson" included a cartoon, which pictured a blackened Cole and Johnson with big lips and eyes. One of the team is pictured sitting at the piano singing "Under the Bamboo Tree," while the cartoon depicts the other members of the group boxing. The caption reads, "He may get over it, but he'll never look the same." The second cartoon that accompanies the article shows one of the group pictured grotesquely blackened with big lips and eyes, lifting a dumbbell and doing the cakewalk with the caption "Dumbbell Cake Walk."[55] Created to present Cole and Johnson as monstrous caricatures, these cartoons could not mask the team's intelligence and dignity that belied the newspaper page as their words revealed their strategy to redefine the black man as educated, talented, physically attractive, and athletic. Through their efforts, a new picture of black masculinity emerged and made its way into the twenty-first century, that of the supremely powerful African American male who fought ferociously. He would reinvent himself in each subsequent historical period in U. S. history, modeled after the quintessential representation—Jack Johnson.

The athlete, scholar, and performer Paul Robeson embodied this new image of African American masculinity. He was the first black All American football player, playing at Rutgers University between 1915–1919; he played professional football with the Akron Pros (1920, 1921) and the Milwaukee Badgers (1922), and excelled at baseball, basketball and track. He belonged to the prestigious Phi Beta Kappa fraternity, graduated summa cum laude from Rutgers, earned a law degree from Columbia University, mastered many languages including African dialects, Russian, Arabic, and Chinese, and became a musicologist and renowned actor and political activist.[56] Like Cole and the Johnsons, he also displayed his muscular body by posing for photographs, sculptures, and drawings that portrayed him as the definitive black masculine form.[57] Between the 1950s and the 1970s boxer Muhammad Ali used his wit and his body to redefine black masculinity, as the most publicly vocal of the athletes of his era. Ali publicly toyed with his opponents with poetic verve and was compared to Jack Johnson because of his vaingloriousness. Like Cole and Johnson, Ali epitomized black manliness coupled with a politicized ideology, by winning the gold medal at the Olympics in 1960 and "in a gesture of racial defiance of American hypocrisy," throwing the medal into the river.[58] In 1964 he wrested the heavyweight title from Sonny Liston, courted controversy by studying with Malcolm X, converted to Islam, and changed his name from Cassius Clay to Muhammad Ali. He refused to fight in the Vietnam War in 1966 on religious grounds; became a college spokesperson against the war, and was censured by the New York State boxing commission, which stripped Ali of his title because of his anti-war stance.[59] He won his case against the commission in 1970 and defeated Joe Frazier in 1973 and George Foreman in 1974, regaining the heavyweight title.[60] Ali personified the ultimate hypermasculine African American übermensch. In the 1960s African American masculinity hit its stride with scholar/athlete/activists such as tennis star Arthur Ashe, an anti-apartheid activist, AIDs activist, and advocate for Haitian immigrants, who blossomed into a gentle, graceful black masculine model. The defiant 1968 black nationalist Olympians John Carlos and Tommy Smith, baseball star Hank Aaron, and former San Antonio Spurs children's advocate David Robinson all embodied the powerful new black male role model through their fusing of athleticism and activism.[61] In *The Shoo Fly Regiment* Cole and Johnson enfolded the hypermasculine African American übermensch and their conception of black masculinity with the manliness of the African American soldiers of the Spanish-American War.

The Restoration of the African American through the Spanish-American War

MANY A FAIR-SKINNED VOLUNTEER GOES WHOLE AND SOUND TO-DAY,
FOR THE SUCCOR OF THE COLORED TROOPS, THE BATTLE RECORDS SAY;
AND THE FEUD IS DONE FOREVER, OF THE BLUE COAT AND THE GRAY;
ALL HONOR THE TENTH, AT LA QUISIMA.

(ST. JOSEPH RADICAL)[62]

One of the most significant aims of the uplift ideology included African Americans' pursuit of citizenship rights. The denial of the basic rights of the "common man" such as voting, education, and land ownership motivated W. E. B. Du Bois, Booker T. Washington, and leaders of the uplift ideology to encourage blacks to prove their patriotism to the United States as a basis for claiming the full fruits and benefits of citizenship. Washington encouraged black participation in the Spanish-American War, but noted in the January 1, 1898, *Bulletin of Atlanta University* that black soldiers aided the United States government even though they encountered apartheid-like laws at home.[63] Washington suggested that the United States "succeeded in every conflict except in the effort to conquer ourselves in blotting out racial prejudices."[64] He argued that black and white men in the North and South must come to a peaceful resolution, and he hoped that the "trenches that we dug together around Santiago [Cuba] shall be the eternal burial place of all that which separates us in our business and civil relations."[65] Washington pointed to the heroism of the black soldiers of the Spanish-American War and argued that because of African Americans' willingness to die for their country, the United States should afford them opportunities.[66] As followers of Washington and DuBois, it remains no surprise that Cole and Johnson placed their heroes within the framework of war, and dealt with the complexities of the role of the black soldier, U.S. racism, and citizenship rights within their productions.

The actual black soldiers who fought this war faced opposition and brutality at home, which prevented them from obtaining basic human rights. Because of the explosion of the U.S. battleship *Maine* in Havana Harbor, the United States joined the black, mulatto, and white Cuban insurgent war against Spain in February 1898.[67] The United States government expected black soldiers to fight in Cuba while at the same time sanctioning the lynch mob and black disfranchisement in the United States. The Spanish-American War in Cuba lasted approximately six months and ended with the Treaty of Paris that required Spain to relinquish ownership of Cuba and ceded Puerto Rico, the Philippines, and Guam to the United States, making it a colonial power.

This war purported to "free" the Cubans from Spanish rule, but it eventually led to U.S. soldiers fighting against the Filipinos seeking independence from the United States as well as from Spain, turning the war into a campaign against people of color. Amy Kaplan suggests that this war worked as a continuation of the Civil War, an "ideological battle against Reconstruction." Kaplan argues that two battlefronts emerged: domestic and international, with blacks at the center in a struggle for civil rights.[68] I would like to argue that four battlefronts emerged—the Haitian Revolution, the Civil War, and the Spanish-American War in Cuba and in the Philippines. Nonwhites remained at the axis of these wars, charged with fighting for civil rights. The core of these crusades for independence lay in the aggrieved communities of color's struggle against European hegemony, and these resistance movements brought into focus the power of people of color. These battles against white domination threatened the concept of white power and white male superiority, which the Spanish-American War represented to white supremacists. The Spanish-American War in the white male imagination worked to reconstruct white masculinity previously destroyed by the Civil War. The hope of restoring white manhood through conquering "the other" would reverberate time and again in U.S. history. By uniting the North and the South "against a common external enemy," African Americans, and other "lesser" races, the nation would reunite and the white male body would revitalize.[69] The war worked symbolically to prove the vitality, vigor, and manliness of the white male body. It also elucidated the power of people of color in their fight for rights and self-rule. Cole and Johnson wrote *The Shoo Fly Regiment* in effect to rejuvenate the black male body through the Spanish-American War.

The Battle for San Juan Hill proved the most prominent cultural icon of the war. Yet by most accounts this battle resulted in a debacle. The sorry state of the U.S. army caused the military failures because of the amateur white soldiers who suffered deadly casualties. The battle was not even fought on the "romantic" San Juan Hill but rather on the mundane and denigratingly titled "Kettle Hill."[70] The other prominent cultural icon of the war, Theodore Roosevelt, tried to rewrite his own history and the history surrounding this battle. Roosevelt redefined himself as a manly imperialist, a cowboy, Indian fighter, warring yet civilized, the ultimate great white conqueror of people of color, the hero of the Spanish American War. He defined white men by what they were not—black, brown, or yellow.[71]

The recruits for Roosevelt's Rough Riders included cowboys, educated men, athletes, Indian fighters, and army personnel. As a Harvard graduate, Roosevelt embodied the civilized white man who in fighting the Spanish American War sacrificed his life of luxury and privilege by taking on the white man's burden by fighting for the black, mulatto, and white Cubans.[72] Thus manhood through the Spanish-American War, as illustrated by Roosevelt's actions, remained connected to his colonialist mentality and his nationalism and racism.

The Spanish-American War provided the perfect opportunity for redefining the black male in the United States, and *The Shoo Fly Regiment* proved the ideal vehicle. African Americans fought in this war side by side with whites, and consequently a certain segment of the white and African American population in the United States perceived them as heroes for their valor. During the war, both the black and the white press cited the black soldiers for their heroism at San Juan Hill. On their return home the soldiers received honors, with the publication of books recounting their bravery; cities gave them homecoming parades, and the U.S. government bestowed congressional medals on these paragons of doughtiness. The city of Philadelphia paid tribute to the "sable hero," First Sergeant George Berry and the Tenth Cavalry, at their Peace Jubilee, where Berry was "pelted with roses from the balconies and stands crowded with people."[73] The print media initially elevated the status of the black soldiers to mythic proportions by recounting their courage in battle. In *Black Troopers* African American Dr. Miles V. Lynk reported that at La Quisima the black Ninth and Tenth Cavalry rescued the Rough Riders from an ambush by Spanish sharpshooters.[74] One southerner wrote in the *Washington Post:* "If it had not been for the Negro cavalry, the Rough Riders would have been exterminated. I am not a Negro lover. My father fought with Mosby's Rangers and I was born in the South, but the Negroes saved that fight. . . ."[75]

The Rough Riders, a group of amateur soldiers, could not really compare to the highly decorated professional black units who had already tested their expertise in battles against Native Americans. Among them stood First Sergeant Berry, who gained his expertise by fighting "the Cheyenne's, Kiowa's, Arapahoe's, Comanche's, Apaches, and Ute's in Colorado, Kansas, Texas, and New Mexico."[76] African American participation in the Indian wars marked a pattern in U.S. history where citizenship rights remained intrinsically linked to fighting other aggrieved communities of color, and seizing their rights and lands. The novel *Captain Blackman* details this pattern through the experiences of Captain Blackman, who fought in *all* the U.S. wars to date, including the Indian Wars. Blackman encounters Native American Man in Rain and offers him a meal and Man in Rain provides the following narrative.

[O]ne day you'll tire of the white man killing you one by one, like stragglers in a buffalo herd, and you'll fight. That will come long after you've helped him kill me. But it will come.

Blackman nodded. That day would surely come, and if it did, and he was still alive and Man in the Rain was still alive, the Indian could have his land back.[77]

The novel underscores the terrible consequences of black participation in U.S. wars against people of color to gain citizenship rights that Blackman comes to realize will never materialize. The African American soldiers of the Spanish-American War did not have the foresight of Blackman and felt certain that they would gain enfranchisement. For the most part the black soldier exhibited a martial spirit and fought proudly for their rights through this war.

Roosevelt and the Black Soldiers

Contemporary accounts acknowledged the bravery and heroism of the African American soldiers, which threatened to diminish the reputation of the Rough Riders. A year after the war, Theodore Roosevelt created a negative image of the performance by black troops. He wrote that they behaved in a cowardly manner by moving to the back and "[t]his I could not allow, as it was depleting my line on the battlefront."[78] In his attempt to debase black soldiers, Roosevelt claimed that they compelled him to draw his revolver, and that he "called out to them that I appreciated the gallantry with which they had fought and would be sorry to hurt them, but that I should shoot the first man who, on any pretense whatever, went to the rear." At this point Roosevelt asserted that his men could attest that he always kept his word, as he cast the Rough Riders in a silly opera. "[M]y cow-puncher, hunters, and miners solemnly nodded their heads and commented in chorus, exactly as if in a comic opera, 'He always does, he always does!'"[79] According to Roosevelt, the black soldiers then "flashed their white teeth at one another and they broke into broad grins, and [he] had no more trouble with them."[80] Roosevelt casts the Rough Riders in a comic opera and the African American soldiers in a blackface minstrel show, simultaneously demeaning both groups and ultimately portraying himself as the only real man in the battle. He neglected to state that black soldiers moved to the rear to transport their wounded and to rejoin their regiment according to standard military practice.

Roosevelt's depiction of them drastically misportrayed their actual heroism. An article saved by Bob Cole entitled "Negroes at Siboney, Too. Twenty-Fourth Infantry's Work in the Fever Camp" illustrates the role the black soldiers played in the war. The Spanish armies underestimated the black soldiers and attacked them, believing in their vulnerability. Their strategy failed because of the black soldiers' valiance, battle skills, and their tactical brilliance. "The Twenty-fourth kept on, meeting the fire from the hilltops unflinchingly, ignoring the galling cross fire, not minding the bullets that pattered on the wire fence ahead."[81]They stayed on San Juan Hill to relieve other commands during the night and returned to the trenches during the day only to face rain, oppressive heat, and no shelter, persevering and keeping their countenance.[82]

A day after the battle of San Juan Hill the *San Francisco Chronicle* reported that a Spanish officer told a white American officer that

> "[W]e didn't leave our positions, until we saw creeping on toward us these black men, these Haitians." "No not Haitians" said the American officer, "but Americans." Spaniards did not retreat—not even from Americans, until they thought Haitians soldiers were in sight! Every race loving Negro's heart must swell within him while he reads these lines![83]

African Americans "swelled with pride," for they linked the Haitian Revolution and the Cuban Insurgent War with their ongoing fight for freedom in the United States. By merging the black soldiers' fearlessness with the gallant Haitians, many African Americans came to envision full enfranchisement as obtainable through insurgency. The amalgamating of the black and Haitian soldiers by the Spaniards, who only retreated when they saw them, illuminates the growing strength of the African American man and his threat to hegemony. The fusing of the black and Haitian soldier, the knowledge that black soldiers like Sergeant Bivens held the "The Distinguished Marksman class," and photographs of black troops bearing arms must have instilled in white supremacists intense fear by elucidating the potential danger of a U.S. black uprising. The courageousness of the "Colored Regiments" and their rescue of Roosevelt and the Rough Riders contested and threatened the very conception of white manhood. The presence of the stouthearted African American soldier magnified the weakening of the white male body and growing black strength. Cole and Johnson took note: *The Shoo Fly Regiment* reflects their careful reading of the African champions of the Spanish-American War and the Haitian Revolution. While the African American soldiers fought for one colonial power against another, Afro-Cuban commissioned officers and generals manned the Cuban Insurgent War and made up 40 percent of the personnel. Their tactical expertise, which secured Cuba's victory against Spain, and Cole and Johnson's knowledge of their existence and their military feats and triumphs surely led the team to center the story of *The Shoo Fly Regiment* around the war. They could not have missed the irony of two black colonial subjects fighting side by side against white hegemony in Cuba. Cole and the Johnsons must have seen the relationship between the struggles of Africans in Cuba and the U.S. and cleverly used the war for its references to the Haitian Revolution in the show in order to aggrandize African Americans by using the tools of hegemony—conquest, war, and masculinity. By alluding to the Haitian Revolution and by overtly positioning African American soldiers at the axis of the Great White Way, that is, Broadway, Cole and Johnson took a stand against white hegemony and unapologetically and unstintingly propounded black power. The Haitian Revolution and the African American and Afro-Cuban soldiers of the Spanish-American War threatened hegemony at its very core. The Great White conqueror had been conquered on all fronts.

By censuring the black soldiers and making them subordinate, Roosevelt insured the denial of the rights the soldiers hoped for, such as equality within the army and the appointment of black officers. Roosevelt destroyed their heroic narrative by creating a narrative built on stereotypes of black men as weak and unable to take charge unless guided by whites. Several political issues framed this portrayal, the most important being the struggle for the appointment of black commissioned officers. Spanish-American War veteran Corporal William T. Goode noted that when African Americans rallied for commissioned officers and the government refused to comply, many African Americans volunteers resigned rather than allow white officers dominion over them.[84]

Roosevelt's account of the war contributed to the argument for white leadership of black soldiers and the argument against black officers, producing a counterplot to the aspirations of African American soldiers who had fought independently. For example, the Twenty-fifth Infantry battled triumphantly under the command of black Colonel First Sergeant S. W. Taliaferro at El Caney, when the white officers were killed "or lay weltering in their life blood."[85]

Another political reason for painting the black soldiers as unqualified for battle included the threat of an uprising. African American soldiers' very presence in the war contested Roosevelt's vision of a United States as distinctly white and raised the fear of black revolt.[86] The black soldier's role in the war threatened to eradicate Roosevelt's iconic white, manly, imperialistic vanquisher. Thus Roosevelt retold the tale and placed himself and the Rough Riders at the center of the war. African Americans fully resisted Roosevelt's account of their role in the war and fought back in the press and in their autobiographies.

For African Americans the pursuit of full citizenship became one of the most important aspects of the uplift movement, and they demanded rights by demonstrating their manhood through war. The Rough Riders' image was created to symbolize white American masculinity, culture, and progress.[87] Because this war took place against nonwhite people in the Philippines and Cuba, Roosevelt attempted to draw parallels between the Spanish-American War and the war against the Native Americans. Roosevelt wanted to assert the necessity of imperialism through the conquest of "lesser races." By creating an image of the Rough Riders as representative of American masculine racial power inside the racialized project of imperialism, African American soldiers faced erasure from the discourse on American masculinity. Returning African American soldiers in uniform defied ideas about their masculinity and virility, their place in U.S. society, and traditional stereotypes, which led to violence against them. Black soldiers faced racism and Jim Crow laws on leaving for war and came home to the same repressive conditions, even though they had displayed their patriotic zeal.

They discovered that no matter how many medals and honors they received for their service, their show of patriotism as soldiers aroused a storm of bitter hostility in white racists. African American Sergeant Horace Bivens recounts that when he and the Tenth Cavalry left the West to fight in the Spanish-American War, they encountered thousands of cheering supporters in Madison, Wisconsin, in Illinois, and in Nashville, Tennessee, but as they moved south, Jim Crow greeted them. Bivens writes that in depot waiting rooms and lunchrooms signs read, "Niggers are not allowed inside." Bivens states "[w]e were traveling in palace cars and the people were surprised that we did not occupy the 'Jim Crow' cars, *the curse of the South*" (emphasis in original).[88] As they stepped out of their assigned positions as a subclass, African American soldiers met tremendous resistance at home, which erupted in harassment and carnage.[89] T. Thomas Fortune reported that upon returning home, black soldiers in Virginia, Georgia, and Florida were subjected to brutal attacks by the "mobocratic ruffianism of Southern soldiers," and in Georgia white soldiers shot black soldiers "in cold blood."[90] They refused to tolerate this abuse, however. Private George Washington returned to the United States only to face being maligned and attacked by a white man with a razor. Private Stephan Patterson, who attended the trial of Washington's attacker, stated, "'[w]e did our duty in Cuba, and we don't think we should be insulted because we are black.'"[91]

Heightened U.S. racial violence in the form of lynchings of blacks coincided with the Spanish-American War. While black soldiers fought for the United States, neither the Republican party nor the Democratic party showed a commitment to protect their political or legal rights. Although the Republican party acknowledged black soldiers' participation in the war and hoped for success in fighting against subjugation and condemned lynching as savage, they made no effort to end it.[92]

James Weldon Johnson's awareness of violence that blacks experienced daily propelled him to write articles condemning lynching. He argued that lynch laws, which allowed whites in the South to take black men from their beds and from jail, became so common that it failed to arouse notice from the general public. He maintained that the South would fail to flourish and develop its resources due to the laws. Johnson advanced the idea that mob law remained antithetical to a civilized and morally sound government; therefore the South could not join ranks with other Christian societies until it "abolishes such cruel and barbaric practices." He contended that the South must practice accountability for the rights and safety of all its citizens.[93]

Beginning with the Black codes in 1865, state after state adopted restrictive policies against African Americans, including grandfather clauses and various tests and qualifications, which ultimately prevented blacks from voting, while exempting whites from these exams. The 1876 withdrawal of federal troops from the South led white supremacists to run amok attacking blacks. Continuing race riots in African American communities, such as Wilmington, North Carolina in 1898, culminated in the murder and mass exodus of the African Americans there.[94] White racialized barbarism proved effective in controlling the black population, given that protection by legal means proved nonexistent. For example, African American women had little legal recourse when assaulted by white *or* black men.[95] Rayford Logan suggests that while the South condoned savagery against African Americans, the Northern press condoned the maintenance of white supremacy through "peaceful means."[96]

Cole and Johnson's Social and Political Thought

Cole and Johnson coupled their black masculinist discourse with Roosevelt's strenuous life rhetoric, as part of a strategy to aggrandize African Americans and to argue that African Americans remained decorous and deserved citizenship rights.[97] The team followed Booker T. Washington's lead by negotiating their support of Theodore Roosevelt while openly criticizing him. Washington steadfastly endorsed Roosevelt and wielded considerable power due to his relationship with him; however, he publicly castigated Roosevelt in

A New Negro for a New Century for his attempt to emasculate and humiliate the African American soldiers of the Spanish American War. Privately Washington asked Roosevelt to reverse his unjust decision to discharge three troops of black soldiers due to the Brownsville Riot in Texas.[98] Cole and Johnson adopted Washington's position by aligning themselves with Roosevelt while publicly contesting Roosevelt's abasement of the valorous African American soldiers of the war in their musical *The Shoo Fly Regiment.*

In 1934 James Weldon Johnson wrote *Negro Americans What Now?,* in which he laid out a plan of action to gain rights and conquer white racism in the United States. Johnson argued that neither socialism nor isolationism proved good methods for the enfranchisement of African Americans. He offered that negotiating with whites and forming biracial coalitions with whites in organizations such as the National Association for the Advancement of Colored People offered the best solution. Cole and Johnson's strategies in combating racism and their alignment to Roosevelt reflected the times in which they lived and the limited but real power which they wielded. While their allegiance to Roosevelt might appear illogical or counterproductive, their use of musical theater to critique Roosevelt and to ennoble the African American fighters in the Spanish-American war remains clever, cunning, and praiseworthy.

Cole and Johnson's connection to Theodore Roosevelt dates back to 1903, when a cartoon appeared with the copyright of the Judge Company of New York. This cartoon depicted Theodore Roosevelt under a tree with a sign hanging on it that reads "Under the Bamboo Tree"(the title of Cole and Johnson's most famous song). The heading of the cartoon states "Dee-lighted, We'll cut the canal, and we ain't going to let any time go to waste." Roosevelt is pictured as saying "I like Panama under the Bamboo Tree," while another sign proclaims that "The Panama Canal will be built." This cartoon points to Roosevelt's move as president for U.S. expansionism and imperialism, as well as to popular awareness of the music of Cole and Johnson.[99] *The Bulletin of Atlanta University* describes the president as bestowing "warm praise" on the music of Cole and Johnson.[100]

Although James Weldon Johnson asserted that he knew "nothing about politics or political organization," when he joined the Colored Republican Club, at the urging of Charles W. Anderson, he remained fully cognizant and aware of the politics of United States racism and its effects on African Americans.[101] In a paper titled "American Democracy and the Negro," Johnson equates U.S. democracy with unbending discrimination against African Americans denied "equal protection of the laws and common justice in the courts" and equitable and fair education due to the structural and institutional practice of funding black schools with less money than their white counterparts.[102] Johnson argued that U.S. democracy equals debt peonage; segregation; Jim Crow; inequity in industry; and the mobbing, lynching, and "burning at the stake" of African Americans.[103] On January 13, 1923, Johnson openly contested the Harvard University president's implementation of segregationists' policies by separating African American students from white students, thus reversing the school's previous liberal policy. Johnson warned that "Harvard's surrender of its tradition and the tradition of liberal America to the slaveholder's prejudice intensifies the very problem which you as Harvard's spokesperson are professing to meet."[104] Johnson's writings illuminate his consciousness of U.S. politics and its effects on African Americans. While Johnson might not have been trained as a politico, the reality remains that the foundation of his schooling in politics occurred through the politics of U.S. racism. Most importantly, his training as a lawyer also offered him some insight into the machinations of politics.

At the time that Johnson joined the Colored Republican Club, their primary campaign included the reelection of Theodore Roosevelt. James Weldon Johnson held the position of chairman of the House Committee, in charge of the finances of the organization, and eventually became the president of the club. In addition, as part of the Colored Republican Club, Cole and Johnson wrote the campaign song "Teddy." The team sent a copy of the song to Theodore Roosevelt, who complimented them on it.[105] Johnson identifies his association with the Colored Republican Club as the time in his life when he became interested in and involved with politics. Because of his work with Charles Anderson in helping to reelect Roosevelt, Booker T. Washington encouraged Elihu Root, Roosevelt's secretary of state, to appoint Johnson to consular posts in Venezuela and Nicaragua.[106] On February 26, 1906, President Roosevelt appointed James Weldon Johnson consul for Cabello, Venezuela.[107] The U.S. State Department denied Johnson's attempt to obtain a promotion as consul to Nice.[108] He also became a member of the "Black Cabinet," which consisted of black men who held positions such as registrar of the treasury, the recorder of deeds of the District of Columbia, the auditor of the Navy Department, assistant United States attorney general, a judge of the municipal court, and the collector for the Port of Washington."[109] As chief advisor to the president, Booker T. Washington wielded an enormous amount of power and brokered many of these positions. Johnson writes of a relationship with Roosevelt in 1915 in which they spoke of issues concerning the black race and American expansionism.[110]

In writing *The Shoo Fly Regiment* Cole and Johnson indited a counternarrative to the attack on the black male by Roosevelt. They also offered an antithesis to the violence against and murder and dehumanization of African Americans. By portraying the black male soldier as hero and the black female subject as educated and feminine, Cole and Johnson in effect used the play to condemn U.S. racial violence and the inhumane treatment of African Americans.

The Black Soldiers in *Shoo Fly Regiment*

The male soldiers in *The Shoo Fly Regiment* and the character of Ned Jackson challenged white America to dare to deny or ignore black patriotism, citizenship, and heroism. Lester A. Walton wrote that white audiences appeared befuddled and perplexed by the serious portrayals of the black soldiers, but that while white audiences displayed their discomfort, black audience members enjoyed the new form of representation.[111] Similar to Buffalo Bill's Wild West Show, which reenacted history, Cole and Johnson reclaimed African American historical events and, in restoring history, educated audience members. By recounting the accomplishments of the black soldiers, Cole and Johnson discarded Roosevelt's distorted narrative and recovered an important part of U.S. history in which African Americans played a central role. Cole and Johnson in effect re-centered the black soldiers' accomplishments in the war.

The U.S. refusal to appoint African American officers in the Spanish-American War informed Cole and Johnson's decision to make J. Rosamond Johnson's character, Edward Jackson, an officer in the production, and to costume him in an officers' uniform. A review in *The New York Age* informed readers that J. Rosamond Johnson's Edward Jackson held the position of sergeant, while Bob Cole's Hunter Wilson initially held the position of private. Both characters received commendations and a higher position in the military on their return from the Philippines.[112] Theodore Pankey also portrayed an officer, while the other male members of the cast portrayed soldiers. In one photograph J. Rosamond Johnson's costumes actually resembled General Wesley Merritt's uniform.[113] Johnson's uniform appeared to be black or blue with a round hat, officer's stripes, and medal on his chest. He also wore a sword and dagger, which signifies his rank as an officer. Bob Cole's uniform also resembled an officer's uniform. He wore a beige uniform with officer's stripes, a dagger, and binoculars (figure 8).

In another photograph of the team (see figure 12), J. Rosamond Johnson appears in a beige uniform, with officers' stripes on his arm and chest, a stiff hat with a rim, a medal insignia, and a gun prominently displayed at his side. The inclusion of officers within the production critiqued U.S. hypocrisy and racism. The very presence of black soldiers on the stage in *The Shoo Fly Regi-*

Figure 8. *Shoo Fly Regiment* and the Threat of
Insurrection. Photograph Department. Moorland-Spingarn Research Center,
Howard University

ment perhaps focused audience attention on the fact that the United States
government expected African American soldiers to fight in Cuba to free
black, mulatto, and white Cubans from Spanish rule while the United States
denied African Americans freedom. The weapons on Cole and Johnson's
bodies also referenced the black and white Cuban insurrection against Spain
and perchance suggested to viewers black insurrection in the United States.
African American soldiers on stage also threatened to bring to light the fact
that the black officers made up 40 percent of the Cuban army, while African
Americans fought in segregated units and their government refused to commission black officers.[114] Cole and Johnson placed unconcealed messages of

protest within the production by presenting themselves in officers' uniforms with guns, swords, and daggers.

In replicating the actual acts of black soldiers during war, Cole and Johnson made the flag the most prominent symbol of their heroism. During the Civil War, Sergeant William Carney, who became the flag bearer of the fifty-fourth Massachusetts Regiment, witnessed the color bearer fall in battle. Carney recalled, "I seized the flag and made rapid strides to the front with my regiment, bearing the flag aloft."[115] All of the white officers lay dead and Carney suffered gunshot wounds, but he continued forward bearing the flag. Upon finding the only surviving officer, Captain Luis F. Emilio, Carney recalled that amid the shouts of the few survivors of the battle that "I responded, amid loud hurrahs, 'Though shot and shell fell all around, boys, the old flag never touched the ground."[116]

Similarly, in 1898, at the height of the war, the professional black soldiers in many cases carried the flags of their regiments as well as the flags of the amateur white soldiers who joined the war to prove their masculinity. During the Battle of San Juan Hill, when the Tenth Calvary rushed to support the Rough Riders, Sergeant Peter McCown of Troop E held aloft the colors of the company even while facing an onslaught of bullets. McCown shouted "Let them shoot, they can't hit this flag." When the Spanish army did in fact puncture McCown's flag, he held it aloft and emerged from the battle unharmed.[117] First Sergeant George Berry of the Tenth Cavalry also showed daring and heroism when charging up San Juan Hill in the face of heavy fire "he waved aloft the Stars and Stripes, and planted the colors of his regiment. . . As he mounted the hill he kept calling as he ran, "'Dress on the colors, boys! Dress on the colors!'"[118] Inspired by these acts of courage and heroism, Cole and Johnson incorporated "the old flag" in the show, making it the focal point of the finale of *The Shoo Fly Regiment*. Their song "The Old Flag Never Touched the Ground," which they dedicated to Sergeant Carney, took center stage in the scene. The show resonated with the historical context of not only the Spanish American War, but the Civil War and the Haitian Revolution as well.

In the show, J. Rosamond Johnson and his "soldiers" captured Allen Hill, replicating the capture of San Juan Hill. Like Sergeant Carney, Sergeant Peter McCown, and First Sergeant George Berry, he stood holding the flag overhead on Allen Hill. *The Indianapolis Freeman* informed their readers that Johnson's Ned Jackson in "a very worthy piece of acting stood waving the American flag insisting that it never touched the ground."[119] They also noted that Cole and Johnson recreated on stage actual events, and that the male chorus, like their real-life counterparts, "march[ed] under 'Old Glory,' prepared to lay down even life itself at that altar of patriotism."[120] The song and the finale symbolized not only a reappropriation of African American history but also the realization of citizenship rights for African Americans. Cole and Johnson's script proclaimed that "When the cry came 'Off to war!' to the front we proudly bore."[121] The scene positioned the African American as a patriot.

They used the musical to reappropriate the black soldier's history of valor in battle and changed black representation by inverting familiar stereotypes of black men as the happy, lazy Sambo, the fast-moving but slow-witted Jim Crow, and the loudly dressed, grandiosely speaking Zip Coon. In their place Cole and Johnson offered the audience black soldiers as courageous heroes of the war, patriots worthy of citizenship rights. The team's progressive political agenda worked to educate and reappropriate.

Mirroring the African American community, Cole and Johnson held the hope that fighting in war proved blacks eligible for equality and full citizenship in the United States, and *The Shoo Fly Regiment* reflected this hope. *The World*, a white-owned newspaper, declared, "Men who have proved their willingness to die for their country are surely entitled, for themselves and for their people, to the ordinary guarantees of life, liberty, and the pursuit of happiness which every white American claims as a birthright."[122]

By introducing the black soldiers on stage as military officers, Cole and Johnson used the image of the black male soldier as a form of protest against white-on-black violence. The team envisioned solidarity between the brown-skinned Filipinos, Cubans, and blacks in the war. Placing black soldiers on stage symbolized a strong political stance against white violence, indicating that African Americans would no longer take abuse by whites, that blacks would fight back. This is what J. Rosamond Johnson and the other black actors in uniform stood for, as evidenced by alliances between the Filipino characters and the African American characters within the production. However, this strategy also ran the risk of connecting black inclusion to participation in policing white supremacy's boundaries of exclusion and subordination.

The Filipino Characters in *Shoo Fly Regiment*

The two Filipino characters within *The Shoo Fly Regiment* reflected the duality of hegemony and imperialism. Siren Nevarro portrayed Grizelle, the Filipino Dancer, and Herbert Amos played the Filipino Spy. Bob Cole's scrapbook allows us to understand his awareness of the duality of U.S. racism and brings to light Cole's empathy for the Filipino subject due to his

"CIVILIZATION BEGINS AT HOME."

Figure 9. "Civilization Begins at Home" *The World,* November 13, 1898. Bob Cole's scrapbook. Dr. Jewel Plummer Cobb Collection

own brushes with U.S. racism and subjugation. Bob Cole saved an illustration from *The World* dated November 13, 1898 (figure 9). The illustration shows a map of the Philippines and a man representing the U. S. government looking at the map. The man appears to be contemplating taking over the Philippines. Next to this man stands Lady Justice with her weights and sword with the word "justice" printed on it. With her left hand she opens a curtain, revealing an illustration of a black man hanging from a tree with a noose around his neck, along with pictures of black men lying dead after being shot by a group of white men who could represent either the Spanish army or white Americans.[123] This illustration clearly demonstrates Cole's knowledge of the nature of U.S. overseas imperialism and the subjugation of African Americans. A year after this illustration appeared, J. Rosamond Johnson and

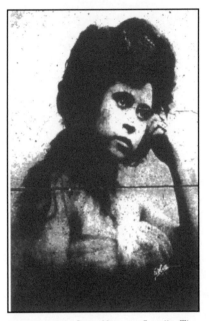

Figure 10. Siren Nevarro, Grizelle, The Filipino Dancer. *The New York Age,* October 21, 1909, 6

Figure 11. Theodore Pankey, Lieutenant Dixon. *The New York Age,* January 21, 1909, 6

James Weldon Johnson wrote the ill-fated *Tolosa,* which satirized the "new American Imperialism."

Cole created Siren Nevarro's Grizelle in *The Shoo Fly Regiment* as an ally and love interest to Theodore Pankey's Lieutenant Dixon (figures 10 and 11).[124] Grizelle appeared in three scenes: as a featured dancer in a ballet, in a duet with Bob Cole entitled "Down in the Philippines," and in the production number that featured the song "On the Gay Luneta" sung by Lieutenant Dixon and danced by Grizelle. Cole and Johnson centered the number on the interracial romance between the two characters in the Philippines and simultaneously broke the love scene taboo and the taboo against interracial romance.[125] With the placement of African Americans and Filipinos in romantic settings, Cole and Johnson contested and fully abnegated these taboos.

The lyrics reflected the romantic nature of the scene. "Twas on the gay Luneta, / One moonlight night I met her, / I never will forget her, This gay Grizelle. / Her midnight Eyes were beaming; / Now I am always dreaming, / Yes! always dreaming of my sweet Manila Belle."[126] This romance replicated actual relationships between black men and Filipino and Cuban women during the Spanish American War. African American rebel David Fagen, who defected and joined the Philippine insurrection against the United States, married a Filipino woman, and many of the five hundred African American men who chose to stay in the Philippines married Filipino women.[127] African American Dr. Curtis, the first lieutenant and company soldier and hospital steward for the Eighth Illinois, recounted that African American soldiers "play[ed] Romeo to Cuban Juliet's" and numerous marriages occurred between African American soldiers and Cuban women of the "pale-face and long-haired variety."[128] Miscegenation, interracial sex, and marriage remain key themes in wars of conquest, and the Spanish-American War proved no exception. World War I led to intermixtures between Africans and German women, producing the Reinhold Children. World War II led to relationships between white and black soldiers with Japanese, Italian, and German women in Europe, Japan, and Hawaii that in some cases led to cohabitation or marriage. Paul Spickard reasons that in many cases starving women in Japan and Germany bartered their bodies for food and shelter due to the dire conditions of the war.[129]

Siren Nevarro choreographed *The Shoo Fly Regiment.* Nevarro might well have performed her dances on pointe because, as the *New York Age* reported, she was "perhaps the only African American woman who has mastered the difficult art of toe dancing."[130] Cole and Johnson's use of Nevarro as the choreographer of the show indicates that they included black women in their creative process, influenced by the active roles their mothers and wives played in business, industry, and African American female uplift. Between 1909 and 1910 Siren Nevarro toured the United States after leaving *The Shoo Fly Regiment,* as part of the vaudeville team Brown and Nevarro.[131]

Grizelle, the sympathetic character, and the Filipino Spy within *The Shoo Fly Regiment* mirror the complex nature of U.S. imperialism and its relation to African Americans. African Americans held several viewpoints concerning the Filipinos and the Spanish-American War, and Cole and Johnson's political thought on this matter remained multilayered. The drawing of "the other" as black regardless of the nationality of the nonwhite persons remains linked in the United States history of racism. The U.S. government made a concerted effort to construct Filipinos and Cubans as blacks, thus racially inferior, not capable of self-government or citizenship rights, and irrevocably unassimilable.[132] Within the imagining of these nonwhite people as black, and Roosevelt's narrative of the black soldier, lay the constant fear of African American, Filipino, Native American, and Cuban insurrection in the United States, the Philippines, and Cuba.

African Americans interpreted the classification of the Cubans and the Filipinos in several ways. Influenced by the oppressive nature of U.S. racism, which left blacks powerless, many in the black community opposed black participation in the process of imperial expansion. An article in the *Colored American* entitled "Negro and Filipino" (1901) argued that while the U.S. government purported to protect the Filipinos' rights and liberate them from Spanish rule, the U.S. government undermined the rights of African Americans through the denial of voting rights and by tolerating lynchings and burnings in New York, Akron, and New Orleans.[133] The article drew comparisons to the Filipino plight and questioned a country that would claim to protect Filipino rights while denying African American rights.[134] Some African American soldiers took this idea a step further and made the connections between their oppression in the United States and that of the Filipinos.[135] These African American soldiers encountered racism, discrimination, and Jim Crow at the hands of white soldiers in the Philippines, and they saw this same white military personnel treat the Filipinos in the same manner. Because of this, many African American soldiers connected their oppression with the suppression of the Filipinos and defected to the Filipino side during the war.[136] Some of the black press took a strong stance against U.S. imperialism, found solidarity with the Filipinos, drew comparisons with their experiences, and remained vehemently against a U.S. colonial project that included the subjugation of Filipinos through Jim Crow laws, disenfranchisement, prejudice, and brutality.[137] Other blacks argued that participation in the war would affirm black male patriotism and masculinity, and work as an "anti-racist" influence in the United States, an argument advanced often by the black community and its soldiers in the many wars and conflicts since.[138] Similarly, some black-owned newspapers expressed a desire for African American inclusion in the "imperial project" as mediators between the colonies and the United States.[139]

Conclusion

Cole and Johnson incorporated a progressive political agenda in which they used the framework of the Spanish-American War, the manliness movement, black power, the conquest of the West, sports, and interracial romance to transfigure theater and society for African Americans.

They adopted the hypermasculine African American übermensch persona of Jack Johnson and brought to the stage the African American heroes of the Spanish-American War, with allusions to brave Afro-Cubans of that same war and the Afro-Haitians of the Haitian Revolution. Cole and Johnson coupled this vision with ideologies of both W. E. B. Du Bois and Booker T. Washington, two seemingly opposing forces, to reconfigure the role of black males as masculine and victorious both off the stage and on it. They restored the black male body from that of degradation to power and used the tools of the dominant culture—masculinity, war, and conquest—to elevate the status of the black male. The model of the new African American superman adopted by Cole and Johnson, which united political activism, black power, and athletic prowess, emerged in their productions and endures in the fame of black champions to this day.

Figure 12. Bob Cole and J. Rosamond Johnson in *Shoo Fly Regiment*.
Dr. Jewel Plummer Cobb Collection.

CHAPTER THREE

THEATRICAL IMAGININGS

Cole and Johnson's *The Shoo Fly Regiment*

~

IN *THE SHOO FLY REGIMENT* education played a role in the images on the stage of uplift. Cole and Johnson placed *The Shoo Fly Regiment* within the setting of a school that bears a striking resemblance to Booker T. Washington's all-black industrial school, Tuskegee Institute in Alabama.[1] Washington describes the living situation of the blacks in Tuskegee as severely impoverished: families living in one-room shacks with nothing to eat except corn bread and pork fat, whole families working in the fields from sunup to sundown with little time to sit down and eat as a family.[2] Yet these impoverished people wanted educational opportunities for their children and for themselves. They petitioned the legislature for a black school and obtained two thousand dollars for the teachers, but not for decent facilities. While Washington expressed apprehension and appeared disdainful of "such people," he determined to "lift them up" from these adverse conditions and educate them.[3] Modeled after Hampton Institute, the school offered an industrial education infused with "practical knowledge" such as hygiene and etiquette, with industrial skills such as housecleaning, laundering, and farming. Washington wanted the students to return to the plantation districts to educate other poor blacks in farming, morals, and religion.[4] Washington's attitudes toward poor, rural blacks may seem regressive and patronizing, but his dedication to educating them remained an inspiration to Cole and Johnson.

Tuskegee Institute did not exist in a vacuum. While the students at Tuskegee learned Victorian morals and industrial skills, so did the students at Hampton Institute and at Atlanta University, Bob Cole's and James Weldon

71

Johnson's alma mater. All these schools utilized the industrial educational model to educate African Americans. Cole and Johnson modeled some of the educational scenes and musical numbers in *The Shoo Fly Regiment* after their educational experiences at Atlanta University. Johnson learned mechanics, mechanical drawing, and printing as part of his practical training.[5] He recalled receiving "practical training" at Atlanta University to prepare him "to earn my living by that trade in any city in which I obtain work."[6] He also received a classical education akin to the educational experience of African Americans at Fisk University in Nashville, Tennessee.

In replicating the educational atmosphere at Tuskegee Institute, Cole and Johnson placed a song within the production which mirrored these institutions' model of education with its emphasis on "practical knowledge." The song details the types of classes the students attended, which included spelling, sewing, cooking, farming, blacksmithing, as well as the loftier Greek, French, Italian, and pedagogy. The farming students sing, "here is the brand new farmer man, We do our farming on the chemical plan; not only do we know how to plow and hoe, But we know what makes the cotton grow." In a similar vein, the female students who learned sewing, sing, "[w]e've learned to cut, and we've learned to sew; we know how to fit both fat and thin, And make them appear just as neat as a pin. . . ."[7] The lyrics of this song reflect James Weldon Johnson's and his mother's positions as principal and assistant principal at the Stanton School. Their use of education as a tool of uplift appears as a paramount component to their agenda. In the fall of 2006 a scholar asked John Hope Franklin why he did not teach at an elite white institution early in his career and why he did not attend an elite white institution as an undergraduate instead of Fisk University. Franklin replied that the choices for African Americans remained limited given Jim Crow and U.S. racism.[8] Similarly, the choices for uplifting African Americans remained few, which is precisely why Cole and Johnson used education to dignify African Americans.

Notes from *The Shoo Fly Regiment* Company

Cole and Johnson promoted contests within their theatrical companies as an extension of their classical educational experiences. They offered cast members contests in which they could exhibit their scholarly prowess. For example, the "Shoo Fly Notes" of March 12, 1908, and March 18, 1908, and the "Notes From Shoo Fly Regiment Company" reported that J. Rosamond Johnson and Bob Cole offered a prize of ten dollars for the best recitation of Kipling's latest poem, and that both Arthur Talbot and Theodore Pankey participated in the competition.[9] In March 1909, while the company toured with *The Red Moon,* Cole and Johnson held a competition in which cast members competed in reciting Longfellow's "Hiawatha." The prize included tuition to "one of Manhattan's best schools in dramatic arts."[10] Over twenty-five entrants registered to compete, "proving that a desire to advance in the profession is the foremost thought among the Red Moon Company."[11] As early as 1898 African American Victoria Earle Matthews taught an African American and African-centered history course at the White Rose Industrial Home for Colored Girls in New York to the female residents and the men in the community. Bob Cole, James Weldon, and J. Rosamond Johnson received a classical education before the emergence of Black Studies programs in higher education, which centered learning on the works of Africans and African Americans; therefore the choice of Kipling would conform to their educational experiences.[12] The selection of Longfellow remains an interesting one given that the heroine in the poem's name is Minnehaha as in *The Red Moon* (which means waterfall in Dakota); the renowned Afro-English composer S. Coleridge-Taylor's most famous composition bore the same name as the Longfellow poem. Perhaps Cole and Johnson chose "Hiawatha" in honor of the Coleridge-Taylor composition, as their aspirations lay in writing classical music. In 1908 Coleridge-Taylor recalled that African Americans attended his concerts in large numbers in all the cities where he played, including Washington, D.C., and that "wherever I went Negroes came to hear the music."[13] Cole and Johnson most certainly remained familiar with Coleridge-Taylor and they quite possibly attended his concerts, which could account for their choice of Longfellow's "Hiawatha."

In the "Notes From Shoo Fly Regiment Company," the author stated, "Edgar Connor and Frank DeLyons have formed a quartette. They will only sing the classics.[14] We can in fact look at Cole and Johnson's musical productions as an extension of their commitment to the tenets of Atlanta University.

While Bob Cole came up with the idea to set *The Shoo Fly Regiment* in a school similar to Tuskegee Institute, James Weldon Johnson, as coauthor, also left his imprint on the production. His meeting with Booker T. Washington at Atlanta University and his commitment to education offered a model that he used for *The Shoo Fly Regiment.* James Weldon Johnson's dedication to teaching, his tenure as principal of the Stanton School in Jacksonville, Florida in the late 1800s, and his election to the position of president of the Florida State Teachers Association in 1901 most certainly informed his writing of the show.[15]

By placing *The Shoo Fly Regiment* within the context of a black industrial institution, Cole and Johnson accomplished several goals: they taught audiences about the importance of education to African Americans, both practical knowledge and higher education; and they instructed audiences about the accomplishments of African American heroes. In addition, the actors and the characters they portrayed became role models for black audiences.

Shoo Fly Regiment: The Operetta

I contend that Cole and Johnson's *The Shoo Fly Regiment* broke the norm for black musical theater during their historical period. African American composer Noble Sissle supports this contention in his essay "The Highlights of the Negro Contributions in the Development of Music and Theatre in the American Scene," that Cole and Johnson and their contemporaries presented black operettas with plotlines "similar in construction to white operettas of the "Blue Danube School."[16] In the 1942 *Theatre Arts Magazine,* Edith J.R. Isaacs gave credence to Sissles's contention and writes that the team wrote "the first true Negro operetta"[17] Cole and Johnson moved past their contemporaries in African American musical theater by discarding blackface and presenting a plotline infused with the uplift ideology that remained fully connected to the music. The 1906 theatrical season gave audiences blackface comedians Bert Williams and George Walker in *Abyssinia* (1906) and *Bandanna Land* (1907); blackface comedian Ernest Hogan in the tour of *Rufus and Rastus* (1905) and *The Oyster Man* (1907), in which Hogan sang coon songs; and blackface performers Flournoy Miller and Aubrey Lyles who appeared in numerous shows at the Pekin Theatre in Chicago, including *The Man From Bam* (1906), *The Mayor of Dixie* (1907), *The Husband* (1907), and the U.S. tour of *The Colored Aristocrats* (1908). African American baritone Theodore Drury's Grand Opera Company performed George Bizet's *Carmen* during the week of May 28, 1906 at the 14th Street Theatre in New York, and the African American opera diva Sissierretta Jones's Black Patti's Troubadours appeared in *Captain Jasper* (1907), *A Trip to Africa* (1908,1910, 1911), and *A Royal Coon* (1909). In addition, the African American vaudeville team The Whitman Sisters performed at the Waldorf Astoria on April 1906, as well as at Grace Chapel in Mount Vernon, Union Baptist Church, and Bethel A.M.E. Church under the direction of Will Marion Cook.[18] While these musical forms advanced African American musical theater, Williams and Walker, Ernest Hogan, and Miller and Lyles adhered to blackface minstrelsy, Black Patti's Troubadours presented what was almost a revue format, and the Whitman Sisters performed in vaudeville. The accomplishments of these artists remained laudatory; nonetheless Cole and Johnson came closest to Washington's ideology of educational uplift in their musicals.

Cole and Johnson, like most of the black community during the nineteenth and twentieth centuries, idolized Booker T. Washington and his accomplishments. Roscoe Conkling Simmons of the *New York Age* reported that Cole and Johnson prominently displayed a picture of Washington of the "Association of Genius" in their study.[19] *The Toledo Blade* newspaper informed its readers that both Bob Cole and J. Rosamond Johnson "are best friends of Booker T. Washington" and that the trio so respected Washington's work with industrial education that they "have written much about it in their play *The Shoo Fly Regiment*. Before being presented to the public the manuscript was sent to Mr. Washington and he edited it and put in several speeches himself."[20] Cole and Johnson's reverence for Booker T. Washington found its way onto the stage with the character of Professor Maxwell, the principal of Lincolnville Institute, played by Arthur Talbot. Washington quite possibly acted as the model for this character.

Female Characters

In a similar vein, Cole and Johnson quite possibly modeled the female characters within the production after women at Tuskegee University, Atlanta University, and the women in their lives. From the inception of the institute in 1881, Booker T. Washington included African American women as students, teachers, and principals so as to educate the newly freed slaves.[21] From 1882 until her death in 1884, Washington's wife, Fannie N. Smith, worked with him to include the students and teachers in their home life.[22] Beginning in 1881, Washington worked with Miss Olivia A. Davidson, a graduate of Massachusetts State Normal School, as a co-teacher and fundraiser for the school. They married in 1885 and worked toward improving Tuskegee Institute until her death in 1889.[23] Washington subsequently hired and then married Fisk University graduate Margaret James Murray in about 1890. Murray worked as a "lady principal" at Tuskegee Institute.[24] Cole and Johnson's use of the lady principal in *The Shoo Fly Regiment* mirrored Washington's use of black women within his uplift agenda. Anna Cook portrayed Martha Jones, the Lady Principal of Lincolnville Institute, and most certainly represented one of Washington's wives.[25]

Anna Cook was described as the prima donna of *The Shoo Fly Regiment* and was an alumna of Bert Williams and George Walker's *In Dahomey*

Figure 13. "The Senior Normal Class in Atlanta University—A Winter Scene."
The Women's class of 1894. *The Bulletin of Atlanta University,* 1894. Robert W. Woodruff
Library, Atlanta University Center

(1903), *Ernest Hogan and His Memphis Students* (1905), and Ernest Hogan's *Rufas and Rastus* (1906).[26] In *The Shoo Fly Regiment* Cook sang "I'll Always Love Old Dixie," which she sang with the "girls," and "Southland," which she performed with Ned (J. Rosamond Johnson) and the male chorus.[27] Although Cole and Johnson moved away from many of the minstrel norms, some of the remnants of minstrelsy made their way into the production as the titles of these two songs suggest. One could surmise that Cole and Johnson included these songs as homage to their southern homeland. Cook's performance of the songs proved noteworthy. Sylvester Russell of the *Indianapolis Freeman* described Cook's voice as "a soprano voice of good quality and rendered in a pleasant manner." A review in *The New York Age* dated March 17, 1906, intimated that audience members recognized and remembered Cook from previous shows, while a review from the same paper dated June 1906 stated that she was "very good" and had a "sweet soprano voice."[28] As a performer Cook did not fit the popular mold of the "beautiful" light-skinned female performer of the 1900s. A photograph from *The New York Age* dated 1908 shows Cook as a gorgeous dark-skinned, full figured woman. She appears reserved and placid, as she looks directly at the camera, conveying aplomb. Cook wears large white earrings, with her hair up and covered with a white lace band. She wears a white form-fitting lace dress with long sleeves and a high neckline. She folds her hands gently in front of her body, maintaining a commanding presence. Cook embodies the classic Lady Principal, thoughtful, authoritative, and stunning. Cook's strong gaze exudes confidence and pride. By casting the dark-skinned Anna Cook, Cole and Johnson abandoned the color-caste code of the African American elite class and the theater community. This challenges the commonly held belief that Cole and Johnson remained unremittingly color conscious. By the time Cook appeared in *The Red Moon* (1908), she had married fellow actor Theodore Pankey.

A photograph of the women's class of 1894 in the *Bulletin of Atlanta University* offers insight into Cole and Johnson's agenda of glorifying African American women (figure 13). Above the photograph is an illustration of a slave woman whose penetrating, yet placid gaze captures the viewer's attention, with the legend, "Behold in this calm face the modern Sphinx with such thoughtful mien."[29] She looks regal in her headscarf, shawl, and earrings. She looks as if she is about to speak, and tellingly a poem surrounds the scene.[30] "No longer here the crude and unformed features of a savage face; / But in those pleading eyes a kindred race / Asks for the highway out of servitude."[31] The photograph that accompanies this illustration includes thirteen well-dressed African American women of every hue —"The Senior Normal Class in Atlanta University—a Winter Scene."[32] Dressed as sophisticates with hats, topcoats, long dresses, bustles, fur scarves, mufflers, and heavy slips, these women exude confidence and dignity. Several of the women gaze pensively past the camera as if contemplating their future. One looks off into the distance, exhibiting serenity, while several look directly into the camera with self-assurance and security. They all look as if they are contemplating their destiny. The photograph reminds us that these women looked to a hopeful and bright future, while at the same time the entire page reminds the viewer that these self-possessed women were only one generation removed from a slave past. The poem that accompanied the photograph conceivably embodied for these women the move away from a slave past to upward mobility through education. It ends,

> Study the problem well,
> For in this Sphinx a message somewhere lies;
> A nation's glory or its shame may rise.
> From out the reading what these features tell.
> —A.T. Worden, in "Judge."[33]

The character of Rose Maxwell, like her real-life counterparts, reflected the departure from a slave past to a future in which education held the key for the children and grandchildren of the slave. As the daughter of the principal of Lincolnville, this character also mirrored Booker T. Washington's own children. One scene from the production offers us a window through which we can view how Cole and Johnson envisioned the black female student. In this scene the female chorus appears in caps and gowns discussing their love for soldiers.[34] This scene evinces the playwrights' strategy to aggrandize African American women and encompassed the importance of education for black women and the great significance of romance and marriage in black relations. The inclusion of educated black women within the production reflected Cole and Johnson's commitment to exalting African American women. Similarly, the photograph of the class of 1894 and the illustration and poem offer us a window into one of the ways in which the team learned to respect the varying experiences of African American women, perusing the "calm face[,] the modern Sphinx," from an enslaved past to the Atlanta University sophisticate. The photograph of the Class of 1894 elucidates Cole and Johnson's deference to African American womanhood.

Both Fanny Wise and Inez Clough played Rose Maxwell, the Professor's Daughter. Of Wise's turn at the part, the *Indianapolis Freeman* stated that "Miss Wise is a singer, a delightful soprano, of high range and as sweet as silver bells."[35] *The New York Age* noted that she "scored an unusually big hit singing 'Wont You Be My Little Brown Bear?'"[36] A review from 1907 states that she sang well and that she handled her role credibly.[37] She appeared in both *The Shoo Fly Regiment* and *The Red Moon*.

Inez Clough also played the part in 1906. Born and educated in Worcester, Massachusetts, Clough trained in voice and piano. She began her professional career singing operatic music in the 1890s in Isham's *Oriental America,* one of the many incarnations of the Creole shows.[38] She also trained vocally in London and Austria, and appeared in Williams and Walker's *Bandanna Land* (1907) and *Mr. Lode of Koal* (1910). She went on to become a renowned actress with the Lafayette Players.[39]

Because the dominant society watched and judged African Americans, the black elite endeavored to present themselves as middle-class and estimable. This Victorian ideology presented an additional burden for black women, who found themselves forced to negotiate or conform to the hegemonic norms of femininity, middle class propriety, and repressive racial ideologies.[40]

Historically the relegation of black women to the position of the "low other," reviled while simultaneously desired, excluded them from political and social power within the dominant society.[41] In theatrical representation black women were barred from dignified parts and fantasy representations, and for the most part they found themselves consigned to roles such as the asexual mammy happy to be in slavery, the oversexed Jezebel, the hyper-frenetic wild child Pickaninny, and the Tragic Mulatto who, due to her one drop of black blood, remains tragic. Beginning in 1798 and continuing into the twenty-first century, these representations gained tremendous popularity in the media in books, advertisements, magazines, the minstrel show, and theatrical and film representations. Hazel Carby notes that in all of these stereotypes, be it the Jezebel, Mammy, or Tragic Mulatto, "Black women repeatedly failed the test of true womanhood because she survived her institutionalized rape, whereas the true heroine (white women) would rather die than be sexually abused."[42]

These stereotypes emerged out of the most revolting conditions. Due to their subjugated position within the labor market as chattel slaves, black women suffered the ravages of slavery physically, psychologically, and socially, through rape, "an instrument of political terror," forced procreation, murder, forced separations from families, and severe inhumane beatings. The Afro-English composer S. Coleridge-Taylor documents another level of abuse that African American women experienced. "No black girl was safe with a white man about. Who fathered thousands nay, millions of mulattoes and

quadroons that one meets on every side in the States." In this sarcastic trea-
tise Taylor underscores the blatant sexual abuse of women and girls during
slavery and upbraids the white male by mordantly asking "[g]ranted that the
black race is inferior, then why did the males of the superior race buy count-
less colored girls some scarcely in their teens—not to work but to become
their paramours?"[43] Coleridge-Taylor also reveals the hypocrisy of the white
male who through inversion created the black male as sexual brute while
he raped African American women and girls. The use of inversion to create
the stereotypes of black women as Jezebels and asexual mammies worked to
justify their enslavement and rape, and these stereotypes soon became central
to theatrical representation.

African American women in theatrical productions, most specifically the
Creole shows (large burlesque productions of the nineteenth century) became
the gazed-upon "other," reduced to "objects" of desire and revulsion. The
very act of these women performing on stage reduced them to the "other"
because of the social stigma attached to women in the theater during this
period.[44] While the hegemony of the dominant white culture and even certain
segments of the black community rejected the links between black women,
the stage, and respectability, Cole and Johnson ennobled African American
women and placed them at the axis of propriety.

Lester A. Walton writes that many of the white reviewers discounted Cole
and Johnson's productions because cast members' "voices nearly all had the
correct English accent and intonation," because some of the members of the
cast were light-skinned, and "[o]nly two or three stuck to the tradition of the
real Negro. Well what is the real Negro from a white man's standpoint?"[45]
While Cole and Johnson subscribed to some forms of color-based casting,
and while many of the women in the shows were alumnae of the Creole
shows, they also cast performers who did not fit the light-skinned mold, such
as Anna Cook and Ada Overton Walker.[46]

In 1890, as the first large black company to present burlesque entertainment and the first to feature beautiful, lavishly costumed black women in
leading roles, the Creole show represented a departure in characterization for
black women. The shows elevated black women's status and afforded them
new chances for employment.[47] James Weldon Johnson describes the Creole
shows as productions to "Glorify the colored girl."[48] Several of these shows
toured the United States, offering viewers extremely light-skinned performers who fueled the white obsession with black skin color. White reviewers
described these women with such exotic names as "white octoroons" and
quadroons, and described them as light as Spanish or French women, and

lighter than Italians.[49] Reviewers of this historical milieu considered these to be "high-born colored people" due to their complexion.[50]

While the stage allowed African American women to raise their status through this form of burlesque, the social stigma of women on stage remained prevalent in some circles in the black community. For example, James Reese Europe, the musical conductor of *The Shoo Fly Regiment*, maintained a long-term affair with a chorus woman named Bessie Simms, whom he met while they both worked on *The Red Moon*. Reid Badger writes that because of his class status and his mother's objections to her theatrical career, and the stain cast on women on the stage, Europe found it difficult to legally legitimize his relationship with Bessie Simms, so they never married. Nonetheless Simms and Europe continued their affair after Europe married Willie Angrom, even until his death in 1919.[51]

Peter Stallybrass and Allon White's concept of the low other and its relationship to low culture helps us understand burlesque during the early 1900s. The creation of low culture such as burlesque for the lower working classes and the invention of "high culture" for the middle and upper classes created a deliberate dichotomy between the working class and the bourgeoisie manufactured by those who held positions of power.[52] Robert Allen maintains that "the creation of the bourgeoisie self was predicated on the exclusion of the popular as that which was not respectable, tasteful, or clean."[53] Thus women performers in burlesque were considered repulsive, yet enthralling, horrible in their prettiness, the "low other," reviled while simultaneously desired.[54] Because of the perception that women of the theater like those who performed in burlesque remained irreparably despoiled and kin to the prostitute, some in the African American community considered women such as Bessie Simms as disgraceful and unworthy of marriage or repute. Others felt that the stage gave African American females the opportunity to raise their rank.

African American actor Leigh Whipper, a contemporary of Cole and Johnson, firmly asserted that the black women who appeared in the Creole shows such as Sam T. Jack's *Oriental America* and John Isham's *Octoroons* "were not like the white women who were featured in the 'strip-tease act' in burlesque, [t]he women of color were sensational in spangled costumes with skirts split at the side," and fleshtone tights.[55] He maintained that unlike the white burlesque shows, the police commissioner never closed a black show. Whipper implies that the black shows offered a higher-caliber production than the white shows and symbolized dignity and venerated black women who appeared in them. Whipper also suggested that the black shows catered to a better class of people then the white shows. Will Marion Cook also attested to the high quality of the Creole shows and asserted that Sam T. Jack's Creoles "was the most classy and best singing Negro show on [the] road," while *Oriental America* appeared later as a "classier and more expensive show."[56]

Part of Cole and Johnson's strategy for aggrandizing African American women included generating an aura around the women, which conveyed their politesse, refinement, and decency. They revered African American women and presented them as role models to the audiences. In effect Cole and Johnson's black musical theater attempted to raise theater from "low culture" to "high culture." Through a concerted effort, which included newspaper articles in the *New York Age,* Cole and Johnson and the actresses in the production changed the image of the black female subject. For example, "The Notes from *The Shoo Fly Regiment*" reported that Miss Oriena Howard, while quiet, practices the piano, and that Miss Ethel James attends dramatic performances and "cries when the villain steals the child, or the wife is deserted at the altar."[57] The article reports that Miss James aspires to become a dramatic actress.

Dr. Jewel Plummer Cobb contended that the theater represented respectability and an allure for her family that did not reflect the hegemonic discourse about stage life: "[Bob Cole and the Johnson Brothers] had several philosophical points that they wanted to make. They wanted to make sure that black women were shown on stage in a very dignified manner and a typical manner for that time period. That was very important to them."[58] Cobb indicates that Cole and Johnson moved away from demeaning images and depictions of African American women common on the stage during the late nineteenth and early twentieth centuries and opted for the quintessential African American women through a more humanistic portrayal. Cobb suggested that her mother so admired her brother Bob Cole and the stage that in 1910 she appeared on stage with her sisters as mechanical dolls for the Upsilon Sigma Club for the benefit of the Hope Nursery and embarked on a career as a dance instructor.[59] Her mother also wrote Cole's biography, and the play titled "What's in a Song," about Cole's life.[60] Cobb gave no indication that her mother or her family felt that the stage degraded black women.

My mother had also been a schoolteacher. She had been to Sargents, which was a physical education school in Boston, and then became involved at Harvard way back then. She went to Washington D.C. to teach physical education and dance. [She taught] classes in dance, this was called interpretive dancing, the precursor of modern dance.[61]

Carriebel Plummer remained so enamored with the stage that she encouraged her daughter in all aspects of performance, including dance and music. Cobb took piano lessons with the famous African American composer and performer Margaret Bonds as a young girl in Chicago. She intimated that her mother's "idol was Isadora Duncan [the renowned white modern dancer and choreographer], so she decided when I was born that my middle name should be Isadora so that's what happened."[62] In "What's in a Song" Plummer created a character named Ada Kingston, who wins a lead role in a Broadway production. Sensing some distress from the mother concerning her daughter's choice of careers, Mr. Kingston informs Mrs. Kingston that "she is not going as a cheap chorus girl. She is a star on Broadway. The first Bronze girl to do so."[63] The mother dismisses the thought that her anxiety comes from her daughter's career choice and tells her husband that she remains troubled that the producers of the show plan on using Cole's music without permission.[64] While Cobb and her mother viewed stage life as a laudable profession, these lines from Plummer's play expose a hierarchy concerning the theatrical roles that remained acceptable within the African American community. While the mother dismisses the suggestion that she is upset about the thought of her daughter as a chorus girl, these lines reveal the caste system that existed concerning African American theater women. Cobb and her mother's experience with theatrical endeavors allows us to understand that viewpoints concerning stage life were not monolithic among African Americans, that they differed along class lines and within social sets. Cobb and her mother's encounters with stage life dispel the perception of the African American theatrical woman as degraded. As Leigh Whipper, James Weldon Johnson, and Will Marion Cook noted, many African Americans' attitudes toward female stage performers diverged from white negative perceptions of stage performers, which indicates that the African American middle class mindset remained multifaceted.

Stereotypes

Some of the characters within the production bear similarities to the actual teachers at Tuskegee Institute. Although no description of the character Randolf the Farmer exists, this character quite possibly evoked associations with George Washington Carver. Yet several comedic and stereotypical characters also appeared in the production, including Bode Edjicashun, Ophelia the Village Pride, and the Pickaninnies. These characters represented stereotypical models and mirrored black minstrel forms.

The show featured "Pickaninnies"—a common vaudeville construct of the time. The Pickaninnies personified a stereotypical image of black women, girls, and boys during the 1900s. The portrayal of the Pickaninny in advertisements, movies, and theatrical productions included that of out-of-control, wild animal-like children, presented as humorous. Usually presented in "comedic" settings, the Pickaninnies always found themselves facing danger, being chased by wild animals such as tigers or lions, in the mouths of alligators, catapulted in the air, or as in *Birth of A Nation* falling out of carriages. All these images were supposed to be funny, and they worked to justify the slavery and abuse of African American children. The stark reality of the Pickaninny included the fact that, like Frederick Douglass, children were sold away from their mothers at young ages; they worked as slave laborers from sunup to sundown, and they died young. In 1991, when builders "discovered" the African Burial Ground (1625) in the Wall Street area of New York, archeologists and anthropologists found that children made up the majority of the four hundred bodies buried there. Upon analyzing the bones they determined that a vast number of these children suffered from developmental defects caused by hard labor. One six-year old child suffered such ailments.

> Orbits of eyes show pitting, characteristic of active anemia . . . lesions in the outer layer of bone caused by infection . . . growth areas of the skull have closed . . . early in development. . . . Lesions at the arm attachments where the brachial muscles [were] strained . . . first and second cervical vertebrae are partially fused due to force or heavy load, trauma to the top of the head.[65]

This was the reality of the Pickaninny. The stage representation of the Pickaninny conveniently omitted the violence inflicted on the children's bodies and psyches. Both Brenda Dixon-Gottschild and Nadine George-Graves describe stage "Picks" as very talented black children who performed as singers and dancers in white vaudeville in finales and backup numbers. Both Dixon-Gottschild and George-Graves define "Picks" as a shortened version of the word "Pickanniny."[66] The Pickaninnies acted as a guaranteed hit for theater owners and performers because these children virtually never failed.[67] George-Graves maintains that Picks usually performed with white female singers such as Sophie Tucker or Nora Bayes, or in the case of Mabel Whitman, with black female singers.[68] The performance style of the Picks consisted of extremely fast-paced movements, which required a mastery of rhythm and speed. White audiences expected speed from black performers.[69]

Margo Webb remembered performing as a Pick in vaudeville in the 1930s in New Jersey. She recalled that the dancers wore bandannas and short skimpy costumes, and that the dance movements included rocking back and forth "like idiots" in plantation scenes, and performing fast-paced dance movements such as Russian and time step movements.[70] These depictions of Picks offer a view into possible types of dances and performance styles that appeared in *The Shoo Fly Regiment*. Daisy Brown, Marion Potter, Marguerite Ward, Edgar Connor, and Emmett Anthony portrayed the Pickaninnies in the production. It appears that Cole and Johnson adhered to this popular minstrel form through their use of the Pickaninny chorus perhaps to guarantee the success of the production both financially and artistically; perhaps the representation remained so commonplace that they saw nothing wrong with the representation, and maybe they incorporated theatrical conventions Cole learned in his previous performance experiences. The team also followed minstrel norms by including the "The Bode Edjicashun."

Booker T. Washington recalled meeting several older black gentlemen in Tuskegee who played an instrumental role in the establishment of the institute by writing and requesting the founding of the school. These older black men facilitated Washington's hiring as the principal of the school. Cole and Johnson conceivably patterned "The Bode Edjicashun" played by Wesley Jenkins and Sam Lucas after these older black men. Sam Lucas was born in 1841 and began his career singing with his family for the Anti-Slavery Society in New York. A veteran minstrel comedian, Lucas appeared in minstrel shows for the Boston Stock Company and Callander's Minstrels and with the Hyer Sisters. He also appeared in *A Trip to Coontown*. According to the reviews, "The Bode Edjicashun" offered audiences comic relief.[71] Given Lucas's theatrical background, we can surmise that these characters reproduced minstrel traditions by presenting audiences with stereotypical forms of performance.

Cole and Johnson incorporated seemingly stereotypical representation when they wrote the character Ophelia the Village Pride played by Andrew Tribble. According to James Hatch and Errol Hill, Tribble was the best of all the female impersonators. He was born in 1879, attended school in Richmond, Kentucky, and began his career as a Pickaninny in African American theatrical productions beginning with *In Kentucky*. He also appeared at the Pekin Theater in Chicago. Tribble graduated from Pickaninny roles to female interpretations. According to George Walker, "[o]ne night in an afterpiece he slipped on a dress and the audience screamed at his action in dresses, which caused him to develop the dress-wearing idea, and found it so effective that he has been working in skirts ever since."[72] Tribble credited

Cole and Johnson with "discovering" him and ensuring his theatrical success.

> One night I was doing my best, not dreaming of anyone watching me, but the manager. I was surprised to learn that among the few in the audience were Cole and Johnson. I was also told that they liked my work. They sent for me and gave me plenty of encouraging talk and pictured a beautiful future for me.[73]

This encounter led to Cole and Johnson contracting Andrew Tribble for *The Shoo Fly Regiment*. Tribble appeared as Ophelia in *The Shoo Fly Regiment*, Miss Lilly White in *The Red Moon*; and in female roles in *His Honor the Barber* (1909) and *Ophelia Snow from Baltimo* (1928), which appears as a homage to his portrayal of Ophelia in *The Shoo Fly Regiment*.[74]

Female impersonators made their way onto the stage at a time when only men performed on stage. Black minstrelsy adopted this form or representation, but it was not central to the genre.[75] Nadine George-Graves identifies cross-dressing as part of black theatrical performance, most specifically vaudeville.[76] Female impersonators popularized two major characters, the Prima Donna or "Wench" role and the low comedy or "Funny Old Gal" character. The Prima Donna/Wench character appeared in white minstrelsy as early as the 1830s with white female impersonator Dan Gardner's portrayal of the role in the 1830s and George Christy's characterization in the 1840s. After the Civil War the Prima Donna gained popularity with white performers and some African American performers, including African American female impersonator Thomas Dilward or Japanese Tommy, who performed with the Hague Minstrels. The Prima Donna character first appeared on the minstrel stage in the guise of "pretty yellow plantation girls," but eventually transformed into an elegantly dressed coquette. The Prima Donna embodied the ultimate Victorian beauty with her diminutive hands, petite feet, and small waist.[77] In the white minstrel show African woman could not fit snuggly into representations of beauty, because of the perception that African women remained unequivocally ugly and undesirable. So the African American Prima Donna embodied the exotic, not really African, but rather "yellow" as in both the plantation girl and Japanese Tommy. With this in mind, the *only* role that African women could fully embody in white minstrelsy was that of the popular low comedy/Funny Old Gal role.

The low comedy/Funny Old Gal, who appeared on stage as mannish and crude, gained popularity in white minstrelsy. To mark this character as truly unfeminine, a big brawny male played the role dressed in unmatched clothing and displaying huge feet in big shoes. This character might also show up dressed in a ball gown, but to mark her as not fully womanly, she wore men's shoes with her gown.[78] The low comedy/Funny Old Gal role in effect was used to degrade and ridicule African American women and to assert that these women remained undeserving of womanhood rights given their masculine tendencies and unattractiveness. This characterization gained incredible popularity in the nineteenth and twentieth centuries, and still remains prominent in twenty-first century representations of African American women by African American and white men. African American performers Martin Lawrence and Eddie Murphy adopted this character and portrayed her in movies such as *Big Mama's House* (2000), *Big Mama's House 2* (2006), *The Nutty Professor I* (1996), *The Nutty Professor II: The Klumps* (2000), and *Norbit* (2007). In African American theater neither the Prima Donna/Wench nor the low comedy/Funny Old Gal character of female impersonation gained the type of popularity that they garnered in the white minstrel shows.

Several reasons exist as to why these images did not become common, including the fact that African American producers placed "beautiful" African American women on the stage and the black audience preferred to view the real thing as opposed to the illusion.[79] The historical period may have also dictated why these characters and female impersonation did not become popular in African American theater. With the push for racial uplift and the protection of African American women, male performers such as Cole and Johnson chose not to deride black women. Thus the female impersonation in African American theater looked quite different from that created by white performers.[80] Andrew Tribble asserted that "I never go on the stage unless I try to do my best. That somehow has always been my motto, and I have been well paid for sticking to it."[81] I contend that Bob Cole, the Johnson Brothers, and Andrew Tribble utilized stereotypes in the characterization of Ophelia Snow to actually reconfigure female impersonation to make it more palatable for the African American audience.

Tribble's characterization of Ophelia Snow in *The Shoo Fly Regiment* fit neither the model of the Prima Donna nor that of the Funny Old Gal. At 5 feet 4 inches, Tribble remained slight in stature and in physicality. A 1908 photograph of Tribble portrays him looking more like a teenage waif then a Prima Donna or the Funny Old Gal. He actually resembles a female Pickaninny, albeit a well-dressed Pickaninny, a reminder of Tribble's childhood career. The photograph pictures Tribble with a large black ribbon prominently placed at the center of his neatly combed hair. He wears Mary Jane shoes, a white dress, and holds a large hat that matches his dress. His finger points coyly at his mouth as he gazes downward at his pigeon-toed feet.[82] *The New*

York Age reported that Tribble's interpretation of Ophelia proved an "instantaneous hit," and that he "plays a part very much like Topsy. He does not have to do anything to get applause. The audience goes wild every time he appears. He acts well, is a great dancer and sings well."[83] From the reviews we can surmise that Tribble relied on his comedic expertise in his pickaninnyesque portrayal of a tough yet kindly Ophelia Snow who, although homely, longed for romance just like her prettier sisters.[84] Ann Marie Bean argues that Tribble's female interpretation fit the mold of Flip Wilson's 1970s television persona Geraldine with a characterization that was about "'us'"—African American men and women and their relationships—not about "'them.'"[85] What I would like to suggest is that Wilson's Geraldine, like Tribble's Ophelia, while stereotypical, reinscribed stereotypes by offering an insider's perspective molded for an African American audience. Toni Morrison argued that while Wilson's Geraldine remained controversial to some in the African American community, Wilson actually inverted stereotypes.

> A shift in semantics and we find the accuracy; for defensive read survivalist; for cunning read clever; for sexy read a natural unembarrassed acceptance of her sexuality; for egocentric read keen awareness of individuality; for transvestite (man in woman's dress) read a masculine strength beneath the glamour.[86]

By creating Geraldine as a clever, individualistic survivor, with a touch of glamour and strength, Wilson affirmed African American women. Like Ophelia Pride who married Hunter Wilson in *The Shoo Fly Regiment,* Geraldine loved and remained faithful to her boyfriend Killer. Geraldine allowed Flip Wilson to discuss political and social issues concerning African American life that he as a black man could not fully articulate out of drag due to societal constrictions on black men in the 1960s and the 1970s. As Wilson noted, "Geraldine doesn't have to bite her tongue, Flip Wilson might have to hold back on something, but Geraldine will jump down your throat. To hell with you . . . Geraldine is in complete control of every situation."[87] Geraldine and Ophelia Pride allowed Flip Wilson, Andrew Tribble, Bob Cole, and the Johnson brothers to unveil their opinions concerning African Americans freely. By rejecting the Prima Donna and the low comedy role and by creating Ophelia Pride, Tribble's female impersonations remained a truly African American invention.

One can draw parallels between the black cowboy westerns of the 1930s, which starred Herb Jefferies, and *The Shoo Fly Regiment.* While Jefferies portrayed the heroic romantic lead in movies such as *Bronze Buckaroo*

(1938) and *Harlem Rides The Range* (1939), his sidekick, the African American composer Spencer Williams, portrayed the stereotypical black male character reminiscent of the Sambo. The presence of Jefferies as the romantic lead worked to dilute the inclusion of Spencer Williams's stereotypical character. *The Shoo Fly Regiment* reflected this softening of stereotypical representations. With the inclusion of the nonstereotypical characters of Ned Jackson, the hero of the Spanish American war and a Tuskegee graduate; Rose Maxwell, a graduate of Lincolnville Institute; Professor Maxwell, the president of Lincolnville Institute; Martha Jones, the Lady Principal of Lincolnville Institute; and the chorus of soldiers and students, *The Shoo Fly Regiment* contested the minstrel forms of representation common for the time and present even within their own production.

I advance this polemic not to dismiss the use of stereotypes, but to point to the fact that Cole and Johnson remained products of their times and incorporated stereotypical forms of representations as well as humane portrayals of African Americans. Because of these characters within their productions, they remained innovators in the realm of musical theater. Through their depictions of actual events in African American history and their placement of African American men and women on stage as educated heroes and heroines, Cole and Johnson made radical changes in black representation that by all accounts would not be replicated until almost two decades after their last show—with Eubie Blake and Noble Sissle's *Shuffle Along* (1921). Sterling Brown aptly notes that "[m]en like Bob Cole and Bert Williams were intelligent enough to know that the comic students they performed were stereotyped. Nevertheless it is inaccurate to magnify the 'chagrin and tears.' They were showmen functioning in the American popular theatre."[88] As showmen and products of the historical period, Cole and Johnson both conformed to and contested stereotypical representations of African Americans within *The Shoo Fly Regiment*. The show reflected the changes in the black image that haunted the black elite in this era, changes that resonated with contradictions about class and color.

Audience Response to Shoo *Fly Regiment*

How did audiences and the press respond to the new forms of representations presented on stage by Cole and the Johnson brothers? How can we understand the impact the new forms of representations as well as the stereotypes had on audience members? While Theodore Roosevelt attempted to rewrite history by omitting the contributions of Native Americans and African American Soldiers in the Spanish-American War, Cole and Johnson's use of the war as a site for African American heroism emphasizes the importance of popular culture in reappropriating African American history.[89]

With ticket prices at twenty-five cents, fifty cents, seventy-five cents and one dollar, Cole and Johnson made it affordable for all people to attend their show.[90] Because of the reasonably priced tickets black audiences and the black press enjoyed the new depictions of African Americans and the narrative, while the white press expressed mixed opinions. The black press and audiences radiated with pride at seeing black men as courageous, and they enjoyed the new representative images of black men and women dressed immaculately and smartly. Some in the white press responded favorably to *The Shoo Fly Regiment* while others appeared baffled. Still others responded antagonistically. Black theatrical critic Lester A. Walton summed up both the black and white responses to the show in a review of Cole and Johnson's *The Red Moon.*

> *The Red Moon* brings to light one thing Cole and Johnson have at least learned, that is they must give the public what it wants and not what they think the public should have. They will be far more successful financially in their new show than in *The Shoo Fly Regiment.* Not because *The Red Moon* is the better for it is not. *The Shoo Fly Regiment* told a much better story than *The Red Moon,* but it did not cater to the tastes of the theatre-goers. Most of the colored people liked *The Shoo Fly Regiment,* but many whites did not care for it being prejudiced against seeing Negro soldiers, but when a show is put out to make money it must produce plays that will be liked by all classes. That is what Cole and Johnson are doing this season.[91]

Underlying Walton's critique of the shows lay the reality that Cole and Johnson incorporated more stereotypes and racially charged words in *The Red Moon* than they did in *The Shoo Fly Regiment* in an attempt to cater to white audiences. *The Shoo Fly Regiment* threatened and challenged hegemony with images of African American soldiers who conjured up the African victors of the Haitian Revolution and the threat of African American insurrection in the white mind. Their message of uplift remained an overt component of *The Shoo Fly Regiment* with its critique of U.S. racism and hegemony for all to see, while *The Red Moon's* uplift agenda appeared more covert. One of the possible reasons for the financial failure of *The Shoo Fly Regiment* lay in the certainty that whites rejected the production. As Walton pointed out, the racism of white audiences prevented them from appreciating the presence of black soldiers on stage and made them uncomfortable. White audience members found it difficult to wrap their minds around the new portrayals of African Americans and, in some cases, they missed the messages of black emancipation through education and war that were embedded in the show. For example while a review in the *Indianapolis Star* praised the production, the author wrote that "[t]he play has a plot which is well carried to logical conclusion—colored logic that is often told in musical numbers. Cole & Johnson certainly have a fine show."[92] While the author enjoyed the show, the messages of black patriotism, education, and even the threat of insurrection were dismissed as "colored logic." The reviewer's unwillingness to acknowledge the messages infused in the production of self-determination through the emancipatory rhetoric of war and education, and his denoting African Americans as simple-minded reveals his racism. Consequently, he refuses to see Cole and Johnson as clever or intelligent. Correspondingly, *Theater Magazine* of September 1907 rejected the production completely and deemed it amateurish, lacking in originality, and not worthy of criticism.[93] The critic for the magazine also failed to see the innovations of the show and missed its social and political critiques.

It appears that black audiences enjoyed the production and remained cognizant of the messages that Cole and Johnson relayed. Cole and Johnson included a review in their advertisement of the production from the March 2, 1907, *Indianapolis Freeman* that complimented them on the show and announced that *The Shoo Fly Regiment* "came and conquered."[94] The reviewer heralded the success of the show and noted that it worked as an educational tool in teaching "most useful lessons concerning American Negro life."[95] The team's educational agenda was not lost on black audiences or black critics. *The New York Age* announced that the show was "a decided hit: it is well laid out, costumed in becoming and elaborate style and with its well-trained company should stay as long as it may desire."[96] This reviewer's glowing account welcomed the new forms of representations and pointed out that "Theodore Pankey, as Lieutenant Dixon Company G. Fifty-fourth U.S.V. makes a capital officer and his soldiers are very well drilled."[97]

We can always look back and find fault in what came before us, but it remains imperative to note the accomplishments together with the faults. Walton, in retrospect, felt that *The Shoo Fly Regiment* proved a far superior show than *The Red Moon*. With the rejection of the former by some in the white community, however, he lamented that Cole and Johnson returned to hegemonic notions of blackness within *The Red Moon*. But did they? *The Red Moon* embodied a politicized message of African American and Native American solidarity for viewers and the importance of education, and it incorporated a move to change representative images of African American

women, Native Americans, and African American men. In writing and presenting *The Red Moon,* Cole and Johnson simply instituted a different and
more covert strategy.

Their production of the play represented a victory in itself. Because of
the nature of structural racism, blacks systematically faced obstacles when
it came to wealth accumulation. Although Cole and Johnson distinguished
themselves as property owners in New York and Florida, they did not own a
viable space in which they could write and perform their own productions.
The dearth of performance spaces in New York still left the group dependent
on theater owners.

Melvin L. Oliver and Thomas M. Shapiro argue that historically blacks
experience constant obstacles and difficulties in their efforts to own property and accumulate wealth. With abolition democracy in the South and
Sherman's Order Fifteen, which redistributed land to former slaves, some
African Americans achieved wealth accumulation for a time, but it was a
definitively short time. The promise to blacks of land redistribution and
forty acres occurred with the confiscation of plantation land, but with the
eventual rescinding of Order Fifteen the government systematically seized
lands owned by blacks. By 1866, the United States government adjusted the
Homestead Act to include African Americans. The Homestead Act set aside
forty-six million acres of public land, but again, this act did not work to
include freed slaves in the distribution of the land.[98] Given the dire situation
surrounding African American wealth accumulation and property ownership, it remains surprising that between 1900 and 1910, black ownership
of theaters remained at a high point and black syndicates emerged during
this time. But racism blocked the growth of black theater due to the absence
of sponsorship, the high cost of transportation, and second-class bookings,
which all marked the demise of these black-owned theaters.[99]

Shoo *Fly Regiment* and Vaudeville

The Shoo Fly Regiment ran for approximately two theatrical seasons and
proved popular among audiences, marking an artistic success; but the show
closed in 1908 due to financial losses. It toured the United States for seven
months, closing in Philadelphia on May 7, 1908. According to James Weldon Johnson, the loss in revenue occurred because, as he states, "not yet had
the fight for Colored companies to play first class houses been won."[100] At
the beginning of the tour the show received favorable bookings, but as they
continued to tour Cole and Johnson found the show booked for one-night

stands at popularly priced, third-rate theaters. They lost money and found it difficult to cover the expenses that a large company accrued. The team eventually used their own money to keep the show going and to bring the company back to New York.[101]

Cole and Johnson began plans for a new show with the closing of *The Shoo Fly Regiment;* in the interim period Bob Cole and J. Rosamond Johnson performed for six weeks in vaudeville on the Williams Circuit. Their act included eight cast members: Bessie Tribble, Edgar Connors, Fannie Wise, Mamie Butler, Lula Coleman, Daisy Brown, and Leona Marshall.[102] Lester A. Walton stated that Cole and Johnson's musicals and vaudeville act dispensed with plantation scenes, buck dancing, and the "old time Negro Songs."[103] Instead their vaudeville act included scenes and songs from *The Shoo Fly Regiment,* which depicted Rosamond as a soldier and a hero while the women in the vaudeville act portrayed college students.[104] Cole and Johnson's vaudeville act also included dialogue and musical selections played by J. Rosamond Johnson on the piano. The finale of the act was the singing of "The Old Flag Never Touched the Ground" accompanied by the cast members.[105] The sophistication of their vaudeville act proved a novelty for the time and Walton lamented that theater owners and booking agents showed resistance to an act that moved away from plantation scenes. He noted that Cole and Johnson "bore the reputation of having the most refined colored acts on the variety stage."[106] W. E. B. Du Bois laid the blame for the failure of Cole and Johnson's productions firmly at the feet of whites. He charged: "In later days Cole and Johnson and Williams and Walker lifted minstrelsy by sheer force of genius into the beginning of a new drama. White people refused to support the finest of their new conceptions like the *Red Moon* and the cycle apparently stopped."[107]

Lester A. Walton hoped that theater-booking agents would cast off their prejudices against civilized portrayals of African Americans as opposed to stereotypes and book Cole and Johnson's vaudeville act. They performed their vaudeville act from May 21 to June 11, 1908. They appeared at the Orpheum Theater in Brooklyn the week of May 21, 1908, the Alhambra Theater on May 28, and the Fifth Avenue Theater on June 4 to June 11, 1908. Walton noted that Cole and Johnson made changes to the act with each performance.[108] It appears that they refined the act while performing, a habit that continued with the touring company of *The Red Moon.* They began rehearsals for *The Red Moon* around July 30, 1908 at the Majestic Theater in Brooklyn, and performed in the "Frolics" for the Frogs, a black theatrical organization, on August 17, 1908 at the Manhattan Casino in the Bronx.[109]

Cole and Johnson planned to begin the tour in August and to play at the best second-class theaters in the United States, which proved a step up from the third-rate houses to which *The Shoo Fly Regiment* had been consigned.[110] They did not control the booking of their shows, and their productions remained blocked from playing first-rate theaters. Their options were few. Ultimately, the success or failure of the production lay in the hands of white booking agents. Walton suggested that the booking of Cole and Johnson's new musical at second-class theaters proved highly encouraging because *The Shoo Fly Regiment* suffered financially since it had played in third-rate houses.[111] Although the booking agent William Morris initially planned on opening *The Red Moon* in New York City, the production opened in Wilmington, Delaware, on August 31, 1908, and then moved to Jersey City, New Jersey. Advertisements for the production reveal that the ticket prices remained the same as for *The Shoo Fly Regiment*.[112]

Conclusion

In the face of seemingly insurmountable obstacles, which included the loss of revenues, Cole and Johnson included a forward-thinking program in which they used uplift and education in changing the theatrical and social landscape for African Americans. They took an unstinting and unapologetic stand and changed the representative images of African American men and women in *The Shoo Fly Regiment*. They rejected stereotypical images of African American women and drew upon their personal history, their romantic relationships, and their life experiences to break the love scene taboo; they created female characters patterned after the women in their families and the female students that they met at Atlanta University.

While Cole and Johnson made progressive changes in the portrayal of African Americans, they also included caricatures—-including a chorus of Pickaninnies and the Bode Edjicashun that reproduced some incredibly degrading stereotypes, which reverberate into the twenty-first century. They likewise included female impersonation in the guise of Ophelia the Village Pride, who, it can be shown, did not really conform to common stereotypes. She plainly broke with the low comedy/Funny Old Gal and Prima Donna representation popularized in blackface minstrel shows performed by whites. Cole and Johnson made a conscientious effort not to deride African American women with this portrayal. We cannot deny that the team conformed to minstrel norms to guarantee the success of the show with white and black audiences, but because they included fully human characters within the musical, and advanced the rendering of the doughty African American male, the educated African American woman, and black romantic love, they tempered these stereotypes and made revolutionary changes in the renderings of African Americans on stage. By aggrandizing African American men and women, and reclaiming African American history through musical theater by setting *The Shoo Fly Regiment* within an educational institution similar to Booker T. Washington's Tuskegee Institute, Cole and Johnson committed the ultimate subversive act by brazenly and unrepentantly claiming black power.

Figure 14. *The Red Moon* sheet music. James Weldon Johnson Papers, Yale Collection of American Literature, Beinecke Rare Book and Manuscript Library

CHAPTER FOUR

THE RED MOON

The Interconnections between Theater and History, the Black and Native Americanization Program at Hampton Institute

THE REDVOLUTION HAS COME
IT HAS BEGUN

IT IS REDVOLUTION OF THE SPIRIT AND OF THE MIND
IT IS FREEING OF THE OPPRESSION, WHICH HAS BOUND US FOR CENTURIES

IT IS THE REALIZATION THAT THE CHAINS WHICH BIND, WHICH BLIND
US

ARE SHACKLED TO OUR SPIRITS NO LONGER
AND THEY NO LONGER BLIND OUR MIND

WAKE UP AND PRAY
WAKE UP AND SPEAK
WAKE UP AND STAND
WAKE UP AND TEACH THE CHILDREN THE TRUTH
OH

NEVER EVER AGAIN SINK INTO THE PRISON OF YOUR ALCOHOL, DRUGS, SELF-HATRED,
    DENIAL OR ANY OF THE OTHER VICES, WHICH SUFFOCATE YOUR SPIRIT

RISE UP AND
TEAR THE CELL WALLS DOWN
    AND LIVE, LIVE, LIVE,
    BREATH
    BREATH IN
    SPEAK THE TRUTH BABY
(LITEFOOT[1] [CHEROKEE/CHICHIMECCA])

The *Red Moon* (1908–1910) introduced audiences to African American and Native American solidarity. To understand the significance of such coalitions we must discuss the creative metamorphosis of the show. The team wrote two versions of *The Red Moon;* during the 1908 theatrical season they revised the production when the show toured the United States and Canada.[2] In 1938 J. Rosamond Johnson wrote a new version of *The Red Moon* with the help of African American film actor Clarence Muse.[3] The original production, written for an all-black cast, took place in Virginia with settings that included a black industrial institution called Swamptown, a Virginia farm, and a reservation in The Land of the Setting Sun. In the introduction to the 1938 edition, J. Rosamond Johnson wrote, "[t]he original story of *The Red Moon* dealt with life among the American Indians and Negroes in a southern community with an industrial school as background."[4] A review by J. D. Howard for *The Indianapolis Freeman* states, "The story of the play has to do with a romantic episode opening in and around a Government school for Indians and Negroes at 'Sunshine Land' (wherever that is). As it unfolds itself, the plot is well sustained throughout."[5] The 1938 production was written for a white cast with situations taking place in 1898 in Oklahoma and the South.[6]

Many scholars describe the 1908 story of *The Red Moon* as revolving around Minnehaha (played by Abbie Mitchell), a half-African American and half-Native American woman who lives in Virginia with her African American mother, Lucretia Martin, "the old chief's wife."[7] In a September 1908 review of the show, Lester Walton explains, "[t]he plot deals with a fight for a girl, who is the daughter of an Indian and a colored woman. While about three years old the Indian leaves wife and daughter and returns to his tribe where he is made chief."[8] J. Rosamond Johnson's 1938 notes describe the 1908 production: Minnehaha "has just graduated from an industrial institution, and is kidnapped by her father, Chief Lowdog (Arthur Talbot), who misses her and takes her back to the reservation in the West."[9] Walton's 1908 review states, "Fourteen years later the Indian [Chief Lowdog] returns the day the daughter is graduating from a Negro-Indian school, and she leaves with her father, amid much commotion."[10]

On the reservation, Minnehaha becomes the object of affection of Red Feather, "an educated Indian" played by Theodore Pankey.[11] Walton relates, "[i]t is only a short time before the girl revolts at the Indian life she is compelled to lead and yearns for civilization."[12] Minnehaha's African American boyfriend Plunk Green, "the lawyer they don't expect," played by J. Rosamond Johnson, and his friend Slim Brown, "the doctor that they don't expect," played by Bob Cole, set out to save her from her father, Red Feather, and reservation life. Walton offered that, "Cole and Johnson do most of the comedy" as these characters.[13]

At the end of the first act, Red Feather and Plunk Green vie for Minnehaha's love through a co-rivalry. According to *The Indianapolis Freeman* review for a performance at the Great Northern, "The battle for the love of Minnehaha began between Red Feather and Plunk Green. The curtain fell on the first act, a beautiful picture, Minnehaha leaving the Government school for the land of the 'Setting Sun.'"[14] Green and Brown ultimately save Minnehaha and also play a role in the reconciliation of Chief Lowdog and Lucretia Martin.[15] In the finale Minnehaha marries Plunk Green as a reward for his bravery in returning her to her family and friends.[16] Walton states that the musical was "unique in many respects" and that "The show ranks high musically, for picturesque scenes and costumes. It should be very successful."[17] Cole and Johnson aggrandized some of the African American and Native American characters through their names and their portrayal, while adhering to degrading representations for other roles. In the case of Minnehaha, they used a name that in Dakota means waterfall and is also the name of the heroine in Longfellow's "The Song of Hiawatha." Given Bob Cole's Black Seminole background, it remains surprising that the team chose the name Chief Lowdog, a racially loaded moniker infused with jokes and preconceptions, which unabashedly and brashly announces negative personality traits.

The Civil War and the Founding of the Black and Native American Program at Hampton

To understand the historical and sociological implications of *The Red Moon*, it remains necessary to discuss the historical epoch in which the team wrote the play. The Civil War proved an important training ground for new race relations and generated models for how the U.S. government would subsequently deal with African Americans and Native Americans through assimilationist programs. After the Civil War, the institutionalization of Radical Reconstruction provided the training grounds for the African American and Native American assimilation programs put into place. The plan included the appropriation of Native American land as the people faced imprisonment or relocation to reservations, and the founding of industrial institutions specifically designed to educate African Americans and Native Americans. White Civil War veterans Captain Richard Henry Pratt and General Samuel Chapman Armstrong gained experience during the Civil War and utilized their "expertise" in schools for Native Americans and blacks, respectively, after the conflict.

Between 1868 and 1876, Radical Reconstruction enfranchised African Americans and impoverished whites in the South. Where African Americans' experience in slavery left them destitute and uneducated, the condition of the poor white was that of a denigrated, uneducated serf. The redistribution of land, the founding of hospitals, and the creation of a school system for the newly freed slaves and poor whites ushered in a new era, one which offered African Americans the opportunity to gain political power as governors, legislators, and in other official capacities. The creation of banks by the Freedman's Bureau for impecunious African Americans enabled wealth accumulation, which allowed them to leave behind poverty for a brief period. Emerging from servitude, slaves fostered a strong desire to better their conditions through education. One of the most important aspects of Reconstruction was the creation of a public school system, ultimately founded by former slaves, with the aid of the Freedman's Bureau, New England teachers, and Northern philanthropy. This paved the way for the founding of schools such as Hampton Institute, Tuskegee Institute, Howard University, and Fisk University by the Freedman's Bureau.[18]

The founding of Hampton typifies the integral part the Union army played in the creation of African American organizations. Because of the presence of the Union army in Southern cities, new governmental institutions emerged, and Union officers such as General Samuel Chapman Armstrong became administrators. Armstrong was raised in Hawaii by missionary parents. In the 1830s he frequently traveled throughout the islands with his father, Richard Armstrong, the minister of public instruction for Hawaiian schools. General Armstrong drew his inspiration for Hampton from Lahainaluna Normal School, founded in 1831, and David B. Lyman's Hilo Boarding and Manual Labor School, founded in 1836. Armstrong observed, "it meant something to the Hampton School, and perhaps to the ex slaves of America, that, from 1820 to 1860, the distinctly missionary period, there was worked out in the Hawaiian Islands, the problem of the emancipation, enfranchisement and Christian civilization of a dark-skinned Polynesian people in many respects like the Negro race."[19] Initially, in 1865, the placement of Captain C. B. Wilder of Boston as an abolitionist superintendent in charge of the Hampton area led to Radical Reconstruction through the redistributing of land to former slaves. Ultimately he faced dismissal and court-martial for following the congressional act, which created the Freedman's Bureau, and the Circular Order Thirteen of July 28, 1865, which directed him to redistribute the abandoned lands to escaped slaves. President Johnson's conservative reconstruction plan, which favored the planter class, led to Wilder's dismissal. The stronghold of the Union army in Hampton and the surrounding area provided a safe harbor for legions of escaped slaves, who by 1862 enjoyed "quasi-freedom." African Americans joined the Union army; cultivated the abandoned farmlands; made alliances with the Northern missionaries; and, according to Robert Engs, defined their freedom as enjoying "all the privileges given free white people in America." [20]

An opponent of Radical Reconstruction, General Samuel Armstrong replaced Wilder and supported the return of Union confiscated lands to former Confederates and the unfair labor contracts negotiated between former slave owners and "free" black workers, but opposed the extension of the franchise to African American males. Armstrong viewed African Americans as an underclass that should be educated primarily as manual laborers and servants to meet the labor need of the white Southern landowners.[21] Hampton Institute was opened in 1868 to provide manual training and literacy skills for the formerly enslaved African Americans, and the school received substantial support from the American Missionary Association, the Union army, and northern philanthropic foundations such as the Slater Fund.[22] The utter absurdity of "educating" blacks in the very skills they had already received training in due to their enslavement seemed lost on Armstrong, his supporters, and white supremacists. Cole and Johnson set *The Red Moon* in a Hampton-like school—Swamptown.

The displacement of Native Americans onto reservations due to westward expansion left the U.S. government with the dilemma of what to do with these indigenous survivors. After the Red River War of 1874, the government imprisoned Native Americans whom they deemed to have committed crimes during the war and sent them to reservations. In 1875 the government placed white Civil War veteran Captain Richard Henry Pratt in charge of these prisoners. After serving four years in the Civil War as a corporal, Pratt became a lieutenant in 1867, and a captain in 1873. He served at Fort Arbuckle, Indian Territory, where he commanded the Tenth Regiment, one of the first all-black regiments, founded in 1866 and consisting of newly freed slaves from Little Rock, Arkansas; Native American scouts from the Tonkawa, Osage, Choctaw, and Cherokee tribes; and white officers. Pratt's experiences with the Tenth Regiment and in the Civil War became the foundation for how he would govern the Native Americans at Hampton.[23]

The imprisonment of Native Americans under Pratt's command at Fort Marion, Florida, in the 1870s began attempts to Americanize Indians through education. In 1875, Captain Pratt controlled Native Americans imprisoned at Fort Sill, Oklahoma, whose legions included Kiowas, Comanche, Cheyenne, and Arapahos. The eventual transfers of seventy-four Native American prisoners to St. Augustine, Florida, under Pratt's command, culminated in Pratt "humanely" removing their shackles and permitting them to police themselves. Part of his project in Florida included teaching them English with the help of missionary teacher, Sarah Mather; indoctrinating them in the idea of "working for wages" in orange groves and packinghouses; encouraging their artistic talents as ledger artists; and assimilating them into European culture. Wealthy northerners wintering at Fort Marion interested in Pratt's project taught them reading, writing, and arithmetic, while the students taught the northerners how to use the bow and arrow. Native American reform advocates such as Episcopal Bishop Henry Whipple, Senator George Pendleton, and Spencer Baird of the Smithsonian Institute wintering at Fort Marion encouraged Pratt in his work with the Indians.[24]

Buoyed by his success, Pratt wrote to the Interior and War Departments in 1878 to propose the education of Native Americans at Hampton Institute in Virginia, after a white school rejected them. Armstrong and the Hampton administrators ultimately accepted the proposal. In 1878, twenty-two Fort Marion prisoners gained admission to Hampton Institute, and Congress agreed to the education of additional Indians at the school. Pratt arranged to transport six students to Hampton, followed by sixty-two others. The government designed the Native American boarding school system to distance the student from their culture and instill in them the U.S. ideologies of citizenship and civilization. The government adoption of the boarding schools system for Native Americans would eventually lead to the founding of Flandreau (South Dakota), Carlisle (Pennsylvania), Haskell (Kansas), and to the Compulsory Attendance Law of 1891, which forced Indian children to attend government boarding schools modeled after Hampton Institute.[25]

Pratt chose a select group of students to attend Hampton; as he recalled, "[s]ide by side with those colored pupils the Indian boys and girls, in perfect harmony with the new life demonstrated their capacity to hold their own in improving the best chances."[26] In a 1878 letter to the Commissioner of Indian Affairs in Washington D.C., Pratt claimed that the Indian prisoners stayed at Hampton by their "own choosing, as even down to the last moment they were offered the privilege of backing down and going home with the others."[27] School administrators assigned the Indian students a black roommate, who taught by example. African Americans remained somewhat reluctant roommates at first because of the perception that Indians were violent. Armstrong assuaged their fears and black students volunteered.[28]

Captain Pratt and General Armstrong worked together to make a smooth transition from an all-black coeducational institution to a biracial institution, despite their differing positions on biracial education. According to Robert Francis Engs, the partnership was brief because "Pratt was a firm believer in the Indian's equality with the white man, and he objected to their education among 'inferior' Negroes."[29] Initially Pratt favored biracial education, though Armstrong opposed it, proposing the education of Native Americans and African Americans in separate campus sites. He feared intimacy between them and worried that they might unite against whites in insurrection and violence.[30] Yet the fear of Native American violence against whites proved unfounded after their defeat in war on the plains against whites and their ultimate subjugation as prisoners at Fort Marion. Despite their tractability, Armstrong hired a jailer for the Native Americans to quell the fears of Hampton administrators and the Virginians in the surrounding areas. Lieutenant Henry Romeyn, a soldier from the Indian territories, acted as the commandant of the school, and Fortress Monroe remained at the disposal of Armstrong in case the Indians rebelled.[31]

Cole and Johnson interpreted biracial education through African American/Native American Minnehaha and Native American Red Feather, students educated at Swamptown, which resembled Hampton. The connections between the Americanization program at Hampton Institute, Booker T. Washington's involvement with the program, and Cole and Johnson's *The Red Moon* enables us to see the connections between what happened off stage and what happened on stage. The team's devotion to Washington influenced their musical about the Indian and African American interaction at Hampton Institute. Before founding Tuskegee Institute, Washington held the position of "House Father" to Native American male students at Hampton in 1880. Washington's job as the housefather included living with the students "and hav[ing] the charge of their discipline, clothing, rooms, and so on."[32] Washington replaced James C. Robbins, an 1876 Hampton graduate who held the position from 1876–1880. While Robbins enjoyed his job, he resigned in 1880 because Armstrong undermined his authority by refusing to give him maximum control over the Indians.[33] Washington's position as their teacher held particular importance, and the success or failure of the project lay firmly in his hands.[34]Armstrong heralded Washington as the primary force in the education of Native Americans.

> Could the black and red races be educated together without too much friction? I selected Mr. Washington as housefather of the Indian boys . . . he settled the whole question most satisfactorily, and, chiefly through his wise initiative, we have for nearly fourteen years educated the two races together.[35]

Armstrong conveniently omits James C. Robbins's contributions to the program. Washington's social welfare and educational agenda included helping and uplifting Indians. In 1905 he traveled to Arkansas, Indian Territory, and Oklahoma to "to see something of the condition of the colored people in the Indian Territory who were classed as Indians, or who were at one time slaves of the Indians."[36] Washington's advocacy work for Native Americans remains noteworthy and most certainly was sparked by his experience teaching Native Americans.

Booker T. Washington believed that interracial cooperation held the key to the success and uplift of Native Americans at Hampton Institute and in the United States. He argued that they must conform to the proven educational program set in place for blacks. Washington initially questioned his ability to teach Native Americans because of what he described as the Indians' feelings of superiority to whites and their higher sense of superiority to blacks due to African submission to slavery. He felt Native Americans would never submit to slavery.[37] Washington found that his trepidation proved unfounded, as he recalled: "[i]t was not long before I had the complete confidence of the Indians, and not only this, but I think I am safe in saying that I had their love and respect. I found that they were about like any other human beings; that they responded to kind treatment and resented ill treatment. They were continually planning to do something that would add to my happiness and comfort."[38]

African American Female
Teachers at Hampton

African American female students and teachers at Hampton found themselves placed in charge of Native American female students. Amelia Perry, an 1879 graduate, supervised the Indian girls in 1876. Lovey Mayo, who graduated in 1880, spent five years managing the Indian girls at Winona, the Indian girls dormitory. Mayo ran the laundry and later became the matron of the dorm.[39] Georgia (Georgiana) Washington, who graduated in 1882, held the position of matron and ran the Winona laundry for ten years.[40] In the summer of 1882, Olivia Davidson, Washington's future wife, trained Indian girls at Hampton in preparation for her fall teaching position at Tuskegee Institute (figures 15 and 16).

Teaching Native American students and employing African American women to teach them provided the foundation for Booker T. Washington's teaching methods at Tuskegee Institute, where he involved women in training and education. This proved exceptional given African American women's

Figure 15. Amelia Perry Pride graduated from Hampton in 1879. She supervised the Indians in 1876. Amelia Perry Pride Papers. Hampton University Archives, Hampton, Virginia. Courtesy of Hampton University Archives

Figure 16. Georgiana Washington graduated from Hampton in 1882. She taught in the Indian Girls Program for fifteen years. Georgiana Washington Papers. Hampton University Archives, Hampton, Virginia. Courtesy of Hampton University Archives

exclusion from higher education, social science, and academic inquiry by colleges, universities, and by people like W. E. B. Du Bois. White foundations and religious institutions also challenged progressive education for blacks and attempted to control black schools.[41] In *A Voice From the South* (1892), Anna Julia Cooper lamented the lack of educational opportunities for black women. She detailed her experience as a student, pointed to the inferior education that black women received compared to black men due to the expectation that women would marry and mother, and she underscored the importance of black women's educational development as integral to ennobling the race.[42] Cooper says "[l]et there be the same flourish of trumpets and clapping of hands as when a boy announces his determination to enter the lists."[43] She argued that schools should raise money for black female education and offer these applicants scholarships as readily as they gave them to male students. Given these many obstacles, Washington's educational institution proved revolutionary in its inclusion of African American women, and his commitment to Native American education also remains noteworthy.

Hampton officials' resistance to biracial education and fear of romance between African Americans and Native Americans originated in the racial hierarchies established at the founding of the institute. These included a romance hierarchy and an education hierarchy, both of which benefited the white administration and teachers at the school. The romance hierarchy set in place by the officials prohibited romance and marriage between blacks and Native Americans, while encouraging romance and wedlock between white teachers and administrators and Native American students. The education hierarchy placed whites as administrators and teachers of preferred courses at the top, blacks as teachers of industrial classes and courses the whites refused to teach in the middle, and Native Americans at the bottom. In addition, one can surmise that to ensure that alliances would not occur between African Americans and Native Americans, white administrators instituted a system in which they used African Americans to physically discipline Native Americans, further complicating race relations.

General Armstrong and the board sat at the top of the racial hierarchy with the white female teachers by their side. Thus an involuted and deliberately divisive racial hierarchy permeated Hampton Institute. The arrival of the Native Americans further snarled the school's racial politics. As citizens, African Americans occupied a higher status than the noncitizen Native American prisoners of war. Whites ruled both groups, but sought to control and supervise African Americans' own supervision of Native Americans. This hierarchy attempted to pit Native Americans and African Americans against each other and undermine the prospects for alliances between the two aggrieved communities of color. Within this racially charged environment African American female teachers and student teachers found common bonds and affinities with Native American students.

White female teachers such as Cora Folsom taught "Advanced Class," "Civilization Class," civics, and economics, while African American female students and teachers Amelia Perry, Lovey Mayo, Georgiana Washington, and Olivia Davidson found themselves relegated to caring for and teaching Indian girls domestic service and running the laundry at Winona. Lovey Mayo gave voice to the disappointment of being trained as a teacher and consigned to the art of domestic science: "Though I did not do much classroom teaching as I had hoped for, there were other points that needed attention, and the greater part of my time and strength went in that direction."[44] Lovey Mayo's experience at Hampton illustrates the fact that her duties left little time for the teaching of elementary education, a duty that it appears Mayo longed for as is evident in her expression of disappointment and disillusionment. Georgiana Washington also taught the Native American girls and, like Mayo, also found that Hampton Institute did not meet her expectations.[45] She recalled that "[h]aving just finished school I was full of the theory and practice of teaching, practice lived, but theory died a natural death."[46] Instead of teaching academic courses, Washington taught domestic science to the Native American girls. She stated: "I had two classes in laundry work in the morning and two in the afternoon, every day except Saturday. One class would wash while the other ironed, so the trial was first at the ironing table, then at the tub."[47] Washington's words elucidate her disenchantment: "practice lived, but theory died a natural death." Lovey Mayo, Georgiana Washington, and the Native American students assigned positions as domestic workers appeared to leave little room for any other aspirations at Hampton. Their experiences also reveal that the administration, with the aid of their white female teachers, blocked the ambitions of the African American female students and teachers because the education was specifically designed to keep them in a marginal position in U.S. society.

They learned sewing and mending, both by hand and machine, as well as washing, ironing, and gardening. The courses also included math, U.S. and English history, English, natural sciences, "moral science," and civics. They worked the majority of the day "learning" domestic skills to support the school and went to classes at night. Hampton and Indian boarding schools reaped enormous financial rewards from this arrangement because the students produced food, made goods for sale, and maintained the campus, and the male students even built campus structures. These schools could not operate without the labor of their students. Many Native American children faced illness and malnourishment, which in numerous cases led to death. They also suffered from incredible bouts of homesickness, which compelled some of them to run away from the boarding schools.[48] The African American female teachers who taught the Native American students at Hampton found that they, too, faced exploitation. Not surprisingly, students at Hampton, Tuskegee, and their Native American government boarding school counterparts two decades later expressed their dissatisfaction and disappointment with their collective educational experience.[49]

Learning and practicing domestic skills proved difficult and dangerous for the girls because the equipment was heavy and cumbersome. In *My Face Is Black Is True: Callie House and the Struggle for Ex-Slave Reparations* (2005), Mary Frances Berry describes what black female domestic laborers experienced. Berry states that washerwomen often made soap from pork grease, used washboards to scrub clothes, made starch by boiling flour, and heated heavy irons on stoves. Domestic work proved both physically challenging and damaging to the body. They ran heavy irons in a continuous pattern back and forth, and "[t]he women's hands were reddened from the harshness of the soap, and they worked with constant pain from bending over to stir the wash kettles and from lifting soaked, wet, heavy bedding."[50] Due to their work as laundresses at Hampton Institute, African American teachers Amelia Perry Pride, Georgiana Washington, and Lovey Mayo's experiences paralleled those of washerwomen. The Native American girls' training in domestic skills also proved harsh and dangerous and certainly secured their position in life as domestic laborers.

Amelia Perry Pride taught the girls how to iron and wrote that they expressed their fear of the hot irons.[51] Pride recalled that, "One [girl] took an iron off to carry it to the tables[,] she did not hold it out away from herself, so it scorched a great place in her dress."[52] Later that day Pride observed: "I found she had got tired of pushing the heavy iron about, so she had just set it down for a few moments here and there on the towel, and of course wherever it had rested it had left a yellow print of itself."[53] Pride's observations demonstrate that the threat of injury and fatigue was high for the teachers and their young students. This type of "education" would manifest itself in the Native American government boarding schools in what David Wallace Adams describes as "never ending drudgery" for the students. Anna Shaw, a student in Phoenix, Arizona, faced "strapping" if she wasn't finished scrubbing the dining room floors by 8:00 A.M.[54] Rebecca Mazakute/Rattling Iron, Lakota (Sioux) wrote about her experience at Hampton in December 1882.

[We] sweep our Halls and steps before we make our beds, and when we ['re] finished [with] that we clean our own rooms, some of us got teachers rooms, [*sic*] So we clean our own rooms before we do the teachers, because they get up later than we do. . . . Right after that I go to school and in [the] afternoon we have sewing at 1 o'clock and stop it at 4 o'clock, after 4 we have study hour. [55]

As with her teachers, little time was allotted for learning academics. Both African American teachers and Native American students at Hampton and their boarding school counterparts all paid a high price for their "education": demoralization, injury, and torturous labor.

All students "trained" in the summer in "outing programs," where they worked for whites as servants and laborers. Booker T. Washington recalled that the girl students "left to spend their vacation north as helpers in strange families."[56] They traveled to New England to continue their domestic education by working for white families. While many of the African American and Native American students attended Hampton Institute due in part to northern philanthropy, the system of sending students out in the summer to train as laborers in northerners' homes remains specious, for the work proved arduous and many students became ill, grew homesick, and died.

Some students attempted to negotiate a return to Hampton. Sarah Walker (Hidasta) wrote to a female benefactor from Pittsfield, Massachusetts, in 1880 that "I want to go back to Hampton and go to school. I am not home sick now. I have very nice time over here. I want to see you all very much."[57] With her assurance that she is not homesick, Walker tries to broker a deal to return home and reveals that she is in fact very much homesick. She continues her letter by stating, "Carrie and I we go to church every Sunday and also to Sunday school. I wash the dishes every day and sweep the kitchen and do my washing and ironing. Mrs. Foot, give me a nice dress. Your friend "'Sarah Walker'"[58] Part of the strategy at Hampton Institute included forcing the Native American students to conform to white ideals and expunge their Indian culture and heritage. It appears that Walker attempted to use the oppressors' tools against them in her negotiations to return home by relaying that her assimilation into white culture was complete. She assured the reader that she conformed to Christianity and accepted domestic labor as her lot and this was why she should be allowed to return home. Other students completely rejected white man's "civilization" and brokered their deals in more profound and heartbreaking ways. White teacher Cora Folsom relayed the following situation.

One girl with the striking misnomer of Happy Road, homesick beyond all reason, would lie prone upon the ground [and could not be] forced from it, and though she scorned not the relief of tear, had to [be] sent home after a few months as hopeless.[59]

By showing her inconsolable despair at being taken away from her family, Happy Road successfully rejected white man's civilization and negotiated her return home.

Other Indian girl students spent their summers at Hampton as "assistant cooks," dining room workers, and waitresses. Booker T. Washington asserted that they "are learning rapidly the many little things necessary to good house keeping."[60] The very young students also stayed behind at Hampton Institute under the charge of black teachers such as Georgiana Washington. As with their teachers, little time was allotted for learning academics.[61]

Even when faced with the harsh reality of the "education" at Hampton, the African American teachers held high ideals and hope for a bright future for both groups. Lovey Mayo asserted that

The Indian race as well as my own, is struggling for recognition as men and though the former has greater encouragements, I considered it a privilege to have contributed even in a small way, toward the accomplishments of the desired end.[62]

In *The Red Moon*, Cole and Johnson's female characters, thankfully, escaped all the degrading and humiliating experiences of the African American and Native American teachers and students at Hampton Institute. Where their real-life experiences offered them a life of domestic service, the play emphasized the importance of a standard education. The show presented audiences with Minnehaha, an African American and Native American woman, attending "Swamptown Institute" for higher education.

Part of the Americanization program at Hampton Institute including donning white's clothing—"citizens' dress." The education emphasized the importance of European clothing and religion, but this is not to say that the Native Americans or the African Americans fully accepted assimilation or that it did not cause humiliation and pain. In a not so thinly veiled criticism of the white man's civilization, Booker T. Washington informs us of the emotionally damaging effects of discarding one's culture.

This thing they [Native Americans] disliked most, I think were to have their long hair cut, to give up wearing their blankets, and to cease smoking; but no white American ever thinks that any other race is wholly civilized until he wears the white man's clothes, eats the white man's foods, speaks the white man's language, and professes the white man's religion.[63]

Washington reveals the arrogance and callousness of hegemony and the psychic effects of "civilizing" Native Americans and other racialized groups. Margaret James Murray's (Mrs. Booker T. Washington) "Practical Leaflet" addressed African American female resistance to relinquishing their heads-carves, a seemingly embarrassing reminder of Africa or African American enslavement.[64] Consequently African American and Native American indoc-trination into white man's civilization included the purging of anything that remotely resembled indigenous culture. Ohet.toint and Toun ke uh, former Fort Marion prisoners, wrote Pratt and discussed their new skills. On July 1878 Ohet.toint wrote, "I am White man now and is not Indian and I think I talk English very soon now because I don't want the Indian clothes now and I like White man clothe very much."[65] On August 23, 1878, Toun ke uh wrote: "But you I want my letter when I come in Hampton so was like I of the white men clothes it to wear and I am very well not sick and I have plenty to eat and good clothes and all I love the white people friend."[66] It remains unclear whether these letters reveal their acceptance of hegemony at Hamp-ton or provide evidence of a strategy of survival for the Indian students. What is clear was the expectation that Native Americans would expunge all remnants of their past and live as "whites." All the students were compelled to wear "citizens' dress."

Despite the obstacles that they faced, the African American female teach-ers saw their work with the Indian girls and their education as affirming, and they worked to draw alliances between the two groups. Brenda Child argues that Native American boarding schools, such as Flandreau and Haskell, forbade students to speak their tribal language, with severe punishments, including beatings, jailing, and having one's mouth washed with soap. One of the school requirements included "cast[ing] off their Indian name" as a mark of civility. Teachers and administrators coupled this with public humili-ation if students used their Native American names, as they were taught to be ashamed of their names and their language.[67]

Hampton Institute's method of Americanization appeared more humane. The school allowed the students to keep their Native American name as a last name, yet required the students to adopt an Anglo first name.[68] The strategy of the African American teachers at Hampton proved quite dissimilar to the methods adopted by the Native American government boarding schools. The African American teachers formed relationships and trust with the Native

American students through language. Lovey Mayo, Georgiana Walker, and Amelia Perry Pride made an effort to learn the students' languages, which certainly forged a bond between them.[69] Taken from their parents for education in Virginia at a young age, many of the Native American female students cultivated warm and loving relationships with their African American female teachers, viewing them as surrogate parents, and they wrote of their mutual affection.

In lamenting Amelia Perry Pride's planned departure from Hampton, Sarah Walker (Hidasta) from Fort Berthold, Dakota wrote on February 1880 in the *Southern Workman,* "I will remember you always. I want you to take care of us all the time. I don't want any body but you. Will cry when you go to teach somebody else please come to see us again."[70] This plaintive expression of grief reveals the strong attachments and quasi-familial relationships that formed between teacher and student. The girls appeared to respect their black teachers and held them in high regard. The Native American student newspaper, *Talks and Thoughts,* noted in 1888, "Miss Georgiana Washington is back from her vacation, and her old friends are glad to see her."[71] White teacher Cora Folsom wrote that Lovey Mayo and Georgiana Washington "were much beloved by the Indian girls who have always held them in grateful remembrance."[72] Anna Dawson, who arrived at Hampton as a little girl, wrote from Framingham, Massachusetts on February 23, 1888: "Miss Lovey Mayo, a colored young lady, . . . was for some years employed in the Indian Department, and she received as much respect and love from the Indian girls as any white teacher we have, and we were all very sorry when she went away."[73]

While it appears that the Hampton administrators attempted to position the white female teachers as superior to the African American teachers, the Native American students rejected this hierarchy. They had fond feelings toward their African American teachers. In the face of the harsh educational environment and their conscription as domestic laborers, the students and their teachers found common ground, mutual admiration, and respect for each other at Hampton Institute. They also committed themselves to education as a means of enhancing the status of both groups.

While these women found the environment at Hampton Institute stifling to their intellectual and social growth, they found meaning for themselves through their work with the Native American female students. They discovered that in order to achieve their aspirations they had to leave Hampton Institute. Upon graduation in 1879 Amelia Perry Pride returned to her home town, Lynchburg, Virginia, where she founded the Polk School, a cooking and sewing school, the Dorchester Home for the Indigent and Aged, and a women's club.[74] Pride also held the position of officer in the Temperance

Society, demanded the termination of the jailing of African Americans, and argued for the end of Jim Crow on steamships and trains.[75] Similarly Georgiana Washington left Hampton Institute after fifteen years teaching the Native American girls.[76] Washington established a school in Alabama to "[lift] the cloud of ignorance and superstition from my brothers and sisters there," and founded the Peoples Village School in Mount Meigs, Alabama, where she held the position of principal.[77] Lovey Mayo left Hampton in 1885 to work at Tuskegee Institute, where she participated in missionary work and held the position of matron.[78]

These women's goals in life came to full fruition upon their departure from the school through their work in establishing self-help organizations to better the lives of African Americans less fortunate than themselves. Despite the prohibitions set in place at Hampton which limited their life opportunities, African American and Native American female students and teachers found meaning for themselves by forming alliances with one another at the school. Once they left Hampton, their chances for personal and intellectual growth became a reality. Comparably, Cole and Johnson fully realized the potential for fighting racism and hegemony in their reimagining of biracial education at Hampton as a setting in which alliance building and interethnic coalitions presented an avenue for the struggle against oppression.

Industrial education proved devastating to African American and Native American students at Hampton. The farming techniques they learned relied on unmechanized operations, low capitalization, and small-scale individualized labor, which proved out of date by the time the students finished their education. In 1882, 90 percent of the black students obtained jobs as teachers and married; three were ministers, and one was a doctor. In 1892 Native Americans went on to work in farming, or as blacksmiths, as wheelwrights, merchants, clerks, missionaries, teachers, and police officers. An infinitesimal percentage of Native American students received higher education and worked as doctors, engineers, surveyors, and lawyers. The majority of them finished the three-year program, and usually returned to the reservation having mastered only an elementary understanding of English, reading, writing, and math. Although African Americans held high hopes for their future because of their education at Hampton, the only professions they actually qualified for after their training were in domestic service and low-wage labor. The promise of small business ownership proved a promise un-kept. Debt peonage in the South, economic depression, racial discrimination, and training on outdated equipment made it nearly impossible for blacks and Native Americans to transcend their condition. Many who gained training in industrial education found themselves at a disadvantage.[79]

Booker T. Washington and Georgiana Washington held high hopes for the black race and the educational opportunities afforded to them. Georgiana Washington wrote that "My aim is to help, in any way I can, both Indian and Negro," and "[h]aving spent fifteen years at Hampton Institute ten as an assistant in the work for Indian girls, I count this experience the great privilege of my life."[80] Booker T. Washington felt that uplift meant self-sufficiency by obtaining land or a business. This seemed to many people the best way for African Americans and Native Americans to advance themselves in white society.[81] Unfortunately, white society had no intention of letting people of color rise.

The real historical events of biracial education at Hampton Institute acted as the foundation and framework for Cole and Johnson's *The Red Moon*. Georgiana Washington felt that interracial unity held the key to dignifying African Americans and Native Americans. Her creed for this unity was "two people down can't help each other, but two people rising can."[82] Correspondingly Cole and Johnson imagined interracial solidarity, mutual education, and romance between African Americans and Native Americans in *The Red Moon*. The musical illustrates this ideological stance. The musical offered Broadway audiences refined and erudite African American and Native American women. The team presented the audience with a chorus of cosmopolitan Gibson Girls and Ada Girls, possibly inspired by Ada Overton Walker—Marie Young, Pauline Hackney, Tootie Delk, Marie Lucas, Mattie Harris, and Millie Dean. They performed the song "Ada My Sweet Potato" with Cole's Slim Brown.[83] This image sharply opposed the lived experiences of the women who attended Hampton. Fanny Wise played Trusculina White, Slim Brown's love interest. Wise performed "I've Lost My Teddy Bear," which Lester Walton asserted "is going to be one of the hits of the show."[84] Ada Overton Walker "the public's favorite," played Phoebe Brown, sang the song of the same name with a chorus of "Spanish senoritas," and choreographed and performed "a new Aboriginal dance," the Native American-inspired "Wildfire."[85] Anna Cook Pankey played Nakomis, the Native American prophetess who sang the hauntingly beautiful slow rag "The Bleeding Moon,"[86] with the lines "When the moon is bleeding, and the clouds are red / 'Tis an awful omen, Jossakeed has said. / Then the skies are crimson, in the month of June. / Oh! My people look not on the bleeding moon."[87] Bob Cole wrote the lyrics, which the team claimed interpreted a Native American omen, and J. Rosamond Johnson wrote the music. The *Red Moon* presented a situation considerably superior to that of domestic or laundry woman assigned to African American and Native American teachers and students at Hampton Institute.

It appears that this production provided audiences with the first rendering of African American and Native American alliances on Broadway, a stellar and unique accomplishment. The musical was based on actual historical events, but the interactions between African Americans and Native Americans within the production presented a far better situation than the historical record. They omitted the problematic whites from their vision of the industrial institution, and by this omission eliminated the racist ideology set in place at Hampton and replaced it with a vision of interracial coalitions. The reality at Hampton painted a far different picture.

African Americans and Native Americans remained segregated from one another at Hampton both academically and socially. Their living facilities, school and church attendance, eating arrangements, military training, and academics all remained separate, except for a few classes. One teacher, Elaine Goodale Eastman, stated that the administration imposed segregation to prevent romantic pairings and fights. Administrators favored cordial relationships between African Americans and Native Americans imbued with chaste, nonintimate behavior. Eastman asserted that the initial reason for racially separating students occurred because the Native American students spoke little, if any, English. In later years, when they came from the reservations already speaking English, they participated in integrated classes. Yet the supporters and "friends" of Indians feared that they would be "contaminated" by associating with the black community and students. Helen Ludlow maintained that administrators kept the interactions between the groups "limited and guarded" to maintain racial purity and personal virtue. These codes of racial purity and morals of conduct did not extend to whites who taught at the institution, as evidenced by the number of marriages that took place between whites and Native Americans.[88] Whites wanted to keep blacks and Native Americans divided through the racial hierarchy created at Hampton because they believed in Native American assimilation into white culture, while they believed that black assimilation would and should never occur.

Industrial education for Native Americans would not last. General Armstrong foretold its demise in 1885. "The entire course includes, or more correctly begins and ends with the essentials of a good English education. Nothing more is attempted, because experience has shown us that nothing more is needed to fit our students for the work which is before them."[89] The commitment by the government to Native American education remained suspect given that they paid for only three years, although the program was designed for five years. According to Armstrong in 1885, Hampton remained "obliged to look to private charity" for the remainder of the school fee. Helen Ludlow reported in 1888 that charity supported the yearly full-time attendance of only fifteen Indian students.[90] By 1900, strong opposition to educating Native Americans began to chip away at the foundation of Indian education. In 1901, the Bureau of Indian Affairs abandoned academic training for Native Americans in favor of vocational and manual labor training. Brenda Childs points out that advocates of Indian education came to doubt full Native American assimilation, so they lowered the educational standards.[91] In his annual report, as the commissioner of Indian Affairs, William Jones detailed other reasons for its demise, including that after thirty-three years it cost the public $240 million dollars, the education remained antiquated, and Native Americans remained dependent on the government, given their lives on reservations. The government expected boarding school–educated students to single-handedly "civilize" all who lived on the reservation, which proved an impossible task.[92] Additionally, those educated at Indian boarding schools faced open hostility, racism, and discrimination in a job market where they could not find work in their respective fields.

The Romance Hierarchy at Hampton

The real experiences at Hampton proved harsh because hegemony prevented the proper education of African American and Native American people. In their musical, however, Cole and Johnson imagined an improved situation. They pictured black and Native American education as affirmative and saw industrial education as useful, and as something that would raise their social standing. Cole and Johnson produced their own form of racial counter lumping together of racial groups, humanizing blacks and Native Americans alike. They drew characters that needed no white supervision, but who decided their own future and welfare. By presenting blacks and Native Americans as more civilized than whites, more respectful and more beautiful, Cole and Johnson placed on stage the antithesis of the hegemonic plan for them. By inverting white domination and expunging whiteness, Cole and Johnson in effect transcended the degradation that white hegemony placed on black and Indian identity.

Cole and Johnson's staged version of life at Hampton differed sharply from the historical model on which it was based. *The Red Moon* featured a serious romantic scene between J. Rosamond Johnson as African American Plunk Green and Abbie Mitchell, an African American singer, as the Indian/black Minnehaha "who has allowed herself to be loved" by him, giving theatergoers interracial romance. The following review of *The Red Moon* confirms the passionate storyline. "This season Mr. Johnson developed into what you might call a romantic actor with a slight touch of tragic in places" as he plays "a very love-sick doctor."[93] This review elucidates the amorous underpinnings of the scenes between Johnson and Mitchell and illuminates the earnestness of the musical, ultimately substantiating the argument that Cole and Johnson broke the love scene proscription. The production also featured romantic intrigue between Minnehaha and the educated, "bold, bad Indian student" Red Feather, played by Theodore Pankey, again offering audiences interracial romance between blacks and Native Americans.[94] Through Minnehaha's parents, Chief Lowdog and African American Lucretia Martin, the audience witnessed interracial romance and its outcome in the birth of Minnehaha.

A hierarchy existed that regulated who actually gained sexual access to other races. Magnus Morner and Ramon Gutierrez argue that an important part of conquest in Latin America entailed white males' sexual access to women. Similarly, at Hampton Institute, conquest also took shape in terms of sexual access, which manifested itself in a romantic hierarchy. White supporters and "friends" of Indians wanted to keep Indians pure and feared that by associating with blacks, Indians faced "contamination."[95] The administrators frowned upon romances between African Americans and Native Americans, which culminated in dismissal of the offenders. However the fact that officials condoned the pairing of whites and Native Americans demonstrated that their codes of racial purity and morality did not extend to the white teachers and administrators at Hampton; eight white men and six white women married Native American students.[96] A concerted effort on the part of the faculty worked to prohibit interracial romantic and sexual relations between blacks and Native Americans.

Helen Ludlow discussed her visit to the Yankton Reservation and detailed the "success" of the Native American assimilation program through outmarriage, that is, marriage outside one's own race. She reported that one "Hampton's star" married a white male industrial teacher for the government, "who has taken her to a pleasant home on another agency, where she is helping him teach her people."[97] While Hampton administrators encouraged intermarriage between whites and Native Americans, they firmly policed and disapproved of wedlock between blacks and Native Americans. In 1888, Ludlow stated that "general social intercourse between the races of opposite sexes is limited and guarded. Trouble might come of it. None ever has. The effort is to build up self respect and mutual respect and we believe that education of the mind and heart tends to individual morality and race purity."[98]

Pratt openly encouraged this hypocrisy. He publicly denounced the lynching of African Americans and dismissed the commonly held notion of blacks as morally corrupt; yet, when having to choose between defending the rights of Native Americans over blacks, he chose the Indian.[99] Armstrong assured readers in *Ten Year's Work,* that "no doubt some low talk and ideas have been brought in from the low life in the South and West; but in ten years not a serious fracas has occurred, not a single case of immorality, between the students of both races and of both sexes."[100] Regardless of the fear of contamination by blacks, the Hampton officials felt that blacks acted as models to Native Americans in terms of civilization, English, and labor.[101] Hampton teacher Elaine Goodale married Charles Eastman (Sioux) in 1891. Rebecca Pond married former Hampton student George Owl (Cherokee) in 1919. Caroline Andrus was engaged to her student, William A. Jones (Sac and Fox tribesman), who, as a Harvard University student on an anthropological study in the Philippines, died in 1909 before they married.[102]

Not all of the relationships between white and Indian ended harmoniously. Native American student Addie Stevens became pregnant in the late 1800s, while administrators expelled Louisa Bissell for getting pregnant by an unmarried white private, Charles Cappizoli, in the 1920s. Both faced the wrath of white teachers Cora Folsom and Caroline Andrus.[103] Whites gained sexual and romantic access to people of color at Hampton; thus we must surmise that they also participated in sexual relations with the African American students, while hypocritically enjoining African American and Native Americans from pursuing romantic relations with one another.

Notwithstanding the ban, interracial romance occurred. The 1888 Hampton faculty notes and discipline files state that three black boys and Indian girls received disciplinary action against them for "midnight strolls." W. T. Penn and Josephine McCarthy (Sioux), James Atkinson and Cora Rulo (Ponca), and Fletcher Ricks and Jennie Ampetu (Assiniboine) found themselves charged with triple dating "for the purpose and engagement in 'criminal conduct.'" The punishment proved severe, as the school expelled Ricks, Penn, and Atkinson, and "sent away" Ampetu. Black students persecuted the informer black student Sydney Williams because students thought that the choice to date interracially was a private matter. In 1902 administrators thwarted James Garvin and Winona Keith's (Sioux) relationship by confiscating, opening, and keeping his letters from Keith, to maintain the racial purity codes. Given that the black students knew of the dating practices of the white faculty members, perhaps they rejected the prohibition as hypocrisy on the part of the faculty. Not surprisingly, the racial hierarchies set in place by the white administrators affected the gender relations between the Indians and blacks and most assuredly affected their relations with whites.

According to the dean of women, Elizabeth Hyde, Indian women deemed black men more desirable then Indian men because of their "civilized" behavior. This tension among the races caused concern among the administrators. Perhaps Indian males felt hostility against black males and found that they must conform to tropes of civilization to compete with the black male at Hampton.[104]

Similarly, a prohibition against romance between Indian men and African American women existed at Hampton, but the two groups pursued each other, renouncing the interdiction. Indian boys and men showed interest in black women and girls at Hampton. The 1888–1889 discipline files state that James Paypay (Cheyenne) was expelled and sent back to Shellbanks for endeavoring to continue "improper" relations with a black girl.[105] In 1879 Helen Ludlow wrote that Indian boys favored African American girls and that one Indian student requested six horses from his father to give to the father of his black fiancée. He promised that while he hunted buffalo his wife would work. If this arrangement failed after one year, he would "throw her away" and acquire another wife.[106] In 1960 David Owl (Cherokee) insisted that while Indian women married black men, no Indian male married a black woman although "sexual interest between Indian men and black women was not unknown."[107] I contend that Owl's observation mirrors the bias against African American women that he learned at Hampton, because the proscription that existed at the school did not completely work to prevent marriage between black women and Indian men. Eleanor Gilman, a Hampton staff member from 1910 until 1975, recalled that Nancy Coleman, who was Cherokee and black, attended Hampton from 1914 to 1922 and married black student Ernest Thornton. "Nancy was a friend with whom Miss Gilman kept in touch over the years; the Thornton's moved to Brookfield, Massachusetts and reared a family of five."[108]

The romantic racial hierarchies that existed at Hampton Institute replicated Armstrong and Pratt's beliefs and reproduced the white Virginians' ideologies pertaining to miscegenation. The foundation of Hampton's race policy lay in local Virginians' initial response and opposition to Native American and black education. They wanted to keep the races separate, because many a white Virginian claimed a noble birthright as a descendant of Pocahontas. Hampton Institute posed a very real menace to them. African blood despoiling the Native Americans at Hampton through romantic relationships threatened to ruin the majestic narrative of the real and imagined progeny of Pocahontas.[109] As long as the Native American legacy remained a thing of the past, given the forced removal of the indigenous Virginians, the heirs and those who claimed kinship to Pocahontas could maintain their noble narrative. With the return of the Native Americans to the area and the threat of the black, a stain threatened to be spilled on their regal status, befouling their racial purity and heritage. A solution was needed. Although officials at Hampton attempted to keep blacks and Native Americans separated, interracial marriages still occurred, and this contributed to the reclassification of Native Americans as black through Virginia's Race Integrity Law in the 1920s.[110]

In *The Red Moon,* Cole and Johnson envisioned the amalgamation of the African American and Native American races as an uplift tool. They discarded the hierarchy established at Hampton and actually placed on stage the very forms of romance completely and utterly forbidden at the school, making a progressive political statement for their time: that African Americans and Native Americans could unite. By eliminating the white presence within the performance, by placing blacks and Native Americans on stage romantically, Cole and Johnson enacted the very thing that white hegemony most feared.

Charles D. Mars underscored the importance of the amorous scenes between blacks and Native Americans during performances of the show, writing: "Rosamond Johnson and Abbie Mitchell in the 'Red Shawl' song was the neatest yet that has been offered in the form of Indian lovemaking. It made many young lovers in the house wish they were Indians."[111] Mars's analysis of the romantic scene remains interesting and unique for the time, given the proscription on African American performance of love scenes during the early part of the twentieth century. Because of the taboo, Mars's statement that the scene "made young lovers in the house wish they were Indians" holds particular meaning and relevance. Mars declared that because of their passionate scenes, viewers experienced so much pleasure that everyone in the audience wanted to be *that* black and Indian couple.

James Weldon Johnson's own love life illuminates how the team patterned theatrical representations after their personal experiences. Johnson's correspondence to his wife illustrates that he fully experienced a serious love in a manner that countered the stereotypical perceptions of black romance as minstrelsy and comedy. He wrote the following letter, dated April 4, 1912 to his wife while serving as the American consul in Nicaragua.

So you miss your old son a little? It is not only hard but odd for us to be separated, because we've been so closely together for two years. Far more constantly together than most couples married for the same length of time, for we have practically spent twenty four hours a day together. I can't describe how much I miss you. I go from the office to the other part of the house, and it seems that I ought to find you. I wake up in the night, and it seems that you must be in your room. One thing, our separation makes me realize more vividly than ever how much I really love my little wife, and yet, I'm glad you are not here; for I can stand what hardships there are better, knowing you don't suffer them, and it won't be for long.[112]

This letter demonstrates the intensity of love and reverence that Johnson held for his wife, and demonstrates that African Americans engaged in romantic lives that communicated their humanity. Cole and Johnson expressed this type of romance and respect for women of color on the stage.

Claudia Tate argues that because whites denied slaves marriage rights, marriage proved incredibly important to the newly freed slaves, representing an emblematic civil right.[113] In late-nineteenth-century African American literary fiction writers appropriated the marriage plot usually associated with white middle-class women for "emancipatory purposes."[114] Similarly, Cole and Johnson utilized the marriage trope throughout *The Red Moon* to delineate the humanity and respectability of African Americans and Native Americans. The song "The Big Red Shawl" reflects this appropriation.

In "The Big Red Shawl," serious romance and courtship between a black man and Native American woman acts as the primary component within the lyrics. J. Rosamond Johnson's Plunk Green describes a Native American man courting a Native American woman. In the song he refers to "a brave of the bold Pawnee," who "[w]hen the wild rose bloomed, / he went eagle plumed to the lodge of the rival band, / 'Neath the big moon red to the maid he said, / as he asked her for her hand." In the song, Abbie Mitchell's Minnehaha replies to the "brave's" marriage proposal by singing: "'Tis de-creed, should a Cherokee give her heart and hand to a Pawnee man, Great wars would the war moon see, but my love is yours."[115] The lyrics mirror Minnehaha's vision of herself as worthy of marriage and in an amorous relationship with a Native American/black man. The song also depicts intergroup marriage, allowed audiences to see the acceptability of romantic pairings between African Americans and Native Americans, promoted the marriage convention as a black citizenship right, and by this claimed citizenship rights for Native Americans.

The song details two very important forms of agency for African Americans and Native Americans. First, it reverses the stereotypes of black men and Native American men as wild, savage, or emasculated, and portrays them as heroic and romantic. By imagining the black and Native American male character as the lover and defender of the black/Native woman in such lines as "cause my love, it is warm and my big right arm will brace the black wolf's call," the team expunges the love scene taboo as the characters symbolize their life experiences. Secondly, the song reflects their insistence that black and Native Americans exhibit romance and love in a humane manner, through the lyric "for my love is true and it's all for you, so let me hold you, love! and fold you, Let me fold you in my big red shawl." Through the male character who promises to protect her and keep her safe and warm, the lyric also portrays black and Native American women as feminized as opposed to common stereotypical renderings. "The Big Red Shawl" foretells the future of the characters because Plunk Green marries Minnehaha as a reward for saving her from the reservation.[116] To the twenty-first-century viewer their marriage appears as patriarchal, but through the lens of late-nineteenth and early-twentieth-century African Americans this remained an emancipatory move, given the marriage prohibitions prescribed for African Americans during slavery. The marriage also exemplified the protection of African American and Native American womanhood, another hard sought-after liberatory right in light of the rampant rape, brutality, and carnage perpetrated on them at the hands of white racists and degenerates. Finally, the union contests hegemony by fully rejecting the interdiction on intermarriages between African Americans and Native Americans.

David Krasner posits that 1908 marked the nadir of race relations in the United States and that the perception of intermarriage among people of color as the "ultimate violation of the social order" permeated white thought.[117] In a similar vein, Katherine Ellinghaus in her study of white female marriage to Native American men at Hampton Institute between 1878 and 1923 states that the prospect of producing additional people of color through the sexual contact of black and Native American proved abhorrent to whites and problematized the racial categories of the nineteenth century.[118]

The fear of nonwhite intermarriage remained at the forefront of social scientific thought and permeated popular racial thought among whites during this time. In Alfred P. Shultz's 1908 book, *Race or Mongrel*, he asserted that intermarriage among people of color led to deterioration, mongrelization, and physical and mental deficiency among their offspring.[119] Shultz contended that race mixing marked the collapse of civilization, threatened United States white racial purity, and that "God made the White man, God made the black man, but the devil made the half-castes."[120] Krasner suggests that Cole and Johnson's possible awareness of the arguments of the social scientists became an impetus for the creation of *The Red Moon*. Krasner surmises that by placing an educated black/Native American woman on the stage and by portraying African American and Native American romance, Cole and Johnson countered the claims of the social scientists.[121]

Native American Authenticity
and *The Red Moon*

The team also capitalized on Native American themes in their music as early as 1906 with "Big Indian Chief," which they wrote for the University of Pennsylvania's sixteenth annual Mask and Wig Club production.[122] Thomas Riis suggests that Indian-themed music gained popularity in the 1900s, and that the team capitalized on the genre by writing *The Red Moon*.[123] The show incorporated Indian motifs within the music. For example the "Bleeding Moon," told the story of an Indian curse, "Life is a Game of Checkers" symbolized red and black admixtures, and "The Big Red Shawl" represented an Indian love song.[124] According to Cole, he and the Johnsons decided to write the musical while performing with their vaudeville act in the "Far West." Yet it appears they actually began writing the musical while performing in *Shoo Fly Regiment*. Bob Cole recalled that they wanted to integrate "traditional or folk elements from both African-American and Indian culture into a musical."[125]

J. Rosamond Johnson's 1938 *Red Moon* production notes specified that "[t]he Indian characters in the sequence are carefully drawn from [t]he authology of the Indians' social life, and marked care has been taken to avoid the usual 'motion picture Indian.' Legends and ceremonial dances are authentic. And in these will be found the mental attitude of the Indian and *not* what some author would want him to be in order to satisfy the formula of his story" (emphasis in original).[126] Johnson felt that the portrayal of Native Americans within the production provided an authentic representation and elevated their position in U. S. culture. In her play about Cole's life, Carriebel Plummer wrote a scene in which Mrs. Kingston (Plummer) reminisces about her brother Buddy's show *The Red Moon* "as one authentic American story of Indian folklore" "registered in Washington, D.C." This scene suggests that Cole and Johnson endeavored to write a true interpretation of Native American life and culture.[127] We can surmise that Cole, whose heritage included Black Seminole ancestry, drew on his own personal knowledge of Indian culture learned from his father for the production. The team performed on an Apache reservation, where they discussed music with their hosts and incorporated what they learned into the musical. I believe that their musical appeared as the first one of its kind to include Native American musical themes on Broadway and the first to portray African American and Native American characters on the Broadway stage. In 1913 the Sioux composer Zitkala-Sa's (Gertrude Simmons Bonnin), a successor of Cole and Johnson, wrote the *Sun Dance* opera with William F. Hanson. The opera integrated original

Native American music and culture in a story of a love triangle between a Winona and Ohiya, a Sioux woman and man, and "the evil Shoshone Sweet Singer."[128] Like *The Red Moon,* the *Sun Dance* endeavored to dignify Native American culture by presenting authentic indigenous traditions.

In *The Red Moon,* Cole and Johnson drew upon their understanding of the shared religious beliefs and moon lore that united blacks and Native Americans, particularly the Apaches.[129] Clara Sue Kidwell and Daryl Cumber Dance contend that ethnoastronomy, cosmology, and moon lore remained integral to the religious beliefs of Native Americans and southern African Americans and played a vital role in their folklore, being used to explain the relationships between the elements and life. Kidwell states that Native Americans time ceremonies by the moon, sun, and stars, and that these elements remain central to their social organization, intellectual thought, sexual and social relations, initiation rights, and calendar systems. Southern African Americans, Mexicans, and indigenous people of the Rio Grande followed similar religious beliefs by abiding by the moon's patterns to farm, cut hair and nails, and hold religious ceremonies. They all accompanied these practices with explanatory tales.[130] Blacks from Georgia and Louisiana believed that the red moon, comets, and shooting stars were signs of trouble, famine, and war, while the Northeastern Seneca (Iroquois) believed in the danger of the meteor fire dragons that must face containment in the water because their embers would ignite the world. In the novel *Cane,* Jean Toomer captured the foreboding the red moon brings to African Americans in Georgia when the "blood-burning-moon" appears, foretelling death. Animals react woefully, the blacks sing "Red Nigger Moon, Sinner, Blood-burning-moon, Sinner," as the red moon casts its ruby dark shadow over the clouds and the town. The Catawba tell of a malevolent woman who steals a mother's infant. When the mother rescues him, the angels are so touched that they lower ropes and mother and son ascend to Heaven. Viewing this, the malevolent woman begs the angels to allow her into Heaven. They lower ropes, but as she climbs they cut them and she plunges headlong, transforming into a comet.[131] Because the woman symbolizes evil, we can surmise that the comet also embodies these qualities. These narratives appear as shared portents between blacks and Native Americans, and they appear as folk beliefs that Cole and Johnson used to authenticate *The Red Moon* and to show the similarities between blacks and Native Americans.

Perhaps Bob Cole's African American mother and Black Seminole father exposed him to Seminole folklore and shared stories about the elements or the Seminole story about the creation of the Spirit Way. According to Seminole lore Hisagita-imisi, "the Breathmaker blew his breath toward the sky and created the Milky Way" as a pathway that leads the souls of good Indians to the City of the West, by way of the Big Dipper, a boat. The Seneca (Iroquois) and the Jicarella Apache also tell of the creation of the Big Dipper. The Seneca (Iroquois) tell the story of two boys' attempt to catch a giant bear, who casts a net over them to avoid capture. The bear throws the net into the sky where the boys are transformed into the handle of the Big Dipper. The Southwest and Jicarella Apache also tell a Big Dipper tale.[132] The Jicarilla Apache's narrative of Holy Boy's failed efforts to create the sun and the moon proceeds with Whirlwind telling him that White and Black Hactcin possess the sun and moon. Holy Boy goes to them and they teach him the ceremony of creating these celestial bodies. Holy Boy completes these rites and the sun and moon rise, illuminating the underworld.[133] The Iroquois and the Apache might have shared these stories with Cole and Johnson when they visited their reservations. Cole and Johnson probably drew upon such folklore to give their musical a sense of cultural authenticity. Perhaps Cole adopted the red moon omen for the musical from stories he heard in childhood and incorporated the augury with tales concerning the elements he heard on the Apache and the Iroquois reservations. Ultimately, the team made use of these shared beliefs as a way of showing the kindred associations that existed between Native Americans and African Americans through their communal and collective memory.[134]

Although many groups of people, including African Americans and Europeans, believed in the prognostications of the red moon, I have found little evidence that points to this belief actually existing in Native American folklore. While Cole and Johnson, as well as Reid Badger, Allen Woll, Henry T. Sampson, and numerous other scholars contend that the team included the presaging of the red moon as a collective belief of African Americans and Apaches, the red moon omen may have been a pseudo-Indian belief. Cole and Johnson probably intertwined the mutual folk beliefs of the groups such as the comet and shooting star as foreboding signs and the African American belief of the red moon as an omen to create the drama within the musical.

Native People's Response to *The Red Moon*

While performing *The Red Moon* in Montreal in March of 1909, Theodore Pankey and Arthur Talbott, who played Native Americans in the show, visited the reservation of the Iroquois tribe on the Caugnawago Reservation on the St. Lawrence River in Montreal as guests of Chief Mitchal Dial Bount. Several Iroquois attended the performance of *The Red Moon* in March of

1909.[135] The Iroquois nation appreciated these efforts to dignify stage representations of Indians and inducted J. Rosamond Johnson into the tribe as a
"sub-chief" of the Iroquois Indian Reserve, Caughnawaga Province, Quebec,
Canada (1921).[136] Johnson's induction into the tribe and the warm reception that the company received on the reservation indicate that the Iroquois
approved of their portrayal of Native Americans; however, one must wonder
how the Iroquois responded to the stereotypical Native American characters
and the narrative that included escaping reservation life for "civilization."
Given the dire living conditions on reservations, and the stripping away of
the traditions and way of life of Indians by the governments of Canada and
the United States, I would surmise that the Iroquois might have appreciated
the Red Feather storyline of revolting against reservation life and Swamptown Institute. I would also like to suggest that given the possibility, the
Iroquois might also have wanted to eschew reservation life. Like Minnehaha,
they surely would have opted to escape the rez for "civilization," Iroquois
civilization. We must remember that Europeans created the reservation
system to control and confine indigenous peoples. As the Native American
rapper Litefoot aptly notes, "Sam and his Crew really take good care of my
FAM, They only killed half of my tribe and stole our land."[137] The reservation system made it possible for Europeans to purloin Native Americans'
land as an invading force and rob them of their freedom. The reservation system worked to indoctrinate Native Americans into European culture through
assimilation, which meant the abandoning of Indian religious practices for
Christianity and the forsaking of traditional ways of life for "civilization."
The Native American artist L. Frank (Tongva) in her drawings likens the
Spanish Mission system to German World War II concentration camps, with
nooses, skulls, crossbones, guillotines, and a never-ending passageway into
the mission that Native Americans could never escape. Litefoot also raps
about the interconnections between the dismal conditions of reservation life
and mortality. He argues that for many Native Americans the reservation
represents death. "Sometimes you know I hear about my friends, my family,
living on the rez, city to city, state to state, rez to rez, and they dying. If they
ain't dying in a physical way, they dying in a spiritual way, or something
much more important is dying."[138] Litefoot raps that the reservation for
many native peoples symbolizes death, a difficult existence, and governmental neglect: "Sometimes I wonder why millions go for aid overseas, while
Indian hospitals can't put band aids on scratched knees," "Sometimes I wish
that Osama Bin Laden hid out on my rez, So that the media would come visit,
and give Indian issues some press."[139] With these types of insurmountable
challenges to reservation life in the twenty-first century, it remains no sur-

prise that the Iroquois welcomed Cole and Johnson's story concerning Minnehaha and Red Feather's escape from the reservation in 1909, for if the rez remains dire in the twenty first century, conditions most assuredly were much worse in 1909. The messages within *The Red Moon* included the narrative that Native American and African American ways of life remained superior to Americanization. Cole and Johnson's critique of the white man's civilization as unworthy of emulation most certainly resonated for the Iroquois, with the African American and Native American characters' full abnegation of "white man's civilization" within the musical. The messages embedded within the play without a doubt carried great meaning for the Iroquois as the messages represented a form of resistance against reservation life and against assimilationist policies.

Clues as to why Cole and Johnson wrote *The Red Moon* when and as they did include their admiration for Booker T. Washington and his project of exalting African Americans and Native Americans, as well as Thomas Riis's identification of the popularity of Native American themed music and musicals. Two additional reasons that have been covered in this text are that the play symbolized a form of protest against scientific racism and social scientists who excoriated intermarriage between people of color, and that the inspiration for the musical stemmed from the team's visit to the West and an Apache Reservation.[140] I argue that all these reasons acted as the framework for the creation of *The Red Moon*, but that Washington's and W. E. B. Du Bois's strategy of ennobling African Americans remained at the foundation for the creation of the project.

Stereotypes, Reality, and *The Red Moon*

For all its good intentions, *The Red Moon* still contained stereotypes. After his successful run in *Shoo Fly Regiment*, Andrew Tribble played Lily White, the Washer Woman in *The Red Moon*. Tribble's female characterizations served primarily as a comedic representation and as a political and satirical commentary on gender.[141] The *Indianapolis Freeman* on October 24, 1908, reported that Tribble was "well received on every entrance, but did not score heavy as usual, yet he worked hard. It must have been the song, for he certainly had the spot."[142] As shown in the previous chapter, as a performer of black musical theater and minstrelsy, Tribble's female impersonations, which he created specifically for black audiences, were infused with insider jokes and proved groundbreaking.[143]

One review of *The Red Moon* reveals that the "chorus was well trained and young blood with plenty of speed. There never was [such] a collection of colored girls."[144] Like Margo Webb's description of pickaninny dancing as fast paced, the chorus of *The Red Moon* danced with "speed," which indicates that the team incorporated this minstrel form into *The Red Moon.*

Cole and Johnson, in their effort to aggrandize African American men, used what George Lipsitz calls turning negative ascription into positive affirmation by inverting the representative image of the Sambo.[145] While the original representation gave audiences a happy, lazy, indolent black man, Cole and Johnson inverted the Sambo in *The Red Moon* to that of the matinee idol, a sex symbol, a member of society, and a well-dressed African American man with realistic stage makeup as opposed to blackface. The lyrics, the reviews, "*The Red Moon* Rays," and Lester A. Walton's columns attest to this characterization. After appearing in *Shoo Fly Regiment* (1906–1908), Edgar Connors originated the role of Sambo Simmons and the Grizzly Bear in *The Red Moon.* Connors sang "Sambo," written by James Reese Europe (music) and Bob Cole (lyrics) in 1908. Sung in the last act with a Virginia homestead as the setting, Leona Marshall and Daisy Brown, who played his sisters Sally and Susan Simmons, accompanied Connors's Sambo.[146]

Cole's lyrics transposed the image of Sambo to that of a freeman, a matinee idol. He discarded dialect, as theatergoers viewed a Sambo who sang in proper articulate English, implying an educated gentleman. Cole also jettisoned the slave image of the Sambo as his Sambo took on the mannerisms of a society "swell" whose etiquette remained impeccable and whose "name is in the 'Blue-books," the antithesis of the disheveled, unkempt, uncouth, but happy slave. Cole provided the audience with a cosmopolitan yet likeable Sambo, a "fashion plate," an urbane man whom children adore. Contrary to the asexual Sambo, Cole sexualized Sambo in the lyrics as the essential "pet of all the ladies," and the idol of the boys."[147]

> Sambo is a card with all the babies, They like him better than they do their toys. For Sambo is a cunning little creature; His manners and behavior they are fine—Sambo! Sambo, a fashion plate, a Flambo; Sambo is a lucky little Shine.[148]

The team's very use of the name Sambo evokes the stereotype, but the song and the characterization by Edgar Connors, his dress, his decorum on and offstage, and the publicity and reviews of *The Red Moon* all worked as a communal effort to overturn the Sambo image. This effort in effect revolutionized the image of the African American man on the stage, in public arenas, and in private life. Both *"The Red Moon* Rays" and Walton's theatrical jottings chronicled the permutation of Sambo. Connor's Sambo Simmons actually metamorphosed into a stunning, charismatic, and desirable man, a suave gentleman whom women could not resist. Charles A. Hunter wrote "[m]en may come and men may go, but the matinee girls go on over 'Sambo' [Edgar Connor] forever."[149] Lester A. Walton wrote "DeWolf Hopper is appearing in a play called 'A Matinee Idol,' but Master Edgar Connors is 'the real matinee idol,' playing 'Sambo' in Cole and Johnson's *The Red Moon* Company."[150] Through these newspaper articles Cole and Johnson transformed the Sambo and African American men into handsome and appealing bon vivants.

Aggrandizing African Americans also included the pursuit of scholarly endeavors such as poetry writing and participating in contests. Reflecting the efforts at transmuting the image of Sambo and of African American men, Walton's "Theatrical Jottings" included commentary on Connors' poetic talents.

Edgar Connor of The Red Moon Company is developing into a rhymer. The Age is in receipt of the following lines from Montreal, Canada: "While this beautiful snow does greatly please, one day in New York would set my heart at ease."[151]

The project to reform the image of black men with the inversion of the Sambo proved a noble undertaking. Unfortunately, the entrenchment of negative stereotypes of blacks remained deeply ingrained within the American psyche. While Cole and Johnson venerated blacks and Native Americans on stage by presenting affirmative images which embodied tropes of uplift, including self determination, marriage, and education, they also offered audiences stereotypes of the hungry Negro, a chorus of Pickaninnies, and at least in one instance, the use of the word "coon." Although these clichés reflected African American theatrical devices of the early 1900s, one cannot deny that these images were damaging to blacks during Cole and Johnson's time and still reverberate reprehensibly today in representations of blacks on stage and film and within rap music.

Bob Cole performed the comedic roles within the Cole and Johnson productions, while J. Rosamond Johnson portrayed the romantic and serious dramatic leads. Cole's portrayal of Silas Brown embodied the stereotype of the hungry Negro. In 1908 Lester A. Walton argued that while Cole's part as Silas Brown in *The Red Moon* offered audiences a better character than the one he played in *Shoo Fly Regiment,* he objected to Cole's characterization of the hungry Negro for laughs. Walton pointed out that while the hungry

Negro remained a component of most black shows, it was a representation that African Americans producers should discard and leave behind. In addition, Cole also used the word "coon" in the production. Walton objected strongly and offers the reader a sample of the dialogue.

> In a dialogue with Rosamond Johnson, Bob Cole puts in a line for the sake of a laugh that could be easily omitted. The dialogue:
> ROSAMOND JOHNSON: "It's a great chance to get some bear meat."
> BOB COLE: "You mean it's a great chance to get some coon meat."[152]

Walton maintained that "the laugh comes from the white portion of the audience not the colored."[153] While Walton avidly supported Cole and Johnson in his articles, he vehemently objected to what he perceived as corrosive and harmful stereotypes. It appears that Cole and Johnson maintained the hungry Negro stereotypes throughout the tour of *The Red Moon*. Charles Hunter notes in the *"The Red Moon* Rays" that around January 28, 1909, a Billy Possum number was introduced in the show. Hunter states that: "[d]espite his mouth-watering description of 'Bre'r Billy Possum' in de pan wid sweet potatoes all around, Bob Cole will ever be remembered as the premier chicken dinner delineator."[154]

Cole and Johnson placed this dialogue and the song within the production to cater to white audiences. Walton warned them that "[a]s the stage is an educator, we should seek to omit all things that we would not like to happen to us in everyday life. The author of the lines would become highly insulted if called a "coon" in public and yet for the sake of a laugh applies the word to himself with apparently good grace."[155]

Several possibilities arise concerning the use of the hungry Negro stereotype and the use of the word "coon." In a September 10, 1908, review of *The Red Moon*, Walton points out that although *Shoo Fly Regiment* was a superior show, with representations that included African American men as soldiers and heroes, the production did not cater to white audience tastes due to the presence of black men as soldiers and the lack of overt stereotypes.[156] He suggested that *The Red Moon* accommodated whites with the presence of the hungry Negro stereotype. Yet while Cole and Johnson used negative stereotypes to indulge white audiences' tastes and consequently profit financially, they also placed on stage new forms of black representations.

Stereotypik
Whatcha know about me
Stereotipik

Absent from history
Stereotipik
Don't pretend to know
Yo, America your letting your ignorance show
(Litefoot[157])

The Red Moon replicated and contested traditional stereotypes about Native Americans. Just as stereotypes of blacks came from the history of slavery, stereotypes of Indians emerged out of the experience of conquest. Three distinct themes emerged in the drawing of Native American stereotypes in U.S. culture: Indians as a monolithic group, Indians as deficient in the eyes of whites, and Indians as morally and spiritually corrupt. Europeans defined Native Americans as monolithic even though they never viewed themselves as a single group. Two thousand cultures and societies existed at the time of conquest with distinct languages, customs, and belief systems. Stereotypes that lump together all Indians include the "good" or Noble Indian, the "bad" or Savage Indian, and the "vanishing Indian."[158]

The Noble Indian is characterized as gentle, submissive, courageous, and at one with nature. The concept of primitivism played a key role in the drawing of Native Americans as noble. It influenced Renaissance explorers who cast them as paradise dwellers, free of the hindrances of modern society, free of a distinct history, and free of complex European society. Anglo and Spanish perceptions of Native Americans as noble included descriptions of them as sexually innocent, physically beautiful, peace-loving, in harmony with nature, and existing with no property, no injustice, and no monarchy.[159]

The perception of Native Americans as gentle and willing to trade with Europeans originated with their first contact with Columbus in San Salvador in 1492, in which he described them as amenable, loving, and giving. In 1524, Verrazano portrayed the native people of New York as "joyful" and friendly. The idea of the new world as diametrically opposed to Europe (which at the time remained impoverished and war torn) played an integral part in the European mentality and worked to encourage European travel to the Americas. Trade encouraged overseas development and made it necessary for Europeans, most specifically English entrepreneurs, to paint Indians as friendly to European traders.[160]

The Noble Savage image coexisted with the image of the uncivilized Indian. European dependence on the Indian kept the uncivilized image tempered, but it persisted nonetheless. For example, not only did Vespucci paint them as friendly and gentle, but he also described Indian women as sexually aggressive, so aggressive in fact that they caused men to lose their sexual organs. The Noble Savage lacked Spanish standards of dress, government, civilization, religion, farming, morals, marriage, and trade.[161]

The stereotype of the Indian as savage emerged to justify the forced removals of Indians in the East and the West from their land. Whites depicted Indians as "semi-human" at the same time they characterized them as noble. As the relationship between them changed due to white land lust, descriptions and perceptions of the Indians permutated from the "noble red man" to the "bloodthirsty savage," a threat to civilization. This change reflected the growing brutal relationship that culminated in the attempt by whites to exterminate the Native American.[162]

The image of the Native American as beast-like, savage, and hostile originated with literature written by the French and Spanish and adopted by the English around 1578.[163] This stereotype of the Savage included descriptions of Native Americans as monolithic and primitive due, in part, to their preference for nudity and their non–Christian status. For example, Pocahontas's father, Powhatan, was described as a savage, both majestic and "cruel yet not pitiless."[164] The description of Caribbean Indians as cannibals, long-haired, and ferocious also made its way into the white imagination.[165] As is usual with white subjugation and stereotyping of people of color, there lay an ulterior motive. The stereotypes emerged to justify the appropriation of Indian lands and to justify Native American genocide by the Spanish and the English. The English found it easy to assert that, due to their uncivilized and non-Christian status, Indians remained unfit for land ownership. By defining the Indian as a savage and a "tawny beast," the English as well as the Dutch, French, Portuguese, and Spanish found it easy to justify robbing Indian lands on moral grounds.[166] Another component of the savage or the bad Indian included the white invention of the Degraded Indian or the Alcoholic Reservation Indian, an inebriated outsider to Indian and white society. Sherman Alexie's novel *Reservation Blues* (1995) introduces the alcoholic Indian Victor to the reader; the real-life descendant of Pocahontas, John Bolling, embodied this cliché.[167]

The forced removal of Indians from the East, expansion in the West, and the reservation system promoted the image of the Indian as a vanishing race. This stereotype paints Indians as facing ultimate extinction due to the expansion of "civilization." The forced removal of the assimilated Cherokee Indians in the 1830s from the point where Georgia, Tennessee, and North Carolina meet to Indian Territory offers an excellent example of how the stereotype of the Vanishing Race emerged in the white imagination.

The Cherokees accommodated whites and assimilated into white culture by adopting white standards such as living in towns, attending schools and churches, and fighting on the American side during the War of 1812. They also held treaties with the United States dating back to 1791 in which the Anglos acknowledged the independence of the Cherokee nation and guaranteed that the Cherokees could keep their lands. Summarily, the Anglos broke the treaties and forcibly removed them from their lands. The Cherokees faced incarceration in 1838 and eventually the government coerced twelve thousand people to march to the Territories; twenty-five hundred people died on the trip known as the Trail of Tears. One Cherokee Chief aptly noted "The truth is if we had no lands, we should have [had] no enemies."[168] Forced removals such as this contributed to the stereotype of the Vanishing Indian, because they no longer inhabited the southern region, and Anglos willingly forgot their existence in the East.

The inconsistent method of Anglo conquest in the West, which ultimately included the attempted genocide of Native Americans, contributed to the Vanishing Indian stereotype in the eighteenth and nineteenth centuries. Because Native Americans inhabited the lands the Anglos wanted, they viewed them as a hindrance to civilization and western expansion. Anglos felt that Indians must disappear either through genocide or assimilation. These perceptions carried over into the nineteenth century with the use of similar methods to make the Native American population vanish. The Vanishing Indian stereotype made its way into fiction with books such as *The Last of the Mohicans* (1826) and in artwork through portraits of Indians on the plains and the prairie by George Caitlin.[169] The concept of the Vanishing Indian through assimilation shaped the assimilationist goals at Hampton Institute. Administrators envisioned Native Americans' assimilation through marriage into the white race, thus marking the end of the Indian race.[170] The half-caste or mixed-race Indian also represented to whites a sign of the Vanishing Race.

Cole and Johnson challenged stereotypes concerning Native Americans in *The Red Moon* through the multilayered and complex character of Red Feather. Red Feather symbolized both Native American and African American resistance to hegemony, the boarding school experience, and reservation life. He embodied actual male students who attended Native American boarding schools and the biracial program at Hampton.

Theodore Pankey, an African American actor, portrayed Red Feather and is described in the *Indianapolis Freeman* as "a bold, bad Indian student at the school who is in love with Minnehaha."[171] Red Feather, an educated brave who Lester Walton notes reads a letter in the play, departed from demeaning portrayals of Native Americans. He represented neither the Bad Indian Savage, the Degraded Indian, the Vanishing Indian, nor even the Noble Indian, but rather a new form of Indian, an educated Indian with a strong sense of agency, and one capable of romantic love.[172]

In the first act, Red Feather falls in love with Minnehaha and assists Chief Lowdog in returning her to her tribe in "The Land of the Setting Sun." This action by a father who misses his daughter and by a young man who loves her sets in motion a struggle for Minnehaha's affections between Red Feather and Plunk Green.[173] Implicit in the action taken by Red Feather is not only love, but also a yearning to leave Swamptown Industrial Institute and return to his family on the reservation. By helping Chief Lowdog, Red Feather exhibits self-determination and agency.

Red Feather's longing to escape school reflected the feelings of some of Hampton's Native American students. Howling Wolf (Cheyenne), a Hampton student, expressed his desire to return West in a June 1879 letter to Captain Pratt from Darlington, Pennsylvania. His yearning to return home remains implicit throughout the letter but his awareness that he must negotiate with and appease Pratt also plays a vital role in the correspondence. Howling Wolf states, "when I was away from hear I had a nuf to eat and cloths to war when I hunted the Bufolo I was not [hungry]." He remains keenly aware that he must bargain with Pratt for the right to return home and assures Pratt, "when I was with you I did not want for any thing but I hear Pam Poos I would like to go out on the plains again whare I could come at will and not come back a gain."[174] At the axis of Howling Wolf's attempt to come to an agreement with Pratt is "but," and with that word he presents the reason why Pratt should allow him to return home, so that he could travel freely to the plains. Throughout the letter he elucidates his awareness that Pratt wields power over him, but Howling Wolf continues to plead his case. He tries to persuade Pratt: "But before I take inch a step I [t]hough[t] best to ask you what you thought about it and hope you will write soon and tell me." Howling Wolf ends the letter by discussing his plans if allowed to return to the plains, writing, "I think thare is a grate meny wild horse in Mexico and if I should got thare I could capture a hurd and bring them back hear then I would not be away. I should not harme any man should be friends to all bare while animals."[175] Like his real-life counterpart, Red Feather also longs to leave Swamptown and return home. Red Feather yearns for the freedom on the reservation to come and go as he pleases, as Howling Wolf so profoundly stated to "come at will and not come back a gain." Similarities exist between Howling Wolf's and Red Feather's longing for home; differences also exist as in Red Feather's recalcitrance and his overt agency in accomplishing his goal, whereas Howling Wolf covertly relays his message and tries to negotiate with his captor, Pratt, and Hampton. The scene in which Red Feather assists Chief

Lowdog in returning Minnehaha to the reservation illuminates Red Feather's conscious and successful escape from the school and reservation life as he travels freely, not confined to the reservation or the school, for, as Native American rapper Litefoot avows, reservation life is no picnic.

> Living in this world
> No hope
> Seeing all the pain in
>
> Got to show your child there's a better place
> Livin' on the rez.
> (Litefoot[176])

The scene with Red Feather reminds audiences that some Native American students rebelled against the Hampton assimilation program. The education of Native American students at Hampton Institute and the government boarding schools gave students a brutal and sometimes deadly indoctrination into "white civilization."

According to Armstrong, the Hampton curriculum included a four-year program with students working during the day to pay for their room and board and taking classes at night. In 1888 and 1894, the male students' classes included farming, blacksmithing, carpentry, printing, wheelwrighting, shoemaking, harness making, tinsmithing, printing, ironwork, farming, and training as "country school teachers." The academic classes included math, English language study, reading, science, geography, history, economics, civil government, student teaching, agriculture, mental science, drawing, woodwork, singing, and gymnastics.[177]

Former Fort Marion prisoners sent letters to Captain Pratt articulating the difficulty of their Hampton school training. Toun ke uh detailed the rigor of his education in a letter dated August 23, 1878, noting that he attended school two days a week "for it days very hard working. I like working and me of every study hard and very much I hope understand me."[178] Doanmoe, a famous ledger artist, writes of the absolute difficulty of the labor expected of him as a student in the summer "outing program." In a July 4, 1879, letter from Lee, Massachusetts, he wrote "I am very sorry to say this, I am not very strong to do hard work, but I would not tell Mr. Hyde about it—how I am getting stronger."[179] Because of the forced labor practices, many of the children became horribly sick and died. The vast number of gravestones at both Hampton Institute and Pennsylvania's Carlisle School bear witness to the suffering of the children and offers a poignant commentary on the cruelty of the school experience. The children's names remain prominently displayed on the markers, one ironically named "Abe Lincoln Son of Antelope Cheyenne January 17, 1880" (Carlisle) and another, "Lasute Whiteback, Gros Ventre, North Dakota Died Jan. 24, 1882 aged 15 yrs" (Hampton).[180] Row upon row of Indian children's gravestones punctuates the landscape at Hampton and Carlisle, resolutely demanding that we not forget them.

Hampton student Doanmoe expressed a strong desire to return home from his "Outing Program" in July 1879. "I has got a letter from home and it very nice letter—it from my brother M-beadle te—and Kiowa against too and they want me to come there. Capt. Pratt I wish to go with you when you goes that way and talk with—them what we can be done for them I wish I do that this summer when I think that way then my feel hurry about doing something for the Indians—Capt. Pratt you know I am trying to doing." [181] Given the harsh reality of his "education," Doanmoe tried to negotiate his escape. Red Feather epitomizes these rebellious students, as opposed to those who languished or perished. He acts as the agent of his own life, openly flouting boarding school by traveling home and returning to the Indian way of life. Red Feather's actions replicated some of the real-life Native American students who took it upon themselves to run away from the oppressive boarding school environment. Charles Eastman, a Lakota, fled from Flandreau, and in 1901, 114 boys ran from Carlisle.[182] Red Feather symbolizes both Native American and African American students who fully resisted and challenged abuse and white domination at boarding schools.

One of the most amazing acts of resistance by the Native American students occurred at Haskell in 1919. They participated in a coordinated full-scale revolt. The students shut down the lights in the auditorium, broke lighting fixtures, helped themselves to the food supply, and one boy proposed lynching the principal, shouting, "Let's string him up."[183] This act of insubordination illustrates how Native American students gained control of their lives. Red Feather symbolizes the spirit of these rebellious students because he made the decision to take command of his life by leaving Swamptown *and* the reservation.

Red Feather to some extent typified a bit of a villain in *The Red Moon* plot, due to his part in kidnapping Minnehaha, but Cole and Johnson's drawing of the character as an educated and a romantic lead who exhibits agency in his quest to return home created a new delineation of Native American men. What the team accomplished with the character of Red Feather was a reinscribing of historical events, a reimagining of the lives of Native Americans from despair and longing to uplift, agency, and freewill. Red Feather represented a major accomplishment, as he personified the Hampton administrators' worst fear, that the Indian student would return to the "blanket."

By placing Red Feather in an industrial institution, Cole and Johnson contested the tensions that existed at Hampton between the two races and presented a school environment in which blacks and Native Americans coexisted peacefully. By drawing Red Feather as a romantic love interest to Minnehaha, they elevated the status of Native American males on campus. Considering that the heroine within *The Red Moon* was black/Native American, the team fully rejected the theatrical love scene proscription and the romance hierarchy at Hampton Institute, by placing on stage passion and love between a Native American man and a black/Native American woman.

In the second act of *The Red Moon*, "In the Land of the Setting Sun," Cole and Johnson romanticized and humanized Red Feather further by allowing him to sing the love song "On the Road to Monterey," with words and music by Bob Cole. This song and the production number mirrored the real-life yet forbidden romances between African American women and Native American men at Hampton. The *Southern Workman* of 1879 reported instances of Native American boys' attraction to black girls and recounted that "When asked if he would take an educated squaw or one of the Indian women at home to wife, [one boy] replied, 'No, I marry a colored girl; she will teach me good English.'" White teacher Caroline Andrus noted in her 1909 report on former student Alex Payer, who returned to Winnebago, Nebraska, that his "wife has Negro blood." [184] "On The Road to Monterey" in essence replicated the types of amorous relationships that emerged between Native American males like Alex Payer and African American women. The song conveys these love affairs as we imagine Red Feather singing the song to Minnehaha as they travel west. A reviewer for the *Indianapolis Freeman* noted, "In this scene is put on one of the most pretentious and best-dressed song numbers I have ever seen staged by colored performers. The song was 'On the Road to Monterey,' sung by Theodore Pankey, backed by a chorus of exquisite sweetness both in voice and costume." [185] The *New York Age* stated that "Theo. Pankey is as pleasing in his new song 'On the Road to Monterey,' as he was in 'On the Gay Luneta.'" [186] Charles D. Mars of the *Indianapolis Freeman* stated, "[t]he lineup of the chorus girls in this number equaled anything that was ever produced on Broadway." [187] These reviews indicate that this scene presented audiences with a big production number. The lyrics tell us that Red Feather sang in standard English as opposed to dialect English—"[W]hen that pretty senorita gave me a tiny kiss, how it filled my soul with such aesthetic bliss." "On the Road to Monterey" explored the romance and tenderness between Red Feather and Minnehaha. [188]

Ultimately, Red Feather personified the lived experiences of many Native American students attending boarding schools. As the "bold, bad Indian student," he represented a hero for Native American students through his resistance to domination both on the reservation and at the school. Red Feather possessed resolve as a lover who romances an African American woman in the face of proscription by contumaciously ignoring the romance hierarchy at Hampton Institute. Finally, he embodied the worst fears of white teachers, administrators, and the surrounding communities by refusing to assimilate, by holding on steadfastly to his culture and heritage, and by defiantly and proudly returning to the blanket.

Arthur Talbot's character Chief Lowdog personified some of the common delineations of Native Americans but at the same time offered audiences new ways of understanding Indians as loving fathers and husbands. Born in 1875 in Dresden, Ontario, Talbot moved with his family to Chatham. At fourteen he moved to Detroit, Michigan, making his stage debut at the age of sixteen as an old man in a dramatic play. Talbot began to appear in churches reciting Shakespeare, eventually performing in Buffalo, New York, in scenes from *Othello,* his favorite play.[189] He studied acting with Professor Schultz and, at twenty-one, moved to New York and studied under Professor Lawrence. Bob Cole discovered Talbot in New York when Talbot recited from *Samson* and *Julius Caesar* at St. Mark's Church. After seeing his performance, Elizabeth Williams, "an actress of ability" who later played Lucretia Martin in *The Red Moon,* asked Talbot to join her successful road company. In 1906 he joined *Shoo Fly Regiment* at Cole's invitation.

At the age of thirty-three, Arthur Talbot joined *The Red Moon,* originating the role of Chief Lowdog. According to Charles Cameron White, after the closing of *Shoo Fly Regiment,* Talbot "was given one of the best dramatic parts ever written for a Negro in the character of 'John [Lowdog],' the old Indian chief and his acting is one of the hits of the play. Mr. Talbott says he owes his success to Bob Cole, to whom he gives credit for 'bringing him out,' and whom he characterizes as a great teacher, a great actor and a great playwright."[190]

A complicated representative image and characterization emerged within the character of Chief Lowdog. One reviewer described the character as adhering to the stereotype of the degraded Indian "charged up with firewater," thus the insulting name Lowdog.[191] Bob Cole's notes also point to this form of representation with the note for Chief Lowdog to say in one scene "Same place no champagne."[192] Although the team adhered to stereotypes, several innovations emerged in Chief Lowdog. The description of Chief Lowdog as an "old Chief," and as "charged up with firewater," offers a radically different perception of the character than that which appears in a publicity photograph. Talbot's photograph in the *New York Age* moves away from conveying the stereotype of the degraded Indian. The portrait offers the viewer a very dignified and handsome Indian.[193] As Chief Lowdog, Talbot does not appear to represent the alcoholic Indian, but rather a very attractive Indian in a strong stance. Talbot wears a feathered headdress, and is dressed in what appears as genuine Native American clothing. I would also like to propose that his portrayal of dramatic Shakespearean roles suggests that Talbot infused Chief Lowdog with an Othello- or a Caesar-like dignity. Talbot's career as a Shakespearean actor gives us some understanding of how Cole and Johnson envisioned Native Americans within *The Red Moon*.

Chief Lowdog also moves away from stereotypical representation because of his romantic pairing with the African American character of Lucretia Martin. This coupling discards the love scene taboo, the prohibition against interracial romance, and the notion that the progeny of mixed couples are doomed.

Several reviews identify Talbot's portrayal of Chief Lowdog as an authentic rendering of Native Americans. Charles D. Mars of the *Indianapolis Freeman* states, "Arthur Talbot as 'John Lowdog' gave the public its first taste of Indian character work with merit by a Negro. His masterly work was as much responsible for the success of *The Red Moon* as any part of the show."[194] Clarence Cameron White described Talbot as one of the "most promising young character actors on the stage."[195] Similarly, Charles A. Hunter asserted that "Arthur Talbot, (John Lowdog) has the best and strongest legitimate part ever written for a colored actor," while Walton stated, "[o]ne would think that he was really an Indian, so true does he play his character."[196] The attempt to portray Native Americans authentically appears an important component to both Cole and Johnson and to the members of the cast. As guests of the Iroquois Tribe on the Caugnawago Reservation in Montreal, both Arthur Talbot and Theodore Pankey bought "several unique and costly Indian relics, namely moccasins, beaded leggings, pipes, arrow heads." They also conceivably learned about the Iroquois, and the presumption that they incorporated their knowledge of the Iroquois into their characterizations remains a very real possibility.[197] According to Charles A. Hunter, Talbot's makeup was so authentic that a letter to the *New York Age* inquired as to his tribal heritage. Cole turned the answer into a joke and answered that after a careful investigation of Lowdog's heritage he discovered that "'Lowdog' was a discreet descendant from the anti-Nomian, but non-anthropohagi (plural)," a fearless tribe in the New York area whose numbers are great.[198]

While *The Red Moon* included some Native American characterizations which deviated from stereotypes, the portrayal of the Indian chiefs' war council in the second act conformed to clichéd portrayals. Cole's theatrical notes allow us a window in which we can view the depiction of the Native American male characters:

DELYON: Speak. How. To law do me here to come about Red Moon. How.

PHELPS: John low dog he me hold a council about Red Moon How?

LUCAS: Must we wait longer for him?

DELYON: No! Red moon say call braves for war dance.

BROWN: Some are came still longer.[199]

We cannot deny that this piece of dialogue replicates the most reprehensible representations of Native Americans as inarticulate speakers of pidgin English, conforming to the historical period in which degrading renderings of Native Americans and African Americans remained the norm. Cole and Johnson's characterization of the Indian chiefs serves as a degrading reminder of the forms of representation that worked to elevate one aggrieved community while deriding another. But like the New Orleans black Mardi Gras Indians who began masquerading in the 1880s as a form of resisting white hegemony and racial and class oppression, we can consider that perhaps Cole and Johnson's Indian Chiefs represented opposition to the dominant society. The African American working-class men of New Orleans who through masquerade, music, and dance subverted white domination by dressing as Plains Indians and claiming a lineage in which the recurring narratives included bellicose and heroic warriors defying white supremacy, allowed them to overcome their oppressive environs, much in the same manner as the African American men masked as Indian chiefs in *The Red Moon*. The Indian Chiefs publicly resisted hegemony by participating in a war dance and other "Native American" forms prohibited by the United States government, like their real-life Lakota counterparts who in 1890 defied white authority by following the Ghost Dance Religion at the Pine Ridge Reservation. The Lakota ultimately faced slaughter by the United States government in the Massacre at Wounded Knee.[200] In a similar vein of resisting white power, Native American boarding school students compelled to play European music, perform in pageants, oratorical debates, and stereotypical plays written about Native Americans by whites, put these cultural productions "to their own social, political, economic, and even religious uses," by returning to the reservation and reviving forbidden Native American dances and songs and becoming political leaders arguing for Native American sovereignty and rights.[201] Surprisingly, these students took no offense to these demeaning portrayals. Like the Mardi Gras Indians and the Native American boarding school children, Cole and Johnson's contumaciousness against white power manifested itself within the reprehensible cliché of the Indian chiefs. By "playing Indian," dancing the prohibited "war dance," and renouncing white man's interdictions, the team claimed agency and freedom from white control in the same vein as the Mardi Gras Indians, even while they replicated virulent stereotypes of Native Americans.

According to Lester Walton, who credited Bob Cole with writing *The Red Moon* script, Cole placed the African American characters in the musical within a context created to dignify the group. The black characters' depiction included the desire for education while showing a great respect for law and order. Some of the Indians within the production on the other hand exhibited total disregard for "White man's laws." The portrayal of the Indians included the characterization of them as nomadic forest dwellers who rejected the white man's civilization.[202] With the placement of two educated Indians within the production and the two romances between Indians and blacks, however, the team portrayed Native Americans and blacks as equals in education and love.

Critiquing White Civilization

It may appear that Cole and Johnson placed blacks over Native Americans by portraying blacks as civilized and by portraying some of the Native American characters as uncivilized, but I believe that Cole intended a critique of white civilization within the production. By characterizing the Native Americans as disrespectful of the white man's law, Cole exposed and reproved the barbaric behavior of whites in his lifetime through the Native American characters. Cole argued that white man's laws and behavior proved unworthy of emulation.

Bob Cole's scrapbook offers some understanding of his views on portraying African Americans as exemplars. In 1893, Cole began collecting a myriad of articles on various subjects concerning blacks at the turn of the century. His scrapbook contained stories about African American heroes and heroines, including twenty-three-year-old Lulie A. Lytle, the first African American woman admitted to the bar in Memphis, Tennessee, on September 8, 1895; Flipper Anderson, the first black to attend West Point; Bishop Abraham Grant, a black philosopher; and Booker T. Washington. Cole also saved articles regarding Menelek, the Ethiopian ambassador to France, and an illustration depicting the Ethiopians' defeat of the Italians. All of this exemplifies Bob Cole's interest in Africans in the Diaspora.[203]

Cole's scrapbook also allows us to discern his viewpoints on "White civilization," which I believe acted as the foundation for his characterization of the black and Native Americans within *The Red Moon*. It contained articles about white on black violence, black self-protection, and political and social injustice. They inform us that Cole showed extreme interest in self-determination, the protection of African Americans, and elevating their status. For example, he saved an article concerning Miss Flagger, a white who shot and killed Ernest Green, a black middle-class youth in Washington D.C. Another article details the lynching of two men in Vicksburg, Mississippi. In addition, Cole saved articles concerning self-defense. A September 9, 1895, article in the *Sun* discussed how a black man protected himself against a white man by hitting him with a rock. The black man ultimately lost his life at the hands of whites. Another article entitled, "Negroes Shot to Kill in Race War" detailed white violence against blacks in their community on Thirty-ninth Street in New York City. This article also discussed how blacks fought back against white violence by shooting to kill. Cole kept articles concerning white supremacists' efforts to disenfranchise blacks in Florida in 1898. In saving stories on white barbarism that included the massive lynching and shooting of blacks, Cole chronicled the violent behavior of whites, which informs us of the possible reasons why the Indian characters within *The Red Moon* spurned "white man's laws" and civilization.[204]

Bob Cole's family history also lends itself to renouncing white civilization, which had proved violent and barbaric for both blacks and Native Americans in Georgia and Florida. As a man who escaped lynching at the age of fifteen in Georgia and as the son of a black Seminole slave whose family probably was captured and enslaved in the white wars against the Seminoles, Cole was no admirer of "White civilization." He most certainly fought on and off stage to dignify African Americans and to demand deference and freewill within his historical milieu. The exclusion of whites from the story of *The Red Moon* and the critique of white civilization all worked to create on stage an environment in which blacks and Native Americans exhibited self-determination, individuality, and respectability. The characterization of the Native Americans within *The Red Moon* might appear retrograde, but I would like to argue that given Cole's background and his erudition regarding U.S. and world events, Cole decisively included a critique of white U.S. barbarism in his Native American characters. Furthermore, Minnehaha departs from any stereotypical, degrading characterization on the stage, shining forth as the epitome of splendor.

Native American Female Stereotypes and Minnehaha

The interracial romance in *The Red Moon* contested taboos against "miscegenation" on and off stage. Cole and Johnson rejected stereotypes of African American women that saturated the American psyche and presented Minnehaha, played by African American singer Abbie Mitchell, as the ideal American woman, as educated and virtuous, effecting changes in perceptions about not only African American women but Native American women as well.

The black female stereotype of the Jezebel and the stereotype of the Native American as overtly sexual, seductive, and carnal particularly permeated the white imagination. The creation of these stereotypes helped to justify the sexual conquest and abuse of Native American and black women. Historically, Native American women faced sexual subjugation by both the Spanish and British due in part to the lack of white women in the Americas. In Georgia and the Carolinas, sexual relations between Anglo men and Indian women in the 1700s remained quite common. In Virginia and North Carolina, legislatures later outlawed marriage between Native Americans and whites, which implies that sexual relations occurred between the two groups.[205] The stereotype of the lascivious woman of color arose out of these very real situations, as a project designed to justify sexual contact and sexual abuse.

At the other end of the spectrum, the characterization in literature and film of Native American women as Noble Savages existed in conjunction with the lustful Native American woman stereotype.[206] The Indian princess Pocahontas offers an excellent model of the Native American woman as noble. In 1607, Powahatan and his tribe kept the Jamestown settlers alive by supplying them with food. Twelve-year-old Pocahontas allegedly saved John Smith from a mock execution and worked as an emissary and an ambassador for her father to the settlers of Jamestown. In 1613, Pocahontas married John Rolfe in a political alliance made by her father as part of a truce with the British. Pocahontas died in 1617 in England after promoting Jamestown and raising money for the Virginia Company. Thus the female Noble Savage was born. Berkhoffer notes appropriately that writers revised nineteenth-century historical figures such as Pocahontas who were "safely dead and historically [in the] past" as the embodiment of Indian nobility.[207]

The mixed-race stereotype of the Native American woman existed with three distinct components: as mongrel and deficient, as doomed, and as member of a dying race. In this view, the Native American, when mixed with another nonwhite race, created a mongrel who remained physically and mentally deficient and posed a danger to white civilization.[208] The stereotype of the doomed, mixed-race Native American made its way into fiction with works such as Mrs. Ann Sophia Winterbotham's *Maleska; the Indian Wife of the Hunter* (1860s). The main theme within this type of literature included the warning that a life of doom and despair awaits women who intermarried and their offspring. In this case Maleska agrees to her dying husband's request to raise her mixed-race child as white as opposed to Indian. Despite her promise, whites take her son away and she returns to her tribe where they plan her execution. Her former Indian suitor helps her to escape, but in the end she and her son die just as her son's marriage to a white woman is about to take place.[209]

Integral to the plot is the prohibition of miscegenation. This theme also made its way onto the Broadway stage and into movies with both the Broadway and film production of *Whoopee*. This show originally played on Broadway from 1928 to 1929 and became a Florenz Ziegfield–produced movie in 1931. The film revolved around the story of Wanenis, who finds that "white people hate me" because of his one drop of Indian blood that prevents him from marrying the white ingénue, Sally. At the end of the movie, Black Eagle, Wanenis's Indian father, reveals that Wanenis is actually white, and that Black Eagle's only relationship to him lay in the fact that he raised him, making it possible for Wanenis to marry Sally.[210] Another component to the mixed-race stereotype is that of the dying race. Hampton Institute's Helen Ludlow and Captain Pratt felt that the amalgamation of the Native American and white race would contribute to their assimilation and to the Native American's demise.

Cole and Johnson made a concerted effort to jettison stereotypes of Native American and African American women in the character of Minnehaha. First and foremost, due to her attendance at Swamptown Institute Minnehaha represented an educated woman. She embodied a chaste and virtuous woman, not a hypersexual one. Minnehaha moved away from the Noble Savage, the half-breed, and the dying race Indian stereotypes.

The role of Minnehaha in many ways acted as a composite of the African American and Native American teachers and students at Hampton. African American student and teacher Amelia Perry Pride personified the ideals of uplift represented in Minnehaha. Upon graduation, Pride returned to Lynchburg, Virginia as a teacher; married Claiborne G. Pride, a barber; and bore three children.[211] Pride asserted that "I am teaching school, and my aim is to remain teaching as long as there is a piece left of me. I find it rather hard though sometimes, but then I love my work. My heart seems to yearn to be among my people, and try and teach them in every way, both educationally and morally."[212]

The character of Minnehaha also mirrored Native American student Anna Dawson's life. Dawson graduated from Hampton in 1885; taught at Hampton from 1885 to 1887; married Byron Wilde (Sioux); and worked as a teacher, a church worker, and as a field matron, a job that entailed teaching domestic skills and the codes of Victorian morals to Native Americans at Fort Berthold.[213] By discarding the stereotypes of African American and Native American women, Cole and Johnson took the positive aspects of the education at Hampton, the glorifying of the race, education that reflected scholarship, and the marriage right—and eliminated the education that included laundry work and domestic labor. The character of Minnehaha replicated the lives of Amelia Perry Pride and Anna Dawson.

Minnehaha also broke the love scene taboo in stage depictions and the interdictions set in place at Hampton Institute which prevented black and Native American romance in the romantic intrigue, which paired her with Native American Red Feather and African American Plunk Green. Minnehaha also sang the romantic ballad "The Pathway of Love" in the production, which symbolized a definitive break of the love scene taboo.

Abbie Mitchell and Minnehaha

The connections between Abbie Mitchell and Minnehaha remain both multifaceted and intriguing and allow us to see that what happens off stage directly effects what happens on stage. Mitchell appeared in *The Red Moon* between 1908 and 1909, but her social thought emerged at the beginning of her theatrical career when she renegotiated her status as a performer by discarding the stigma associated with black women on the stage. She reimagined the stage as a place to ennoble African American women and worked to dignify theatrical life. In doing this, she carved a site for herself and others in African American and white society, despite attempts by some in the black and white communities to degrade her due to her career choice. The character of Minnehaha conveyed Mitchell's effort to dignify the stage and, in effect, symbolized a new and emancipatory black female subject.

Abbie Mitchell's early family life played a central role in her development and in her social thought. Mitchell's family consisted of loving and supportive black aunts who worked as domestics and a kind and caring Jewish father. Her family encouraged the young Mitchell in all aspects of life, including her educational pursuits. This family instilled in Mitchell self-assurance, a sense of her worth as a human being, and an unbreakable pride. Insulated from the prescripts of hegemony concerning her mixed-race background, when faced with prejudice, Mitchell fully rejected any labels. The part of Minnehaha mirrored Mitchell's idea of self through its abnegation of Native American and African American stereotypes and celebration of intermarriage. The character embodied a Mitchellesque persona. Mitchell also used education as a form of freedom from the restrictions placed on theatrical women. Cole and Johnson envisioned the character of Minnehaha as educated, and that mirrored Mitchell.

Abbie Mitchell was born on September 25, 1884, on East Third Street in New York City to a dark-skinned African American mother and a Jewish father.[214] Mitchell recalled that her mother died in childbirth and "bequeathed me to her oldest sister, Alice."[215] Raised by her aunt Alice in Baltimore, Maryland, Abbie recalled being reared "with tenderness and understanding."[216] Her Aunt Josephine as well as her grandparents also played an instrumental role in her upbringing. After Mitchell's mother's death, her father actively participated in her nurturing. She remembered her father as a "serene and kindly" man and recalled with affection "[t]he quiet father whose gentleness I shall never forget."[217] Mitchell remembered a loving relationship with her father, a father who made her shoes, built her dollhouses, and who "never felt I needed chastisement for anything."[218] At the age of thirteen, she moved to New York to spend the summer with her Aunt Josephine.[219]

Abbie Mitchell's social thought emerged around this time. When she was thirteen and living with her Aunt Josephine on West 33rd Street, Billy English, a black vaudevillian, heard her singing and asked her Aunt Josephine to allow Abbie to audition for the African American composer Will Marion Cook's *Clorindy: or The Origin of the Cakewalk*. Mitchell recalled her aunt's reaction: "'But she's only a child,' my aunt objected, 'and besides, nice girls don't go on the stage.'"[220] Reluctantly, Aunt Josephine allowed Mitchell to display her talents.[221] Abbie Mitchell later recalled that at the time she herself disapproved of African American music and women on the stage. She most certainly acquired this viewpoint from her family. Yet she auditioned for the famous African American composers Will Marion Cook and H. T. Bureleigh, as well as the respected African American poet Paul Laurence Dunbar. She won a place in the show.

After appearing in *Clorindy* throughout the summer of 1898, Mitchell returned to Baltimore and to school, only to discover that her foray into the world of the theater irrevocably stained her reputation. She discovered, after "proudly" giving her Aunt Alice the "small fortune" she made on stage, that her aunt cried when informed how Mitchell earned the money. Given the

Figure 17. Abbie Mitchell circa 1898. Photograph Department. Moorland-Spingarn Research Center, Howard University

stigma attached to stage life, Mitchell's aunt forced her to return to school. She recalled that "[b]ack to school I went, to find myself snubbed by all my former playmates. What was wrong? What had I done? I was stunned."[222] Not only did she face the disapproval of her aunt, but her friends and classmates suddenly looked down upon her as a result of her life on the stage. She later recalled:

> Gradually I was made to understand that I had committed the unforgivable crime: I had been on the stage, which meant that I had become a lewd girl at thirteen. The narrow-mindedness, the stupidity of my Baltimore friends astounded me, and yet I could understand it.[223]

Abbie Mitchell's playmates ostracized her because of her foray into the theater. She received unwanted attention from men and boys as a result of the perception that she was a "lewd girl." Mitchell recounted one such occasion, "a young man much older than I decided that I was easy prey and proceeded to get fresh. I whipped him, scratched his face, and tore his clothes. He went home considerably wiser about 'women of the theatre.'"[224]

Mitchell refused to accept societal attempts to debase her. She transcended the perception of the immoral woman of the theater and physically fought for respect. Mitchell writes that this experience as well as the banishment by her classmates deeply hurt her and proved emotionally painful. Despite her pleas to attend school in another city, her Aunt Alice insisted she remain in Baltimore. She cried herself to sleep nightly and recounted that "[w]ith morning, I'd go back to my torture with a heavy heart. My pride upheld me during this trying time, plus the conviction that I really was a good girl. "[225]

Abbie Mitchell's Aunt Alice eventually relented and allowed her to return to New York, where she rejoined the tour of Cook's *Clorindy*. Upon her return to the production, Mitchell won the leading lady role and received seventy-five dollars a week for her performances.[226] According to Mitchell, this turn of events deflected the stigma attached to the stage. As a result of her new prominent position in the production she gained the respect and admiration of both the African American and the theater community. Mitchell realized at the age of thirteen that she could invert ideas about girls on the stage. She negotiated her social rank through her association with the theater, and adopted a strong persona. The character of Minnehaha mirrored Mitchell's renegotiation of her class status and symbolized a new and emancipatory black and Indian female subject.

A photograph of a teenage Abbie Mitchell, probably taken around 1898, offers us a window through which we can discern her resilience, self-assurance, and unbreakable spirit (figure 17).

Nan Enstad argues that during the early part of the twentieth century, working-class European immigrant women factory workers dressed elegantly to demand the status of a lady and the respectability denied them because of their position in society. Similarly black women used dress to signify class status and dignity. Abbie Mitchell made a concerted effort to convey stature through her attire. In the photo, Mitchell wears white pear-shaped earrings and her hair is wrapped elaborately, with flowers placed prominently on the right side of her head. She displays two metal bracelets on her right arm, one near her elbow and one below. On her left wrist she wears a white bracelet. Mitchell's attire consists of an ornate virginal white dress, with a scooped neck and a flower close to her left shoulder. Flowers adorn the center of the waist, while flowers and lace drape down the center of the dress, and lace sleeves add a complementary touch to the garment. She dresses in virginal white intentionally to command respectability, signify her purity, and connote a class status that she would not be denied. The picture captures Mitchell with her hands clasped firmly in front of her, tightly, almost protectively, conceivably guarding her from outside forces.

The photograph also offers us a view of Mitchell's spirit. Her big black eyes stare at the camera and convey both sadness and defiance, with not a hint of a smile threatening to part her lips. She looks small yet steely and strong, and her straight back and proud stance suggest a strong personality. Mitchell appears both somber and bold, a determined little girl who commands deference. Perhaps her experience with overcoming the stain attached to the stage, or her plucky personality, elicited such a provocative gaze from an amazingly resilient little girl.

Abbie Mitchell soon learned that marriage raised her repute still higher and enabled her metamorphosis. Marriage offered an avenue through which blacks gained propriety and projected middle-class normalcy in a society that attempted to denigrate and lower their status at every turn. Abbie Mitchell married composer Will Marion Cook in New York after touring with *Clorindy* in 1899.[227] Mitchell described him as "a man more than twice my age, a giant in experience, a sincere student of music despite all statements to the contrary." She recalled "the doors of the most important offices opened to him without hesitation."[228] The marriage allowed Mitchell to reconfigure her place in society by wedding one of the most prominent black composers of the day and by becoming a well-respected singer. Ultimately, marriage and stage life allowed Abbie Mitchell to achieve middle class propriety and status.

The role of Minnehaha proved the ultimate means to reconfiguring the rank of both Native Americans and African Americans. Most importantly, playing the character worked to ennoble Mitchell. In the play, Minnehaha's marriage to the lawyer Plunk Green enhances her reputation and rank. Abbie Mitchell used marriage in her life to transcend her background. Her marriage to the middle-class Cook enabled Mitchell to transfigure her position as a performer. Similarly, the character of Minnehaha garnered middle-class politesse through the fictional marriage to Plunk Green.

Abbie Mitchell reached the meridian because of her marriage, but she soon discovered that Cook's middle-class family scorned her because of her Jewish background. Their opinion reflected the African American elite's response to interracial relationships in both the North and the South.

In the South the black elite believed that relationships between African American women and white men equaled sexual depravity. For the black elite these relationships and their offspring signified an unwanted reminder of slavery. Northern black elites held similar viewpoints and saw interracial unions as a threat to the African American family, "class survival," and propriety.[229] Both groups subjected those who became involved in interracial marriages to gossip and ridicule, and argued against miscegenation based on the grounds that it would weaken the race. They viewed those involved in these unions as "race traitors" who rejected racial solidarity and tried to pass for white.[230] The majority of the black elite rejected miscegenation; but some, including many light-skinned members, felt that to raise their status they should marry white or marry light. Willard B. Gatewood notes that in New York between 1877 and 1918 the majority of outmarriages occurred between African Americans of the lower and middle classes, with a minute number of marriages occurring among the black upper class, for example, the African American sisters Maud and Cora Clamorgan of St. Louis, who married white men. Gatewood attests that during this period the number of marriages between African American women and white men matched those of African American men and white women. Because of the interdiction, the black elite for the most part avoided interracial marriages and dating for fear of marrying a white not of their same class or economic ilk, thereby losing their class status. Coercion by the greater African American and white community also acted as a potent prohibition against marrying whites, and those who stepped over the color line faced the wrath of the African American community.[231] For example, many African Americans expressed extreme repugnance for Frederick Douglass's second marriage, to a white woman. Douglass addressed the animosity he experienced in a March 18, 1884, letter:

> My marriage has brought to me clouds, and darkness, and stormy criticism for offending popular prejudice, but there is peace and happiness within. I was unwilling to allow the world to select a wife for me, but preferred to select for myself, and the world is displeased with my independence. Dust will rise, but if well let alone will settle. It has already begun to do so in this case.[232]

Douglass experienced great resistance to his marriage, but felt that the African American community would eventually accept his union. They did not.

The resistance to interracial unions took on added meaning when the romantic relationships occurred with those aggrieved communities that the dominant society designated as not white. The nineteenth century signaled the rise in nativism and anti-Semitism with the arrival of white ethnics including Jewish people, who posed an economic threat to the white Anglo nation. Because of their working-class background in construction, the garment industry, as factory workers, longshoreman, coachmen, artisans, and tailors, and their menace to hegemony due to their very presence in the United States, the white power structure assigned to Jewish people the marginal status of nonwhite.[233] If the black elite remained antipathetic to marrying whites not of their social ilk, then marriage to Jewish people remained completely verboten given their low caste status in U.S. society. The African American elite *had* to position Jewish people as unworthy of them; the risk that their rank would decline remained *too great.* Victoria Earle Matthews expressed the sentiment of some of the black elite in the 1800s when she wrote of the danger that the Jewish man posed to the working-class southern black women relocating north for work. Matthews warned that these women should steer clear and beware of Jewish men, for she suspected them of luring African American women into immoral sexual activities.[234] In spite of the proscription against these unions by the black elite, it appears that no such ban existed among the working class, and in some cases the black middle and upper class married Jewish men.

Physical location influenced the relationships that might manifest themselves between African Americans and Jewish people. In many communities across the country African Americans lived side by side with Jewish people and found kindred spirits and like interests, which culminated in romance and marriages. Paul Spickard affirms that between 1700 and 1800, with the first two waves of Jewish immigration to the United States, a large number of Jewish people married outside their race and religion, with the Gentiles absorbing a large component of the Sephardic Jewish population.[235] In the nineteenth century, because of the lack of Jewish women in their locale, German Jewish men intermarried, as occurred in New Orleans where they married African American women. According to Joshua D. Rothman, between 1796 and 1837 David Isaacs, a Jewish mercantile business owner in Charlottesville, Virginia, maintained a marital relationship with Nancy West, a free black woman who bore him seven children.[236] While these marriages occurred, some in the African American community expressed antipathy toward them. As members of the black elite, the Cook family belonged to the category of those who remained antagonistic to such unions and considered Jewish people inferior to African Americans, given their working-class backgrounds. Abbie Mitchell remained outside of the Cook family's elite circle because of her mother's and aunts' careers as domestics and her working-class Jewish father.

Lynn Nottage's play *Intimate Apparel* (2005) reflects the types of associations that blossomed between African Americans and Jewish people at the turn of the twentieth century. The play is set in 1905 in the Lower East Side of New York. Esther, a thirty-five-year-old African American seamstress, lives in a boarding house that resembles the White Rose Industrial Home for Colored Girls.[237] Esther makes intimate apparel for both the ladies of the night and ladies of leisure. She buys fabrics of splendor, brilliance, and beauty for these garments from Mr. Marks, a Jewish fabric merchant who lives in her neighborhood. The play alludes to the real lived experiences of African Americans and Jewish people at the turn of the century who, because of their class status, lived in the same communities as Esther and Mr. Marks and Abbie Mitchell's parents.[238]

Mr. Marks's and Esther's friendship appears as a casual one in which they share similar affinities, but just below the surface of their relationship is an attraction that threatens to erupt. On a visit to his "shop," a one-room tenement flat, Mr. Marks and Esther participate in a romantic dance of words concerning gorgeous fabrics. Marks encourages Esther to buy a piece of beautiful Japanese silk to make something nice for herself, or he suggests, probing into her personal life, that perhaps she could make a smoking jacket for her "gentleman friend." Embarrassed by Marks's suggestion, Esther informs him that she remains without a gentleman suitor. As the conversation comes to an uncomfortable halt, they somehow return to commenting on the brilliant fabrics, an interaction which causes Esther so much happiness that she warmly grabs Mr. Marks hand. He pulls his hand away from her, offending Esther, who tells him scornfully "the color won't rub off on you."[239] He tries to right the misunderstanding by telling Esther that in his religion he must not touch a woman who is not his wife; he also informs her that his fiancée through an arranged marriage lives in Romania. Esther offers "'I bet you miss her something awful' (*Marks rubs his hand where Esther touched him. He laughs, a bit self-consciously*)." Marks states, "'I haven't even met her, actually.'"[240] Later in the play Esther visits Marks to buy material and they again bond and laugh over textiles and, as his back is turned, she touches him very lightly, leaving the audience to wonder if Marks felt her touch and pretended not to notice. Later in the play as Esther fits white society woman Mrs. Van Buren for a garment Esther confides that she disregarded a taboo: "'I touched someone, who I knew I wasn't supposed to touch. I touched them because I wanted to, it was wrong but I couldn't help myself.'"[241] At the end of the play after some life disappointments, which culminated in a loveless marriage for Esther that dissolved humiliatingly, she presents Mr. Marks with the fine Japanese silk smoking jacket that he suggested she make for her "gentleman friend." This jacket represents marriage and love to both Esther and Mr. Marks, which I believe signals the beginning of their amorous relationship and the end of the play. *Intimate Apparel* in some respects mirrors the real-life relationships that manifested itself between African American women like Abbie Mitchell's mother and her Jewish father. Mitchell in some ways symbolizes the offspring of the union between Mr. Marks and Esther. The play also represents the types of romance that the black elite, like the Cooks, vehemently opposed and helps explain why they treated Abbie Mitchell so cruelly.

Mitchell discovered that her family background caused the Cook family and some of the black elite to question her rank and worthiness. While she achieved a level of veneration because of her marital status, Cook's family rebuffed her because of her family background. After a difficult delivery of their daughter, Mitchell recuperated at the Cook family home where she confronted hostility.[242] Mercer Cook, Abbie Mitchell's son, states that the Cook family was

[e]xcessively caste and class conscious. The Cooks violently resented Abbie. "A child of miscegenation," as they called her, because her father had been a Jew. The family complained that Cook had "turned up with a little nobody, almost twenty-three years his junior." "She's nothing but a chorus girl," Abbie [could] hear Will's mother, Aunt Mick, brother, and sister-in law [state] in the next room the very first night of her arrival. "She hasn't even a high school education. And she was reared by two aunts who work as domestics!"[243]

Mitchell insisted that her husband remove her from the Cook family home, telling him, "'Mr. C. get me out of this house today or I'll crawl down the steps!'" Will Marion Cook removed her immediately and housed her with his white friend Miss Louise Lamprey, an editorial staff writer at the *Washington Star*.[244] Mitchell proved herself a strong-willed, determined woman who would not put up with mistreatment. Mitchell did not fit into the upper-class mold of the Cooks, which certainly led to and compounded her humiliating rejection by the family. To the Cook family she remained an affront, degraded because of her Jewish father and her mother's and aunts' working-class background. Mitchell never expressed embarrassment toward her family, and, when given the opportunity to pass as white by her father's side of the family, she refused and chose to live her life as a proud African American. She rejected any and all prohibitions against her marriage to Will Marion Cook, given her perceived lower-caste status and her mixed-race heritage. Mitchell used her career in the theater and her marriage to Cook to demand respect, and she reconfigured herself as the essence of culture, prepossessed and decorous.

Reminiscent of Abbie Mitchell, Cole and Johnson's Minnehaha diverged from the stereotype of the debased mixed-race subject by incorporating marriage as a trope of uplift. The musical theater team also discarded the love scene interdiction in plays and the Hampton romance ban and portrayed on stage what was forbidden off stage. Similarly Mitchell dismissed the prohibition that would have prevented her from marrying Cook due to her perceived lower-caste status and her mixed-race heritage.

An integral component to uplift for African Americans included the pursuit of education. Abbie Mitchell believed in the importance of education and made it an integral part of her life. Mitchell fondly recalled that her father encouraged her thirst for learning.

> I can even remember his saying so often, learn to love books they will help you in life—will lead you to a knowledge of people—of life and will never disappoint you. Read and remember. I know now he had great hopes for me—he believed I had something to develop. How he loved me!!"[245]

This early exposure to education instilled in Mitchell a love of learning and a desire to better herself. Mercer Cook wrote that his mother attended school up until her sophomore year of high school and relayed that "she studied informally all of her life."[246] Education for Mitchell worked as a form of racial uplift and legitimized her as dignified, decent, and upright. She took voice and language lessons. This training helped to advance her operatic career and validated her as a professional singer and actress. Abbie Mitchell's musical career, including *The Red Moon*, offered her an avenue into middle-class respectability.[247] In 1908 Lester A. Walton, a key proponent of aggrandizing the race, praised Abbie Mitchell for avidly and unremittingly studying her craft. He asserted that because of her studies Mitchell excelled as a "great artist," singing "high class songs," and her scholarship propelled her to "the head of [her] respective class."[248] Her erudition enabled Mitchell to live as the African American quintessence of repute.

Abbie Mitchell's educational pursuits began informally at the beginning of her career, helped by composers Will Marion Cook and H. T. Burleigh and poet Paul Laurence Dunbar. She maintained that at this juncture in her life, "[m]y colossal conceit and ignorance stood me in good stead at this, my first audition."[249] When asked if she knew any music written by black composers, she recalled later, "'No,' I replied quite pertly. 'I'm a nice girl, I only sing classics.' [Will Marion Cook] laughed and pulled his hat further down over his eyes."[250] According to Mitchell, her response exposed and reflected her ignorance of the importance and beauty of black music, black literature, and black theater. Her response perhaps mirrored the notion that "nice girls" don't perform on the stage.

Despite this viewpoint, both Cook and Dunbar imparted knowledge to Mitchell about the beauty of black culture, thus beginning her informal education. In her autobiographical notes, Mitchell detailed Cook's attempt to educate her at the audition for *Clorindy* by playing two of his compositions, "Love in a Cottage" and "Darktown Is Out Tonight." She recalled that his music affected her profoundly and that she was struck dumb by hearing the brusque Cook's magnificent music. After his performance she remembered that he chastised her, "'That's the kind of music you should sing, that's Negro music, and you're ashamed of it!' I tried to defend myself by explaining that decent, colored girls did not sing coon songs or ragtime, as it was then called. Again he laughed, bitterly."[251] She noted that it was interesting that fifty years later blacks appreciated the beauty of black art naturally, while she had to be taught.

Mitchell elucidated the importance of this educational encounter concerning the importance, charm, and magnificence of African American music. She suggested that her education regarding black music by Cook remained so significant that she made a conscientious effort to perform black music during her career as a concert singer.

Abbie Mitchell also began informal classes with Paul Laurence Dunbar. According to Mitchell, the inception of her education in poetry began when Dunbar told her Aunt Josephine "he would enjoy teaching me the beauty of Negro poetry and music if she would permit." [She adds,] "Josephine accepted in confusion, and Paul kept his word, became my teacher for about ten years intermittently."[252] She greatly respected Dunbar and it appears she treasured her educational experience with him. Mitchell's quest for education continued even after her daughter's birth, when she studied with Madame Emilia Serrano.[253] While performing concerts in 1905, Mitchell studied French and continued lessons in Europe while performing with the New York Syncopated Orchestra. Mitchell exuded culture and grace as a soloist on the operatic stage, a performer of spirituals and Will Marion Cook's compositions.[254] Her thirst for knowledge led her to mentor others. She opened a music and dramatic school in New York later in her career and taught voice.[255] Abbie Mitchell personified the definitive lady, urbane, courageous, audacious, brazen, and confident.

Abbie Mitchell used education to elevate her status in U.S. society and found herself aligned with several of the most influential black male creative forces of her time. Comparably, Cole and Johnson's Minnehaha mirrored Mitchell's educational life by positioning Minnehaha as a highly educated graduate of Swamptown/Hampton. The team drew Minnehaha as an educational model for African American women to emulate, which resonated for Mitchell. Her thirst for knowledge and her educational pursuits proved emancipatory and enabled her to rise above society's assigned position. The character of Minnehaha also worked as an emancipatory force for the audiences about the importance of learning. Finally, Mitchell's emancipation occurred through her display of her educational achievements on the stage as Minnehaha for all to see and honor.

In August 1908, Mitchell divorced Cook. It was announced that she would appear in *The Red Moon*.[256] Mercer Cook wrote that "[t]hey offered Mother the role of Minnehaha [and] she accepted. After rehearsing for six weeks, they tried out in Wilmington, Delaware."[257] Lester Walton noted that the team featured Mitchell prominently in the show. He heralded the fact that this role offered a departure from her previous singing roles because "she has lines galore to speak, and what's more she speaks them!"[258] When the show opened in September, Mitchell received excellent reviews from Walton, who wrote, "Mitchell lives up to her reputation of possessing an overabundance of personal magnetism and charms her audience whenever she is on the stage."[259] Mercer Cook remembered seeing the show as a six-year-old and recalled in 1978 that he "still remember[ed] some of Rosamond Johnson's catchy tunes: 'On the Road to Monterey,' 'Let Me Wrap You in My Big Red Shawl,' and 'Bleeding Moon.'" Abbie Mitchell recalled that she "co-starred with Bob Cole and J. Rosamond Johnson," and remembered *The Red Moon* as one of "[t]ruly the most spectacular plays to be done by Negroes at that time or any other," and that "New York yelled 'thumbs up!' as did Boston, Philadelphia, and Chicago."[260]

One of the main innovations Cole and Johnson made with Minnehaha was the overcoming of the love scene interdiction. Not only did Minnehaha attract the attention of two amorous suitors, Plunk Green and Red Feather, but she also sang three love songs within the production in the light operatic tradition. Walton wrote that Mitchell sang "As Long as the World Goes Round" in the second act in the "Mitchellesque style." He recounted that the audience responded positively to her rendition of the song and "she was compelled to respond to several encores before the audience had enough of her rendition."[261] J. Rosamond Johnson wrote the words and music to the highly dramatic song. The song's introduction reflects a wistfulness and a youthful air "What shall I say, What shall I do? Teach me the way, love to woo you." It built to a dramatic tension with the chorus "As long as the world goes round constant and true I'll be round, say you'll be mine, and love, I'll be thine, as long as the world goes round."[262] According to Bob Cole's notes, Johnson and Mitchell sang "Big Red Shawl" in the second act. This was followed by a scene with Cole, the Indian characters, J. Rosamond Johnson, and Abbie Mitchell. After this scene Abbie Mitchell sang "The Pathway of Love, with lyrics by Bob Cole and music by J. Rosamond Johnson."[263] This song illuminates Cole's romanticism:

> There's a pathway that leads to a beautiful land, Somewhere, some how,
> A pathway that only those few reach the end, who dare! I vow
> 'Tis a pathway so rough and so rocky, they say
> With poor broken hearts strewn along on the way;
> Yet new trav'lers will journey this pathway, each day,
> They call it the pathway of Love,
> The beautiful pathway of love.[264]

This song in some respects conveys Abbie Mitchell's struggles in life, "a pathway so rough and so rocky, they say," while also communicating her resiliency and her successful stride down "the beautiful pathway of love." Through her strength and unbreakable spirit, Abbie Mitchell embodies the very essence of the African American female, majestic, brilliant, charismatic, and refined. Mitchell's whole public and private persona radiated imperial bearing, with pluck.

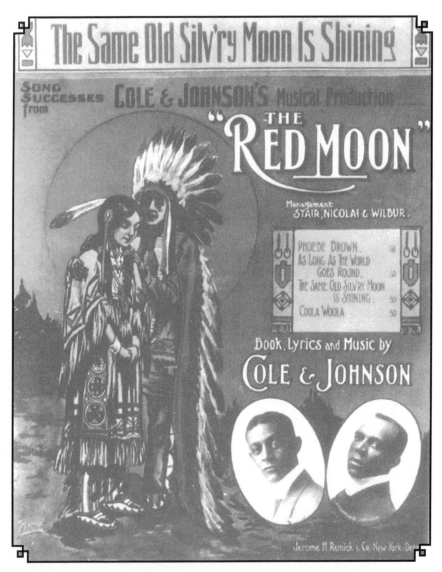

Figure 18. *The Red Moon* sheet music. Manuscripts, Archives & Rare Books Division, The Schomburg Center for Research in Black Culture.

CHAPTER FIVE

COLE AND JOHNSON AND THE GIBSON GAL

Gender, Race, and Uplift

~

THE BATTLE OF WOMANHOOD IS THE BATTLE FOR THE RACE
(MRS. BOOKER T. WASHINGTON [MARGARET JAMES MURRAY])[1]

O NE OF COLE and Johnson's most important innovations in the way of performative African American female uplift came through their featuring of an all-female chorus called the "Gibson Gals."[2] These African American women appeared on stage as sophisticated, pure, and respectable. The team's Gibson Gals performed in regular stage makeup, with the repulsive practice of "blacking up" discarded, which replicated Bob Cole's 1891 performance as the white-faced character Willie Wayside, the Tramp. The Gibson Gals contested negative notions of African American women during this period by exemplifying the ideals of the Cult of True Womanhood—appearing as pious, innocent, submissive, domestic, virtuous, weak, and fragile: attributes denied African American women both on stage and off.[3] Through the Gibson Gals, Bob Cole, J. Rosamond Johnson, and James Weldon Johnson communicated a politics of uplift and racial pride.

Charles Dana Gibson created the Gibson Girl, illustrations of well-bred and cosmopolitan women, for *Life Magazine* in 1890. Gibson himself described the Gibson Girl as the ultimate"[a]ll American girl to all the world."[4] His sister, Mrs. Josephine Gibson Knowlton, maintained that

[m]y brother wanted to portray a totally American type. The Gibson Girl was symbolic of a wholesome, healthy, utterly American Girl. She liked

sports, was a little ahead of her time, definitely athletic, and certainly did not smoke or drink—then. Importantly, she carved a new type of femininity," suggestive of emancipation.[5]

Stephen Warshaw asserts that the Gibson Girl represented American womanhood, with a sarcastic and realistic edge, embodying "[m]ore than the American girl, certainly; but more like what the American girl hoped to be was the Gibson Girl."[6] The popularity of the Gibson Girl lasted for two decades, and many white society women claimed they modeled for the original rendering, although Woody Gelman in *The Best of Charles Dana Gibson* maintains that Josephine Gibson Knowlton, Gibson's sister, posed for the illustrations. The Gibson Girl appeared in illustrations as youthful, fashionable, and blue-blooded: a woman of noble birth.[7] White women of the era tried to pattern themselves after her, copying her hairstyle, dress, and gestures. Therefore, it comes as no surprise that African American women would also follow the fashion and style of the Gibson Girl.[8]

Nan Enstad argues that fashion signified white women's class and privilege. She maintains that certain articles of white women's dress connoted their sexual purity and standing in society. A small waist, curved back, petite hands and feet, corsets, and petticoats denoted that a white woman belonged to the middle-class, led a life of leisure, and, most importantly, her dress marked her as a lady.[9] Fashion magazines in the nineteenth century depicted African American women as the opposite of white women, that is, as fat, crude, unchaste, and far removed from a lady given her slave past or working-class status.[10] Thus U.S. society positioned African American women as the antithesis of The Cult of True Womanhood. African American women confronted extreme obstacles in their fight for womanhood rights during the early part of the twentieth century. They came up against the menace of rape, a horrific inevitability in many African American women's lives, and they found themselves routinely and derisively called racial epithets or "girl" instead of being properly addressed as "lady," "Miss," or "Mrs." The use of the image of the Gibson Girl as symbolic of African American womanhood, therefore, proved a powerful tool for emancipating them from the dictates of white society and from the obstacles they dealt with physically and psychologically. While they were excluded by whites from womanhood rights, respect, and middle-class standing, and were situated as the antithesis of womanhood, the positioning of African American women as the Gibson Girl, all-American, fashionable, and patrician, proved an incredibly progressive and praiseworthy claim. Thus the use of the Gibson Girl iconography in black vaudeville and in *The Red Moon* proved a deliberate and calculated attempt to uplift African American women's status.

The Whitman sisters appeared on stage in the 1900s in "full Gibson Girl style with high pompadours."[11] By performing on stage as cosmopolitan women dressed exquisitely and at the height of fashion, they presented a dignified image on stage of African American femininity. They communicated that African American women exuded beauty, politesse, and sophisticated fashion sensibilities. This contrasted sharply with common representations of African American women as the asexual Mammy, the oversexed Jezebel, the wild, childlike, dancing Pickanniny, and the Tragic Mulatto.

Cole and Johnson also used the image of the Gibson Girls, *a la* the "Gibson Gals," to elevate African American women's social position. The placement of the "Gibson Gals" in *The Red Moon* worked to legitimate African American women as refined, reputable, and extremely well dressed. The Gibson Gals worked as a lesson to audience members and specifically to white people about the decorum of African American women, their womanhood, and their moral character. Just as black writers like Jessie Fauset presented extremely conservative depictions of African American female virtue, fidelity, and chastity in order to make credible arguments for citizenship and marriage rights for African American women, the Whitman Sisters and Cole and Johnson deployed portrayals of black respectability as part of a broader strategy of uplift.

Cole and Johnson situated African American women at the axis of true womanhood by christening African American women in their production the Gibson Gal. The contention here is that the team recast African American women as the Gibson Gal to signify their blackness; to reappropriate the pejorative term girl, which was assigned to African American women; and to affirm African American womanhood.[12] Cole and Johnson envisioned the Gibson Gals as wealthy, reputable, and cosmopolitan, "the social leaders" of their town. Mollie Dill portrayed Amanda Gibson, while Bessie Tribble, Lulu Coleman, Mayme Butler, Tillie Smith, Bessie Sims, and Blanche Deas portrayed the Gibson Gals.[13] Bob Cole's notes for the production indicated that in the second act an "[a]uto horn [is] to toot on entrance of [the] Gibson Gals."[14] The car represented middle-class standing, upward mobility, polish, and the gentility of the Gibson Gals.[15] Henry Gant portrayed Bill Gibson, the saloonkeeper, who, although he is the richest man in town and finances his daughter's forays into "Negro society," is nevertheless excluded from "Negro society."[16]

During the 1908–1910 theatrical seasons of *The Red Moon,* a column entitled *"The Red Moon* Rays" appeared in the Booker T. Washington–owned newspaper, *The New York Age.*[17] The column, written by Charles A. Hunter, the stage manager and press agent for the production, followed the company as they toured the United States and Canada.[18] This column featured varied topics, including light gossip and brief reviews, as well as other relevant issues about the show and the cast members. The articles offered insight into the strategies used to elevate African Americans. Four important themes threaded through the column in relation to the female entertainers: the importance of marriage, racial uplift, the positioning of the women cast members as Gibson Girls, and the use of women's clubs started by them to promote women's rights while on tour. Through "*The Red Moon Rays*" Cole and Johnson and the female performers made a conscious and strategic effort to venerate African American women.

The projects of uplift, marriage, and the protection of African American women proved essential elements to Cole and Johnson's program for raising the rank of African Americans on and off stage. Bob Cole's scrapbook offers insight into the reasons why uplift and protection proved necessary for African American women, and reveals some of Cole's influences. One such article from the 1895 Republican newspaper *The Press* recounted the murder of black men in Georgia's Brooks County by white men which culminated in "their wives' and daughters' subject[ion] to [the] most inhuman indignities."[19] The brutal treatment the women encountered most likely included rape, beatings, and torture, but the paper felt that the atrocities proved too horrible to print in detail. Before their brutalization by white men, many of the women dealt with the horror of witnessing their husband's murder. Others found their spouses dead upon returning home. The article also related that the inhumane treatment they experienced proved as barbaric and as terrible as the Armenian genocide.[20]

These types of articles acted as reminders that Bob Cole himself escaped lynching at the age of fifteen. These incidents and the many other atrocities committed against African American people during his lifetime influenced Cole to protect blacks, most specifically African American women, and to raise their societal rank. His family life influenced his efforts to aggrandize African American women because he adored his mother and his four sisters. Because of these warm familial relationships, Cole promoted respectability through the marriage trope in both *Shoo Fly Regiment* and *The Red Moon*.

In 1900 African American clubwoman Fannie Barrier Williams contended that African American women met extreme challenges in gaining womanhood rights and the safeguards it afforded.

There has been no fixed public opinion to which [African American and I will add Native American] women could appeal; no protection against libelous attacks upon their characters, and no chivalry generous enough to guarantee their safety against man's inhumanity to woman.[21]

Figures 19–20. Bessie and Andrew Tribble. *The New York Age.*
November 25, 1909, 7; December 24, 1908, 6

Williams argues that as insurmountable as these obstacles appeared, African American women persevered, and by 1900 they ascended to American womanhood. The character of Minnehaha and the Gibson Gal chorus represented this ascension. Like her white Gibson Girl counterpart sitting in the park with her beau in "In The Park" (1898), the African American/Native American Gibson Gal fit firmly in this mold, precious and deserving of all the protections and comforts of womanhood.[22] "*The Red Moon* Rays" also worked to uplift African American women through marriage and propriety.

While marriage proved central to the plot of *The Red Moon*, it also dominated the lives of Cole and Johnson and the cast members. Married couples in the company included Bessie and Andrew Tribble, Theodore Pankey and Anna Cook Pankey, and Bessie O. Brown and Frank Brown (figures 18 and 19). Abbie Mitchell, recently divorced from Will Marion Cook, and Ada Overton Walker, who married George Walker, rounded out the married cast (figure 21).

Marriage played an important role in the personal lives of Cole and Johnson as well. Cole married soubrette Stella Wiley early in his career, while James Weldon Johnson married Grace Nail in 1910, and J. Rosamond Johnson married Nora Johnson in 1913[23] (figures 22, 23, and 24).

Figure 21. Ada Overton Walker and George Walker.
The Schomburg Center for Research in Black Culture

Figure 22. Bob Cole and Stella Wiley. James Weldon
Johnson Papers, Yale Collection of American Literature, Beinecke
Rare Book and Manuscript Library

Figure 23. James Weldon Johnson and Grace Nail Johnson.
Special Collections Department, Robert W. Woodruff Library,
Emory University. Protected by Copyright Law, Title 17 U.S. Code

Figure 24. Nora Johnson and Baby Mildred. Special Collections Department, Robert W. Woodruff Library, Emory University. Protected by Copyright Law, Title 17 U.S. Code

Figure 25. Gertrude Townsend Robertson. *The New York Age.* May 11, 1911, 6

"*The Red Moon* Rays" also promoted marriage and touted the women of the company as attractive and good marriage material. For example, "Sam Lucas, in speaking of pretty women in the profession, says that were *The Red Moon* Company's ladies in the matrimonial market, a suitor could easily be blindfolded, grasp the first one near and be happy ever after."[24] *The New York Age* also reported that Gertrude Townsend Robertson met and married a wealthy Canadian while on tour[25] (figure 25).

Articles about the married couples appeared in "*The Red Moon* Rays," with accounts of gift giving among them. Bessie Oliver Brown gave her husband a birthday present of "a silver filigreed fountain pen and a gilt edge morocco bound check book" which, according to the article, left "no loophole for the forthcoming ever ready '*touch*' for spring millinery."[26] "*The Red Moon* Rays" made a clear attempt to reverse not only the cruelty that African Americans encountered, but reinscribed their status from victims to people with agency. The discussion of marriage within the article and the marriages of the cast members accomplished the goal of seizing civilizing and respectability tropes for African Americans in the face of the savagery of whites in the United States.

"*The Red Moon* Rays" promoted the female performers as reputable due to their marriages and as the embodiment of the Gibson Girl. The female cast members' women's clubs celebrated African American womanhood and intellect. Some of the women such as Abbie Mitchell belonged to the larger African American women's organizations such as the National Council of Negro Women, while others, including Mitchell and Ada Overton Walker, participated as clubwomen, performers, and financial supporters of local New York women's clubs such as Victoria Earle Matthews's White Rose Mission and the Travelers Aid Society.[27] Theatrical women like Abbie Mitchell, Ada Overton Walker, and the women of *The Red Moon* followed in the footsteps of Hampton University teachers Georgiana Washington and Amelia Perry Pride, who belonged to women's clubs and who through these clubs founded organizations, agitated against racism, and fought for civil rights.[28] In 1898 in the "Afro-American Notes," T. Thomas Fortune detailed the activities of African American clubwomen. He noted that the Woman's Auxiliary of the Summer State League of Connecticut and women in Pine Bluff, Arkansas, endeavored to build homes for orphans and homes for the aged. Fortune reported that Atlanta Clubwomen's Carrie Steele orphanage in Atlanta flourished, and that the Women of the Soldiers Aid Society of Boston sent supplies to African American soldiers in "Porto Rico." *The Crisis* also reported on the activities of clubwomen, while Cornelia Bowen, Principal of Mt. Meigs Institute, the school that Georgiana Washington founded, wrote of the efforts made by the National Federation of Colored Women's Clubs in Mount Meigs to operate a reformatory to prevent the criminalization of African American youth imprisoned with "hardened criminals."[29] Some famous clubwomen belonged to the black bourgeoisie like Mrs. Booker T. Washington (Margaret Murray), the Mississippi Senator Blanche K. Bruce's wife, Fannie Barrier Williams, Victoria Earle Matthews, who founded the New York Black Women's Club, and Washingtonian Mary Church Terrell, who founded the National Association of Colored Women. Others, like Madame C. J. Walker, a former washerwoman and the first African American female millionaire, discovered that the elite clubwomen rejected her application to join the NACW, but eventually relented.[30] These elite women, while more than willing to aid the less fortunate, drew distinct color-caste and class distinctions.

The women of *The Red Moon* yearning to learn propelled them to the center of the disputations surrounding raising the status of African American women and the Gibson Girl. They organized two women's clubs, *The Red Moon* Mending Club, with Bessie Tribble as president, and a dramatic class, organized and taught by Elizabeth Williams.[31] Williams was no novice to acting and teaching given that in 1905 she organized The Elizabeth Williams' Oriental Empire Stock Company.[32] Through these clubs the women presented themselves as not only intellectual but also cultured and concerned about the issues African American women encountered in U.S. society. Their efforts replicated the work of African American clubwomen across the country like Mrs. Fannie L. Gordon of Fargo, North Dakota, who in 1903 held the position of president of the H. P. C. Literary Club of Fargo. In 1898 T. Thomas Fortune lauded clubwomen and wrote that "[i]n all directions there are signs that Afro-American women are taking hold of the race problem with intelligence and are finding that those who help themselves have plenty of people to help them."[33] The importance of respectability appeared a concern for *The Red Moon* clubwomen. For example, at one of the biweekly meetings of *The Red Moon* Mending Club, Mrs. Bessie Tribble asked the participants, "What is a lady?" Mrs. Bessie O. Brown stated:

A lady, in a true sense is one who abhors vulgarity of both thought and speech; one who dislikes to be conspicuous in any way and avoids notoriety; she sets higher store by personal cleanliness and neatness than by fine clothes. One who tries to look and dress like a lady and is ever willing to behave and act like one.[34]

The women of the club worked to change the perception of African American

Figure 26. Grace Nail Johnson as the Gibson Gal in Nicaragua.
James Weldon Johnson Papers, Yale Collection of American Literature. Beinecke Rare
Book and Manuscript Library

women to that of a "lady": well spoken, clean, neat and well dressed.

Middle-class standing, and the right to call one's self a lady, proved essential to African American women at the turn of the century. The women of *The Red Moon* appeared acutely aware of the obstacles African American women met with in the struggle for rights and respect within U.S. culture. Blackface minstrelsy, coon songs, and virulent stereotypes all worked to denigrate African American women through ugly and reprehensible images and ideas. By claiming the title "lady," by abjuring vulgarity, and by dressing immaculately, the African American women of *The Red Moon* steadfastly seized womanhood as their own.

Similarly, the drama class taught by Elizabeth Williams advanced the notion that the women of the company embodied culture and superior mental abilities. The drama club, described as "[t]he latest of the many intellectual and social organizations connected with *The Red Moon* Company," positioned the African American women of the company as concerned with intellectual as well as social issues of the day.[35] The participants in the group, Bessie O. Brown, Mayme Butler, Bessie Tribble, Blanche Deas, and Lulu

Coleman, were, according to the column, "rapidly advancing in this art." Williams stated that she "is very proud of the class and says that the time is not far distant when there will be six new character artists in the profession."[36] The female cast members of The Red Moon aspired to broaden their knowledge base and present themselves as well-bred women. Like the Gibson Girl in "All's Well That Ends Well" who sits at the piano dressed exquisitely in a mutton-sleeve dress while accompanying her Gibson Girl friend who dreamily sings off into the distance, the female cast members of The Red Moon pursued musical, theatrical, physical, and literary knowledge and aspired to broaden their overall knowledge base and present themselves as well-bred women.[37] One could easily locate the women of The Red Moon in this drawing, as they fully encompass the essence of the Gibson Girl as students, teachers, and performers through their pursuit of erudition and culture. While society routinely afforded white women the privilege of womanhood and education, African American women seized womanhood rights through the creation of clubs whose primary object included uplift.

Correspondence between James Weldon Johnson and his wife Grace Nail also illustrates the significance of elevating the African American female through education. Nail belonged to the black aristocracy of Brooklyn, and was known as a notable and popular hostess of the New York elite, a woman with "schooled sensitivity to the finest art and literature, and a deep concern for community welfare"[38] (figure 26).

While Johnson acted as the American consul in Venezuela in 1912, his wife lived in Florida with his parents. The interconnections between perceptions of theatrical African American women and laywomen is illuminated by the couple's attention to her cultural and scholarly pursuits as evidenced by Johnson's May 8, 1912, inquiry from Corinto as to her progress in her French and piano lessons:

And how are you getting on Chicken? Still sticking to your French? Don't slow down on it. Try and do a little work on your piano if you find time, but I suppose its already getting too hot for that. But your French is fine outdoor work for you. Nothing nicer for whiling away a few morning hours in the Park.[39]

Nail's pursuit of enlightenment and James Weldon Johnson's encouragement of these endeavors follow both the ideology of W. E. B. Du Bois and Booker T. Washington, who saw the importance of ennobling African American women. Washington and Du Bois's daughters attended elite white institutions, and pursued music and other markers of the upper class. We must remember that while Washington publicly promoted industrial training over higher education, he felt that edification at the university level and the pursuit of culture remained key to elevating African Americans. Although Francille Rusan Wilson notes that Du Bois did not encourage Atlanta University female students to further their education, he did support his daughter's efforts at higher learning.[40] Another important trope of uplift illuminated within the correspondence between the Johnsons included his respect for African American womanhood. The correspondence elucidates Johnson's reverence and regard for his wife. He wrote from Corinto on May 18, 1912:

> Don't get discouraged with your French, you can only master it by constant repetition—you know it was the same with your Spanish, hour after hour of repetition, then suddenly you found out that you could speak Spanish and that you knew more than you had any idea that you knew. It would be fine if you could find some little French shop in the neighborhood where you could stop in every day or two, spend a dime and get a dollar's worth of French in return.[41]

While Grace Nail enjoyed a life of leisure, the reality of the majority of African American women's lives at the beginning of the twentieth century included working as domestics, washerwomen, and laborers. According to Kali Gross in *Colored Amazons,* even in northern cities such as Philadelphia, African American women found themselves confined to domestic service, given the discriminatory hiring practices which barred them from factory work.[42] Nail's membership in the black aristocracy of Brooklyn freed her from this type of life.

Grace Nail's 1912 diary offers us a view into how African American women carved a space in society and positioned themselves at the center of the spheres of womanhood and respectability. Nail made entries in the diary when she stayed with her family in New York while James Weldon Johnson acted as the consul in Venezuela. She detailed her daily activities, which included taking French lessons at the Berlitz School, shopping for clothing, lunching with her friends and family, and attending the theater. These activities not only exemplify Nail's status as a lady of leisure, a true Gibson Girl, but also evince edification and the theater as tropes of uplift.[43] The correspondence and the diary illustrate the Johnsons' use of uplift to position African American women at the center of womanhood, intellect, and repute. By utilizing the tools of uplift, that is, African American female estimation, education, and deference for African American womanhood, the Johnsons repositioned and reimagined the status of the African American female.

"*The Red Moon* Rays" also promoted the female performers as fashionable Gibson Girls, cosmopolitan and honorable. Correspondingly, by positioning them as well bred, Cole and Johnson and the female performers contested the notion of stage life as unseemly. Like the Gibson Girl drawings, witty and spirited comments on the fashion sense of the female entertainers dominated the column. A February 18, 1909, article offered that many of them wore fur coats and that "Judging from the number of fur coats worn by *The Red Moon* chorus girls one would believe that their route laid directly to the North Pole."[44] In a similar vein, "*The Red Moon* Rays" reported with mock alarm that the female chorus including Fanny Wise, Zennie Hunter, Mollie Dill, Marie Lucas, Pauline Hackney, and Marie Young had fallen ill and suffered from "millinery hysteria." The symptoms included "the desire to possess the latest creations in headgear," but the author assured the reader "that they will probably be cured by pay day."[45]

Photographs of the female cast members accompanied the articles and presented them as dignified and stylish. A photograph of Zennie Hunter shows her as a slender woman standing sideways with her hair styled in a fashionable roll, wearing a black dress with long sleeves that puff at the shoulders. Her hands rest delicately on a mantle and she glances at the camera displaying just a hint of a smile. Hunter appears as a tranquil and serene presence. In another photograph, Leona Marshall appears serene. She is a large woman who looks directly at the camera, slightly smiling. Marshall wears a white headband knotted at the left side, and a white lace dress with a high neck and long sleeves. The slight smile that plays off Marshall's lips glows with mischief that the author hints at in the commentary. Finally, Lulu Coleman emerges as the most flamboyantly dressed of the women, as she appears dressed in full costume for the song "On the Road to Monterey." She stands in a side profile, with her head tilted looking directly at the camera. Coleman wears a mantilla of shoulder-length black lace with flowers that frame her face. She also wears a white high-necked, long-sleeved blouse with a large broach at her throat and a black skirt. She crosses her hands in front of her body and looks placid. All these women radiate a quiet eminence that reflects Charles A. Hunters' witty comments and a Gibson Girl mystique.

James Weldon Johnson's letters from Corninto, Venezuela in 1912 to Grace Nail reveal the importance of fashion to the uplift of African American women. In these letters Johnson expresses his desire to see his wife exquisitely dressed and as the most beautiful of the women in their circle. On May 24, 1912, he states, "I'm glad your new dress is pretty. I always want you to look pretty, as pretty as anybody and a great deal prettier than most of them."[46] Part of the uplift strategy meant introducing African American women to the pub-

Figure 27. Grace Nail Johnson in "Men's Clothing." Special Collections Department, Robert W. Woodruff Library, Emory University. Protected by Copyright Law, Title 17 U.S. Code

lic as the ultimate in sophistication, style, and dress. In her diary, Grace Nail described shopping excursions which took her to Stern's for stockings, Wanamaker's for shoes, Gimbel's for lunch, Macy's for Macy's, the beauty salon to have her hair "waved," and dress fittings at home.[47] These jaunts proved an important part of situating Nail as the quintessence of African American womanhood. To some this may appear problematic, given Grace Nail's membership in black society and the color-caste system so ingrained within the group, which placed Nail over other blacks due to her light complexion. But we must remember that *all* African American women struggled for womanhood rights and experienced extreme racism and discrimination *regardless of color*. We also must keep in mind that Cole and Johnson argued for womanhood rights for all the women of the cast of different hues. On August 9, 1912, Johnson reveals that not only was he pleased to see pictures of Nail, but that he shared the photos with his colleagues in Corinto (figure 27).

The pictures came. They are fine! I gave Mrs. May hers, and she is delighted. I was so proud that I took mine in my pocket and showed it to several of my friends. It is now my favorite picture of you. Your hat and your suit show up splendidly. Little Carlota May admired the picture very much, but wanted to know why you had on men's clothes.[48]

Little Carlota's comments elucidate the significance of Cole and Johnson's battle to elevate African American women in U.S. society. Carlota's question exposes the hegemonic codes of womanhood, which exclude African American women, codes that placed Nail firmly within the stereotype of the masculinzed woman. The comment speaks to why it proved necessary to situate Nail at the center of African American womanhood. No matter how cosmopolitan Nail appears, regardless of Johnson's efforts to glorify her, her womanhood comes into question when faced with white preeminence in the guise of Little Carlota. The correspondence between the Johnsons reveals the necessity of presenting African American women as refined and decorous not only to one's husband, but to the public. The diary also illustrates how Nail participated fully in centering herself within the discourse of uplift.

The uplift of the female cast members also included presenting themselves as well bred and pious. Religion proved a central aspect in the uplift of African Americans beginning with slavery, the missionary industrial institutions, and African American adherence to religious doctrine. "*The Red Moon* Rays" and Cole and Johnson utilized religion and fashion sensibilities to prove African American women deserved citizenship and womanhood rights. In a column dated March 18, 1909, "Edgar Connor claims that when to church a soubrette goes it's mostly to show her clothes. Our Six Saucy Soubrettes, headed by Daisy Brown, think he is slurring."[49] The strategy of uplift through the church remains very similar to the vaudeville team the Whitman Sister's methods. The sisters used the church to dignify and legitimate the women of their vaudeville act. Similarly, "*The Red Moon* Rays" also used the church to legitimate the women of the production.

Cole and Johnson and the female entertainers of the show utilized "*The Red Moon* Rays" to promote the uplift of African American women through the Gibson Girls, women's clubs, and religion to show the moral character, politesse, middle-class status, and intellect of the African American female.[50] The women created meaning for themselves through these symbols. By positioning African American women at the center of such hegemonic tropes, Cole and Johnson used uplift and demanded respect for African American women. Despite the denial of citizenship rights, human rights, and the privileges of the Cult of True Womanhood, these African American women fixed onto the title of "lady" and held firmly to that status.

African American female performers experienced many obstacles in changing perceptions about stage life. In the novel *The Sport of the Gods,* Paul Laurence Dunbar illustrates the negative perceptions of the musical stage, characterizing the stage as low class with its cheap costumes, "pale yellow and sickly green" women, and "tawdry music and inane words."[51] Dunbar's novel demonstrates African American women on stage falling from grace, as evidenced by the two characters Hattie Sterling and Kitty Hamilton. Hattie Sterling, although good looking, lost her youth and maintained an affinity for whiskey. Although she attracted the much younger Joe, an innocent from the South whom she likes in a "half-contemptuous, half-amused way," Dunbar characterizes her as bad to the bone.[52] He states, "Hattie Sterling had given [Joe] both his greatest impulse for evil and for good."[53] She drove Joe first to drink, then to financial excess by compelling him to lavish his money on her, then to humiliation, and finally to murder.[54]

Dunbar also details Kitty Hamilton's descent brought about by the evils of the theater. Kitty Hamilton was young, African American, and beautiful and arrived in New York with her doomed brother Joe. After meeting Sterling through her brother, she auditioned and joined Hattie's Broadway show, in the face of her mother's disapproval.[55] Her mother vehemently rejected stage life and would rather see Kitty dead, despite Kitty's retort that "nowadays everybody thinks stage people respectable up here."[56] Like Hattie, Kitty eventually showed the signs of age, and worked to maintain an illusion of beauty with the aid of cosmetics. Kitty became self-involved, obsessed with clothes, and fixated on the attention and adoration that the theater brought her. Ultimately, Kitty experienced estrangement from her parents, who felt she was worse then dead, and continued a downward spiral because of her association with the stage.[57]

Dunbar paints a bleak picture of stage life. He writes: "It is strange how the glare of the footlights succeeds in deceiving so many people who are able to see through other delusions. The cheap dresses on the street had not fooled Kitty for an instant, but take the same cheese-cloth, put a little water starch into it and put it on the stage, and she could see only chiffon."[58] Although his theatrical affiliation dated back to 1898, Dunbar painted a depressing picture of theatrical life in the novel. One could ascribe Dunbar's frustration and contempt for the stage to his assigned position as a dialect poet and finding himself locked into the genre even when writing the librettos for *Clorindy: or The Origin of the Cakewalk* (1898), *Jes Like White Folks* (1900), and *The Cannibal King* (1901), which he wrote with J. Rosamond Johnson while Cole produced the show. His close association with show business and his conflicted relationship with women may also account for his insensitive portrayal of African American theatrical women and his total dismissal of the theater as a place for ennobling them.[59]

While Dunbar envisioned the negative connotations of stage life, *The New York Age* attempted to invert the unfavorable perceptions of the stage. Through what appears as a carefully constructed and planned ideological campaign, the newspaper ran a series of articles in 1909 that advanced the positive aspects of performance life. They promoted a theatrical career as a form of racial uplift in articles with titles such as "College Girls and the Stage," and "The Church and the Stage." These articles elevated the status of African American artists by lauding their ethics and religious standards.

"College Girls and the Stage" asserted that although a large portion of college women chose a career on the stage, they failed almost in all instances due to their feelings of superiority. They felt their high breeding, education, and moral character placed them above theatrical women with less education.[60] The college girl's family and friends warned her to remember her social standing and status as a lady, as a Christian to hold herself above the other performers through disassociation, and the family expressed sorrow concerning the "evil associations of the theatre."[61] This attitude, the author asserted, accounted for the failure of college girls in the theatrical arena. He concluded that college girls who pursued the stage must discard their judgmental attitude toward performers if they wanted to succeed, and avoid judging other theatrical women whose self-sacrifice might enable one woman to support her mother, another woman to send her brother to school, and still another to go without food and clothing to care for an invalid sister.[62]

Similar efforts to dignify stage performers appear in an article entitled "The Church and the Stage." In *The New York Age* Lester A. Walton asked ministers to respond to comedian Ernest Hogan's contention published in a previous issue that church people felt antagonistic toward entertainers. Bishop Alexander Walters responded and assured the readers that his followers respected performers. He asserted that many performers such as Madame Selika, Miss Edna Nahar, and Madame Floretta Batson Bergen began their careers in the church. Walters also assured the readers that the church supported performers "at every stage of the career" and explained that while he pastored at the Mother Zion Church from 1888 to 1892, he introduced Sissieretta Jones to New York audiences.[63] Similarly, Reverend Reverdy Ransom also noted that many female artists, including Sissieretta Jones, either received their early training in the church or were discovered there. Ransom contends that these women "graduated from our church choirs into a theatrical career."[64] He suggests that while the church and the stage, to some extent, lay at two different ends of the spectrum, as a minister he commends those who go into the theatrical profession.

While Bishop Walters felt that a lower class of people attended vaudeville, he assured the readers that appropriate entertainment included light comedy and dramas. He praised the shows of Cole and Johnson and Williams and Walker, asserting that both ministers and laymen enjoyed them. Bishop Walters maintained that the church welcomed performers as long as they declared their "willing[ness] to live up to Christian principles," and noted that his friends included some distinguished African American performers.[65]

Reverend Reverdy Ransom of the Bethel AME Church held views comparable to Bishop Walters. Because his family included an uncle, Mr. Sam Lucas, who, according to Lester Walton, held the title of "the dean of the theatrical profession among Negroes," Ransom sympathized with Hogan's argument. He offered that not only did some church folk express hostility towards theater people, but they also unveiled hypocritical views because many clergymen attended the theater when out of town. He concluded that since they attended the theater, their opinion and attitude toward the stage were due more to "religious public opinion and inherited prejudices than to anything based on moral or religious scruples."[66] The black press's participation in debates concerning the theater makes clear that theatrical representations, the image of the stage performer, and their careers proved important to the entire African American community, not just to the entertainers and entrepreneurs.

Ada Overton Walker and the Gibson Girl

The Words of pity dwelt upon her lip
And in her heart good will to all mankind.

But o'er her grave shall hearts to mem'ry warm,
And tears bedew the pious lady's tomb
(Romeo L. Doughterty, "Aida Overton Walker in Memoriam"[67])

Theater as a place for "staging" a battle for racial inclusion permeated the writings of Ada Overton Walker. In *The Red Moon* she played Phoebe Brown. Walker's performance glorified African American and Native American women. Her choreographic achievements remained incredibly impressive, given that men dominated the theatrical profession. Walker successfully carved out a space for herself in the theater, emerging as one of the most renowned African American female choreographers and performers of the time.[68] Because of these accomplishments Ada Overton Walker symbolized the ultimate African American Gibson Girl, modern, independent, self-assured, creative, and womanly. She contended that the stage offered a dignified and acceptable profession for African American women. In her effort to change their station, Walker adopted the principles of The Cult of True Womanhood and the persona of the Gibson Girl.

Walker was born Ada Reed in 1880 on Cornelia Street in New York City. She began her formal dance training with Mrs. Thorp on Seventh Avenue and Thirty-fourth Street.[69] In 1896 Ada Overton Walker joined Bob Cole's All Stock Theater Company, and performed with them for two years as a dancer, actress, and singer.[70] In 1898 she joined Black Patti's Troubadours. Bob Cole also performed with the troop as Willy Wayside.[71] This proved a radical career choice given the negative perceptions surrounding theatrical women. Walker assumed the role of the definitive cultured African American female performer. She epitomized an alluring Gibson Girl and closely resembled her white replica in "Studies in Expression: The 'Chorus Girl's' Visit Home." Gibson envisaged this Gibson Girl from the chorus draped in pearls, a large feathered hat, and a beautiful gown, with her astonished family.[72] Ada Overton Walker at this early stage in her career possessed the style and glamour of Gibson's chorus girl. Her unique charisma and charm would lead African American theatrical critic Lester A. Walton to proclaim in 1908 that Walker was a "great artist," "a soubrette second to none in America and whose dancing marks her a genius no. 1."[73] Her experience with the Troubadours and Cole's ultimate imprisonment and censure left an indelible mark on Walker, who with Cole and his supporters discovered that the management of the Black Patti Troubadours conspired to blacklist them, as discussed in chapter 1. By supporting Bob Cole and demanding equal pay, Ada Overton Walker exhibited a strong sense of social justice, agency, and determination. This pivotal event most certainly informed her social thought and her strategy concerning racial uplift. Walker's home decorations also reflected her social and political ideology, and revealed her as a forward-thinking Gibson Girl. She displayed photographs of Frederick Douglass and Booker T. Washington, underscoring her modern and revolutionary philosophy concerning African American uplift.[74] Her loyalty to Bob Cole and her steadfastness in some ways replicated the Gibson Girls in "Rival Beauties," who brandished axes while radiating propriety."[75] In the vein of these Gibson Girls, Walker radiated decorum, charm, and refinement, while at the same time exhibiting a headstrong nature. Ada Overton Walker remained resolute in her beliefs and stood ready to go to battle for equity and justice.

The experience with Black Patti's Troubadours left an ineradicable imprint on Walker and most certainly taught her how to advocate for her rights. This incident colored the ways in which she would argue for the womanhood and civil rights of the African American female entertainer later in her career. Because of the episode with the Troubadours, Ada Overton Walker retired from the stage temporarily only to return later in 1898.[76] Walker joined the African American dancer Stella Wiley, Bob Cole's wife, and the African American blackface comedians Bert Williams and George Walker for a tobacco advertisement, which featured them cakewalking and led to Walker's return to the stage.[77] A producer wanted to present a show featuring the quartet cakewalking. Ada Overton Walker initially refused in part because of her bad experience with the Troubadours. She later relented and joined the Williams and Walker Company for New York performances only.[78] Walker's career blossomed and she was transformed into a famous soubrette, dancer, choreographer, singer, and producer within the Williams and Walker theatrical company.

Ada Overton Walker incorporated lessons learned from Bob Cole and publicly claimed ownership of her creative product as a choreographer and theatrical producer, shaping her image as that of an imposing, confident, yet poised Gibson Girl.[79] Walker performed in the tour of *Clorindy: or The Origin of the Cakewalk*, *The Octoroons* (1899), Williams and Walker's Policy Players (1899) as the choreographer, *Son of Ham* (1900), *The Cannibal King* (1901), *In Dahomey* (1902), *Abyssinia* (1906) as the choreographer and rehearsal director, *Bandanna Land* (1907) as the choreographer, *The Red Moon* (1908–1910), *His Honor The Barber* (1911), and the "Salome Dance"(1912) as the dancer and choreographer.[80]

While performing in these shows, Walker cultivated her Gibson Girl persona by coupling her work as an artist with strategies learned from her experience with the Black Patti's Troubadours to campaign for African American rights. She publicly addressed the experiences of African Americans who confronted racism both on stage and off and tackled the question of the love scene interdiction for African American performers. While she promoted African American rights, her creative talents also gained the notice of the press. The *Brooklyn Eagle* announced that she transcended the color line by performing with "grace and distinction of style which add a touch of Gallic eloquence to the work of Aida Overton Walker."[81] As the essence of the progressive African American Gibson Girl, Walker reached the zenith at her time.

Walker also incorporated her writings, her career, and photographic

Figure 28. Ada Overton Walker and the Gibson Gal.
Fisk University, Special Collections

Figure 29. "Mercy Hospital Benefit: Aida *[sic]*
Overton Walker in Vaudeville, March 26, 1910." Cullen
Jackman Memorial Collection. Special Collections and
Archives, Atlanta University

images of herself as part of her approach to uplifting African American women in the United States. In a photograph that accompanies an article written by Walker, she embodies the very essence of a Gibson Girl, as she looks directly at the camera with large, piercing black eyes (figure 28). Ada Overton Walker is stunning with her smooth dark brown skin, her hair piled high, her figure adorned with a beautiful crisp white blouse with mullet sleeves, a high neckline, and a silver brooch. Not only did she write articles as part of her strategy for elevating the status of African American women, she also participated in charity work to aid them (figure 29). She performed in the Charity Bee for the benefit of the White Rose Industrial Home, The Home for Protection of Colored Women, Mercy Hospital, and St. Philips Parish Home.[82] In her writings Ada Overton Walker also includes African American men in the project of uplifting African American women. Walker writes

> [African American men] have duties on and off the stage, to women as well as to yourselves. Remember this fact: good men help women to be good; and remember also, that in helping women you are really helping yourselves. We must work together in the uplift of all and for the progress of all that is good and noble in life.[83]

Including men in her uplift project, Walker maintains that this partnership will assure the success of not only African American theatrical women, but also the entire race. Walker also alludes to society's perception of stage life.

Ada Overton Walker addresses the negative connotations that the stage evinced during the 1900s. She suggests that some people such as "so-called [black] society people" perceive stage life as undignified and "regard the stage as a place to be ashamed of."[84] Walker proposes that performers in fact act as representatives of the race. Walker places herself above "society people" as an actress by saying that "[w]henever it is my good fortune to meet such persons, I sympathize with them for I know they are ignorant as to what is really being done in their own behalf by members of their race on stage."[85] By first displaying sympathy for the ignorant "so-called society people," and by placing herself above them, Walker demonstrates that society people remain unaware of the uplift agenda of artists.

In one fell swoop, Walker dignifies the African American female performer; reimagines her as respectable, cosmopolitan; and through her argument, illustrates the intelligence of the African American female performer. One could say that Walker places herself at the center of society as a "Gibson Girl." Through this form of self-representation, Ada Overton Walker annihilates the argument that stage life is a disreputable profession.

While one of Ada Overton Walker's concerns was the relationship between black society people and performers, she also involved herself with working to eradicate white racism. Fighting white racism seems most important to Ada Overton Walker's project of uplift. She considers that, "In this age we are all fighting the one problem—that is the color problem! I venture to think and dare to state that our profession does more toward the alleviation of color prejudice than any profession among colored people."[86]

Walker presents performers as freedom fighters whose success challenges racism. She notes that as part of the Williams and Walker Company, she performed and instructed the wealthy white class in the United States and in Europe, including King Edward VII and Lady Constance Mackenzie. Walker asserts, "I can truthfully state that my profession has given me entrée to residences which members of my race in other professions would have a hard task in gaining if ever they did."[87] By entrée into these circles Walker suggests that she and the Williams and Walker Company raised the level of African Americans to a prominent position through their positive representation of African American performers. Walker in effect transformed attitudes toward the theatrical profession to that of a highly regarded occupation. She contended that African Americans must show that they are as skilled as whites in all arenas, including the stage, and that the theatrical community must train great performers to "demonstrate that our people move along with the progress of the times." [88] This statement exposes Walker as a progressive and modern theorist concerning African American theater. Ultimately, she holds racism accountable for preventing African American performers from fully "moving along with the progress of the times." In the end, Walker reveals her idealistic and at the same time pragmatic nature and argues that African American entertainers would succeed fully in theater if given the opportunities.

Ada Overton Walker's most important intervention in the perceptions of African American women performers included arguing that the stage promoted the uplift of African American women and that their morals remained uncompromised. She asserted that "a woman does not lose her dignity to-day as used to be the case—when she enters upon stage life." Rather than blaming the "avocation," one must look at the reasons a woman chooses the stage life.[89] Walker insisted that the quality of the girl rather than the profession mattered, and predicted:

If a girl is gay and easily dazzled by the brilliant side of life on the Stage or off, then I should say to that girl: "Choose some other line of work; look to some other profession for the Stage is certainly no place for you." But if she be a girl of good thoughts and habits, and she chooses the stage for the love of the profession and professional work, then I should say to her, "Come, for we need so many earnest workers in this field; and by hard work, I am sure the future will repay you and all of us."[90]

Ada Overton Walker maintained that the quality of the girl rather than the nature of the profession mattered. Through her writing and her charity work, Ada Overton Walker situated herself at the center of womanhood as a Gibson girl and reinscribed the status of African American women on and off stage.

Taking a page out of Ada Overton's Walker's perception of stage life, Jessie Fauset's novel *Comedy American Style* (1933) introduces the very respectable, successful actress and dancer Marise Davies to the reader. Fauset portrays the stage as something favorable and emancipatory. The dark-skinned Marise with her "nut-brown skin with its hint of red on the cheek-bones" represents a sophisticate at the height of fashion, desirability, and reputability who took New York by storm as an entertainer.[91] In painting Marise as an extremely successful artist in New York, Fauset upgrades the perceptions of African American women on the stage. Marise in many ways epitomizes Ada Overton Walker. Marise marries the highly successful Nick, and this marriage symbolizes her respectability, middle-class values, and station in life.[92] Fauset, in this way, immortalized Walker. Ada Overton Walker crested as the iconic Gibson Girl; her career stands as a record of her unstinting efforts to exalt African American women and the stage.

Ada Overton Walker, Abbie Mitchell, and an Audience with the King

The year 1903 proved pivotal for Ada Overton Walker and Abbie Mitchell, who continued their transformation into Gibson Girls. Their connections with the Williams and Walker production of *In Dahomey* in London allowed them to fully embrace the image of the Gibson Girl as their personas.

The popularity of *In Dahomey* and the adventures of the cast members in Europe caused quite a stir, given the numerous articles written detailing the popularity of the show and the performers' escapades. The musical offered audiences the story of Shylock Homestead (Bert Williams) and Rareback Pinkerton (George Walker), detectives hired by Mr. Cicero Lightfoot for a reward of $500 to search for his silver box with an etching of a cat. Because they cannot find the box, Homestead and Pinkerton present Lightfoot with a counterfeit box and collect the reward. With the recompense in hand, the detectives travel to Dahomey with the African Colonization Society. In the end, the original box is recovered, Lightfoot finds a pot of gold and gains wealth, and Pinkerton and Shylock become the kings of Dahomey. Ada Overton Walker portrayed Rosetta Lightfoot and sang "Vassar Girl" and "I Want to Be an Actor Lady" in the show.[93]

Ada Overton Walker and Abbie Mitchell used the stage to change the perceptions of African American women through their 1903 audience with King Edward VII of England. Walker appeared in Williams and Walker's *In Dahomey* at the Shaftsbury Theater, while Abbie Mitchell accompanied her husband, Will Marion Cook, the composer of the show.[94]

Abbie Mitchell remembered her initial exclusion from the performance for the king at Buckingham Palace, but she recalled that "[t]he King's coat of arms with coachman and footman [arrived] at my home in Regents Park" and [t]he King held up [the] performance until I arrived."[95] By bestowing on her this grand honor, the king symbolically ennobled Mitchell, and she submerged herself fully in the experience and surfaced graciously to accept the emblematic regal title conferred upon her. Mitchell recalled, "I remembered that I was now a great lady, so I put on all the airs I knew and walked with dignity, I hope to the carriage."[96] Thus the experience transformed Mitchell into a "great lady." Influenced by the affirming reception and the deference displayed to her by the king, Mitchell constructed a public identity as a lady, by embodying all the attributes of The Cult of True Womanhood and the Gibson Girl: deference, innocence, purity, and virtue.

Abbie Mitchell crafted a majestic persona as a Gibson Girl that forever linked her to the monumental event. She incorporated the audience into her legend as a performer, and her publicity notices and biographies in playbills announced that she sang before King Edward VII and the queen.[97] Mitchell also used her status as a lady to advocate for the rights of African American women, by performing in benefit concerts for the White Rose Industrial Home for Colored Girls and participating in the African American Women's Club movement.[98]

Jo A. Tanner argues that when Mitchell reached her forties, her training and her uncompromising need for perfection dictated her behavior. Reminiscent of royalty, she did not socialize or form friendship bonds with those she worked with. Similar to the monarchs, she struck fear in both African American and white colleagues; her Mitchellesque persona led her to "possess a sharp tongue, which she wielded like a weapon."[99] Her early life experiences informed her strong personage, which safeguarded her from harmful outside forces. Abbie Mitchell's autobiographical notes indicate that at this early point in her life she developed a steely attitude and created a strong mechanism for self-preservation. This indestructible spirit in some respects replicated the image of the aloof Gibson Girl "Waiting for Tables at the Waldorf." This Gibson Girl who sits demurely, while at the same time looking intently and impassively at the viewer, conveys the traits that Abbie Mitchell adopted at the age of thirteen to fortify and protect herself from hostile forces.[100] This Gibson Girl façade would follow her throughout her life and would dictate her reserved interactions with people she worked with both on Broadway and in Harlem with the Lafayette Players in the 1920s and 1930s.

Ada Overton Walker also discovered that the king and the English treated her deferentially. Walker gained social prominence in the United States and England as a result of her performance in the show *In Dahomey* at the Shaftsbury, but her performance before the king of England worked to elevate her class position as a lady. Upon their return to the United States, the Williams and Walker Troupe became the toast of New York City as a result of their triumph at the Shaftesbury Theater. Ada Overton Walker learned that some of the white upper classes in the United States considered her a lady and treated her reverentially. One notable example was Walker's encounter with the white southerner Mr. Robert L. Hargous, who belonged to the upper crust of New York society.

On May 3, 1903, Mr. and Mrs. Robert L. Hargous hired the *In Dahomey* company, Ada Overton Walker, and her husband, George Walker, to entertain General Sir Arthur Paget and his American-born wife, Lady Paget, at Delmonico's.[101] To the dismay of some of the guests, Hargous actually introduced Ada Overton Walker, joined her in the cakewalk, and invited her to waltz. Hargous's treatment of Walker caused a racial incident, with the *New York Sun* reporting "some of the women guests thought it was time to leave, and the party did break up shortly afterward."[102]

Richard Newman argues that the incident became the talk of the town, and he surmised that Hargous quite possibly "crossed the color line by treating a black woman virtually as a guest and equal."[103] Newman also suggests that the wives at the event exhibited jealousy and resented the attention their husbands paid to Ada Overton Walker. While Walker promoted her womanhood and middle-class position, the *New York Sun* maligned her by referring to her in derogatory terms.[104] The members of the white upper class and some of the New York papers disapproved of Hargous's deference to Walker; the *New York Times* suggested that Hargous's behavior "made Mrs. Walker . . . a fad of the season."[105] Despite the print media and society folk who attempted to dismiss Ada Overton Walker as unworthy of reverential treatment, the audience with the king repositioned Walker's place in United States society. The very fact that *The New York Times* referred to her as Mrs. Walker, whether in jest or not, attests to the shift in her rank.

Conclusion

Performing in front of the king of England in London reconfigured Ada Overton Walker's and Abbie Mitchell's place in U.S. society, and positioned them at the pinnacle of upper middle-class standing, aspiration, and woman-hood rights. In addition, performing in front of the king worked to erase the taint associated with the stage and helped to configure theatrical work as respectable. In response to the question of how the king treated her, Walker aptly noted that the king treated her as any king would treat another, which exhibits not only wit, but also her thoughts on her social position.

Influenced by the affirming reception and the deference displayed to them by the king of England, Abbie Mitchell and Ada Overton Walker used their audience to elevate their status in U.S. society and legitimate the African American theatrical woman. Finally, both women successfully constructed an identity which combined all the attributes of the Gibson Girl to demand womanhood rights and respectability as stage performers during a time when U.S. society denied these very rights to African American women. Through the iconic image of the Gibson Girl, the marriage right, the women's club movement, religion, and education, Abbie Mitchell, Ada Overton Walker, the women of *The Red Moon*, Cole and Johnson, and the African American print media endeavored to glorify African American women. Cole and John-son reconfigured the Gibson Girl to that of a chorus of Gibson Gals to claim womanhood rights for African American women on and off the stage, while James Weldon Johnson and Grace Nail shaped her public persona into that of the Gibson Girl. Through their public and private personas, Ada Overton Walker and Abbie Mitchell became the agents of their own lives by fully inhabiting the Cult of True Womanhood, molding themselves into quintes-sential African American women. Through unremitting agency, political activism, and their audience before the king of England they demanded in no uncertain terms the rights of woman for themselves and their sisters.

Cole and Johnson infused their musicals and their lives with one of the most essential tropes of uplift—education. They coupled the ideology of Booker T. Washington and W. E. B. Du Bois and set their philosophies firmly into their musicals and their lives. By adopting the ideologies of these two seemingly discordant figures' philosophies, the team created musical theater imbued with Du Bois and Washington's educational goals and those established at Atlanta University, Tuskegee Institute, and Hampton Institute. Because they loved and admired the women in their families, respected theatrical women and those women they met at school, Cole and Johnson easily embraced Washington's Womanist strategy as their own, and seamlessly weaved African American women into their theatrical, political, and social ideology. By including tropes of masculinity—the iconic Jack Johnson and the hypermasculine übermensch persona, sports, the gallant African American soldiers of the Spanish American war, and the conquest of the West, Cole and Johnson changed the image of African American men. This change resounds into the twenty-first century through champions such as Paul Robeson, Muhammad Ali, and Arthur Ashe.

While Cole and Johnson's flaws appeared in a number of stereotypical representations of African Americans and Native Americans, they did in fact change the theatrical map for African Americans by incorporating African American, Native American, and Filipino romantic love in their stage presentations; by including the dauntless African American soldiers of the Spanish American War; by infusing education into their musicals; and by humanizing African American men and women through the manliness movement and the iconic Gibson Girl in so many of their characters. These were incredible accomplishments for their historical milieu, so noteworthy in fact that they influenced a generation of African American writers, directors, performers, and producers.

EPILOGUE

CCORDING TO THE July 1908 *The Colored American Magazine,* Cole and Johnson's strategy for avoiding the types of financial difficulties they encountered with *Shoo Fly Regiment* included trying to book *The Red Moon* in large houses. The team, however, faced an insurmountable obstacle. White producers and booking agents remained unwilling to book black shows into first-rate theaters.[1] The blocking of Cole and Johnson's *The Red Moon* from first-rate theaters contributed to the closing of the show.

The Red Moon met with moderate success with houses packed in cities such as Chicago and Washington, D.C. The show closed in Washington on May 14, 1910 after playing successfully there.[2] Cole and Johnson retired temporarily from musical comedy but then, according to Bob Cole, made plans to produce a new show, *Phoebe Brown,* which would star Ada Overton Walker.[3] The theater owners Stair and Havlin assured the team that their new show would only play in their first-class theaters around the country, but Stair and Havlin reversed themselves, and offered the team second-class theaters instead.[4] Lester A. Walton suggested that because Stair and Havlin had begun leasing their first-class theaters for the showing of movies, the increasing popularity of the moving picture industry caused some of the problems Cole and Johnson experienced in terms of booking their new show. Because of Stair and Havlin's reversal, Cole and Johnson canceled their plans for the new show for the fall of 1910.[5]

J. Rosamond Johnson and Bob Cole attempted to return to vaudeville after *The Red Moon* closed, but Cole became ill and they subsequently retired from vaudeville. Cole died on August 2, 1911. After his death J.

Rosamond Johnson embarked on a solo vaudeville career in London, and James Weldon Johnson continued his work as the consul of Nicaragua and Venezuela. He eventually became the secretary of the NAACP. The death of Bob Cole marked the end of the Cole and Johnson team.[6]

In 1913 James Weldon Johnson hoped to continue his career as a diplomat, but the United States blocked his ambitions because of their unwillingness to send an African American man to the Azores. J. Rosamond Johnson left the United States for England in the hopes of building a career in the theater that he could not have in the United States. On May 13, 1913, James Weldon Johnson wrote a response to J. Rosamond Johnson who asked for his advice about whether he should remain in England and send for his pregnant wife Nora. Johnson's letter offers a commentary on the United States and its relationship to African Americans. James Weldon Johnson wrote, "[f]rom my point of view, if I was going to be his daddy I'd have him born an Englishman; for there's nothing in being an American of colored hue."[7] This comment expresses the frustrations and difficulties that African Americans encountered during the early part of the twentieth century when their hopes remained so high for the future but they were defeated by structural racism at every turn.

Several forms of black musical theater emerged after Cole and Johnson's career came to a close in 1910. These included musical theater, which relied on minstrel forms, revues, and multiracial musicals. The book musical became a rare commodity with the appearance of these new forms of musical theater, and blacks, for the most part, lost control of black musical theater. In *Black Manhattan* James Weldon Johnson concluded that with the end of the Cole and Johnson musicals came a period in black theater which he called the "term of exile." Johnson asserted that black theater faced exile from downtown New York theaters from 1910 to 1917, resulting in a thriving theater in Harlem which catered exclusively to black audiences.[8] During the "term of exile" black performers found themselves free from the constraints placed upon them when playing in front of white audiences, allowing them to dismiss the minstrel forms.[9] Dramatic theater companies such as The Lafayette Players and the Lincoln Players performed melodramas with *Shoo Fly Regiment* and *The Red Moon* alumni Abbie Mitchell and Inez Clough, who both appeared with The Lafayette Players. The "term of exile" ended on April 5, 1917, when the Colored Players appeared at the Garden Theater in a series of plays by white author Ridgely Torrence, which in effect marked the beginning of white control over black theatrical representations.[10] A black show would not appear on Broadway for another four years, not until 1921, when black composers and writers Sissle and Blake's *Shuffle Along* appeared.

NOTES

Introduction

1. James Weldon Johnson, "What Atlanta University Has Done for Me," *The Bulletin of Atlanta University* 64 (April 1895), Atlanta University Center, Robert W. Woodruff Library. 1.

2. Lizabeth Cohen, *Making a New Deal: Industrial Workers in Chicago 1919–1939* (New York, Port Chester and Melbourne, Sydney: Cambridge University Press, 1990), 5.

3. Ibid.

4. In 1904 Cole and Johnson's contemporary, theatrical critic Sylvester Russell, proposed that black shows should include black women of every color. The team followed his suggestion (Helen Armstead-Johnson, "Some Late Information on Some Early People." *Encore American and World Wide News*, 23 June 1975, 48–55. The Schomburg Center for Research in Black Culture 1971, 52).

Chapter One

1. Lester A. Walton, "The Death of Bob Cole," *New York Age*, 10 August 1911; Stella Wiley Scrapbook, James Weldon Johnson Papers, Yale Collection of American Literature, Beinecke Rare Book and Manuscript Library, Yale University. The Negro in the Theatre: XI Scrapbook.

2. Jewell Plummer Cobb, April 24, 2003, interview.

3. Carriebel C. Plummer, "Under the Bamboo Tree: The Bob Cole Story," n.d., 11. Jewell Plummer Cobb Collection; Thomas Laurence Riis, "Black Musical Theatre in New York, 1890–1915," Ph.D. diss., University of Michigan, 1981; Walton, "The Death of Bob Cole"; Henry T. Sampson, *Blacks in Blackface: A Sourcebook on Early Black Shows* (Metuchen, NJ, and London: The Scarecrow Press, 1980), 66.

4. Plummer, "Under the Bamboo Tree," 11.

5. Ibid., 6; Walton, "The Death of Bob Cole"; Riis, "Black Musical Theatre," 51;

Sampson. *Blacks in Blackface,* 66.

6. Plummer, "Under the Bamboo Tree," 12; Riis, "Black Musical Theatre," 52.

7. Plummer, "Under the Bamboo Tree," 12; Carriebel C. Plummer, "What's in a Song: Highlights of a Songwriter's Career as Told by His Sister," 6, The Leigh Whipper Papers, MSS 47, box 1, Manuscripts and Rare Books Collection, The Schomburg Center for Research in Black Culture.

8. W. E. B. Du Bois, *Black Reconstruction in America* (New York: Athenaeum, 1935), 700.

9. Plummer, "What's in a Song," 7.

10. Riis, "Black Musical Theatre," 52.

11. Plummer, "Under the Bamboo Tree," 2.

12. Walton, "The Death of Bob Cole"; Riis, "Black Musical Theatre," 52; *Bulletin of Atlanta University,* 1903, Atlanta University Center, Robert W. Woodruff Library, Atlanta Georgia; *Colored American* 3 (June 1901): 139–40, Fisk University Special Collections, Nashville, Tennessee.

James Hatch, Erroll G. Hill, and others maintain that Cole worked at Atlanta University and did not attend the school. I contend that the *Bulletin* of *Atlanta University* and the sources cited above point to the conclusion that he attended AU (James Hatch and Errol G. Hill, *A History of African American Theatre* [Cambridge, Cambridge University Press, 2003], 156).

13. Stella Wiley's scrapbook, the 1911 *New York Age,* the *New York Times,* and scholars Thomas Riis, Allen Woll, Errol G. Hill, James Hatch, and Karen Sotiropoulos all confirm that Wiley married Bob Cole. The scrapbook states, "Stella Wiley was wife of Bob Cole. Gave her book to Jim for *Black Manhattan* facts. Grace. To Carl. Sept. 11" (Wiley Scrapbook, Walton, "The Death of Bob Cole"; "Robert Cole A Suicide," *The New York Times,* 3 August 1911; Riis, "Black Musical Theatre," 52; Allen Woll, *Black Musical Theater: From Coontown to Dreamgirls* (New York: DaCapo Paperback, 1991), 5; Hatch and Hill, *A History,* 156; Karen Sotiropoulos, *Staging Race* (Cambridge, MA: Harvard University Press, 2006), 46, 186.

14. Plummer, "Under the Bamboo Tree," 2; Sylvester Russell, "Cole Gives Private Lecture," *The Indianapolis Freeman,* 7 October 1905 (page number cut from microfilm).

15. Leigh Whipper Papers, box 114–5 folder 125, "The Negro Actor's Guild Scoreboard," 71, Moorland Spingarn Research Center, Howard University.

16. Mercer Cook Papers, box 157–4, Mercer Cook, "From Clorindy to 'The Red Moon' and Beyond." Paper presented on October 26, 1978, 18. Moorland-Spingarn Research Center, Howard University.

17. James Weldon Johnson, *Black Manhattan* (New York: Athenaeum, 1930), 98.

18. Thomas L. Riis, *Just Before Jazz: Black Musical Theater in New York, 1890–1915* (Washington, D.C.: Smithsonian Institution Press, 1989), 26, 28; Sotiropoulos, *Staging Race,* 38.

19. Wiley: n.d., B. Wiley Scrapbook; D: Cook, Will Marion, "The Black Patti Troubadours: The Best Colored Company on the Road Notes and Comments." Newspaper article about Cole and Johnson by Will Marion Cook. N.d. Johnson, James Weldon. James Weldon Johnson Collection. Beinecke Rare Book and Manuscript Library, Yale University.

20. Wiley: n.d., B. Wiley Scrapbook; Johnson, *Black Manhattan,* 102: E: "Seized Black Patti Music." Newspaper article about Bob Cole's financial disagreement with the Black Patti Troubadours. N.d. Johnson, James Weldon. James Weldon Johnson Collection. Beinecke Rare Book and Manuscript Library, Yale University.

21. William Foster, "Pioneers of the Stage," *The Official Theatrical World of Colored Artists National Directory and Guide* 1, no. 1 [April 1928]: 48, Black Culture collection contents by Reel, UCSD Geisel Library.

22. Foster, "Pioneers of the Stage," 48–49; Riis, "Black Musical Theatre," 140–41.

23. Foster, 48–49.

24. The relationship between Du Bois, Cole, and his family proved longstanding. Dora Cole Norman, Cole's sister, helped Du Bois produce the *Star of Ethiopia Pageant* in Philadelphia around 1916. W. E. B. Du Bois, "The Drama Among Black Folk," *The Crisis* 12, no. 4 (August 1916): 173.

25. Foster, "Pioneers of the Stage," 48.

26. Ibid., 48.

27. *A Trip to Coontown* Program, Grand Opera House, 1898. The Museum of the City of New York.

28. Bernard Peterson, *African American Theater Directory* (Westwood, CT: Greenwood Press, 1997), 12–13.

Performers who worked with Cole maintained longstanding professional relationships, performing together in *Porgy and Bess,* the Lafayette Players, and the Pekin Theater, Chicago. The majority of them also belonged to the Negro Actors Guild (1904–1982). Clara and Pauline Freeman, Jesse Ship, and Sam Lucas appeared with Cole in the Black Patti's Troubadours and *A Trip to Coontown.* Shipp and Inez Clough worked with J. Rosamond Johnson in *Oriental America.* Clough, Lucas, Theodore and Anna Cook Pankey, Andrew Tribble and Bessie Tribble, Fanny Wise, Edgar Connors, Sam Lucas, William Phelps, Mollie Dill, Daisy Brown, Maymie Butler, Henry Gant, Lula Coleman, Wesley Jenkins, Frank DeLyons, Rebecca Allen, and Elizabeth Williams appeared in *Shoo Fly Regiment* and *The Red Moon* (Edward A. Robinson, "The Pekin: The Genesis of American Black Theater," *Black American Literature Forum* 16, no. 4, Black Theatre Issue [Winter 1982]: 137; Negro Actors Guild of America Booklet, 1946–1961. Lester A. Walton Papers Entertainment Career, Coordinating Council for Negro Performers, box 6, MG, 183, folder 8, Rare Books and Manuscripts Collection, The Schomburg Center for Research in Black Culture; Abbie Mitchell, Mercer Cook Papers, box 157–7, folder 29, folder 24, Moorland-Spingarn Research Center, Howard University; *Shoo Fly Regiment* program; Robinson Locke Collection, Lincoln Center Library for the Performing Arts, 1906; *New York Age,* January 28, 1909, 6; *New York Age,* August 26, 1909, 6; Foster, "Pioneers of the Stage," 1; Sotiropoulos, *Staging Race,* 132).

29. *Colored American,* June 1901, Vol. III: 139–40, Fisk University Special Collections, Nashville, Tennessee.

30. *A Trip to Coontown* program; David Krasner, *Resistance, Parody, and Double Consciousness in African American Theatre, 1895–1910* (New York: St. Martin's Press, 1997), 30.

31. Krasner, *Resistance, Parody, and Double Consciousness,* 130. Both Hatch and Hill maintain that Cole performed Willie Wayside in whiteface as a form of defiance, and Carriebel Plummer argues that Cole performed sans cork and originated the Kirk

Soap Tramp. An image of Cole as Willie Wayside appears in *Black Magic: A Pictorial History of the Negro in American Entertainment* as white with reddish hair, confirming that Cole's performance was in whiteface (Hatch and *Hill, A History,* 156; Carriebel Plummer, *Biographical Sketch,* n.d., Jewell Plummer Cobb Collection; Langston Hughes, *Black Magic: A Pictorial History of the Negro in American Entertainment* [New Jersey: Prentice-Hall, Inc., 1967], 52).

32. Camille F. Forbes, "Dancing with Racial Feet: Bert Williams and the Performance of Blackness," *Theater Journal* 56, no. 4 (December 2004): 604; Hatch and Hill, *A History,* 97, 104.

33. Plummer, "Under the Bamboo Tree."

34. Plummer, "What's in a Song,"10.

35. Wiley: n.d., C. Wiley Scrapbook.

36. J. Rosamond Johnson, *Rolling Along in Song* (New York: Viking Press, 1937), 14. Sotiropoulos, *Staging Race,* 82.

37. Henry T. Sampson, *The Ghost Walks: A Chronological History of Blacks in Show Business 1865–1910* (Metuchen, NJ: The Scarecrow Press, Inc., 1988), 101.

38. Ibid., 103.

39. Ann Charters suggests that if Bert Williams had refused to blacken up he would not have gained theatrical success (Ann Charters, *Nobody* [London: MacMillan Company, 1970], 14; Nathan Irvin Huggins, *Harlem Renaissance* [Oxford: Oxford University Press, 1971], 250).

40. Plummer, "Under the Bamboo Tree," 2; Russell, "Cole Gives Private Lecture," *The Indianapolis Freeman* 7 (October 1905) (page number cut from microfilm).

41. Wiley, n.d., C. Wiley Scrapbook.

42. William Durbin, *Yale Daily News,* 20 February 1999, 1–2; Marc Wiznia, *Yale Daily News,* 17 November 2000, 1; Diane Scarponi, *South Coast Today,* 19 November 2000, 2; Sigmund Spaeth, *The History of Popular Music* (New York: Random House, 1948), 292; Plummer, "Under The Bamboo Tree,"10; Riis, *Just Before Jazz,* 83–84.

43. Plummer, "Under the Bamboo Tree," 9.

44. James Weldon Johnson, *Along This Way: The Autobiography of James Weldon Johnson* (New York: Viking Press, 1933), 5.

45. ASCAP: n.d., J. Rosamond Johnson Obituary, *New York Times,* "J. R. Johnson, 81, Composer, Dead,"1954. Billy Rose Collection, Lincoln Center Library for the Performing Arts, New York City.

46. E. Franklin Frazier, *Black Bourgeoisie: The Rise of a New Middle Class* (New York: Free Press, 1957), 11–12, 20.

47. Kevin G. Gaines, *Uplifting the Race: Black Leadership, Politics, and Culture in the Twentieth Century* (Chapel Hill: University of North Carolina Press, 1996), 14.

48. Frazier. *Black Bourgeoisie,* 26.

49. Willard B. Gatewood, *The Aristocrats of Color: The Black Elite, 1880–1920* (Bloomington:, Indiana University Press, 1990), 50.

50. *Colored American,* n.d., James Weldon Johnson Papers, G: Earle, Victoria. *The Colored American.* Washington, D.C. N.D. Johnson, James Weldon. James Welcon Johnson Collection. Beinecke Rare Book and Manuscript Library, Yale University.

51. Johnson, *Along This Way,* 64.

52. Gatewood, *Aristocrats of Color,* 176–77.

53. Huggins, *Harlem Renaissance,* 22–23. Louise Thompson Patterson (1901–1999) was a communist, a social worker, and the founder of the Harlem Suitcase Theater who married the prominent Black communist lawyer William Patterson (Mark Naison, *Communists in Harlem during the Depression* [New York: Grove Press, 1983], 42–43, 67–68, 70, 72, 74, 136, 144, 145, 179, 182, 218).

54. Johnson, *Along This Way,* 141.

55. James Weldon Johnson: n.d., A: "Lynch Laws in the South"; C: *Lutheran Courier.* Oldest Scrapbook, James Weldon Johnson Papers, Yale Collection of American Literature, Beinecke Rare Books and Manuscripts Library, Yale University.

56. Johnson, "What Atlanta University Has Done for Me."

57. *The Bulletin of Atlanta University,* May 1894, 41. Atlanta University Center, Robert W. Woodruff Library.

58. James Weldon Johnson, George A. Towns Papers, box 2, folder 12, December 30, 1896, Special Collections, Atlanta University Center, Robert W. Woodruff Library.

59. James Weldon Johnson, George A. Towns Papers, box 2, folder 12, May 14, 1914, Special Collections, Atlanta University Center, Robert W. Woodruff Library.

60. *Bulletin of Atlanta University,* no. 56, May 1892; *Bulletin of Atlanta University,* June 1894, 1; *Bulletin of Atlanta University,* no. 38 (June 1892): 2, Atlanta University Center, Robert W. Woodruff Library.

61. *Bulletin of Atlanta University,* no. 51, December 1893, 8, Atlanta University Center, Robert W. Woodruff Library.

62. Wiley, n.d., E: Wiley Scrapbook; Jacksonville newpaper that announced James Weldon Johnson's resignation from the Stanton School, n.d. Johnson, James Weldon. Johnson Collection. Beinecke Rare Book and Manuscript Library. James Weldon Johnson Biography, James Weldon Johnson Collection, Fisk University Special Collections. In 2005 I visited the Stanton School and discovered that the school is now a highly competitive college preparatory school with a majority white student body.

63. James Weldon Johnson, B: *Daily American* newspaper, n.d., James Weldon Johnson Papers, Yale Collection of American Literature, Beinecke Rare Books and Manuscripts Library, Yale University; James Weldon Johnson Collection, Fisk University Special Collections, Nashville, Tennessee; Wiley, n.d., E.: Wiley Scrapbook; Russel Crouse, "One of Gershwin's Actors Has Some Tunes to His Credit Too," *New York Herald Tribune,* 22 December 1935, box 7, 21, Scrapbook 1930s miscellaneous, James Weldon Johnson Papers. Yale Collection of American Literature, Beinecke Rare Book and Manuscript Library; Yale University, box 2, Scrapbook 1, The Stage 1905–1910, James Weldon Johnson Papers, Yale Collection of American Literature, Beinecke Rare Book and Manuscript Library.

64. The song was published in 1900.

65. Johnson, *Along This Way,* 154; Crouse, "One of Gershwin's Actors"; Wiley, n.d. D. Wiley Scrapbook.

66. "Atlanta University Edition of Lift Every Voice and Sing," J. W. Johnson Collection, box 2, folder 28, James Weldon Johnson Collection, Special Collections Department, Robert W. Woodruff Library, Emory University; George A. Towns Papers, box 2, folder 12, Atlanta University Center, Special Collections, Robert F. Woodruff Library; f: "From Sunday School to Stage." Newspaper article about Cole and Johnson's musical writing practices. Johnson, James Weldon. James Weldon Johnson Collection. Beinecke Rare Book and Manuscript Library, Yale University.

67. Johnson, *Along This Way,* 154–55; Julian Bond and Sandra Kathyrn Wilson, *Lift Every Voice and Sing* (New York: Random House, 2000), xix.

68. J. W. Johnson Collection. "Atlanta University Edition," Bond and Wilson, *Lift Every Voice,* 3–4.

69. *Bulletin of Atlanta University,* no. 93, June 1898, 1, Atlanta University Center, Robert F. Woodruff Library, Clark Atlanta University.

70. Isham produced *Oriental America* from 1896 to 1897 for high-quality houses. According to William Foster it was the first black show produced on Broadway. It featured a large professional black cast, including Inez Clough and Jessie Shipp. The show discarded the minstrel format and offered audiences an extravagant spectacle, with operatic selections, beautiful costumes, beautiful sets, and special lighting effects (Foster, "Pioneers of the Stage," 40; Riis, *Just before Jazz,* 22; Woll, *Black Musical Theater,* 5).

71. ASCAP, n.d. J. Rosamond Johnson Papers, "J.R. Johnson, 81, Composer, Dead," 1954; Wiley, n.d. D, Wiley Scrapbook.

72. Luzviminda Francisco, "The Philippine-American War," 8–21, in *The Philippines Reader: A History of Colonialism Neocolonialism, Dictatorship and Resistance,* ed. by Daniel B. Schirmer and Stephen Rosskamm Shalom (Boston: South End Press, 1987), 9–21; *Colored American:* August 1909, 123, Special Collections, Fisk University Library, Nashville, Tennessee; Rienzi B. Lemus, Company K, Twenty-fifth Infantry, "The Enlisted Man in Action or, The Colored American Soldier in the Philippines," *Colored American,* no. 5 (May 1902), Special Collections, Fisk University Library, Nashville, Tennessee, 46–54; Lemus, "The Negro and the Philippines," *Colored American* 6, no. 4 (February 1903), Special Collections, Fisk University Library, Nashville, Tennessee, 314–18; Sergeant Carney, "Sergeant Carney," *Colored American* 7 (10 October 1904), Special Collections, Fisk University Library, Nashville, Tennessee, 636.

73. Cole and Johnson, *New York Age,* December 24, 1910.

74. Johnson, *Along This Way,* 149–50, 179, 187; Walter White, "A Biographical Sketch by Walter White, Exec Secy., NAACP," James Weldon Johnson Collection, Fisk University Special Collections.

75. Ella Shohat and Robert Stam, *Unthinking Eurocentrism* (New York: Routledge, 1994), 180–81.

76. Jacqui Malone, *Steppin' On the Blues* (Urbana and Chicago: University of Illinois Press, 1996), 51–52.

77. Deborah Gray White, *Ar'n't I A Woman? Female Slaves in the Plantation South* (New York and London: W.W. Norton & Company, 1985), 28–29.

78. Peter Stallybrass and Allon White, *The Politics and Poetics of Transgression* (Ithaca, NY: Cornell University Press, 1986), 191–93; Robert C. Allen, *Horrible Prettiness* (Chapel Hill and London: University of North Carolina Press, 1991), 26.

79. Ibid. At the forefront of United States media representations are hypersexualized animalistic Jezebels in the films *American Gangster* (2007), *Hustle and Flow* (2006), and *Monster's Ball* (2001); asexual mammies in *Bringing Down the House* (2003); masculinized Mammies in *Chicago* (2003); and the Mammyesque television host Sherri Shepard on the *View,* who boasts about her criminal record. Broadway shows such as *Marie Christine* (2000), rap songs such as "Cameltoe" by Fanny Pack, and rap artists such as Lil' Kim further propagate stereotypes. (Elvis Mitchell, "How Out of It Can You Be? Here's Going All the Way. Review of 'Bringing Down the House,'" *New York Times,* 7

March 2003; *The View* (1997–present); Kelefa Sanneh, "Fashion Tip in Rap for Brooklyn Girls," *New York Times,* 23 May 2003; Lynette Holloway, "Media; Lil' Kim Surprises Critics as CD Catches On," *New York Times,* 17 March 2003.

80. Americo Paredes, *With His Pistol in His Hand* (Austin: University of Texas Press, 1958), 20.

81. Hazel V. Carby, *Reconstructing Womanhood: The Emergence of the Afro-American Woman Novelist* (Oxford: Oxford University Press, 1987), 22.

82. Stanley J. Lemons, "Black Stereotypes as Reflected in Popular Culture, 1880–1920," *American Quarterly* 29, no. 1 (Spring 1977): 102.

83. Ibid.

84. George Lipsitz, *Time Passages: Collective Memory and American Popular Culture* (Minneapolis: University of Minnesota Press, 1990), 9.

85. William J. Mahar, *Behind the Burnt Cork Mask: Early Blackface Minstrelsy and Antebellum American Popular Culture* (Urbana and Chicago: University of Illinois Press, 1999), 332–33, 343.

86. Ibid., 332; Hatch and Hill, *A History,* 104; Malone, *Steppin' on the Blues,* 51–52; Eric Ledell Smith, *Bert Williams: A Biography of the Pioneer Black Comedian* (Jefferson, NC, and London: McFarland & Company, 1992), 11; Huggins, *Harlem Renaissance,* 250–51.

87. John Waters, Leslie Dixon, Mark O'Donnell, and Thomas Meehan, *Hairspray* (2007); Jerry Lewis, Bill Richmond, David Sheffield, Barry W. Blaustein, Tom Shadyac, and Steve Oederkerk, *The Nutty Professor* (1996).

88. Robert C. Toll, *Blacking Up: The Minstrel Show in Nineteenth-Century America* (New York: Oxford University Press, 1974), 36, 54, 67.

89. Huggins, *Harlem Renaissance,* 253–54, 257.

90. David Krasner, "The Mirror up to Nature: Modernist Aesthetics and Racial Authenticity in African American Theatre, 1895–1900," *Theatre History Studies* 16 (June 1996): 120–21.

91. Du Bois, "The Drama among Black Folk," 171; W. E. B. Du Bois, "Criteria of Negro Art," *The Crisis* 32, no. 6 (October 1920): 296; Lisa M. Anderson, *Mammies No More: The Changing Image of Black Women on Stage and Screen* (Lanham: Rowman & Littlefield, 1997), 6; Rena Fraden, "A National Negro Theater That Never Was: A History of African American Theater Production, Performance and Drama in the US," *American Visions* 9, no. 5 (October–November 1994): 2.

Du Bois's call to action remained unremitting. In 1913 he proposed that blacks should develop a new "Negro drama" to teach their history, humanity, and emotional life. By 1926 his views evolved as he coupled black creative production, beauty, civil rights, and propaganda together. He used his writings as "propaganda for gaining the right of black folk to love and enjoy," and proposed that black artists should do the same. In 1926 Du Bois reflected on people's response to "black" Americans if by 1926 the only representations in literature and theater that existed were stereotypes created by whites and proposed that blacks *must* generate their own Afrocentric projects infused with "the kind of people you know and like and imagine" (Du Bois, "The Drama Among Black Folk," 171; Du Bois, "Criteria of Negro Art," 296). Cole and Johnson preceded Du Bois in advancing these ideas and remained in the vanguard of developing a strategy of racial uplift through theater.

92. James Weldon Johnson, *The Autobiography of an Ex-Coloured Man* (New York: Garden City Publishing, 1912), 210–11.

93. Q: Conkling Roscoe Simmons, "Afro American in the Musical World," *New York Age*, n.d., Wiley Scrapbook. James Weldon Johnson Collection. Beinecke Rare Book and Manuscript Library, Yale University.

94. Pauline Hopkins, "Famous Men of the Negro Race. Booker T. Washington," *Colored American* 3, no. 6 (October 1901): 438; letter to Francis Garrison, from Booker T. Washington, January 10, 1906, Booker T. Washington Collection MG 182, box 1, Manuscripts, Archives, and Rare Books Division, The Schomburg Center for Research in Black Culture.

95. Rayford W. Logan, *The Negro in American Life and Thought: The Nadir 1877–1901* (New York: Dial Press, Inc., 1954), 277; Booker T. Washington, *Up From Slavery: An Autobiography of Booker T. Washington* (New York: Bantam, Doubleday, Doran & Company, 1901); Harold Cruse, *The Crisis of the Negro Intellectual* (New York: William Morrow & Company, Inc., 1967), 558.

96. Letter to Francis J. Garrison from Booker T. Washington, 31 August 1903, Booker T. Washington Collection MG 182, box 1, Manuscripts, Archives, and Rare Books Division, The Schomburg Center for Research in Black Culture.

97. Ibid.

98. Manning Marable, *W. E. B. Du Bois, Black Radical Democrat* (Boston: Twayne Publishers, 1986), 30; Louis H. Harlan and Raymond W. Smock, *The Booker T. Washington Papers Volume 7, 1903–1904* (Urbana: University of Illinois Press, 1977), 455–56.

99. *The Crisis* 1, no. 1 (November 1910): 5; Gatewood, *Aristocrats of Color,* 313.

100. David Levering Lewis, *W. E. B. Du Bois: Biography of a Race, 1868–1919* (New York: John McCrae Book, Henry Holt and Company, 1993), 321–22; Elliott M. Rudwick, "Booker T. Washington's Relations with the National Association for the Advancement of Colored People," *Journal of Negro Education* 29, no. 2 (Spring 1960): 134–43; James Weldon Johnson Collection, Special Collections Department, Robert W. Woodruff Library, Emory University; Gatewood, *Aristocrats of Color,* 313, 316, 318–19.

101. Letter from James Weldon Johnson to W. E. B. Du Bois, December 16, 1905, *The Correspondence of W. E. B. Du Bois: Volume 1 Selections, 1877–1932,* ed. Herbert Aptheker (Amherst: University of Massachusetts Press, 1973), 115–16; *The New Yorker,* 30 September 1933, 23–24, Fisk University Archives.

James Weldon Johnson and his wife's roles as committee members for the Du Bois Dinner in 1924 substantiate their close association, as does *The New Yorker,* which reported that his relationship with Du Bois began early in his life ("Dinner in Honor of Dr. W. E. Burghardt Du Bois, April 13, 1924," W. E. B. Du Bois Papers, folder 8, Rare Books and Manuscript Collection, The Schomburg Center for Research in Black Culture; *The New Yorker,* 30 September 1933, 23–24).

102. "G.O.P. The First Annual Souvenir Liberty Ball of the Colored Republican Club of the City of New York will be given at Tammany Hall," *New York Age,* 22 February 1906; "Hon. Charles W. Anderson Elaborately Banqueted," *New York Age,* 6 February 1908; Bernard Eisenberg, "Only for the Bourgeois? James Weldon Johnson and the NAACP, 1916–1930," *Phylon* 43, no. 2 (Second Quarter, 1982): 111–12.

103. "Tuskegee Institute: Report of the Seventeenth Annual Session of the Tuskegee Negro Conference," *New York Age,* Thursday, 5 March 1908.

Correspondence between Washington, William E. Curtis of the *Chicago Record-Herald*, Francis Garrison, and Fred R. Moore, the President of the *New York Age*, details Washington's promotion of the National Negro Business League, black-owned businesses, and his co-ownership of the *New York Age* (letter to William E. Curtis from Booker T. Washington, 24 January 1905; letter to Francis Garrison from Booker T. Washington, 31 August 1903; letter from Fred R. Moore to Booker T. Washington, 23 March 1910, Booker T. Washington Collection MG 182, box 1, Manuscripts, Archives, and Rare Books Division, The Schomburg Center for Research in Black Culture).

104. Letters between the Johnson brothers discuss their land holdings in Jacksonville, Florida, and New York City and detail their financial situation. On April 1, 1913, the president of the State Bank of Florida, John C. L'engle, describes the properties the Johnson's owned and the unpaid mortgages (J. W. Johnson Collection, box 1, folder 3, Special Collections Department, Robert W. Woodruff Library, Emory University). J. W. Johnson apparently managed the family's properties and financial holdings. On December 15, 1913, Johnson wrote to Rosamond and addressed the precarious financial situation that the family faced and their holdings and investments. He expressed concern about Rosamond's inability to help the family financially, reprimanded him for not saving money, and wrote that his brother-in-law, Jack Nail, offered financial assistance to him (ibid.).

105. On March 2, 1928, J. W. Johnson wrote to Rosamond and discussed the team's music copyrights and the ethics of providing the Cole sister's royalties when they re-copyrighted the music. Johnson felt that "there was a moral obligation—that if Bob was alive he would stand in the same position that you and I stand in and that we were morally obligated to secure for his next of kin the same benefits that he would have if he was alive. Max [Marx] said he would re-draft the contracts so as to make the royalty four cents instead of the three in order that we could arrange for a certain part of the royalties to be paid to the Cole girls" (J. W. Johnson Collection, box 1, Special Collections Department, Robert W. Woodruff Library, Emory University). On July 23, 1942, Max Marks wrote to Carriebel Plummer to inform her that he had sent her several royalty checks for Cole's music. (Jewel Plummer Cobb Collection, 23 July 1942.) Questions of authorship and ownership of the team's music continued to surface. ASCAP denied Plummer's request to join the organization or renew Cole's copyrights as a successor because they claimed he died before their establishment (Carriebel Plummer. Jewel Plummer Cobb Collection, 21 July 1942). Plummer wrote the play "What's in a Song," which told Cole's life story and advocated for his legal and publishing rights. In the play, after Ada becomes the star of a Broadway show which utilizes Cole's music, her mother laments "to think that the Modern Musician's are robbing the "Old timers' of music and their rights. Look at this, my brother's songs—a list of forty of them. All new copyrights must still bear his name. I won't let them take this honor from the memory of Bob Cole. I'll see Attorney Wimbush" (Plummer, "What's in a Song," 12). Ownership surfaced in a 1944 letter from Plummer to Leigh Whipper concerning Grace Johnson's claims that the Johnsons co-authored Cole's music. "And say I had a near fist fight with Grace Nail Johnson (another chapter) in the lobby of Theresa the Wednesday before leaving. It was that she claims the three wrote together 'Under the Bamboo Tree' as many other songs. It was written by only one of the three and that one was Bob Cole." Plummer committed her adult life to aggrandizing Cole, and questions of authorship centered on Plummer's pride in her brother and on insuring that the descendants of Cole were not cheated of his royalties (letter to Leigh Whipper from Carribel Plummer,

20 February 1944, Leigh Whipper Papers, MSS 47, box 1, Manuscripts and Rare Books Collection, The Schomburg Center for Research in Black Culture).

106. J. W. Johnson Collection, box 6, folder 1, James Weldon Johnson Collection, Special Collections Department, Robert W. Woodruff Library, Emory University.

107. Ibid. Companies controlled by white and black producers advertised their shows in newspapers and posters. While they promoted their shows, it is worth noting that Cole and Johnson's strategy of sending out postcards appears unique (The Black Patti's Troubadours Thirteenth California Tour 1908–1909, Jessie Shipp Collection, Manuscript Department, Moorland-Spingarn Research Center, Howard University; "Theodore Drury's Grand Opera Company at the 14th Street Theater," *New York Age,* 5 April 1906; Williams and Walker in *Bandanna land, New York Age,* 12 March 1908; James Reese Europe's "The Clef Club Orchestra at the Manhattan Casino," *New York Age,* 11 August 1910; "A Royal Coon," *New York Age,* 13 April 1911; "The Smart Set," *New York Age,* 4 May 1911).

108. Lester A. Walton, *New York Age,* 10 September 1908, 6.

109. Bob Cole, "Mr. Cole's Letter and Thanks" under Walton's "Music + the Stage," *New York Age,* 25 June 1908, 6.

110. Ibid.

111. Ibid.

112. Ada Overton Walker, "Colored Men and Women on the Stage," *The Colored American 9,* no 4 (June 1905): 571, Special Collections, Fisk University Library, Nashville Tennessee; Helen Armstead-Johnson, "Some Late Information on Some Early People," *Encore American and World Wide News,* June 23, 1975, 52, The Schomburg Center for Research in Black Culture.

113. Walker, "Colored Men and Women on the Stage," 571; Johnson, "Some Late Information," 52. Walker joined *The Red Moon* in 1909. Abbie Mitchell starred in *The Red Moon* in the first season, and Fannie Wise replaced her (*New York Age,* 26 August 1909, 6).

114. Theodore Pankey, "How to Make Good," *New York Age,* 18 March 1909, 6.

115. Ibid.

116. Ibid.

117. Riis, *Just Before Jazz,* 54.

118. Johnson, *Along This Way,* 172–73; James Weldon Johnson, "NAACP Farewell Speech," 1931, J. W. Johnson Collection, box 2, 34, James Weldon Johnson Collection, Special Collections Department, Robert W. Woodruff Library, Emory University.

119. Sterling Brown, "The Negro on the Stage," *The Negro in American Culture,* vols. 1–2 (1940): 36, The Schomburg Center for Research in Black Culture, New York City.

120. Through the careful analysis of the lyrics from the musicals, written reviews, fragments of *The Red Moon* found at Howard University, and evaluating the writing of James Weldon Johnson, Bob Cole's descendants, Abbie Mitchell, and members of the casts, I reconstructed the storylines of *Shoo Fly Regiment* and *The Red Moon.* In addition, I analyzed a 1938 script of *The Red Moon* written by J. Rosamond Johnson and Clarence Muse for an all-white cast that allowed me to ascertain how the story unfolded on stage. Some may question the validity of using the 1938 script of *The Red Moon,* especially considering that it was written for an all white cast, but I have come to the conclusion that this script differed little from the original. *The New York Times* reported on May 4, 1909 that "A flimsy and uninteresting story of an Indian maiden Minnehaha,

who was taken away from boarding school by her chieftain father to 'the land of the set-ting sun only to be rescued and happily married in Bill Gibson's parlor in Swamptown, served as the structure on which hang about twenty songs with tunes of more or less familiarity'" ("'Red Moon' Uninteresting," 4 May 1909, *The New York Times*). This description matches almost word for word the Johnson and Muse 1938 script. From my analysis of the materials mentioned above I stand by my assertion that that both shows included storylines integrated with music, a first in the history of African American musi-cal theater.

121. J. Rosamond Johnson Papers, 1905–06, B, Libretto *Shoo Fly Regiment* 1905–1906. J. Rosamond Johnson Papers, box 6, folder 15, Irving S. Gilmore Music Library, Yale University.

122. Johnson, *Black Manhattan*, 171. *New York Age* details the romantic scenes that occurred in *Shoo Fly Regiment* with the Filipina Grizelle and African American Lieuten-ant Dixon, and Rose Maxwell who sang "Won't You Be My Little Brown Bear" to Ned Jackson. The *Red Moon Review* in the W. C. Cawley Collection details the romantic underpinnings of *The Red Moon* with the romantic scenes between Plunk Green and Minnehaha, and Minnehaha and Red Feather (Cole and Johnson Collection, Schomburg Center for Research in Black Culture, *New York Age*, June 6, 1907, W. C. Cawley Col-lection, Lincoln Center Library for the Performing Arts).

123. Johnson, *Black Manhattan*, 171.

124. Lester Walton, "Abyssinia's Star Actress," *Indianapolis Freeman*, 6 October 1906.

125. Malone, *Steppin' on the Blues*, 77.

Chapter Two

1. Will Marion Cook, Mercer Cook Papers, box 1, folder 4, 3, Moorland-Spingarn Research Center, Howard University

2. Will Marion Cook, letter addressed to the Teachers Association (Carter), Novem-ber 23, 1934, Jewel Plummer Cobb Collection.

3. *New York Evening Journal*, 1893. Jewell Plummer Cobb Collection, Bob Cole scrapbook.

4. Johnson, "NAACP Farewell Speech," 1931.

5. Bob Cole, Manuscript Department, Moorland-Spingarn Research Center, How-ard University

6. Bob Cole, Manuscript Department, Moorland-Spingarn Research Center, How-ard University, "Shoo Fly Regiment" Review, *Indianapolis Freeman*, January 14, 1908; "Shoo Fly Regiment" Review, January 27, 1908, Robinson Locke Collection, The Lin-coln Center Library for the Performing Arts; *New York Age*, 1 June 1906, 6; *New York Age*, 26 July 1906, 5.

7. Bob Cole: OG 605, Manuscript Department, Moorland-Spingarn Research Cen-ter, Howard University.

8. Ibid.

9. Ibid.

10. Ibid.; Plummer, "What's in a Song," 7.

11. Ann Marie Bean, "Black Minstrelsy and Double Inversion, Circa 1890," *African American Performance and Theater History: A Critical Reader*, edited by Harry J. Elam

and David Krasner (Oxford: Oxford University Press, 2001), 178.

12. *Dayton Journal,* March 19, 1907. Bob Cole, Manuscript Department, Moorland-Spingarn Research Center, Howard University; Robinson Locke Collection B.

13. *St. Louis Dispatch Post,* March 25, 1907. Bob Cole, Manuscript Department. Moorland-Spingarn Research Center, Howard University.

14. Bob Cole, Manuscript Department. Moorland-Spingarn Research Center, Howard University.

15. Reid Badger, *A Life in Ragtime: A Biography of James Reese Europe* (Oxford: Oxford University Press, 1995), 31–32.

16. The show offered important advances by portraying black men as stouthearted, patriotic, and erudite. Woll contends that one of the most important breakthroughs included a serious love scene between a black man and woman, thus breaking the "love scene taboo." A January 14, 1908, review reported that the show presented "three love stories," confirming its romantic underpinnings (Woll, *Black Musical Theatre,* 23–24; "Shoo Fly Regiment Review," *Indianapolis Freeman,* 14 January 1908; Johnson, *Black Manhattan*).

17. Washington, *Up From Slavery,* 121, 124–25, 146–47, 198–99, 267–68.

18. Walton, "Abyssinia's Star Actress."

19. Davarion Baldwin, *Chicago's New Negroes: Modernity, The Great Migration, and Black Urban Life* (Chapel Hill: University of North Carolina Press, 2007), 196.

20. Booker T. Washington, *A New Negro for A New Century: An Accurate and Up-To-Date Record of the Upward Struggles of The Negro Race* (New York: American Publishing House, 1900; reprinted by Arno Press and *The New York Times,* 1969), 54–62.

21. Conkling Roscoe Simmons, "Afro American in the Musical World," *New York Age,* n.d. Stella Wiley Scrapbook. The admiration between the team and Du Bois remained longstanding. Du Bois praised Johnson at an NAACP dinner given in Johnson's honor. Johnson also won the 1933 Du Bois Literary Prize ("James Weldon Johnson Honored," *New York Times,* May 15, 1933, 18; "Negro Poet Gets Prize," *New York Times,* December 28, 1933, 17 [ProQuest Historical Newspapers, New York Times]).

22. Quoted in Arthur Ashe, *A Hard Road To Glory, Boxing, African American Athlete in Boxing* (New York: Amistad, 1993), 11.

23. Ibid.; Michael S. Kimmel, *Manhood in America, A Cultural History* (New York: Oxford University Press, 2006), 67–68. See Paula Marie Seniors, "Jack Johnson, Paul Robeson and The Hyper Masculine African American Ubermensch," *Harlem Renaissance Politics, Letters, Arts,* ed. Jeffrey Ogbar (Baltimore: Johns Hopkins University Press, forthcoming).

24. James Oliver Horton and Lois E. Horton, "Violence, Protest and Identity: Black Manhood in Antebellum America," in *A Question of Manhood,* edited by Darlene Clark Hine and Earnestine Jenkins (Bloomington: Indiana University Press, 1984), 383.

25. James Baldwin, *Nobody Knows My Name* (New York: Dial Press, 1961), 217; Patricia Hill Collins, *Black Sexual Politics* (New York: Routledge, 2004), 160–61, 207.

26. T. Thomas Fortune, "Race War in Alabama, Riot and Bloodshed in the Town of Blossburg," *The Sun,* Wednesday, 28 June 1899, T. Thomas Fortune Scrapbook, Manuscripts, Archives and Rare Books Division, The Schomburg Center for Research in Black Culture.

27. Robert F. Williams. *Negroes With Guns* (New York: Marzani & Munsell, 1962), 58–61.

28. Maurice O. Wallace, *Constructing the Black Masculine* (Durham, NC: Duke University Press, 2002), 103–4.

29. Nell Painter, *Creating Black Americans* (New York: Oxford University Press, 2005), 189; Davarion Baldwin, *Chicago's New Negroes: Modernity, The Great Migration, and Black Urban Life* (Chapel Hill, NC: University of North Carolina Press, 2007), 5.

30. "Igerje meg, hogy, ezt" nem Irja meg" (Budapest, 1933), Jack Johnson Scrapbook, box 1; "Former Champ in Paris," Photo of Johnson and his "beautiful wife," Jack Johnson Scrapbook, box 3; photo of Johnson rowing, *Le Sports Illustrés*, France (1933), Jack Johnson Scrapbook SCM90–87, box 3; "Jack Johnson L'ancien Champion du Monde De Boxe Arrive Ce Soir à Paris" (1913), Jack Johnson Scrapbook, box 3; "Jack Johnson is fined $25 for Speeding," "Auto Speed Costs Jack Johnson $20," n.d. Jack Johnson Scrapbook SCM90–87 box 1; "He is an accomplished linguist, speaking both French and Latin," "Jack Johnson with the Carnival" by James R. Scott of the Review Staff, n.d. [1940s], box 2, Manuscripts, Archives, and Rare Books Division. The Schomburg Center for Research in Black Culture.

31. Ashe, *A Hard Road To Glory, Boxing*, 16.

32. "The Man They All Dodge," n.d., Jack Johnson Scrapbook, box 3.

33. "Business Man Urges Jeffries," *New York Times,* 31 January 1909; "Sullivan Offers $75,000," *New York Times,* 21 January 1909; "Two More Challenge Johnson," *The New York Times,* 30 December 1908; "Jeffries to Sell Ranch: Then He Will Go Into Vaudeville—May Fight Again," *New York Times,* 31 January 1909; "Johnson Wins; Police Stop Fight," *New York Times,* 26 December 1908; John L. Sullivan, "Johnson wins in 15 Rounds; Jeffries Weak," *New York Times,* 5 July 1910; "Life Looks Back, 28 Years Ago to the Johnson-Jeffries Fight in Reno" (1938), The Jack Johnson Scrapbook, box 3.

34. Tex Rickard, "Tex Rickard Tells How Ring Champions Are Made" (Copyright, 1925 North American Newspaper Alliance. Jack Johnson Scrapbook SCM90–87 box 2).

35. "I Outclassed Him, Johnson Declares," *New York Times,* 5 July 1910.

36. Henry Lee Moon, *The Emerging Thought of W. E. B. Du Bois: Essays and Editorials from the Crisis with an Introduction, Commentaries, and a Personal Memoir by Henry T. Moon* (New York: Simon and Schuster, 1972), 296–97.

37. On March 23, 1909, Emmett J. Scott asked J. Frank Wheaten, a black lawyer, to speak to Johnson concerning his boasting about beating Jeffries. Louis H. Harlan et al., eds., *The Booker T. Washington Papers,* vol. 10, 1909–1911 (Urbana: University of Illinois Press, 1981), 75–76; Louis H. Harlan and Raymond W. Smock, eds., *The Booker T. Washington Papers,* vol. 12, 1912–1914 (Urbana: University of Illinois Press, 1982), 43–44; *New York Evening Graphic,* n.d. [probably 1929], The Jack Johnson Scrapbook, box 2.

38. *Along This Way,* in *James Weldon Johnson, Writings,* ed. William L. Andrews (New York: The Library of America, 2004), 360. Newspapers noted Johnson's infectious smile. "[H]is famous golden smile stopped trading on the Stock Exchange" ("Jack Johnson is fined $25 for Speeding," n.d.; "Li'l Artha Panics Bears and Bulls on 'Change Visit,'" Jack Johnson Scrapbook).

39. Johnson, *Along This Way* in *James Weldon Johnson, Writings,* 360–61.

40. Johnson, "The Passing of Jack Johnson," 1915, in *James Weldon Johnson, Writings,* 614–16.

41. Ibid.; Ashe, *A Hard Road To Glory,* 9–12; Johnson, *Along This Way,* in *James Weldon Johnson, Writings,* 360–61.

42. Johnson. "The Passing of Jack Johnson," 615–16; Johnson, *Along This Way,* in

James Weldon Johnson, 360–61.

43. Wiley, n.d., F, *The World,* Stella Wiley Scrapbook.

44. *The Bulletin of Atlanta University,* no. 51, December 1893, 8, Special Collections, Atlanta University Center, Clark Atlanta University; *The New York Age.* N.d. Article about Cole and Johnson as athletes and musicians. Johnson, James Weldon. James Weldon Johnson Collection. Beinecke Rare Book and Manuscript Library, Yale University.

45. Wiley, n.d., G, Stella Wiley Scrapbook; *The New York Age.* N.d. Article about Cole and Johnson as athletes and musicians. Johnson, James Weldon. James Weldon Johnson Collection. Beinecke Rare Book and Manuscript Library, Yale University.

46. O: *Plain Dealer,* 1903, James Weldon Johnson Papers, Yale Collection of American Literature, Beinecke Rare Book and Manuscript Library, Yale University. Scrapbook.

47. Walton, "Music and the Stage" *New York Age,* 12 March 1908, 6.

48. Walton, *New York Age,* 10 January 1910, 6.

49. Walton, *New York Age,* 12 May 1910, 6.

50. Charles A. Hunter, "Rays from 'The Red Moon,'" from "Music and the Stage," *New York Age,* 10 February 1910, 6.

51. Walton, *New York Age,* 19 May 1910, 6.

52. Walton, *New York Age,* 26 May 1910, 6.

53. Plummer, "Under the Bamboo Tree," n.d., 12.

54. Wiley, n.d., G, Stella Wiley Scrapbook.

55. *The World,* n.d., James Weldon Johnson Papers, Scrapbook, Yale Collection of American Literature, Beinecke Rare Book and Manuscript Library, Yale University.

56. Susan Robeson, *The Whole World In His Hands, A Pictorial Biography of Paul Robeson* (New York: Citadel Press, 1981); Paul Robeson, *Here I Stand* (New York: Beacon Press, 1988. Originally published 1958); Paul Robeson Jr., *The Undiscovered Paul Robeson: An Artist's Journey, 1898–1939* (New York: John Wiley and Sons, 2001), 49, 53, 69.

57. Nude photograph of Paul Robeson, Paula Marie Seniors Collection; Mora J. Beauchamp-Byrd, Curator, "Body and Soul: Paul Robeson Race and Representation," The Robert and Sallie Brown Gallery and Museum, The Sonja Haynes Stone Center for Black Culture and History, University of North Carolina, Chapel Hill.

58. Ashe, *A Hard Road to Glory: A History of the African-American Athlete since 1946* (New York: An Amistad Book, 1988), 96

59. "The Draft, Cassius vs. Army," *New York Times,* 30 April 1967, 190.

60. Arthur Ashe, *A Hard Road To Glory: A History,* 96–100

61. Arthur Ashe with Neil Amdur, *Off The Court* (New York and Scarborough, Ontario: New American Library Books, 1981), 167–89, 98, 101, 102, 146–47, 151; Arthur Ashe, with Arnold Rampesard, *Days of Grace* (New York: Alfred A. Knopf, 1993), 256–57, 262–63, 7–16; Ashe, *A Hard Road to Glory,* 168–73, 190–91, 194–95, 18–19; Renford Reese, *American Paradox, Young Black Men* (Durham, NC: Carolina Academic Press, 2004),105, 95.

62. St. Joseph Radical, in Miles V. Lynk, *The Black Troopers or The Daring Heroism of The Negro Soldiers in the Spanish American War* (Jackson, TN: M.V. Lynk Publishing House, 1899), 35–36, Manuscripts, Archives, and Rare Books Division, The Schomburg Center for Research in Black Culture.

63. *The Colored American,* 8, no. 4 (29 December 1900): 10.

64. Booker T. Washington. "From Mr. Washington's Jubilee Address," 3, *The Bulletin*

of Atlanta University, January 1, 1898, Atlanta University Center, Robert W. Woodruff Library.

65. Ibid.

66. Ibid.

67. Ada Ferrer, *Insurgent Cuba: Race, Nation and Revolution, 1868–1898* (Chapel Hill: University of North Carolina Press, 1999), 196–97; Edward A. Johnson. *The History of the Negro Soldiers in the Spanish American War, and Other Items of Interest* (Raleigh: Capital Printing Co., Printers and Binders; 1899; New York and London: Johnson Reprint Corporation), 6.

68. Amy Kaplan, "Black and Blue on San Juan Hill," in *Cultures of United States Imperialism* (Durham, NC: Duke University Press, 1993), 219–20.

69. Ibid., 219.

70. "Roosevelt to Colored Men," *The New York Times*, October 15, 1898; Theodore Roosevelt, *The Rough Riders* (New York: Charles Scribner's Sons, 1899), 121.

71. Roosevelt described the Filipinos as "half-caste and native Christians, warlike Moslems and wild pagans" unsuitable to self-rule; Chinese remain ignoble and feminine, and blacks need constant guidance by whites. He maintained that the Philippines, Cuba, and Puerto Rico needed the "manly" United States to guide them toward civilization. Theodore Roosevelt, *The Strenuous Life: Essays and Addresses* (New York: The Century Co., 1900), 17–18, 4–7; Theodore Roosevelt, "The Rough Riders," *Scribners Magazine* 25 (January 1899): 5; Theodore Roosevelt, "Cavalry at Santiago," *Scribners Magazine* 25 (April 1899): 436; Theodore Roosevelt, *Hunting Trips of a Ranchman: Sketches of Sport on the Northern Cattle Plains* (New York and London, G.P. Putnam, 1902), 11–12; Gail Bederman, *Manliness & Civilization* (Chicago: The University of Chicago Press, 1995), 180, 192.

72. Roosevelt, *The Strenuous Life*, 4–7; Roosevelt, "The Rough Riders," *Scribners* (June 1899): 8–12; Theodore Roosevelt. *Theodore Roosevelt: An Autobiography* (New York and Boston, Macmillan Company, 1913), 28–249; Lynk, *The Black Troopers*, 24, 25.

73. Chaplin Jas. M. Guthrie, *Camp-Fires of the Afro-American: or, The Colored Man as a Patriot, Soldier, Sailor, and Hero, in the Cause of Free America: Displayed in Colonial Struggle, in the Revolution, the War of 1812, and in Later Wars, Particularly the Great Civil War—1861–5, And the Spanish-American War—1898: Concluding with The Filipinos—1899* (Philadelphia: Afro-American Pub Co., 1899), 692–93. Manuscripts, Archives and Rare Books Division, The Schomburg Center for Research in Black Culture (hereafter *Camp-Fires of the Afro-American*).

74. Lynk, *The Black Troopers*, 30.

75. Herschel V. Cashin, Charles Alexander, William T. Anderson, Arthur M. Brown, and Horace W. Bivens, *Under Fire with The Tenth U.S. Cavalry* (London, New York, Chicago: F. Tennyson Neely, 1899), 160. Manuscripts, Archives and Rare Books Division, The Schomburg Center for Research in Black Culture.

76. Lynk, *The Black Troopers*, 17, 24; Guthrie, *Camp-Fires of the Afro-American*, 692, 52–53; Cashin et al., *Under Fire With The Tenth U.S. Cavalry*, 59–60.

77. John A. Williams, *Captain Blackman* (Minneapolis: Coffee House Press, 1972, 1988, 2000), 76.

78. Roosevelt, *The Rough Riders*, 144–45; "Cavalry at Santiago," *Scribners Magazine* 25, April 1899, 436.

79. Ibid.; Washington, *A New Negro for a New Century*, 54–62.

80. Roosevelt, *The Rough Riders*, 144–45; Washington, *A New Negro for a New Century*, 54–62.

81. Newspaper clipping, n.d. Jewel Plummer Cobb Collection, Bob Cole Scrapbook.

82. Ibid.

83. Lynk, *The Black Troopers*, 29–30.

84. William T. Goode, *The Eighth Illinois* (Chicago: The Blakely Printing Company, 1899), 232–33; Guthrie. *Campfires of the Afro-American*, 692; Washington, *A New Negro for A New Century*, 54–62; Willard B. Gatewood, *Smoked Yankees and The Struggle for Empire* (Urbana: University of Illinois Press, 1971), 92–97.

85. Lynk, *The Black Troopers*, 77; Cashin et al., *Under Fire with The Tenth U.S. Cavalry*, 80. (Books published by blacks attests to their military expertise.)

86. Lynk, *The Black Troopers*, 29, 30, 39, 40, 43; Goode, 225; Guthrie, *Campfires of the Afro-American*, 684–86, 688; Cashin et al., *Under Fire with The Tenth U.S. Cavalry*, 89–90, 124.

Roosevelt details his and the Rough Riders' ineptitude and their confusion in the Cuban jungles. "I had an awful time trying to get into the fight and trying to do what was right in it; and all the while I was thinking that I was the only man who did not know what I was about, and that all the others did—whereas as I found out late, pretty much everybody else was as much in the dark as I was." (Theodore Roosevelt, *Theodore: An Autobiography* [New York: The Macmillan Company, 1913], 128, 256–57)

87. Bederman, *Manliness & Civilization*, 101.

88. Cashin et al., *Under Fire with The Tenth U.S. Cavalry*, 61–62.

89. Gaines, *Uplifting the Race*, 26.

90. T. Thomas Fortune, "Afro-Americans Not Cowards," *Sun*, August 1898. T. Thomas Fortune Scrapbook, Manuscripts, Archives and Rare Books Division, The Schomburg Center for Research in Black Culture.

91. Michael C. Robinson and Frank N. Schubert, "David Fagen: An Afro-American Rebel in the Philippines, 1899–1901," *Pacific Historical Review*, February 1975, 70.

92. Logan, *The Negro in American Life and Thought*, 187.

93. James Weldon Johnson, A: "Lynch Laws in the South"; C: *Lutheran Courier*, n.d. Oldest Scrapbook, James Weldon Johnson Papers, Yale Collection of American Literature, Beinecke Rare Books and Manuscripts Library, Yale University.

94. Logan, *The Negro in American Life and Thought*, 89; Franklin, *From Slavery to Freedom*, 341.

95. Du Bois, *Black Reconstruction in America*, 699.

96. Logan, *The Negro in American Life and Thought*, 89.

97. Roosevelt, *Strenuous Life*, 2.

98. Moorefield Storey, "Athens and Brownsville," *Crisis* 1, no. 1 (November 1910): 13; letter to Washington from Theodore Roosevelt, November 5, 1906; letter to Washington from Frances J. Garrison, December 3, 1906, Booker T. Washington Collection MG 182 box 1 (1), The Schomburg Center for Research in Black Culture; Franklin, *From Slavery to Freedom*, 441–42.

99. Wiley, 1903 H: Stella Wiley Scrapbook; K: Cartoon dated 1903 with copyright of the Judge Company of New York. References to "Under the Bamboo Tree" and Theodore Roosevelt and the Panama Canal appear. Johnson, James Weldon. James Weldon Collection. Beinecke Rare Book and Manuscript Library, Yale University.

100. "Musical Composition by Negroes," *Bulletin of Atlanta University,* no. 140, November 1903, 5.

101. Johnson, *Along This Way,* 218–20. Anderson was the collector of internal revenue for the Wall Street area and political leader within the black community.

102. James Weldon Johnson, "American Democracy and the Negro," Cullen Jackman Memorial Collection, box 20 folder 4, Atlanta University Center, Robert W. Woodruff Library, 8–9.

103. Ibid.

104. James Weldon Johnson, "Attacks Harvard on the Negro Question: J. Weldon Johnson Denounces the Exclusion of Negroes from its Dormitories," *The Historical New York Times,* January 13, 1923, 5.

105. Johnson, *Along This Way,* 218–19.

106. Louis R. Harlan, *Booker T. Washington: The Wizard of Tuskegee 1901–1915* (New York: Oxford University Press, 1983), 18–19; *Bulletin of Atlanta University,* April 1906; *Bulletin of Atlanta University,* June 1907; letter to Towns from Johnson, George A. Towns Papers, box 2, folder 12. Special Collections, Atlanta University Center.

107. 26 February 1906 letter from the State Department to Johnson, J. W. Johnson Collection, box 1, folder 2, James Weldon Johnson Collection, Special Collections Department, Robert W. Woodruff Library, Emory University.

108. Johnson, *Along This Way,* 250–51.

109. Ibid., 239.

110. Ibid., 345.

111. Krasner, *Resistance, Parody, and Double,* 140.

112. "Shoo Fly Regiment Review," January 27, 1908, Robinson Locke Collection, Lincoln Center Library for the Performing Arts [no page no., uncited clipping]; *Dayton Journal,* 19 March 1907, Bob Cole Manuscript Department, Moorland Springarn Research Center, Howard University.

113. Jerry Keenan, *Encyclopedia of the Spanish-American and Philippine-American Wars* (Santa Barbara, CA: ABC-CLIO, 2001), 256.

114. *The Cleveland Gazette* reported that the "War Department Opposes Negro Officers," in George P. Marks, *The Black Press Views American Imperialism (1898—1900)* (New York: Arno Press, 1971), 75.

115. Carney, "Sergeant Carney."

116. Ibid.

117. "New York and The Fighting Tenth," in *The Colored American* 16, no. 2 (August 1909). Special Collections, Fisk University, Nashville, Tennessee.

118. Guthrie, *Camp-Fires,* 692.

119. Krasner, *Resistance, Parody, and Double Consciousness,* 140.

120. Bob Cole, Manuscript Department, Moorland-Spingarn Research Center, Howard University.

121. Bob Cole, James Weldon Johnson, and J. Rosamond Johnson, "The Old Flag Never Touched the Ground," 1901, Cole and Johnson Archives, The Schomburg Center for Research in Black Culture.

122. "New York and The Fighting Tenth," 127.

123. Jewel Plummer Cobb Collection, Bob Cole Scrapbook.

124. "Shoo Fly Regiment Review," *Indianopolis Freeman,* January 14, 1908.

125. Robinson Locke Collection. *Indianapolis Freeman,* 1908, Europe, Cole: 1905.

126. Cole and Johnson Collection, Schomburg Center for Research in Black Culture, New York City.

127. Robinson, Schubert, "David Fagen," 80; Gary Okihiro, "Is Yellow Black or White?" in *Margins and Mainstreams: Asians in American History and Culture* (Washington: University of Washington Press, 1994), 57; letter from Chaplain George W. Prioleau, Ninth Cavalry from the Philippines to the *Colored American,* March 1901, in Gatewood's *Smoked Yankees,* 300–302.

128. Goode, *The Eighth Illinois,* 234.

129. Paul R. Spickard, *Mixed Blood: Intermarriage and Ethnic Identity in Twentieth-Century America* (Madison: University of Wisconsin Press, 1989), 125–126, 133, 276, 70, 80.

130. *New York Age,* "Their Newest Hit: Young Authors Produce Another Musical Comedy," 26 July 1906.

131. Walton, *New York Age,* 14 January 1909, 17 February 1910, 31 March 1910, 12 May 1910.

132. Roosevelt, *The Strenuous Life,* 6–7, 9, 15; Robinson and Schubert, "David Fagen," 63–83. White soldiers and their wives referred to the Filipinos as "gugus," "niggers," and "Black devils." (Ibid.)

133. "Negro and Filipino," *The Colored American* 1, no. 5 (1901): 334.

134. Ibid.

135. Robinson and Schubert, "David Fagen," 68–83.

136. Ibid.

137. Kaplan, "Black and Blue on San Juan Hill," 228; Robinson and Schubert. "David Fagen," 68–83; Gatewood, *Smoked Yankees,* 237, 244, 257, 269–71, 279–81, 304–6.

Sgt. Patrick Mason, the *Cleveland Gazette:* "I don't believe they will be justly dealt by. The first thing in the morning is the 'Nigger' and the last thing at night is the 'nigger.' You have no idea the way these people are treated by the Americans here." Gatewood. *Smoked Yankees,* 257.

138. Gaines, *Uplifting the Race,* 26–27. The article "New York and the Fighting Tenth" in the August 1909 edition of *The Colored American* and in 1902 "The Enlisted Man in Action" by Rienzi B. Lemus of the 25th Infantry lauded the accomplishments of the black soldiers in the war in the Philippines and Cuba. Rienzi Lemus, "The Enlisted Man in Action," 46–54, 123–27.

139. Kaplan, "Black and Blue on San Juan Hill," 228; Guthrie, *Campfires,* 706–10. Chaplin Guthrie argued that the United States brought democracy to the Philippines and maintained that the end of the war in the Philippines "will not come until the colored man has had a share in the toils, dangers, and sacrifices of a war with the Filipinos as he has had in other wars to establish, perpetuate and extend the principles of American free government" (ibid., 710). Guthrie remained unaware of the impending Jim Crow in the Philippines.

Chapter Three

1. Washington, *Up From Slavery,* 74.
2. Ibid., 78–80.
3. Ibid., 83.

4. Ibid., 89.

5. Johnson, "What Atlanta University Has Done for Me."

6. Ibid.

7. John Rosamond Johnson Papers: 1905–06 B, Irving S. Gilmore Library, Yale University.

8. John Hope Franklin Plenary Session, The Association for the Study of African American Life and History, Atlanta, Georgia, Fall 2006. See: John Hope Franklin, *Mirror to America: The Autobiography of John Hope Franklin* (New York, Farrar, Straus and Giroux, 2005).

9. Walton, *New York Age,* 12 March 1908, 6.

10. Hunter, "Rays from 'The Red Moon,'" from "Music and the Stage," edited by Lester A. Walton, *New York Age,* 18 March 1909, 6.

11. Ibid.

12. "White Rose Industrial Association: An Appeal to Our Friends," April 6, 1910, 3, White Rose Mission and Industrial Association Collection, SCMS 565 Manuscripts, Archives, and Rare Books Collections, The Schomburg Center for Research in Black Culture.

13. S. Coleridge-Taylor, "The Negro Problem in America," *New York Age,* 3 September 1908, 6.

14. Walton, *New York Age,* 12 March 1908, 6.

15. *Bulletin of Atlanta University,* no. 90 (March 1898): 1; *Bulletin of Atlanta University,* no. 94 (October 1898): 1; *Bulletin of Atlanta University,* no. 120 (June 1901): 1, Atlanta University Center, Robert W. Woodruff Library.

16. Noble Sissle, president of the Negro's Actor's Guild of America, Inc., "Highlights of the Negro's Contribution in the Development of Music and Theatre in the American Scene," 3–4, Leigh Whipper Papers, MS 47, box 1, The Schomburg Center for Research in Black Culture.

17. Edith J. R. Isaacs, "The Middle Distance: 1890–1917," *Theatre Arts, The Negro in the American Theatre,* August 1942, 527, Lester A. Walton Papers, The Schomburg Center for Research in Black Culture.

18. *New York Age,* 18 October 1906; Eileen Southern, *Biographical Dictionary of Afro American and African Musicians* (Westport, CT: Greenwood Press, 1982), 115, 222–23, 272, 387, 404; Bernard Peterson, *A Century of Musicals in Black and White* (Westport, CT: Greenwood Press, 1993), 184, 86, 227–29, 295, 264, 394–96; Woll, *Black Musical Theater,* 11, 55, 60; Johnson, *Black Manhattan,* 106–7; Maude Cuney Hare, *Negro Musicians and Their Music* (New York: G.K. Hall & Co.,1936), 158–59; Gerald Boardman, *American Musical Theater: A Chronicle* (New York: Oxford University Press, 1978), 240, 44–45, 295, 358; "Drury Grand Opera Co. The Secret and Benevolent Organization of Greater New York," *New York Age,* 29 March 1906; "Drury Grand Opera Company Week beginning May 28, 1906," *New York Age,* April 5, 1906; *New York Age,* 18 May 1905, 1; Sampson, *Blacks in Blackface,* 173–74, 319–21; Peterson, *African American Theater Directory,* 295, 358; "Music and the Stage," *New York Age,* 5 April 1906, 8; Isaacs, "The Middle Distance," 527–29; Sissle, "Highlights of the Negro's Contribution," 3–4.

When *Shoo Fly Regiment* opened on Broadway, Viennese-style operettas proved popular among white composers and audiences. The stage was overwhelmed with musicals, including *Naughty Marietta,* European imports including *The Merry Widow* (1907), and the Ziegfield Follies, whose origins were a Paris revue. Little room remained for American musicals. (Boardman, *American Musical Theater,* 230, 231, 236) White composers emulated European styles, while black artists created an original American form, which included minstrelsy, grand opera, vaudeville, and book musicals. They wrote coon songs, ragtime, and light opera.

19. Conkling Roscoe Simmons, "Afro American in the Musical World," n.d.

20. *Toledo Blade,* 1906, Stella Wiley Scrapbook.

21. Booker T. Washington, *Up From Slavery,* 121.

22. Ibid., 146–47.

23. Ibid., 124–25, 198–99.

24. Ibid., 267–68. Because whites denied black women deference when it came to addressing them as Miss, Mrs., or Lady, blacks named their children Queen, Lady, or Mrs., to insure that whites would address them properly, and they included these titles in their job descriptions—lady principal of Tuskegee.

25. Ibid., 231-32; Robinson Locke Collection: n.d. F, 1906 G; Sampson, *The Ghost Walks,* 291, 347-48, 364.

26. Sampson, *The Ghost Walks,* 291, 347–48, 370, 364; Robinson Locke Collection: 1906 G.

27. *New York Age,* "Notes From the *Shoo Fly Regiment,*" 12 March 1908.

28. Sampson, *The Ghost Walks,* 370; *New York Age,* 1906.

29. *Bulletin of Atlanta University,* no. 48 (July 1893).

30. Ibid.

31. Ibid.

32. Ibid.

33. Ibid.

34. Walton, "Music and the Stage," *New York Age,* 14 May 1908, 6.

35. Sampson, *The Ghost Walks,* 394; "Review of *Shoo Fly Regiment,*" *Indianapolis Freeman,* 23 March 1907.

36. *New York Age,* 6 June 1907. The Schomburg Center for Research in Black Culture, New York City.

37. Bob Cole: OG 605, Manuscript Department, Moorland-Spingarn Research Center, Howard University.

38. Susan Curtis, *The First Black Actors on the Great White Way* (Columbia, MO: University of Missouri Press, 1998), 36; Johnson, *Black Manhattan,* 172.

39. Ibid., 178.

40. Gaines, *Uplifting the Race,* 217.

41. Allen, *Horrible Prettiness,* 32.

42. Jo A. Tanner, *Dusky Maidens: The Odyssey of the Early Black Dramatic Actress* (Westport: CT: Greenwood Press, 1992), 8; Carby, *Reconstructing Womanhood,* 34.

43. Coleridge-Taylor, "The Negro Problem in America," 6.

44. Badger, *A Life in Ragtime,* 71.

45. Curtis, *The First Black Actors,* 51.

46. Both the *Toledo Blade* and the *Brooklyn Eagle* noted that *The Red Moon* chorus included women of all shades. The *Toledo Blade* stated that the chorus consisted of "dusky damsels, ranging in color from sable black to a pinkish white." *Toledo Blade,* 14

December 1908, *Brooklyn Eagle*, 29 December 1908, The Robinson Locke Collection.

47. Sampson, *The Ghost Walks*, 70–71; Isaacs, "The Middle Distance," 527.

48. Johnson, *Black Manhattan*, 95.

49. *Sun*, 13 November 1904. Stella Wiley Scrapbook.

50. Stella Wiley, n.d., I: Stella Wiley Scrapbook, L: "Flowers for Another Caused Trouble"; N: "The Matinee Girl," *The New York Dramatic Mirror*. N.d.; M: "The Theatres/Another Visit of the Octoroons' Other Plays." Syracuse newspaper. N.d; P: "Prima Donnas of African Blood: A Recent Development in the Musical World. Some sing Negro songs written by Negro poets and set to music by Negro composer—appreciated by White audiences as as by people of their own race." *The Sun*, 13 November 1904, Stella Wiley Scrapbook, Johnson James Weldon, James Weldon Johnson Collection. Beinecke Rare Book and Manuscript Library, Yale University.

51. Badger, *A Life in Ragtime*, 71.

52. Peter Stallybrass and Allon White, *The Politics and Poetics of Transgression* (Ithaca, NY: Cornell University Press, 1986), 5, 191–93; Allen, *Horrible Prettiness*, 26, 146, 150.

53. Allen, *Horrible Prettiness*, 150.

54. Stallybrass and White, *The Politics and Poetics*, 5, 191–193; Allen, *Horrible Prettiness*, 26, 26, 132–37.

55. Whipper, "The Negro Actor's Guild Scoreboard," 31.

56. Will Marion Cook, "Autobiographical Notes," Mercer Cook Papers, box 4, folder 6, Moorland-Spingarn Research Center, Howard University.

57. Walton, *New York Age*, 12 March 1908, 6.

58. Interview with Dr. Jewel Plummer Cobb 2003, Los Angeles, California.

59. Walton, *New York Age*, 17 May 1910, 6.

60. Plummer, "What's in a Song."

61. Interview with Dr. Jewel Plummer Cobb 2003. Los Angeles, California.

62. Ibid. Margaret Bonds was born in Chicago on March 3, 1913. She studied music with William L. Dawson and Florence Price, received a bachelors and a masters of music from Northwestern University, attended the Juilliard School of Music, and studied composition with H. T. Burleigh and Will Marion Cook. Bonds composed symphonies, ballets, piano music, a cantata, and musicals. She received awards from the National Association of Musicians, Roy Harris, the Rosenwald Foundation, and Rodman Wanamaker. Southern, *Biographical Dictionary*, 40–41; Barbara Smith, *Black Women in America* (Brooklyn, New York, Carlson Publishing, 1993), 147–48.

Self-dubbed a "Puritanical Pagan," the famous modern dancer Isadora Duncan was born in San Francisco/Oakland in 1877 or 1878. Duncan was considered revolutionary because she performed with her hair down, in loose fitting clothing, and barefoot. She founded dance schools in Russia, Germany, and Paris, and is known for her tragic death. On September 19, 1927, her scarf became intertwined in the wheels of her car on the Riviera (Jack Anderson, *Dance* [New York, Newsweek Books, 1974], 89–92; "On this day: September 15 1927: Scarf Strangles Dancer Isadora Duncan in Car," *Guardian* [London] —Final Edition, 15 September 1927, 36; John Martin, "Isadora Duncan Danced Like a 'Puritanical Pagan,'" *New York Times*, 8 January 1928 [ProQuest Historical Newspapers, The New York Times (1851–2004), 62]).

63. Plummer, "What's in a Song, 11.

64. Ibid.

65. Warren R. Perry, "Archeology as Community Service: The African Burial Ground Project," New York City, 1999, 3. http://www.stpt.usf.edu-jsokolov/burialgr.htm

66. Brenda Dixon-Gottschild, *Waltzing in the Dark* (New York: St. Martin's Press, 2000), 42–43; Nadine George-Graves, *The Royalty of Vaudeville* (New York: St. Martins Press, 2000), 25.

67. Ibid.

68. George-Graves, *The Royalty of Vaudeville*, 25.

69. Dixon-Gottschild. *Waltzing in the Dark,* 42–43.

70. Ibid. The pickanninny characterization remains an enduring legacy in films, including the Wayans Brothers *Scary Movie* (2000), where a wild, loud, animal-like, chicken-eating pickanninny disrupts the film *Shakespeare in Love.*

71. Whipper, "The Negro Actor's Guild Scoreboard," 69; Cook, "From Clorindy," 18; Cole, OG 605; Robinson Locke Collection: n.d. F.

72. George Walker, "Bert and Me and Them," *New York Age* 22, no. 13 (24 December 1908): 4.

73. Ibid.

74. Walker, "Bert and Me and Them," 4; Hatch and Hill, *A History,* 128–29.

75. Bean, "Black Minstrelsy," 178.

76. George-Graves, *The Royalty of Vaudeville,* 77.

77. Toll, *Blacking Up,* 139–40; Mahar, *Behind The Burn't Cork Mask,* 316; Hill and Hatch. *A History of African American Theatre,* 120.

78. Ibid., 140; Mahar. *Behind The Burn't Cork Mask,* 311.

79. Bean, "Black Minstrelsy," 178.

80. The black female impersonator C. Adam La Rose held "the record as the only colored female impersonator doubling band in America," and prepared to perform the Salome dance (*Freeman,* 22 May 1909, 5). LaRose's performance style of female impersonation which included performing in the band and the Salome dance appears as something quite unique and distinctly African American and appealed to black audiences. It does not fit into the mold of white female impersonation.

81. Walker, "Bert and Me and Them," *New York Age,* 24 December 1908, 4.

82. Ibid.

83. *New York Age,* 6 June 1907, 6.

84. Bean, "Black Minstrelsy," 179.

85. Ibid., 180.

86. Toni Morrison, "What the Black Woman Thinks about Women's Lib," *New York Times,* 22 August 1971, SM 14.

87. George O. Brome, "Geraldine? She Isn't So Flip," *New York Times,* 3 September 1972, D 11.

88. Brown, "The Negro on the Stage," 43.

89. Richard Slotkin, "Buffalo Bill's 'Wild West' and the Mythologization of the American Empire," in Amy Kaplan and Donald Pease, *Cultures of United States Imperialism* (Durham, NC: Duke University Press, 1993), 177.

90. The *New York Age* advertisement of "The First American Negro Play," *Shoo Fly Regiment* at the Grand Opera House on Thirty-third Street and Eight Avenue listed the price of the tickets (*New York Age,* June 1907).

91. Walton, *New York Age,* 10 September 1908.

92. Bob Cole: OG 605. Manuscript Department, Moorland-Spingarn Research Center, Howard University.

93. "Shoofly Regiment," *Theater Magazine,* September 1907, The Billy Rose Collection, Lincoln Center Library for the Performing Arts.

94. Bob Cole: OG 605. Manuscript Department, Moorland-Spingarn Research Center, Howard University.

95. Ibid.

96. *New York Age,* 6 June 1907. The Schomburg Center for Research in Black Culture, New York City.

97. Ibid.

98. Melvin Oliver and Thomas Shapiro, *Black Wealth/White Wealth* (New York: Routledge, 1997), 14–15.

99. Rena Fraden, "A National Negro Theater That Never Was," ed. Erroll Hill (Englewood Cliffs, NJ: Prentice-Hall, 1980), 210–11, 26, 4. Between 1895 and 1915 a vibrant black theater emerged in black communities around the country, which led to the rise in black theater ownership and the formation of black syndicates. As early as 1820 blacks founded theater companies such as the Shakespearean African Grove Theater, which lay the foundation for the founding of the Pekin Stock Theater Company in 1906, and the Anita Bush Stock Company in New York in 1915, which would become the Lafayette Players. With the advent of black shows, black theater ownership increased across the country with the opening of Chicago's Robert T. Mott's Pekin Theater (1905) and Columbia Theater; Washington, D.C.'s The Howard; Jacksonville, Florida's The Lincoln Theater (1912); St. Louis's Booker T. Washington Theater (1913); Baltimore's Colonial Theater (1916); and Norfolk, Virginia's Attucks Theater (1919). The emergence of cheap movie tickets, the high cost of transportation, second-class bookings, and overt racism which blocked the sponsorship of black shows, all marked the demise of black theater ownership (Rena Fraden, "A National Negro Theater That Never Was," 26, 2, 4; Sister M. Francesca Thompson, OSF, "The Lafayette Players 1915–1917," in *The Theater of Black Americans [Volume II],* ed. Erroll Hill [Englewood Cliffs, NJ: Prentice-Hall, 1980], 15–17; Tanner, *Dusky Maidens,* 78; Edward A. Robinson, "The Pekin: The Genesis of American Black Theater, *Black American Literature Forum* 16, no. 4., Black Theatre Issue [Winter 1982]: 136–37; Peterson, *African American Theater Directory,* 28–29).

100. Riis, *Just Before Jazz,* 36.

101. Johnson, *Along This Way,* 239–40.

102. Walton, *New York Age,* 7 May 1908, 6; 14 May 1908, 6.

103. Walton, *New York Age,* 14 May 1908, 6.

104. Ibid.

105. Ibid.

106. Ibid.

107. Du Bois, "The Drama among Black Folk," 169.

108. Walton, *New York Age,* 21 May 1908; 28 May 1908; 4 June 1908; 11 June 1908.

109. Walton, *New York Age,* 20 August 1908.

110. Walton, *New York Age,* 30 July 1908, 6.

111. Ibid.

112. Walton, *New York Age,* 6; 20 August 1908; 27 August 1908, 6; 3 September 1908, 6. The 1909 advertisement for *The Red Moon* at the Majestic Theater in Brooklyn, New York, and the Folly Theatre in Williamsburg lists the price of the tickets at twenty-five cents, fifty cents, seventy-five cents, and one dollar. *New York Age,* 24 December 1908; 28 January 1909, 6.

Chapter Four

1. Litefoot, "Tribal Boogie," on *Litefoot Redvolution* (Seattle, WA: Limited Release, Collectors Edition, 2005). Litefoot (Cherokee/Chichimecca) is an inspirational speaker, rapper, and actor.
2. *New York Age,* 1909–1910.
3. John Rosamond Johnson Papers, Irving S. Gilmore Music Library at Yale University, box 6, folder 14.
4. R. Johnson Papers, box 6, folder 14.
5. Sampson, *The Ghost Walks,* 443.
6. Woll, *Black Musical Theatre,* 24–27; R. Johnson Papers, box 6, folder 14. While the 1938 script of *The Red Moon* was written for an all-white cast, the notes within the script include commentary on the 1908 version and illuminate the performance practices of the black show. The 1938 script also sheds light on the original script.
7. Cole and Johnson Collection, Museum of the City of New York, Majestic Theater Program of *The Red Moon,* May 3, 1909.
8. Lester A. Walton, "Music and the Stage," *The Colored American* 14, no 8 (September 1908): 459, Fisk University Special Collections.
9. J. R. Johnson Papers, box 6, folder 14; Riis, *Just before Jazz,* 244–45; Badger, *A Life in Ragtime,* 38–39; Woll, *Black Musical Theatre,* 24–27.
10. Walton, *The Colored American,* 459.
11. Majestic Theater Program of *The Red Moon* May 3, 1909; Badger, *A Life in Ragtime,* 38.
12. Walton, "Music and the Stage," 459.
13. Ibid., 459; Majestic Theater Program of *The Red Moon* May 3, 1909; Riis, *Just before Jazz,* 244; Badger, *A Life in Ragtime,* 38–39; Woll, *Black Musical Theatre,* 24–25.
14. Sampson, *The Ghost Walks,* 443.
15. Badger, *A Life in Ragtime,* 38; Woll, *Black Musical Theatre,* 24–27.
16. Sampson, *Blacks in Blackface,* 287.
17. Walton, "Music and the Stage," 459.
18. Du Bois, *Black Reconstruction,* 325–26, 431, 637–38; Du Bois, *The Souls of Black Folk* (New York: Premier Americana, 1961, originally 1900), 36.
19. (Mrs.) M. F. Armstrong, "A Teacher's Witness," 38; Donal Lindsey, *Indians at Hampton Institute* (Urbana and Chicago: University of Illinois Press, 1995), 1–3. Mrs. Armstrong states that the Lahainaluna School taught the Native Hawaiians Christianity, citizenship, and manual labor and that "[General Armstrong] had seen the successful working of such schools among semi-civilized natives of the Sandwich Islands, and his own views were strengthened by the testimony of some of the oldest of the pioneer missionaries" (Armstrong. "A Teacher's Witness," 38, 43–45).

20. Armstrong, "A Teacher's Witness," 18; Robert Francis Engs, *Educating The Disenfranchised and Disinherited* (Knoxville: University of Tennessee Press, 1999), 61–62; M. F. Armstrong and Helen W. Ludlow, *Hampton and Its Students by Two of Its Teachers* (New York: Putnam's Sons, 1874), 20–21; General Samuel Chapman Armstrong, *Hampton Institute 1868–1885: Its Work for the Two Races* (Hampton, VA: Hampton Virginia Normal School Press Print, 1885), 6, Hampton University Archives; Lindsey, *Indians at Hampton Institute*, 7.

21. Armstrong, *Hampton Institute 1868–1885*, 61–62; James D. Anderson, *The Education of Blacks in the South 1860–1935* (Chapel Hill: University of North Carolina Press, 1988), 33–78; Spivey, *Schooling for the New Slavery*, 6–7.

22. Frederick E. Hoxie, *Indians in American History* (Arlington Heights: Harlan Davidson, Inc., 1988), 216–17; Armstrong, *Hampton Institute 1868–1885*, 6–7; Engs, "Red, Black, and White," 243. According to Mrs. Armstrong, contributors to Hampton included Mrs. Augustus Hemenway of Boston, $1000 for a printing office, New York companies Richard Hoe & Company of New York, "hand stop cylinder press," and Farmer, Little & Co, $300. (Armstrong, "A Teacher's Witness,"38, 43–45.)

23. Robert Utley, *The Indian Frontier* (Albuquerque, NM: University of Albuquerque Press, 1984), 176–77, 218–19; Lindsey, *Indians at Hampton Institute*, 22.

24. Utley, *The Indian Frontier*, 176–77, 218–19; *Southern Workman* 7, no. 5 (May 1878): 36, Hampton University Archives; Frederick E. Hoxie, *The Final Promise: The Campaign to Assimilate the Indians, 1880–1920* (Lincoln: University of Nebraska Press, 1984), 55; *Harpers Weekly*, May 11, 1878. Ledger Art—Anonymous, 1876, "Mounted Kiowa Warrior in Action"; Anonymous, 1876, "Mounted Kiowa Warrior going on War Path"; Anonymous, [1876], "Indian Hunter Shooting Arrow at Elk, Comanche Peyote Man, Photograph—Indians At Fort Marion, The United States Department of the Interior, National Park Service, Fort Caroline National Memorial, Timucuan Ecological and Historic Preserve, Jacksonville, Florida; Cora Folsom, "Indian Days at Hampton" [incomplete manuscript], 1–2, 1918, Hampton University Archives; Cora Folsom, *Friends Intelligencer* (vol. 38, 1881–1882), Hampton University Archives; Helen Ludlow, *Southern Workman*, December 1878, 91, Hampton University Archives; Ludlow, "An Indian Raid on Hampton Institute," 36; Armstrong and Ludlow, *Ten Years Work for Indians at Hampton Institute* (Hampton: Normal School Press, 1888), 9; Lindsey, *Indians at Hampton Institute*, 28.

25. *Ten Years Work*, 9–10; James E. Gregg, *The Southern Workman* 51 (August 1922): 393–94, Hampton University Archives; Lindsey, *Indians at Hampton Institute*, 28–30; R. H. Pratt Papers WAMSS S-1174 series I, box 10, folder 342, Outgoing letters, The Western Americana Collection, Beinecke Rare Book and Manuscript Library, Yale University; Hoxie, *Indians in American History*, 216–17; Ludlow, "An Indian Raid on Hampton Institute," 36; Hoxie, *The Final Promise*, 55, *Harpers Weekly*, May 11, 1878; Folsom, "Indian Days at Hampton," 1–2; Hoxie, *Indians in American History*, 216–17; Brenda Child, *The Boarding School Seasons: American Indian Families 1900–1940* (Lincoln: University of Nebraska Press, 1998), 13, 43; Robert Francis Engs, "Red, Black, and White: A Study in Intellectual Inequality," *in Region, Race, and Reconstruction: Essays in Honor of C. Vann Woodward* (New York: Oxford University Press, 1982), 241, 242.

26. R. H. Pratt Papers, series I, box 10, folder 342.

27. R. H. Pratt Papers, Pratt Wa MSS S-1174, Letter Press Bound Volume #3, 1877

Nov–1878 Apr, in the Western Americana Collection, Beinecke Rare Book and Manuscript Library, Yale University.

28. Engs, "Red, Black, and White," 245.

29. Engs, *Educating the Disenfranchised*, 119.

30. The threat of retaliation against conquest by Indians proved very real. Ramon Gutierrez argues that New Mexican Indians appeared converted to Christianity, but in fact practiced their own religion, and eventually grew tired of Spanish rule, eventually murdering missionaries and burning churches and missions in the Revolt of 1680. The fear of retribution colored the ways in which administrators dealt with Native American and Blacks at Hampton. (Ramon A. Gutierrez, *When Jesus Came, the Corn Mothers Went Away: Marriage, Sexuality, and Power in New Mexico, 1500–1846* [Stanford: Stanford University Press, 1991], 133–34; Lindsey, *Indians at Hampton Institute*, 30–31)

31. Lindsey, 31; Folsom, "Indian Days At Hampton," 6; Ludlow, "An Indian Raid on Hampton Institute," 36.

32. Washington, *Up from Slavery*, 97.

33. Folsom, "Indian Days At Hampton," 37, 51, 29; "Class of 1876. J.C. Robbins," *Twenty-Two Years Work of the Hampton Normal and Agricultural Institute at Hampton Virginia* (Hampton Normal School Press, 1893), 37, 51, 73, Hampton University Archives; Lindsey, *Indians at Hampton Institute*, 95.

34. Lindsey, *Indians at Hampton Institute*, 95.

35. Ibid.

36. Letter to Francis J. Garrison from Booker T. Washington, November 25, 1905, Booker T. Washington Collection MG 182, box 1(1), Correspondence 1905–1913, Rare Books and Manuscript Collection, The Schomburg Center for Research in Black Culture.

37. Washington. *Up from Slavery*, 98.

38. Ibid.

39. "Lovey A. Mayo, Class of 1880," *Twenty-Two Years Work*, 145, Hampton University Archives; Folsom, "Indian Days at Hampton," 82; Joseph Willard Tingey, "Indians and Blacks Together: An Experiment in Bi Racial Education at Hampton Institute (1878–1923)," dissertation Teachers College, Columbia University, 1978, 178.

40. Georgia (Georgiana) Washington's School Records, Hampton University Archives; H.B. Frissell, "Georgia Washington," *Hampton Graduates, 1871–1899*, 95, Hampton University Archives.

41. Stephanie Y. Evans, *Black Women in the Ivory Tower 1850–1954: An Intellectual History* (Gainesville: University of Florida Press, 2007), 42–46; Francille Rusan Wilson, *Segregated Scholars* (Charlottesville: University of Virginia Press, 2006), 102–5.

42. Anna Julia Cooper, *A Voice From the South* (New York: Negro Universities Press, 1892), 61. Anna Julia Cooper, *A Voice from the South, by a Black Woman of the South* (New York: Oxford University Press, 1988).

43. Ibid., 79.

44. "Class of 1880, Lovey A. Mayo," 145. Please see Paula Marie Seniors, "Cole and Johnson's *The Red Moon*, 1908–1910: Reimagining African American and Native American Female Education at Hampton Institute," *The Journal of African American History* 93, no. 1 (Winter 2008): 21–35.

45. Georgiana Washington, "'A Resident Graduate's Fifteen Years at Hampton' by Georgiana Washington, Class of '82," Essay read at the Hampton Anniversary, May

19, 1892, *Southern Workman* 21, no. 7 (July 1892): 116–17; *Twenty-Two Years Work; Southern Workman*, February 1893, Hampton University Archives.

46. Washington, "A Resident Graduate's."

47. Ibid.

48. Ludlow, *Ten Years Work*, 29; Spivey, *Schooling for The New Slavery*, 21–22; Engs, *Educating the Disfranchised*, 102, 103, 121; Adams, "Education in Hues," 166; Engs, "Red, Black, and White," 248; Katherine Ellinghaus, "Assimilation by Marriage," 298–99; Child, *The Boarding School Seasons*, 32, 36, 82, 88, 35–36, 79; Adams, *Education for Extinction*, 156, 213–14, 224, 239; Robert Francis Engs, *Freedom's First Generation: Black Hampton, Virginia, 1861–1890* (Philadelphia: Africa World Press, 1979), 149, 156.

49. Engs, *Educating the Disenfranchised*, 106, 101, 102, 112; Child, *The Boarding School Seasons*, 74, 70, 71; Donald Spivey, *Schooling for The New Slavery: Black Industrial Education 1868–1915* (Westport, CT: Greenwood Press, 1978), 56–58.

50. Mary Frances Berry, *My Face Is Black Is True: Callie House and The Struggle for Ex-Slave Reparations* (New York: Alfred A. Knopf, 2005), 54.

51. "Pioneer Teacher Ends Busy Life: Amelia Perry Pride, Teacher in Negro Schools for 33 Years Dies Today"; *Hampton Questionnaire*, 16 January 1928, 1–2; letter from Amelia Perry Pride to General Armstrong dated 12 November 1888, Hampton University Archives; Amelia Perry Pride, "Incidents of Indian Life at Hampton" (February 1880), 19, Hampton University Archives (hereafter, "Pioneer Teacher Ends Busy Life").

52. Amelia Perry Pride, "Incidents of Indian Life at Hampton," 19.

53. Ibid.

54. Adams, *Education for Extinction* , 151–53.

55. *Southern Workman* (December 1882), 123, Hampton University Archives.

56. Booker T. Washington, "Magnanimity of the Negro toward The Indian," *The Southern Workman* (October 1880), 103, Hampton University Archives.

57. Ibid.

58. Ibid.

59. Folsom, "Indian Days at Hampton," 53.

60. Washington, "Magnanimity of the Negro toward the Indian," 103.

61. *Southern Workman*, December 1882, 123.

62. "Class of 1880. Lovey A. Mayo," 145.

63. Washington, *Up from Slavery*, 98.

64. Margaret James Murray, "Practical Help Leaflet No. 1," Hampton University Archives.

65. R. H. Pratt Papers, Pratt Incoming letters, WAMSS S-1174 series I, box 7, folder 235, The Western Americana Collection, Beinecke Rare Book and Manuscript Library, Yale University.

66. R. H. Pratt Papers, Pratt Incoming letters, WA MSS S-1174 box 8, folder 296.

67. Child, *The Boarding School Seasons*, 28, 29, 72, 97.

68. Adams, *Education for Extinction*, 110.

69. Amelia Perry Pride, "Incidents of Indian Life at Hampton," 19; Georgiana Washington, "Vacation in Winona," 103; Washington, "A Resident Graduate's."

70. Sarah Walker, Fort Berthold, Dakota (Hidasta), "Incidents of Indian Life at Hampton" [February 1880], 19, Hampton University Archives.

71. Thomas Sloan, *Talks and Thoughts of the Indian Students,* eds. Sam Defond, Rebecca Mazakute, Richard Powless, manager, vol. 3, no. 5 (September 1888): 2, Hampton University Student Newspaper Archives.

72. Folsom, "Indian Days at Hampton," 87.

73. *Talks and Thoughts* (October 1895), Hampton University Archives; *Talks and Thoughts* (1898),

74. The Amelia Perry Pride Papers: letter addressed to Mrs. Cleveland, December 1892; obituary. *Hampton University Questionnaire,* January 1928; letter addressed to Dr. Frissell, President of Hampton (1901); letter to Dr. Frissell (President of Hampton University) from Amelia Perry Pride 1901; *Twenty-Two Years Work.* The Polk School survives and is renamed The Paul Laurence Dunbar Middle School, High School, and Alternative School (called The Amelia Perry Pride House). Personal visit to Lynchburg, Virginia, fall 2007.

75. Amelia Perry Pride, "Report of the Committee on Domestic Economy, by A. E. Pride," The Amelia Perry Pride Papers, Hampton University Archives.

76. Washington, "A Resident Graduate's."

77. *Southern Workman* (July 1892). When Georgiana Washington died in 1952 at the age of 91, the community and the school administrators named the school in her honor. (*Hampton Graduates 1871–1899*, box 42, Peoples Village School Correspondence 1917–1988, Hampton University Archives.)

78. "Lovey Mayo, Class of 1880," 145.

79. Ellinghaus, "Assimilation by Marriage, 298–299; Engs, "Red, Black, and White," 247–48; Laura Wexler, *Tender Violence: Domestic Visions in an Age of U.S. Imperialism* (Chapel Hill: University of North Carolina Press, 2000), 149; Ludlow, *Ten Years,* 14–15.

80. "Class of 1882; Georgiana Washington," *Twenty-Two Years Work,* 145; Outgrowths of Hampton Peoples Village School, Georgia Washington, box 45 G, Washington Papers; *Southern Workman* folder March 1916, *Southern Workman,* March 1916, 199, Hampton University Archives.

81. Washington, *Up from Slavery,* 88–89.

82. Folsom, "Indian Days At Hampton," 87, 95; *The Southern Workman* (July 1892).

83. *The Red Moon* program, Lester Walton, *New York Age,* 10 September 1908, 6.

84. *The Red Moon* program; Walton, *New York Age,* 6.

85. "Music and the Stage," from "Music and the Stage," edited by Lester A. Walton, *New York Age,* 26 August 1909, 6.

86. C.A.H. [Charles A. Hunter], *New York Age,* 1 April 1909, 6.

87. J. Rosamond Johnson Papers, Irving S. Gilmore Music Library, Yale University.

88. Adams, "Education in Hues," 169–71.

89. Armstrong, *Hampton Institute 1868–1885,* 8.

90. Engs, "Red, Black, and White," 248; Armstrong, *Hampton Institute 1868–1885,* 7; Ludlow, *Ten Years Work,* 12.

91. Child, *The Boarding School Seasons,* 14.

92. Ellinghaus, "Assimilation by Marriage," 301; Engs, *Educating the Disenfranchised,* 106; Child, *The Boarding School Seasons,* 74; Adams, *Education for Extinction,* 307.

93. *Red Moon* review, W. C. Cawley Collection, Lincoln Center Library for the Performing Arts.

94. Ibid.; Johnson, *Black Manhattan,* 171; Riis, *Just before Jazz,* 175; Sampson, *The Ghost Walks,* 439, 442–43; Badger, *A Life in Ragtime,* 38–39. All reviewers indicate that the show *did* break the love scene taboo with romantic scenes and a storyline in the vein of light opera (review of *The Red Moon, Toledo Blade,* 14 December 1908, Robinson Locke Collection). The passion imbued in the musical accounts for white reviewers discomfort when evaluating the musical, given that the norm was to lampoon black love. The *New York Times* identifies a plotline with a finale, which saw Minnehaha happily married to Plunk Green ("'Red Moon'" Uninteresting," *New York Times,* 4 May 1909, 9; "Few Novelties in the Waning Theatrical Season," *New York Times,* 2 May 1909, X8). The love songs within the musical, including "Won't You Be My Little Brown Bear," a playfully romantic ditty, also substantiate the ardent nature of the show. J. Rosamond Johnson's 1938 notes on the 1908 production confirm the sentimentality of the play. Finally, contemporary scholars Henry T. Sampson, Thomas Riis, Reid Badger, and Karen Sotiropoulos all write of the romantic nature of *The Red Moon.*

95. Adams, "Education in Hues," 171.

96. Ellinghaus, "Assimilation by Marriage," 291.

97. Helen Ludlow, "Hampton Indian Students at Home," *Hampton Institute 1868 to 1885: Its Work for Two Races* (Hampton: Virginia Normal School Press Print, 1885), 13–17, Hampton University Archives.

98. Armstrong and Ludlow, *Ten Years Work,* 14.

99. Lindsey, *Indians at Hampton Institute,* 27.

100. Samuel Chapman Armstrong, preface to (M. F.) Armstrong and Ludlow, *Ten Years Work,* 4.

101. Adams, "Education in Hues," 172.

102. Eastman was a physician at the Pine Ridge Reservation. The HBO movie *Bury My Heart at Wounded Knee* presents composites of the Eastmans (Elaine Goodale Eastman, *The Voice at Eve* [Chicago: The Bookfellows, 1930], 28–29, Hampton University Archives). Owl the tribal chairman of the Eastern Cherokees married Ponds after World War I. Ponds died in childbirth. Owl recalls their courting in 1911. "'We weren't allowed to be socially mixed with female teachers,'" but he took a job gardening for teachers and they became romantically involved "as she found excuse to assist him in the flower beds" (Tingey, *Indians and Blacks Together,* 235–36). Jones graduated from Hampton in 1892, and was the first Indian graduate from Harvard and the first to receive a PhD from Columbia University under Franz Boas in 1904. He taught at Columbia College, studied Indian languages in Canada and Minnesota, and was killed in March 1909 by the Illgnot tribesmen while conducting anthropological research in the Philippines (*Talks and Thoughts* 18, no. 7 [January 1904]: 2; "William Jones Obituary." *Southern Workman* 37, no. 5 [May 1909]: 263, Hampton University Archives; Lindsey, *Indians at Hampton Institute,* 165).

103. Lindsey, *Indians at Hampton Institute,* 173.

104. Ibid., 169, 170.

105. Ibid., 169

106. Ludlow, "Incidents of Indian Life at Hampton," *Southern Workman* 9, no. 7 (July 1879): 77, Hampton University Archives.

107. Lindsey, *Indians at Hampton Institute,* 169.

108. Tingey, *Indians and Blacks Together,* 182.

109. Wyndham Robertson, *Pocahontas alias Matoaka and Her Descendants through the Marriage at Jamestown, Virginia in April 1614 with John Rolfe, Gentleman* (Richmond, VA: J.W. Randolph & English Publishers and Booksellers, 1887, CS 71 R747, Special Collections University Libraries, Virginia Tech). Pocahontas's descendants included Anne Bolling, who displayed her majesty through her "awe-inspiring bearing of her great Indian progenitor, Powhatan," and John Bolling, who married Thomas Jefferson's sister, who rescued him from the "Circe cup" and helped him ascend to the aristocracy (Robertson, *Pocahontas,* 61, 59).

110. "Racial Integrity or 'Race Suicide': Virginia's Eugenic Movement, W. E. B. Du Bois and the Work of Walter A. Plecker," *Negro History Bulletin,* April–September 1999, 1–4, 10; Lindsey, *Indians at Hampton Institute,* 32, 1–4,10.

111. Sampson, *The Ghost Walks,* 439.

112. James Weldon Johnson Papers, Yale Collection of American Literature, GNK James Weldon Johnson to series no. III, folder no. 21, Beinecke Rare Book and Manuscript Library, Yale University.

113. Claudia Tate, "Allegories of Black Female Desire; or, Rereading Nineteenth-Century Sentimental Narratives of Black Female Authority," in *Changing Our Own Words,* ed. Cheryl A. Wall (New Brunswick: Rutgers University Press, 1989), 103.

114. Ann duCille, *The Coupling Convention* (New York: Oxford University Press, 1993), 3.

115. James Weldon Johnson Papers, Yale Collection of American Literature, JWJV3J633B49, Yale University James Weldon Johnson Papers, Beinecke Rare Book and Manuscript Library, Yale University.

116. Sampson, *Blacks in Blackface,* 287.

117. Krasner, *Resistance, Parody, and Double Consciousness,* 141.

118. Ellinghaus, "Assimilation by Marriage," 294.

119. Krasner, *Resistance, Parody, and Double Consciousness,* 141.

120. Ibid.

121. Ibid.

122. James Weldon Johnson Papers, Yale Collection of American Literature, JWJV3J633B49.

123. Indian inspired songs included Harry Williams Egbert Van Alstyne's "'Navajo'" (1903), James T. Brymn's "'Rowena'" (1904), and Thurland Chattaway and Kerry Mill's "'Red Wing'" (1907). Cole and Johnson wrote several songs in the genre for *The Red Moon* (Riis, "Black Musical Theatre in New York," 129–30).

124. Krasner, *Resistance, Parody, and Double Consciousness,* 141.

125. Badger, *A Life in Ragtime,* 38.

126. J. R. Johnson Papers, box 6, folder 14.

127. Plummer, "What's in a Song," 9–10.

128. P. Jane Hafen, ed., *Dreams and Thunder: Stories, Poems, and The Sun Dance Opera, Zitkala-Sa* (Lincoln: University of Nebraska Press, 2001), 126–27. Hanson claimed to have been the sole writer of the opera, performed in 1938 by the New York City Opera. (Hafen, *Dreams and Thunder,* 128.)

129. Badger, *A Life in Ragtime,* 38; Woll, *Black Musical Theatre,* 24; J. R. Johnson Papers, box 6, folder 14.

130. Clara Sue Kidwell, "Ethnoastronomy as the Key to Human Intellectual Develop-

ment and Social Organization," in *Native Voices: American Indian Identity and Resistance,* ed. Richard A. Grounds, George E. Tinker, and David E. Wilkins (Lawrence: University Press of Kansas, 2003), 6–7, 12–13; John G. Bourke, *Journal of American Folk-lore* 7, no. 25 (April–June, 1894), 136; Newbell Niles Puckett, *Folk Beliefs of the Southern Negro* (Chapel Hill: University of North Carolina Press, 1926), 463–64; "Signs from the Hampton Folk-Lore Society, from *Southern Workman* 23 January 1894," in *From My People,* ed. Daryl Cumber Dance (New York: W.W. Norton and Company, 2002), 564.

131. Bourke, *Journal of American Folk-lore,* 136; Newbell Niles Puckett, *Folk Beliefs of the Southern Negro,* 463–64; "Signs from the Hampton Folk-Lore Society," 564; Sam D. Gill and Irene F. Sullivan, *Dictionary of Native American Mythology* (Santa Barbara: ABC-CLIO, 1992), 95; Jean Toomer, *Cane* (New York: Liveright, 1923, reprint 1975), 28–35; Alain Solard, "Myth and Narrative Fiction in *Cane:* 'Blood Burning Moon,'" *Callaou,* no. 25, Recent Essays from Europe: A Special Issue (Autumn 1985): 551–52; Hilda Roberts, *Journal of American Folklore* 40, no. 156 (April–June1927): 185; "Comet," told by Sally Brown Gordon, in *Voices from Four Directions: Contemporary Translations of the Native Literatures of North America,* ed. Brian Swann (Lincoln: University of Nebraska Press, 2004), 389–90; Gill and Sullivan, *Dictionary of Native American Mythology,* 320.

132. Margot Edmonds and Ella E. Clark, "The Milky Way," *Voices of the Winds Native American Legends* (New York: Facts on File, 1989), 307–8; Sam D. Gill and Irene F. Sullivan, "Hisagita-misa," "Great Bear Constellation," "Apache Creation and Emergence," in *Dictionary of Native American Mythology,* 123, 105; Margot Edmonds and Ella E. Clark, "Creation," in *Voices of the Winds,* 100–104.

133. Told by John Armstrong, translator Wallace Chafe, "Seneca Creation Story," *Voices from Four Directions,* 523–24; Sam D. Gill and Irene F. Sullivan, "Apache Creation and Emergence," Jicarella Apache, Southwest, *Dictionary of Native American Mythology,* 13–14; Edward Morris Opler, *Myths and Tales of the Jicarilla Apache Indians* (New York: Kraus Reprint, 1969; originally published in 1938), 10–14.

134. Badger, *A Life in Ragtime,* 38; Woll, *Black Musical Theatre,* 24; J. R. Johnson Papers, box 6, folder 14.

135. Charles A. Hunter, *New York Age,* 25 March 1909, 6.

136. John Rosamond Johnson Papers, box 8, *New York Amsterdam News,* January 29, 1938, 1921, photograph of John Rosamond Johnson, J. Rosamond Johnson Collection, Irving S. Gilmore Music Library at Yale University.

137. Litefoot, "Stereotipik," on *The Messenger* (Seattle, WA: Red Vinyl Records, 2002).

138. L. Frank, "Mission Times," from *Acorn Soup,* 26; Litefoot, "The Life and Times," on *Litefoot Redvolution* (Seattle, WA: Limited Release, Collector's Edition, 2005).

139. Litefoot, "Seein' Red," on *Litefoot Redvolution.*

140. Riis, "Black Musical Theatre in New York," 129–30; Krasner, *Resistance, Parody, and Double Consciousness,* 141.

141. Bean, "Black Minstrelsy,"180.

142. Sampson, *The Ghost Walks,* 440.

143. Bean, "Black Minstrelsy," 180.

144. Sampson, *The Ghost Walks,* 438.

145. George Lipsitz, "Noises in the Blood," *Crossing Lines: Race and Mixed Race*

across the Geohistorical Divide (Lanham, MD: Alta Mira Press, 2005), 21.

146. Hunter, *New York Age,* 21 October 1909, 6; "Rays from 'The Red Moon,'" from "Music and the Stage," edited by Lester A. Walton; *Shoo Fly Regiment* Program 1906, Robinson Locke Collection, 1906; James Weldon Johnson Papers, Yale Collection of American Literature, Beinecke Rare Book and Manuscript Library, Yale University; Majestic Theater Program of *The Red Moon,* 3 May 1909; Sampson, *Blacks in Blackface,* 288; Badger, *A Life in Ragtime,* 39.

147. "Sambo," James Weldon Johnson Papers, Yale Collection of American Literature, JWJV3J6335a, folder 44, Beinecke Rare Book and Manuscript Library, Yale University.

148. Ibid.

149. "Red Moon Rays," from "Music and the Stage," edited by Lester A. Walton; Hunter, *New York Age,* 25 March 1909, 6.

150. Walton, "Music and the Stage," *New York Age,* January 10, 1910, 6.

151. Walton, "Music and the Stage," *New York Age,* 17 February 1910, 6.

152. Walton, "Music and the Stage," *New York Age,* 10 September 1908, 6.

153. Ibid.

154. Hunter, "Rays from 'The Red Moon,'" from "Music and the Stage," edited by Walton, *New York Age,* 18 March 1909, 6.

155. Walton, *New York Age,* 10 September 1908, 6. The Hungry Negro reverberates in the movies today. The Nappy Roots album's name "Watermelon, Chicken & Gritz" also perpetuates the stereotype. Psyche A. Williams-Forson argues that the stereotype is enduring, originating during slavery. Like stereotype-infused rap music which conforms to white audiences' tastes, Cole and Johnson adhered to white tastes while at the same time giving black people affirmative characters. The line between glorifying blacks and ridicule remained thin. (*Entertainment Weekly,* 20 May 2002, 107; Psyche A. Williams-Forson, "Black Men, Visual Imagery, and the Ideology of Fear, in *Building Houses Out of Chicken Legs: Black Women, Food, & Power* [Chapel Hill: University of North Carolina Press, 2006], 38–78.)

156. Walton, "Music and the Stage," *New York Age,* 10 September 1908, 6.

157. Litefoot, "Stereotipik," from *The Messenger,* Red Vinyl Records, 2002.

158. Robert Berkhoffer, *The White Man's Indian* (New York: Alfred A. Knopf, 1978), 3, 10, 26.

159. Ibid., 3, 10, 72–73.

160. Gary Nash, *Red, White, and Black* (Englewood Cliffs, NJ: Prentice Hall, 1974), 35.

161. Berkhoffer, *The White Man's Indian,* 7–8, 10.

162. Steinberg, *The Ethnic Myth,* 14–15.

163. Nash, *Red, White, and Black,* 38.

164. Robertson, *Pocahontas,* 1–2.

165. Berkhoffer, *The White Man's Indian,* 7.

166. Nash, *Red, White, and Black,* 39–40; Robertson, *Pocahontas,* 1–2.

167. Sherman Alexie, *Reservation Blues* (New York: Atlantic Monthly Press, 1995, Warner Books, 1996), 219, 233, 240–41; Robertson, *Pocahontas,* 61.

168. Steinberg, *The Ethnic Myth,* 16–17.

169. Berkhoffer, *The White Man's Indian,* 30, 88. George Catlin's *Wi-Jun-Jon, the Pigeon's Egg Head (The Light), Going to and Returning from Washington* (1832) depicts

the Vanishing Indian as noble.

170. Frances B. Johnston's 1899–1900 photographs details the Hampton Indian's transformation with "before" images in traditional attire and "after" pictures in Anglo dress.

171. Sampson, *The Ghost Walks,* 442.

172. Ibid.

173. J. D. Howard, *Indianapolis Freeman,* 1909–1910; Sampson, *The Ghost Walks,* 439.

174. R. H. Pratt Papers WAMSS S-1174, Pratt incoming letters, box 4, Howling Wolf, The Western Americana Collection, Beinecke Rare Book and Manuscript Library, Yale University.

175. Ibid.

176. Litefoot, "The Life and Times," on *Litefoot Redvolution* (Seattle, WA: Limited Release, Collector's Edition, 2005).

177. Armstrong, *Hampton Institute 1868–1885,* 8; 298–99; Armstrong and Ludlow, *Ten Years Work,* 25–29; Katherine Ellinghaus, "Assimilation by Marriage: White Women and Native American Men at Hampton Institute, 1878–1923," *The Virginia Magazine of History and Biography* 108, no. 3 (2000): 298–99; Child, *The Boarding School Seasons,* 32, 82, 88; David Wallace Adams, *Education for Extinction: American Indians and the Boarding School Experience, 1878–1928* (Lawrence, KS: University of Kansas Press, 1995), 156, 213–14, 224, 239.

178. R. H. Pratt Papers, WA MSS S-1174 box 8, folder 296, Pratt Incoming Letters, Toun ke uh, The Western Americana Collection, Beinecke Rare Book and Manuscript Library, Yale University.

179. R. H. Pratt Papers, box 2, folder 67 WA MSS S-1174, Pratt Incoming Letters, Doanmoe, The Western Americana Collection, Beinecke Rare Book and Manuscript Library, Yale University.

180. I photographed the gravesites at Hampton in 2005 and Carlisle School in 2007.

181. R. H. Pratt Papers, box 2, folder 67 WA MSS S-1174, Pratt Incoming Letters, Doanmoe, The Western Americana Collection, Beinecke Rare Book and Manuscript Library, Yale University.

182. Charles Alexander Eastman, 1858–1939, *Indian Boyhood* (Omaha: University of Nebraska Press, 1902, prepared for the University of Virginia Library Electronic Text, Electronic Text Center, University of Virginia Library, 1999), 289; Adams, *Education for Extinction,* 239, 240, 225.

183. Child, *The Boarding School Seasons,* 32.

184. Ludlow, "Incidents of Life at Hampton"; Caroline Andrus, box 2, biography Andrus Booklet "C.W. Andrus 1909 Recorded C.W. Andrus Summer 1909 All notes marked entered on records," 37, Hampton University Archives.

185. Sampson, *The Ghost Walks,* 442. The song reflected the popularity of Latin dances with its "habanera ostinato" (Riis, *Just Before Jazz,* 135).

186. Hunter, "Rays from 'The Red Moon,'" from "Music and the Stage," edited by Walton, *New York Age,* 14 January 1909, 6.

187. Sampson, *The Ghost Walks,* 439.

188. Bob Cole, "On The Road To Monterey," James Weldon Johnson Papers, Yale Collection of American Literature, JWJV3J633, Beinecke Rare Book and Manuscript Library, Yale University.

189. Charles Cameron White, "The Negro in Musical Europe," *New York Age,* 24 December 1908.

190. Ibid.

191. Sampson, *The Ghost Walks,* 439.

192. Robert Allen Cole Theatre Directions for Red Moon (play), n.d. [1908–1910], OG248, Moorland-Spingarn Research Center, Howard University.

193. White, "The Negro in Musical Europe."

194. Sampson, *The Ghost Walks,* 439.

195. White, "The Negro in Musical Europe."

196. Hunter, "Rays from 'The Red Moon,'" edited by Walton, *New York Age,* 14 January 1909, 6; Walton, "Music and the Stage," *New York Age,* 10 September 1908, 6.

197. Hunter, "Red Moon Rays," from "Music and the Stage," edited by Walton, *New York Age,* 25 March 1909, 6.

198. Hunter, "Music and the Stage," edited by Walton, *New York Age,* 28 January 1909, 6.

199. Robert Allen Cole Theatre Directions for Red Moon (play), n.d.

200. George Lipsitz, "Mardi Gras Indians," from *Time Passages,* 236, 247.

201. Margaret L. Archuleta, Brenda J. Child, and K. Tsianina Lomawaima, *Away from Home: American Indian Boarding School Experiences, 1879–2000* (Phoenix, Heard Museum, 2000), 61, 72.

202. Walton, "Music and the Stage," *New York Age,* 10 September 1908, 6.

203. Jewel Plummer Cobb Collection: *The Journal,* Sunday, March 1, 1896; *The World,* September 8, 1895; *The World,* 1896, Bob Cole's Scrapbook, illustration of the Ethiopian Defeat of the Italians and Menelek.

204. Jewel Plummer Cobb Collection, *The Evening Telegram,* August 2, 1898; *The World, Florida Times Union, Boston Herald, New Orleans Picayune, New Orleans Times Democrat, Kansas City Star,* 1895.

205. Nash, *Red, White, and Black,* 281–82.

206. Berkhoffer, *The White Man's Indian,* 90.

207. Nash, *Red, White, and Black,* 56–57; Edmund S. Morgan, "The Jamestown Fiasco," in *American Slavery, American Freedom* (New York: W. W. Norton and Company, 1975), 76, 83; Robertson, *Pocahontas,* 1–2; John Gould Fletcher, *John Smith—Also Pocahontas* (New York: Brentano's Publisher, 1928), 124, 105, 259–61 (F229S7174), Special Collections University Libraries, Virginia Tech; Benjamin Woolley, *Savage Kingdom: The True Story of Jamestown, 1607, and the Settlement of America* (New York: Harpers Collins Publishers, 2007), 311–12, 316–18, 132, 134; Camilla Townsend, *Pocahontas and the Powhatan Dilemma* (New York: Hill and Wang, 2004), 52, 104, 115–18; David A. Price, *Love and Hate in Jamestown* (New York: Borzoi Book, 2003), 68–69, 148–51; Berkhoffer, *The White Man's Indian,* 90; Paula Gunn Allen, *Pocahontas, Medicine Woman, Spy, Entrepreneur, Diplomat* (San Francisco: Harper San Francisco, 2003), 21, 57–58, 84–85, 175; Asebrit Sundquist, *Pocahontas & Co., The Fictional American Indian Woman in Nineteenth-Century Literature: A Study of Method* (Atlantic Highlands, NJ: Humanities Press International, 1987), 51–51. John Smith changed the Pocahontas narrative from a rescue narrative to a self-aggrandizing romance between Pocahontas and himself. Virginia's Jamestown settlement features a life-size romanticized statue of Pocahontas that reinscribes Smith's narrative.

208. Krasner, *Resistance, Parody, and Double Consciousness*, 141.

209. Berkhoffer, *The White Man's Indian*, 99.

210. Ibid; Michael Rogin, *Blackface, White Noise: Jewish Immigrants in the Holly-wood Melting Pot* (Berkeley, Los Angeles, London: University of California Press, 1998), 13, 127, 153–54; *Whoopee*, 1931.

211. "Pioneer Teacher Ends Busy Life"; letter from Amelia Perry Pride to the General dated November 12, 1888. I discovered that Amelia Perry Pride's family gravestone in the Old City Cemetery in Lynchburg, Virginia, is a very prominent monument that connotes her stature.

212. "Amelia Perry, Class of 1879," In *Twenty-Two Year Work*, 124–25; "Pioneer Teacher Ends Busy Life"; letter from Amelia Perry Pride to the General dated 12 November 1888.

213. *Talks and Thoughts* 3, no. 6 (3 (November 1888): 1895; Mary Lou Hultgren and Paulette Fairbanks Molin, *To Lead and to Serve: American Indian Education at Hampton Institute 1878–1923* (The Virginia Foundation for the Humanities, 1989), 21, Hampton University Archives

214. Abbie Mitchell, Mercer Cook Papers, box 157–7, folder 24, Cook, "From Clorindy," 18, Moorland-Spingarn Center, Howard University.

215. Abbie Mitchell's Autobiographical Notes, Mercer Cook Papers, box 157–7, folder 27, 1, Moorland-Spingarn Center, Howard University.

216. Abbie Mitchell, Abbie, Mercer Cook Papers, box 157–7, folder 24, 2–3.

217. Ibid.

218. Ibid. Mitchell's father played an active role in her wellbeing. Jo Ann Tanner conducted an interview with Mitchell's granddaughter who conveyed that Mitchell's relationship with her father thrived. (Tanner, *Dusky Maidens*, 109.)

219. Abbie Mitchell, Mercer Cook Papers, box 157–7, folder 27, 1.

220. Ibid.

221. Abbie Mitchell, Mercer Cook Papers, box 157–7, folder 24, Cook, "From Clorindy," 7.

222. Abbie Mitchell, Mercer Cook Papers, box 157–7, folder 24, 9–10.

223. Ibid.

224. Ibid.

225. Ibid.

226. Abbie Mitchell, Mercer Cook Papers, box 157–7, folder 24, 12.

227. Abbie Mitchell, Mercer Cook Papers, box 157–7, folder 17, 6.

228. Abbie Mitchell, Mercer Cook Papers, box 157–7, folder 24, 14.

229. Gaines, *Uplifting the Race*, 122–23.

230. Michelle Mitchell, *Righteous Propagation: African Americans and the Politics of Racial Destiny after Reconstruction* (Chapel Hill: University of North Carolina Press, 2004), 199.

231. Gatewood, *Aristocrats of Color*, 178–80.

232. Letter to W. E. B. Du Bois from Arturo Schomburg, 18 November 1931, W. E. B. Du Bois Correspondence 1911–1957, MG 109 box 1, Rare Books and Manuscript Collection, Schomburg Center for Research in Black Culture. Interest abounded in Douglass's marriage. Both Schomburg and Du Bois wanted to analyze the union. Du Bois wanted possession of the letter. (Letter from W. E. B. Du Bois to Arturo Schomburg, Cor-

respondence 1911–1957, Letter 20 November 1931, Du Bois MG 109 box 1, Schomburg Center for Research in Black Culture.)

233. Steinberg, *Ethnic Myth,* 225; Gutman, *The Black Family in Slavery and Freedom,* 523. By 1913 anti-Semitism became so pronounced that Jewish pencil factory manager Leo Frank was convicted of raping and murdering Mary Phagan in Atlanta, Georgia. The anti-Semitic feeling ran so high that white supremacists dismissed the common practice of accusing a black, in this case a janitor, and lynched Frank in 1915. The musical *Parade* was based on this case.

234. Mitchell, *Righteous Propagation,* 197–98. The White Rose Home worked to protect Southern black women from those who "lay in wait," namely, "Jewish men." ("Report of the White Rose Home for the Summer of 1906," White Rose Mission and Industrial Association Collection, Manuscripts, Archives, and Rare Books Collections, The Schomburg Center for Research in Black Culture.)

235. Spickard, *Mixed Race,* 170, 172; Joshua D. Rothman, "'Notorious in the Neighborhood': An Interracial Family in Early National and Antebellum Virginia," *Journal of Southern History* 67, no. 1 (February 2001): 73–74.

236. Ibid. Rothman's article remains unclear as to whether the marriage was a common law marriage or legal.

237. "Report of the White Rose Home for the summer of 1906"; Hudsey Smith, "Partial History of White Rose Mission and Industrial Association," White Rose Mission and Industrial Association Collection, SCMS 565 Manuscripts, Archives, and Rare Books Collections, The Schomburg Center for Research in Black Culture. The Great Migration brought Southern black women north for work, which fueled the need for safe, affordable housing. This proved incredibly important given the threat of violence in the homes of some employers, and limited accommodations in areas where there were houses of prostitution, or in gambling/vice districts. Black women like Victoria Earle Matthews and clubwomen resolved to remedy the situation by establishing homes, including the White Rose Mission Home in New York City, to help the Colored "Stranger Girl." The home provided shelter for women and their children from the U.S., the Caribbean, Brazil, and Hawaii; helped find safe employment; and offered training and classes. ("Report of the White Rose Home for the summer of 1906"; Hudsey Smith, "Partial History of White Rose Mission and Industrial Association"; "White Rose Industrial Association: An Appeal To Our Friends," April 6, 1910; "Our Appeal," The White Rose Mission and Industrial Association, Inc. AKA "The White Rose Home," Mary Kendall Hyde and Mrs. S.E. Wilkerson, Treasurer; "White Rose Home: Its Work and Need," probably 1898–1899; "Certificate of Incorporation of The White Rose Mission and Industrial Association, 1899, 1; n.d.; Rental Agreement between Abraham C. Quackenbush and The White Rose Industrial Association (1908); Mortgage, White Rose Mission and Industrial Association (1930), White Rose Mission and Industrial Association Collection, SCMS 565 Manuscripts, Archives, and Rare Books Collections, The Schomburg Center for Research in Black Culture; Deborah Gray-White, *Too Heavy A Load: Black Women in Defense of Themselves 1894–1994* (New York and London: W.W. Norton & Company, 1999), 30–31.

238. Steinberg, *Ethnic Myth,* 91, 93, 95.

239. Lynn Nottage, *Intimate Apparel* (New York: The Dramatists Play Service, Inc, 2005), 18.

240. Ibid., 17–18.

241. Ibid., 28.

242. Mercer Cook Papers, box 157–9, folder 39, Moorland-Spingarn Center, Howard University.

243. Ibid. Mercer Cook was professor and chair of Romance Languages at Howard University (1950s–1970). He served as the ambassador to Niger for three years and Senegal for two years. ("Abbie Mitchell Goes to Perpetual Summertime," *New York Amsterdam News,* 23 March 1960; "Abbie Mitchell, Actress, Is Dead; Singer was Widow of Composer," *The New York Times,* 20 March 1960, Mercer Cook Papers, Moorland-Spingarn Research Center, Howard University; "Will Mercer Cook," *The New York Times,* 7 October 1987.)

244. Mercer Cook Papers, box 157–9, folder 39.

245. Abbie Mitchell, Mercer Cook Papers, box 157–7, folder 24, 2–3.

246. Mercer Cook Papers, box 157–4, 18, Moorland-Spingarn Research Center, Howard University.

247. Mercer Cook Papers, 157–9, folder 39. In 1908 Abbie Mitchell sang a classical selection for the Benefit for the Industrial Home for Colored Working Girls. (Walton, "The Benefit," *New York Age,* 11 June 1908, 6.)

248. Lester A. Walton, "Bandanna Land," *New York Age,* 6 February 1908.

249. Mercer Cook Papers, box 157–7, folder 27.

250. Ibid.

251. Abbie Mitchell, Mercer Cook Papers, box 157–7, folder 27.

252. Ibid.

253. Abbie Mitchell, Mercer Cook, 157–9, folder 39.

254. *The Tuskegee Student,* 18 April 1903, Mercer Cook Papers, box 157–7; "Abbie Mitchell in a Song Program," "The Musical Courier Says," "Heifetz and Abbie Mitchell Heard in Recitals," *The New York Evening Journal,* n.d., Mercer Cook Oversize, Moorland-Spingarn Center, Howard University. Mitchell paid for several advertisements for her school in support of the White Rose Home. ("The White Rose Home Gypsy Tea," Program, 26 October 1952, 2, White Rose Mission and Industrial Association Collection, SCMS 565. The Schomburg Center for Research in Black Culture. Manuscripts, Archives, and Rare Books Collections.)

255. Tom Fletcher, *100 Years of the Negro in Show Business* (New York: Burdge, 1954), 131, 132; Mitchell, Abbie, Mercer Cook Papers, box 157–7, folder 17, 11.

256. Walton, "Music and the Stage," *New York Age,* 6 August 1908, 6.

257. Cook, "From Clorindy," 18.

258. Walton, "Music and the Stage," *New York Age,* 10 September 1908, 6.

259. Ibid.

260. Cook, "From Clorindy," 18.

261. Lester A. Walton, "Red Moon Improves with Age," *New York Age,* 2 September 1909, 6.

262. J. Rosamond Johnson Papers, box 6, folder 15, Irving S. Gilmore Music Library, Yale University James Weldon Johnson Papers, Yale Collection of American Literature, Beinecke Rare Book and Manuscript Library, Yale University.

263. Robert Allen Cole Theatre Directions for Red Moon.

264. J. R. Johnson Papers, box 6, folder 15.

Chapter Five

1. Margaret James Murray, "Practical Help Leaflet No. 1."

2. Lester A. Walton, "Music and the Stage," *New York Age*, 1911; Riis, "Black Musical Theatre," 52; Plummer, "Under the Bamboo Tree," 10.

3. White, *Ar'n't I A Woman?*, 29. *Birth of a Nation* (1915) perfectly illustrates The Cult of True Womanhood. The white ingénue Flora Cameron leaps off a cliff to her death rather than face despoilment by Guy, the black union officer "rapist." This action exemplifies the characteristics of the stereotype and magnifies the black female's failure as a woman due to her rape during and after slavery.

4. gibsongirls.com, 2002, 2.

5. Woody Gelman, *The Best of Charles Dana Gibson* (New York: Bounty Books, 1969), viiii; gibsongirls.com, 2002, 1.

6. Steven Warshaw, *The Gibson Girls* (Berkeley, CA: Diablo Press, 1968), 1.

7. Gelman, *The Best of Charles Dana Gibson*, viiii.

8. Henry C. Pitz, *Gibson Girl and Her America* (New York: Dover Publications, 1969), xi.

9. Nan Enstad, *Ladies of Labor, Girls of Adventure* (New York: Columbia University Press, 1999), 27.

10. Ibid.

11. Graves, *The Royalty of Vaudeville*, 52–53.

12. I will use Gibson Gal when discussing *The Red Moon*, and Gibson Girl when discussing how Abbie Mitchell and Ada Overton Walker used the icon.

13. Walton, "Music and the Stage," *New York Age*, 10 September 1908, 6; The Majestic Theater Program, 3 May 1909.

14. Robert Allen Cole Theatre Directions for *Red Moon* (play), n.d. [1908–1910].

15. Ibid. Almost one hundred years later in the Broadway shows *Ragtime* and *The Color Purple* (2006), the Model T Ford and the Packard represented middle-class attainment and standing for blacks. In *Ragtime* Coalhouse Walker buys a Ford as a symbol of his status, and in *The Color Purple* the Packard signifies refinement and upper-class status.

16. Walton, "Music and the Stage," *New York Age*, 10 September 1908, 6.

17. In 1907 T. Thomas Fortune, the original owner of the *New York Age*, sold stock in the paper to Fred R. Moore, who acted as Washington's agent. Fortune remained unaware that he was selling the *Age* to Washington, who also co-owned *The Colored American Magazine* with Doubleday, Page and Company, while publicly denying his ownership. (Letter to Booker T. Washington from Fred B. Moore, March 23, 1910, Booker T. Washington Collection MG 182 box 1(1), The Schomburg Center for Research in Black Culture Rare Books and Manuscripts Collection; Louis R. Harlan and Raymond W. Smock, *Booker T. Washington in Perspective* [Jackson and London: University Press of Mississippi, 1988], 145.)

18. Walton, *New York Age*, 10 February 1910, 6.

19. *The Press*, New York, August 7, 1895, The Jewell Plummer Cobb Collection.

20. Ibid.

21. Fannie Barrier Williams, "The Club Movement among Colored Women of America," in Booker T. Washington, *A New Negro for A New Century*, 382.

22. C. D. Gibson, "A New York Day," "Evening," *Scribners Magazine* 24 (July–December 1898): 417; Gelman, *The Best of Charles Dana Gibson;* Pitz, *Gibson Girl and Her America;* Warshaw, *The Gibson Girls.*

23. In 1909 James Weldon Johnson wrote to George A. Towns to announce his engagement and pending marriage to Grace Nail. They married on February 3, 1910. (George A. Towns Papers, box 2, folder 12, Special Collections, Atlanta University Center; J. W. J. Johnson Collection, wedding announcement box 2, folder 13, James Weldon Johnson Collection, Special Collections Department, Robert W. Woodruff Library, Emory University; "Robert Cole A Suicide," *The New York Times,* 3 August 1911, 5.

24. Hunter, "Red Moon Rays," from "Music and the Stage," edited by Lester A. Walton, *New York Age,* 25 March 1909, 6.

25. *New York Age,* 4 May 1911, 6.

26. Hunter, "Red Moon Rays," from "Music and the Stage," edited by Lester A. Walton, *New York Age,* 25 March 1909, 6.

27. Mercer Cook Papers, National Council of Negro Women, Award to Abbie Mitchell from the National Council of Negro Women, box 157–8, folder 8, Moorland-Spingarn Research Center, Howard University; "The White Rose Home Gypsy Tea," 26 October 1952, 2, White Rose Mission and Industrial Association Collection, SCMS 565 Manuscripts, Archives, and Rare Books Collections. Mitchell advertised her vocal studio, and her student Massey Lowery's recital. ("The White Rose Home Gypsy Tea," 26 October 1952, 2, White Rose Mission and Industrial Association Collection, SCMS 565 Manuscripts, Archives, and Rare Books Collections.)

28. The Amelia Perry Pride Papers: Letter addressed to Mrs. Cleveland December 1892 Obituary, *Hampton University Questionnaire* (January 1928); letter addressed to Dr. Frissell, president of Hampton (1901); letter to Dr. Frissell from Amelia Perry Pride (1901); *Twenty-Two Years Work;* Amelia Perry Pride, "Report of the Committee on Domestic Economy, by A. E. Pride," The Amelia Perry Pride Papers, Hampton University Archives; Washington, "A Resident Graduate's Fifteen Years at Hampton," *Southern Workman* (July 1892), Hampton University Archives.

29. T. Thomas Fortune, Afro American Notes, *The Sun* 1898, T. Thomas Fortune Scrapbook, The Schomburg Center for Research in Black Culture, Rare Books and Manuscripts Collection; "Along The Color line," *The Crisis* 1, no. 1 (10 November 1910): 5; Cornelia Bowen, "Women's Part in the Uplift of Our Race, *The Colored American* 12, no. 2 (February 1907): 222–23.

30. George True, "In the Woman's Behalf," *The Colored American* 9, no. 19 (10 August 1901): 10; "The National Association of Colored Women's Clubs," *The Colored American* 14, no. 8 (September 1908): 498–508, Fisk University Archives; "Report of the White Rose Home for the summer of 1906": Hudsey Smith, "Partial History of White Rose Mission and Industrial Association"; "White Rose Industrial Association: An Appeal To Our Friends," April 6, 1910; "Our Appeal": "The White Rose Mission and Industrial Association, Inc., aka "The White Rose Home"; Mary Kendall Hyde and Mrs. S. E. Wilkerson, Treasurer, "White Rose Home Its Work and Need," probably 1898–1899; "Certificate of Incorporation of The White Rose Mission and Industrial Association, 1899, 1; n.d., White Rose Mission and Industrial Association Collection, SCMS 565 Manuscripts, Archives, and Rare Books Collections, The Schomburg Center for Research in Black Culture; Noliwe M. Rooks, *Ladies Pages: African American Wom-*

en's Magazines and the Culture That Made Them (New Brunswick: Rutgers University Press, 2004), 30; "The National Association of Colored Women's Clubs," *The Colored American* 14, no. 8 (September 1908): 498–508; "The Sixth Bi-ennial Convention Held in Brooklyn Ends with Great Enthusiasm," *New York Age,* 3 September 1908, 3; A'Lelia Bundles, *On Her Own Ground: The Life and Times of Madam C. J. Walker* (New York: Washington Square Press), 74–75.

31. Hunter, "Red Moon Rays," from "Music and the Stage," edited by Walton, *New York Age,* 21 January 1909, 6; 25 March 1909, 6.

32. Helen Armstead-Johnson, "Some Late Information on Some Early People," *Encore American and World Wide News,* June 23, 1975, 53, The Schomburg Center for Research in Black Culture, New York City.

33. T. Thomas Fortune, "Afro American Notes," *The Sun* 1898, T. Thomas Fortune Scrapbook, The Schomburg Center for Research in Black Culture, Rare Books and Manuscripts Collection; "Here and There, *The Colored American Magazine* 7, no. 3 (3 January 1903): 213, Fisk University Archives.

34. Hunter, "Red Moon Rays," from "Music and the Stage," edited by Walton, *New York Age,* 21 January 1909, 6.

35. Hunter, "Red Moon Rays," from "Unclean Productions," edited by Lester A. Walton, *New York Age,* 25 March 1909, 6.

36. Ibid.

37. C. D. Gibson, *Drawings by C. D. Gibson* (New York, R. H. Russell & Son, 1894), NC 1075 G4, 1894 Folio, Special Collections, Virginia Tech.

38. J. W. Johnson Collection, Scrapbook BV 6, *New York Amsterdam News,* A2, November 6, 1976, *The Crisis,* March 1977, James Weldon Johnson Collection, Special Collections Department, Robert Woodruff Library, Emory University; Gatewood, *Aristocrats of Color,* 107. In the autobiographical *Along This Way,* Johnson maintains that "[a] number of these older families in Brooklyn were positively rich; their money, made in the days when Negroes in New York were successful caterers, fashionable dressmakers, and the janitors of big buildings having come down through two or three generations." Grace Nail came from such a family because her father owned a tavern. (Johnson, *Along This Way,* 202.)

39. James Weldon Johnson Papers, Yale Collection of American Literature, JWJ MSS Johnson box 41, folder 21, Beinecke Rare Books and Manuscripts Library, Yale University.

40. Du Bois's daughter Yolande attended Bedales and Fisk University, and he gave her a lavish wedding. Washington's daughter Portia attended Bedford Academy, Wellesley, and studied music in Germany, while his son Booker attended Drummer Academy, Phillips Academy, Exeter, and Fisk. (Gatewood, *Aristocrats of Color,* 306; David Levering Lewis, *W. E. B. Du Bois,* 452; David Levering Lewis, *W. E. B. Du Bois: The Fight For Equality and the American Century 1919–1963* (New York: John Macrae Book, Henry Holt and Company, 2000), 31, 220–21; Louis Harlan, *Booker T. Washington: 1901– 1915* (New York and Oxford: Oxford University Press, 1983), 110–13, 115; Francille Rusan Wilson, *Segregated Scholars* (Charlottesville: University of Virginia Press, 2006), 102, 103, 104, 105.

41. James Weldon Johnson Papers, Yale Collection of American Literature. JWJ MSS Johnson box 41, folder 5, Beinecke Rare Books and Manuscripts Library, Yale University.

42. Nell Painter, *Creating Black Americans* (New York: Oxford University Press,

2007), 163; Mary Frances Berry, *My Face Is Black Is True: Callie House and the Struggle For Ex-Slave Reparations,* 52–54; Kali Gross, *Colored Amazons: Crime, Violence, and Black Women in the City of Brotherly Love, 1880–1910* (Durham, NC: Duke University Press, 2006), 40–41.

43. Grace Nail, J.W. Johnson Collection, box number 1, James Weldon Johnson Collection, Special Collections Department, Robert Woodruff Library, Emory University.

44. Hunter, *New York Age,* 18 February 1909, 6.

45. Ibid.

46. James Weldon Johnson Papers, Yale Collection of American Literature, JWJ MSS Johnson box 41 folder 6, Beinecke Rare Book and Manuscript Library, Yale University.

47. J. W. Johnson Collection, box number 1, James Weldon Johnson Collection, Special Collections Department, Robert F. Woodruff Library, Emory University.

48. James Weldon Johnson Papers, Yale Collection of American Literature, JWJ MSS Johnson box 41 folder 12, Beinecke Rare Books and Manuscript Library, Yale University. Johnson as a diplomat kept a photograph of Grace Nail on his desk, so it remains possible that this was the photograph he showed Carlotta.

49. Hunter, "Rays from 'The Red Moon,'" from "Music and the Stage," edited by Walton, *New York Age,* 18 March 1909, 6.

50. Elizabeth Clark-Lewis observed a luncheon in Washington, D.C., held by her eighty-year-old aunt's Bible club in the 1990s and surmised that their main goal included promoting black female reputability. She noticed their elegant and expensive dress, with their matching hats and gloves. She noted their pride in presenting themselves as "proper ladies," sophisticated, and middle class. Elizabeth Clark-Lewis, *Living In, Living Out: African American Domestics in Washington D.C., 1910–1940* (Washington and London: Smithsonian Institution Press, 1994), 2.

51. Paul Laurence Dunbar, *The Sport of the Gods* (New York: Signet Classic, 1901), 58.

52. Ibid., 92–93, 95, 113–120, 75.

53. Ibid., 113.

54. Ibid., 71–72, 119–20.

55. Ibid., 93–95.

56. Ibid., 95.

57. Ibid., 124–125, 144.

58. Ibid., 58–59.

59. Johnson, *Along This Way,* 175; Allen Woll, *Black Musical Theater,* 10; Richard Newman, "'The Brightest Star': Aida Overton Walker in the Age of Ragtime and Cakewalk," in *Prospects: An Annual of American Cultural Studies,* vol. 18 (New York University Press, 1993); Eric Ledell Smith, *Bert Williams: A Biography of the Pioneer Black Comedian* (Jefferson, NC, and London: McFarland Press, 1992), 49; "Jes Like White Folks—A Negro Operetta," *The New York Times,* 24 June 1900, 17.

60. Lester A. Walton, "Music and the Stage," *New York Age,* 14 January 1909, 6.

61. Ibid.

62. Ibid.

63. Walton, "Music and the Stage," *New York Age,* 28 January 1909, 6.

64. Ibid.

65. Ibid.

66. Ibid.

67. Romeo L. Doughterty, "Aida Overton Walker In Memoriam, A Star among Stars Lies Dead," in "Rambling 'Round," Leigh Whipper Papers, mss 47, Writings and Typescripts, other artists, Rare Books and Manuscript Collection, The Schomburg Center for Research in Black Culture.

68. Lester A. Walton, "Music and the Stage," *New York Age,* 26 August 1909, 6; "Cole and Johnson in 'The Red Moon,'" *New York Age,* 26 August 1909, 6. Ada Overton Walker changed her name to Aida, like the opera, later in her theatrical career. Walker accrued ten years' experience choreographing and producing Williams and Walker's shows. She "arranged," danced, and, according to the *New York Dramatic Mirror,* trained the dancers for "The Dance of the Amhara Maid" in *Abyssinia.* She gained renown for her interpretation of the Salome dance in *Bandanna Land* (1907), and performed the dance for William Hammerstein's 1912 production. ("Williams and Walker *Bandanna Land,* Ada Overton Walker as SALOME," *The New York Times,* 24 August 1908; "Ada Overton Walker in Salome Dance," *The New York Times,* 29 June 1912; Abyssinia Program 1906, "Majestic–Abyssinia," *The New York Dramatic Mirror,* 20 February 1906, Helen Armstead-Johnson Miscellaneous Theater Collection, Rare Books and Manuscripts Division, The Schomburg Center for Research in Black Culture; Lester A. Walton, "Abyssinia's Star Actress," *Indianapolis Freeman,* 6 October 1906, 5–6)

69. Richard Newman, "The Brightest Star," 466; Foster, "Pioneers of the Stage," 46–48.

70. Bernard Peterson Jr., *The African American Theater Directory* (Westport, CT, 1997), 12.

71. Foster, "Pioneers of the Stage," 46–47, 48.

72. Pitz, *Gibson Girl and Her America,* 116.

73. Lester A. Walton, "Bandanna Land," *New York Age,* 6 February 1908.

74. Lester A. Walton, "Abyssinia's Star Actress," *Indianapolis Freeman,* 6 October 1906, 4–5.

75. Pitz, *Gibson Girl and Her America,* 74; Gelman, *The Best of Dana Gibson;* Warshaw, *The Gibson Girls.*

76. Foster, "Pioneers of the Stage," 46–47.

77. Ibid.; "The Brightest Star," 467.

78. Ibid.

79. Abyssinia Program 1906, "Majestic–Abyssinia"; Lester A. Walton, "Abyssinia's Star Actress," *Indianapolis Freeman,* 6 October 1906, 4–5.

80. "'The Brightest Star': Aida Overton Walker in the Age of Ragtime and Cakewalk," in *Prospects: An Annual of American Cultural Studies,* vol.18 (New York University Press, 1993), 467–71; Walton, "Abyssinia's Star Actress"; "Williams and Walker *Bandanna Land,* Ada Overton Walker as Salome," *The New York Times,* 24 May 1908; "Negro Company Has Season at Majestic [*His Honor the Barber*]," *The New York Times,* 9 May 1911; "Ada Overton Walker in Salome Dance," *The New York Times,* 29 July 1912.

81. Lester A. Walton, "Art Knows No Color Line, Says the Brooklyn Eagle," *New York Age,* 30 April 1908, 6.

82. Cullen/Jackman Collection: box 36 folder 14, "Mercy Hospital Benefit Ada Overton Walker in Vaudeville" Program, May 26, [1889/1898], "Souvenir Programme Ada

Overton Walker's Benefit for White Rose Industrial Home for Colored Working Girls,"
Grande Central Palace June 3, 1908, "Souvenir Program The Charity Bee's Benefit for
Mercy Hospital and the Home for the Protection of Colored Women, May 29, 1913,
Atlanta University Center, Robert W. Woodruff Library; "St. Philip's Parish Home Given
by Ada Overton Walker at Grand Central Palace," *New York Age,* April 8, 1909, 6; Les-
ter A. Walton, "The Benefit," *New York Age,* 8 June 1908, 6; "Special Announcement:
Benefit. Ada Overton Walker on Behalf of White Rose Industrial Association Home for
Colored Working Girls," *New York Age,* 7 May 1908, 6.

    83. Walker, "Colored Men and Women on the Stage," 575.

    84. Ibid., 571.

    85. Ibid.

    86. Ibid.

    87. Ibid.

    88. Ibid., 573.

    89. Walker, "Colored Men and Women on the Stage," 574.

    90. Ibid.

    91. Jessie Fauset, *Comedy American Style* (New York: Negro Universities Press,
1933), 58, 110, 278.

    92. Ibid., 296.

    93. "Dahomey on Broadway," *The New York Times,* 19 February 1903; Allen Woll,
Black Musical Theater, 36–38; Lester A. Walton, "The Benefit," *New York Age,* 11 June
1908, 6; "News of the Theater *In Dahomey: A* Musical Comedy in Two Acts," Helen
Armstead-Johnson Miscellaneous Theater Collection, Rare Books and Manuscripts Division, The Schomburg Center for Research in Black Culture.

    94. Richard Newman, "The Brightest Star," 470; Mercer Cook Papers, box 157–7,
folder, 17, pg. 9, 19–20, folder 29, pg. 2, Moorland-Spingarn Research Center, Howard
University. See Paula Marie Seniors, "Ada Overton Walker, Abbie Mitchell and the Gibson Girl: Reconstructing African American Womanhood," *The International Journal of
Africana Studies* 13, Issue 2 (Fall 2007): 38–67.

    95. Abbie Mitchell, Mercer Cook Papers, box 157–7, folder 17, 11, Moorland-Spin-
garn Center, Howard University.

    96. Abbie Mitchell Autobiographical Notes, 157–7, Moorland-Spingarn Center,
Howard University.

    97. Leigh Whipper Papers, Moorland Spingarn Center, Howard University. Mitchell's
biography for *Stevedore* and newspaper obituaries all mentioned her audience with the
King of England. (Abbie Mitchell Papers, Moorland Spingarn Center, Howard University.)

    98. "Souvenir Programme, Ada Overton Walker's Benefit for White Rose Industrial
Home for Colored Working Girls," Lester A. Walton, *New York Age,* "The Benefit," 11
June 1908, 6.

    99. Tanner, *Dusky Maidens,* 119. Mitchell's anticipated responses to insults and
slights instilled intense fear in those she who worked with. When Ethel Barrymore saw
Mitchell in *Coquette* (1930) with the white actress Helen Hayes, she asked "[w]ho's
that marvelous nigger back there?" Hayes, who both respected and feared Mitchell,
responded frantically, "Please, please, Oh God! Please don't let her hear you say that"
(Tanner, *Dusky Maidens,* 119). Mitchell refused to allow *anyone* to disrespect her, and
Hayes's response indicates that if Mitchell had heard the slur she would have given both

women a humiliating tongue-lashing.

100. Gibson, "A New York Day," "Evening," 1898.

101. "What is Doing In Society," *The New York Times,* 3 May 1903. Robert L. Hargous was a wealthy southerner known for his elaborate New York parties for society folk.

102. Brown, "The Negro on the Stage,"36

103. Richard Newman. "The Brightest Star," 471.

104. Brown, "The Negro on the Stage," 36.

105. "Robert L. Hargous Dead," *The New York Times,* November 26, 1905, 9.

Epilogue

1. Lester A. Walton, *The Colored American* 14, no 7 (June 1908): 409–10, Fisk University Special Collections, Nashville, Tennessee; Nadine George Graves, *The Royalty of Vaudeville* (New York: St. Martin's Press, 2000), 99.

2. Henry T. Sampson, *The Ghost Walks: A Chronological History of Blacks in Show Business 1865–1910* (Metuchen, NJ, and London: The Scarecrow Press, Inc., 1988), 438; Lester A. Walton, "Music and the Stage," *New York Age,* 12 May 1910, 19 May 1910, 6. *The Indianapolis Freeman* suggested that while *The Red Moon* was not a "storming hit or boisterous, [it was] just a plain big success. The music is the best that was ever offered by Negroes. Every number received an equal amount of encores and was well placed throughout the program. The comedy was exceptionally light; nothing to scream at, but keep smiling, not laughing. The piece is so well balanced that any two good comedians could do the show justice" (Sampson, *The Ghost Walks,* 438).

3. In a letter addressed to Grace Nail, Bob Cole congratulated her on her marriage to James Weldon Johnson and detailed his commitment to theater: "[A]though the show closes for the season I see no vocation for me as I should be busy on our new piece right away. Mrs. Walkers play *Phoebe Brown.*" (J. W. Johnson Collection, box number 1, folder number 3, James Weldon Johnson Collection, Special Collections Department, Robert W. Woodruff Library, Emory University.)

4. Lester A. Walton, "Music and the Stage," *New York Age,* July 14, 1910, 6.

5. Ibid.

6. Walton, "Music and the Stage," *New York Age,* 3 August 1911, 6; Lester A. Walton, "Music and the Stage," *New York Age,* 10 August 1911, 6; Bob Cole Memorial Service Program, Jewell Plummer Cobb Collection, Los Angeles, California.

7. J. W. Johnson Collection, box number 1, folder number 3, May 13, 1913, James Weldon Johnson Collection, Special Collections Department, Robert W. Woodruff Library, Emory University.

8. James Weldon Johnson, *Black Manhattan* (New York: Athenaeum, 1930), 170.

9. Ibid.

10. Ibid.

BIBLIOGRAPHY

Books

Adams, David Wallace. *Education for Extinction: American Indians and the Boarding School Experience, 1878–1928*. Lawrence: University Press of Kansas, 1995.

Alexie, Sherman. *Reservation Blues*. New York: Atlantic Monthly Press, 1995; Warner Books, 1996.

Allen, Robert C. *Horrible Prettiness*. Chapel Hill and London: University of North Carolina Press, 1991.

Allen, Robert C. *Channels of Discourse*. Chapel Hill and London: The University of North Carolina Press, 1987.

Anderson, Jack. *Dance*. New York: Newsweek Books, 1974.

Anderson, James D. *The Education of the South 1860–1935*. Chapel Hill, NC, 1988.

Anderson, Lisa M. *Mammies No More: The Changing Image of Black Women on Stage and Screen*. Lanham, MD: Rowman & Littlefield Publishers, Inc., 1997.

Andrews, William L., ed. *Along This Way*. In *James Weldon Johnson Writings*. New York: The Library of America, 2004.

Aptheker, Herbert. *The Correspondence of W. E. B. Du Bois: Volume 1 Selections, 1877–1932*. Boston: University of Massachusetts Press, 1973.

Archuleta, Margaret L., Brenda J. Child, and K. Tsianina Lomawaima. *Away From Home: American Indian Boarding School Experiences, 1879–2000*. Phoenix: Heard Museum, 2000.

Armstrong, General Samuel Chapman. *Hampton Institute 1868–1885: Its Work for the Two Races*. Hampton Virginia Normal School Press Print, 1885.

Armstrong, Mrs. M.F. "A Teacher's Witness." *Hampton and Its Students by Two of Its Teachers*. New York: Putnam's Sons, 1874, Hampton University Archives.

Ashe, Arthur. *A Hard Road to Glory: A History of the African-American Athlete since 1946*. New York: An Amistad Book, 1988.

———. *A Hard Road to Glory, Boxing, African American Athlete in Boxing*. New York: Amistad, 1993.

Ashe, Arthur, with Neil Amdur. *Off The Court*. New York and Scarborough, Ontario: New American Library Books, 1981.

——, and Arnold Rampesard. *Days of Grace*. New York: Alfred A. Knopf, 1993.

Badger, Reid. *A Life in Ragtime: A Biography of James Reese Europe*. Oxford: Oxford University Press, 1995.

Baldwin, Davarion. *Chicago's New Negroes: Modernity, the Great Migration, and Black Urban Life*. Chapel Hill: University of North Carolina Press, 2007.

Baldwin, James. *Nobody Knows My Name*. New York: Dial Press, 1961.

Bean, Ann Marie. "Black Minstrelsy and Double Inversion, Circa 1890." In *African American Performance and Theater History: A Critical Reader*. Edited by Harry J. Elam and David Krasner. New York: Oxford University Press, 2001.

Bederman, Gail. *Manliness & Civilization*. Chicago: The University of Chicago Press, 1995.

Bennett, Lerone. *Before the Mayflower: A History of Black America*. Chicago: Johnson Publishing Company, Inc., 1969.

Berkhoffer, Robert. *The White Man's Indian*. New York: Alfred A. Knopf, 1978.

Berry, Mary Frances. *My Face Is Black Is True: Callie House and the Struggle for Ex-Slave Reparations*. New York: Alfred. A. Knopf, 2005.

Bierhorst, John. *Latin American Folktales*. New York: Pantheon, 2002.

Boardman, Gerald. American *Musical Theater: A Chronicle*. Oxford: Oxford University Press, 1978.

Bogle, Donald. *Toms, Coons, Mulattos, Mammies, & Bucks*. New York: Continuum, 1990.

Bond, Julian, and Sandra Kathryn Wilson. *Lift Every Voice and Sing*. New York: Random House, 2000.

Brown Gordon, Sally. "Comet." In *Voices from Four Directions: Contemporary Translations of the Native Literatures of North America*. Edited by Brian Swann, 389–90. Lincoln: University of Nebraska Press, 2004.

Bundles, A'Lelia. *On Her Own Ground: The Life and Times of Madam C. J. Walker*. New York: Washington Square Press, 2001.

Carby, Hazel V. *Reconstructing Womanhood: The Emergence of the Afro-American Woman Novelist*. Oxford: Oxford University Press, 1987.

Charters, Ann. *Nobody*. London: MacMillan Company, 1970.

Child, Brenda. *The Boarding School Seasons: American Indian Families 1900–1940*. Lincoln: University of Nebraska Press, 1998.

Clark-Lewis, Elizabeth. *Living In, Living Out: African American Domestics in Washington D.C., 1910–1940*. Washington and London: Smithsonian Institution Press, 1994.

Cohen, Lizbeth. *Making a New Deal: Industrial Workers in Chicago 1919–1939*. New York: Cambridge University Press, 1990.

Collins, Patricia Hill. *Black Feminist Thought*. New York and London: Routledge, 1991.

——. *Black Sexual Politics*. New York: Routledge, 2004.

Connell, R. W. *Masculinities*. Berkeley and Los Angeles: University of California Press, 2005.

Cooper, Anna Julia. *A Voice from the South by a Black Woman of the South*. New York: Negro Universities Press, 1892.

――――. *A Voice from the South by a Black Woman of the South*. New York: Oxford University Press, 1988.

Cruse, Harold. *The Crisis of the Negro Intellectual*. New York: William Morrow & Company, Inc., 1967.

Cumber Dance, Daryl, ed. "Signs from the Hampton Folk-Lore Society from *Southern Workman* 23 January 1894." In *From My People*, 564. New York: W.W. Norton and Company, 2002.

Cuney-Hare, Maude. *Negro Musicians and Their Music*. New York: G.K. Hall & Co., 1936.

Curtis, Susan. *The First Black Actors on the Great White Way*. Columbia: University of Missouri Press, 1998.

Dixon-Gottschild, Brenda. *Waltzing in the Dark*. New York: St. Martin's Press, 2000.

Du Bois, W. E. B. *The Autobiography of W. E. B. Du Bois; A Soliloquy on Viewing My Life from the Last Decade of Its First Century*. New York: International Publishers, 1968.

――――. *Black Reconstruction in America*. New York: Athenaeum, 1935.

――――. *The Souls of Black Folk*. New York: Premier Americana, 1961.

duCille, Ann. *The Coupling Convention*. New York: Oxford University Press, 1993.

Dunbar, Paul Laurence. *Sport of the Gods*. New York: Signet Classic, 1901.

Eastman, Charles Alexander. *Indian Boyhood*. Omaha: University of Nebraska Press, 1902. Prepared for the University of Virginia Library Electronic Text, Electronic Text Center, University of Virginia Library, 1999.

Edmonds, Margot, and Ella E. Clark. *Voices of the Winds Native American Legends*. New York: Facts on File, 1989.

Engs, Robert Frances. "Red, Black, and White: A Study in Intellectual Inequality." In *Region, Race, and Reconstruction: Essays in Honor of C. Vann Woodward*, 241–66. New York and Oxford: Oxford University Press, 1982.

Engs, Robert Frances, Morgan J. Kousser, and James M. McPherson. *Region, Race and Reconstruction: Essays in Honor of C. Vann Woodward*. New York and Oxford: Oxford University Press, 1982.

Engs, Robert Frances. *Educating the Disfranchised and Disinherited*. Knoxville: University of Tennessee Press, 1999.

――――. *Freedom's First Generation: Black Hampton, Virginia, 1861–1890*. Philadelphia, 1979.

Enstad, Nan. *Ladies of Labor Girls of Adventure*. New York: Columbia University Press, 1999.

Evans, Stephanie Y. *Black Women in the Ivory Tower 1850–1954: An Intellectual History*. Gainesville: University Press of Florida, 2007.

Fauset, Jessie. *Comedy American Style*. New York: Negro Universities Press, 1933.

Ferrer, Ada. *Insurgent Cuba: Race Nation and Revolution, 1868–1898*. Chapel Hill and London: University of North Carolina Press, 1999.

Fletcher, Tom. *100 Years of the Negro in Show Business*. New York: Burdge, 1954.

Foner, Philip S., ed. *Paul Robeson Speaks*. Secaucus, NJ: Citadel Press, 1978.

Fraden, Rena. "'A National Theater that Never Was.' A History of African American Theater Production, Performance, and Drama in the United States." *American Visions* 9, no. 5 (October–November 1994): 26

Francisco, Luzviminda. "The Philippine-American War." In *The Philippines Reader: A History of Colonialism, Neocolonialism, Dictatorship and Resistance.* Edited by Daniel B. Schirmer and Stephen Rosskamm Shalom, 8–19. Boston: South End Press, 1987.

Frank, L. *Acorn Soup.* Berkeley, CA: Heyday Books, 1999.

Franklin, John Hope. *From Slavery to Freedom.* New York: Knopf, 1947.

Frazier, E. Franklin. *Black Bourgeoisie: The Rise of a New Middle Class.* New York: Dryden Free Press, 1957.

———. *The Negro Family in the United States.* New York: The Dryden Free Press, 1951.

Gaines, Kevin G. *Uplifting the Race: Black Leadership, Politics, and Culture in the Twentieth Century.* Chapel Hill and London: University of North Carolina Press, 1996.

Gatewood, Willard B. *The Aristocrats of Color: The Black Elite, 1880–1920.* Bloomington: Indiana University Press, 1990.

———. *Smoked Yankees and The Struggle for Empire.* Urbana: University of Illinois Press, 1971.

Gelman, Woody. *The Best of Charles Dana Gibson.* New York: Bounty Books, 1969.

George-Graves, Nadine. *The Royalty of Vaudeville.* New York: St. Martins Press, 2000.

Gill, Sam D., and Irene F. Sullivan, eds. *Dictionary of Native American Mythology.* Santa Barbara: ABC-CLIO, 1992.

Gross, Kali. *Colored Amazons: Crime, Violence, and Black Women in the City of Brotherly Love, 1880–1910.* Durham, NC: Duke University Press, 2006.

Gunn Allen, Paula. *Pocahontas, Medicine Woman, Spy, Entrepreneur, Diplomat.* San Francisco: HarperSan Francisco, 2003.

Gutierrez, Ramon A. *When Jesus Came, the Corn Mothers Went Away: Marriage, Sexuality, and Power in New Mexico, 1500–1846.* Stanford, CA: Stanford University Press, 1991.

Gutman, Herbert G. *The Black Family in Slavery and Freedom.* New York: Vintage Books, 1976.

Hafen, P. Jane. *Dreams and Thunder: Stories, Poems, and The Sun Dance Opera, Zitkala-Sa.* Lincoln: University of Nebraska Press, 2001.

Harlan, Louis. *Booker T. Washington: 1901–1915.* New York and Oxford: Oxford University Press, 1983.

———. *Booker T. Washington: The Wizard of Tuskegee 1901–1915.* New York and Oxford: Oxford University Press, 1983.

———, ed. *The Booker T. Washington Papers: Volume 5, 1899–1900.* Urbana: University of Illinois Press, 1976.

———, and Raymond W. Smock, eds. *The Booker T. Washington Papers: Volume 7, 1903–1904.* Urbana: University of Illinois Press, 1977.

Harlan, Louis H., Raymond W. Smock, and Barbara S. Kraft, eds. *The Booker T. Washington Papers: Volume 6, 1901–1902.* Urbana: University of Illinois Press, 1977.

Harlan, Louis H., Raymond W. Smock, and Geraldine McTigue. *The Booker T. Washington Papers: Volume 8, 1904–1906.* Urbana: University of Illinois Press, 1979.

Harlan, Louis H., Raymond W. Smock, and Nan E. Woodruff. *The Booker T. Washington Papers: Volume 9, 1906–1908.* Urbana: University of Illinois Press, 1980.

Harlan, Louis H., Raymond W. Smock, Geraldine McTigue, and Nan E. Woodruff. *The*

Booker T. Washington Papers: Volume 10, 1909–1911. Urbana: University of Illinois Press, 1981.

Harlan, Louis H., and Raymond W. Smock. *The Booker T. Washington Papers: Volume 12, 1912–1914.* Urbana, University of Illinois Press, 1982.

Harlan, Louis H., and Raymond W. Smock. *Booker T. Washington in Perspective.* Jackson and London: University Press of Mississippi, 1988.

Hay, Samuel A. *African American Theatre: An Historical and Critical Analysis.* New York: Cambridge University Press, 1994.

Hatch, James, and Errol G. Hill. *A History of African American Theatre.* Cambridge, Cambridge University Press, 2003.

Horton, James Oliver, and Lois E. Horton. "Violence, Protest and Identity: Black Manhood in Antebellum America." In *A Question of Manhood.* Edited by Darlene Clark Hine and Earnestine Jenkins. Bloomington: Indiana University Press, 1984.

Hoxie, Frederick E. *The Final Promise: The Campaign to Assimilate the Indians, 1880–1920.* Lincoln: University of Nebraska Press, 1984.

———. *Indians in American History.* Arlington Heights: Harlan Davidson, Inc., 1988.

Huggins, Nathan Irvin. *Harlem Renaissance.* Oxford: Oxford University Press, 1971.

Hughes, Langston, and Milton Meltzer. *Black Magic: A Pictorial History of the Negro in American Entertainment.* Englewood Cliffs, NJ: Prentice-Hall, Inc., 1967.

———. *A Pictorial History of the Negro in America.* 2nd ed. New York: Crown Publishers, 1963, 1968.

Jasen, Donald. *Tin Pan Alley: The Composers, the Songs, the Performers and their Time. The Golden Age of Popular American Music from 1886–1956.* New York: Donald I. Fine Inc., 1980.

Johnson, Edward A. *History of Negro Soldiers in the Spanish-American War, and Other Items of Interest.* Raleigh: Capital Printing Co., Printers and Binders, 1899. New York and London: Johnson Reprint Corporation.

Johnson, J. Rosamond. *Rolling Along in Song.* New York: Viking Press, 1937.

Johnson, James Weldon. *Along This Way: The Autobiography of James Weldon Johnson.* New York: Viking Press, 1933.

———. *The Autobiography of an Ex-Coloured Man.* New York: Garden City Publishing, 1912.

———. *Black Manhattan.* New York: Athenaeum, 1930.

———. *James Weldon Johnson, Writing.* Edited by William L. Andrews. New York: The Library of America, 2004.

———. "The Passing of Jack Johnson" (1915). In *James Weldon Johnson, Writings,* edited by William L. Andrews. New York: The Library of America, 2004.

———. *Self Determining Haiti.* New York: The Nation, 1920.

Kaplan, Amy. "Black and Blue on San Juan Hill." In *Cultures of United States Imperialism,* edited by Amy Kaplan and Donald Peare, 219–36. Durham, NC: Duke University Press, 1993.

———, and Donald Pease. *Cultures of United States Imperialism.* Durham, NC: Duke University Press, 1993.

Keenan, Jerry. *Encyclopedia of the Spanish-American and Philippine-American Wars.* Santa Barbara, CA: ABC-CLIO, 2001.

Kidwell, Clara Sue. "Ethnoastronomy as the Key to Human Intellectual Development and Social Organization." In *Native Voices: American Indian Identity and Resistance*, edited by Richard A. Grounds, George E. Tinker, and David E. Wilkins. Lawrence: University Press of Kansas, 2003.

Kimmel, Michael S. *Manhood in America, a Cultural History*. New York and Oxford: Oxford University Press, 2006.

Krasner, David. *Resistance, Parody, and Double Consciousness in African American Theatre, 1895–1910*. New York: St. Martin's Press, 1997.

Lewis, David Levering. *W. E. B. Du Bois: Biography of a Race, 1868–1919*. New York: John McCrae Book, Henry Holt and Company, 1993.

Lewis, David Levering. *W. E. B. Du Bois: The Fight for Equality and the American Century 1919–1963*. New York: John McCrae Book, Henry Holt and Company, 2000.

Lindsey, Donal. *Indians at Hampton Institute*. Urbana and Chicago: University of Illinois Press, 1995.

Lipsitz, George. "Noises in the Blood: Culture Conflict and Mixed Race Identities." In *Crossing Lines: Race and Mixed Race across the Geohistorical Divide*, 19–44. Lanham, MD: Alta Mira Press, 2005.

———. *Time Passages: Collective Memory and American Popular Culture*. Minneapolis: University of Minnesota Press, 1990.

Logan, Rayford W. *The Negro in American Life and Thought: The Nadir 1877–1901*. New York: The Dial Press, Inc., 1954.

Mahar, William J. *Behind the Burnt Cork Mask: Early Blackface Minstrelsy and Antebellum American Popular Culture*. Urbana and Chicago: University of Illinois Press, 1999.

Malone, Jacqui. *Steppin' on the Blues*. Urbana and Chicago: University of Illinois Press, 1996.

Marable. Manning. *W. E. B. Du Bois Black Radical Democrat*. Boston: Twayne Publishers, 1986,

Marks, George, P. *The Black Press Views American Imperialism 1898–1990*. New York: Arno Press, 1971.

Massey, Douglas S., and Nancy Denton. *American Apartheid*. Cambridge, MA: Harvard University Press, 1993.

Mitchell, Michelle. *Righteous Propagation: African Americans and the Politics of Racial Destiny after Reconstruction*. Chapel Hill: University of North Carolina Press, 2004.

Moon, Henry Lee. *The Emerging Thought of W. E. B. Du Bois: Essays and Editorials from the* Crisis *with an Introduction, Commentaries, and a Personal Memoir by Henry T. Moon*. New York: Simon and Schuster, 1972.

Morgan, Edmund S. "The Jamestown Fiasco." In *American Slavery, American Freedom*, edited by Edmund S. Morgan, 71–91. New York: W.W. Norton and Company, 1975.

Morner, Magnus. *Race Mixture in the History of Latin America*. New York: Little, Brown & Co., 1987.

Naison, Mark. *Communists in Harlem during the Depression*. New York: Grove Press, 1983.

Nash, Gary. *Red, White, and Black*. Englewood Cliffs, NJ: Prentice Hall, 1974.

Nottage, Lynn, *Intimate Apparel*. New York: The Dramatists Play Service, Inc., 2005.

Okihiro, Gary Y. *Margins and Mainstreams*. Seattle: University of Washington Press, 1996.

Oliver, Melvin, and Thomas Shapiro. *Black Wealth/White Wealth*. New York: Routledge, 1997.

Opler, Edward Morris. *Myths and Tales of the Jicarilla Apache Indians*. New York: Kraus Reprint, 1969. Originally published 1938.

Painter, Nell, *Creating Black Americans*. New York: Oxford University Press, 2005.

Paredes, Americo. *With His Pistol in His Hand*. Austin: University of Texas Press, 1958.

Peterson, Bernard. *African American Theater Directory*. Westwood, CT: Greenwood Press, 1997.

———. *A Century of Musicals in Black and White*. Westport, CT: Greenwood Press, 1993.

Pitz, Henry C. *Gibson Girl and Her America*. New York: Dover Publications, 1969.

Price, David A. *Love and Hate in Jamestown*. New York: Borzoi Book, 2003.

Puckett, Newbell Niles. *Folk Beliefs of the Southern Negro*. Chapel Hill: University of North Carolina Press, 1926.

Reese, Renford. *American Paradox, Young Black Men*. Durham, NC: Academic Press, 2004.

Riis, Thomas Laurence. "Black Musical Theatre in New York, 1890–1915." Ph.D. diss., University of Michigan, 1981.

———. *Just Before Jazz: Black Musical Theater in New York, 1890–1915*. Washington, D.C., and London: Smithsonian Institution Press, 1989.

Robeson, Paul. *Here I Stand*. New York: Beacon Press, 1988. Originally published 1958.

Robeson, Paul, Jr. *The Undiscovered Paul Robeson: An Artist's Journey, 1898–1939*. New York: John Wiley and Sons, 2001.

Robeson, Susan. *The Whole World in His Hands: A Pictorial Biography of Paul Robeson*. New York: Citadel Press, 1981.

Robinson, Cedric J. *Black Movements in America*. New York and London: Routledge, 1997.

Rogin, Michael. *Blackface, White Noise: Jewish Immigrants in the Hollywood Melting Pot*. Berkeley and Los Angeles: University of California Press, 1998.

Rooks, Noliwe. *Hair Raising*. New Brunswick: Rutgers University Press, 1997.

———. *Ladies Pages: African American Women's Magazines and the Culture That Made Them*. New Brunswick: Rutgers University Press, 2004.

Roosevelt, Theodore, *Hunting Trips of a Ranchman: Sketches of Sport on the Northern Cattle Plains*. New York and London: G.P. Putnam, 1902.

———. *The Rough Riders*. New York: Charles Scribner's Sons, 1899.

———. *The Strenuous Life: Essays and Addresses*. New York: The Century Co., 1900.

———. *Theodore Roosevelt: An Autobiography*. New York and Boston: Macmillan Company, 1913.

Ross, Marlon B. *Manning the Race*. New York: New York University Press, 2004.

Rusan Wilson, Francille, *Segregated Scholars*. Charlottesville and London: University of Virginia Press, 2006.

Sampson, Henry T. *Blacks in Blackface: A Sourcebook on early Black Shows*. Metuchen, NJ and London: The Scarecrow Press, Inc., 1980.

———. *The Ghost Walks: A Chronological History of Blacks in Show Business 1865–1910*. Metuchen, NJ and London: The Scarecrow Press, Inc., 1988.

Seniors, Paula Marie. "Jack Johnson, Paul Robeson and the Hypermasculine Übermench." In *Harlem Renaissance, Politics, Arts, Letters,* edited by Jeffrey Ogbar. Baltimore: Johns Hopkins University Press, forthcoming.

Shohat, Ella, and Robert Stam. *Unthinking Eurocentrism.* New York and London: Routledge, 1994.

Slotkin, Richard. "Buffalo Bill's 'Wild West' and the Mythologization of the American Empire." In *Cultures of United States Imperialism,* edited by Amy Kaplan and Donald Peale, 164–82. Durham: Duke University Press, 1993.

Smith, Barbara. *Black Women in America.* Brooklyn: Carlson Publishing, 1993.

Smith, Eric Ledell. *Bert Williams: A Biography of the Pioneer Black Comedian.* Jefferson, NC and London: McFarland Press, 1992.

Southern, Eileen. *Biographical Dictionary of Afro American and African Musicians,* Westport CT: Greenwood Press, 1982.

Sotiropoulos, Karen. *Staging Race.* Cambridge: Harvard University Press, 2006.

Spaeth, Sigmund. *The History of Popular Music.* New York: Random House, 1946.

Spicer, Edward Holland. *Cycles of Conquest: The Impact of Spain, Mexico and the United States on the Indians of the Southwest 1533–1960.* Tucson: University of Arizona Press, 1962.

Spickard, Paul R. *Mixed Blood: Intermarriage and Ethnic Identity in Twentieth-Century America.* Madison: University of Wisconsin Press, 1989.

Spivey, Donald. *Schooling for the New Slavery: Black Industrial Education 1868–1915.* Westport, CT: Greenwood Press, 1978.

Stallybrass, Peter, and Allon White, *The Politics and Poetics of Transgression.* Ithaca, NY: Cornell University Press, 1986.

Steinberg, Stephan. *The Ethnic Myth: Race, Ethnicity, and Class in America.* Boston: Beacon Press, 1981.

Sundquist, Asebrit. *Pocahontas & Co., The Fictional American Indian Woman in Nineteenth-Century Literature: A Study of Method.* Atlantic Highlands: NJ: Humanities Press International, 1987.

Tanner, Jo A. *Dusky Maidens: The Odyssey of the Early Black Dramatic Actress.* Westport, CT: Greenwood Press, 1992.

Tate, Claudia. "Allegories of Black Female Desire; or, Rereading Nineteenth-Century Sentimental Narratives of Black Female Authority." In *Changing Our Own Words,* edited by Cheryl A. Wall, 98–126. New Brunswick: Rutgers University Press, 1989.

Thompson, Sister M. Francesca, OSF. "The Lafayette Players 1915–1917." In *The Theater of Black America (Volume II).* Edited by Erroll Hill. Englewood Cliffs, NJ: Prentice-Hall, 1980.

Thornbrough, Emma. *T. Thomas Fortune: Militant Journalist.* Chicago and London: The University of Chicago Press. 1972.

Toll, Robert C. *Blacking Up: The Minstrel Show in Nineteenth Century America.* New York: Oxford University Press, 1974.

Toomer, Jean, *Cane.* New York: Liveright, 1923; reprint 1975.

Townsend, Camilla. *Pocahontas and the Powhatan Dilemma.* New York: Hill and Wang, 2004.

Utley, Robert. *The Indian Frontier of the American West, 1846–1890.* Albuquerque: University of Albuquerque Press, 1984.

Van Deberg, William L. *Slavery & Race in American Popular Culture.* Madison: The

University of Wisconsin Press, 1984.

Wallace, Maurice O. *Constructing the Black Masculine*. Durham, NC: Duke University Press, 2002.

Warshaw, Steven. *The Gibson Girls*. Berkeley, CA: Diablo Press, 1968.

Washington, Booker T. *A New Negro for a New Century: An Accurate and Up-To-Date Record of the Upward Struggles of The Negro Race*. New York: American Publishing House, 1900; reprinted Arno Press and *The New York Times*, 1969.

———. *Up from Slavery: An Autobiography of Booker T. Washington*. New York: Bantam, Doubleday, Doran & Company, Inc., 1929.

West, Cornel. *Keeping Faith*. New York and London: Routledge, 1993.

———. *Race Matters*. Boston: Beacon Press, 1992.

Wexler, Laura. *Tender Violence: Domestic Visions in an Age of U.S. Imperialism*. Chapel Hill and London: University of North Carolina Press, 2000.

White, Deborah Gray. *Ar'n't I a Woman? Female Slaves in the Plantation South*. New York and London: W.W. Norton & Company, 1985.

———. *Too Heavy A Load: Black Women in Defense of Themselves 1894–1994*. New York and London: W.W. Norton & Company, 1994.

White, L., and James H Cones III. *Black Emerging Man*. New York: W. H. Freeman and Company, 1999.

Williams, John A. *Captain Blackman*. Minneapolis: Coffee House Press, 1972.

Williams, Robert W. *Negroes with Guns*. New York: Marzani & Munsell, Inc., 1962.

Williams-Forson, Psyche A. "Black Men, Visual Imagery, and the Ideology of Fear." In *Building Houses Out of Chicken Legs: Black Women, Food, & Power*. Chapel Hill: University of North Carolina Press, 2006.

Woll, Allen. *Dictionary of the Black Theatre*. Westport, CT and London: Greenwood Press, 1983.

Woll, Allen. *Black Musical Theatre: From Coontown to Dreamgirls*. Baton Rouge and London: Louisiana State University Press, 1989.

Woolley, Benjamin. *Savage Kingdom: The True Story of Jamestown, 1607, and the Settlement of America*. New York: HarperCollins Publishers, 2007.

Manuscript Collections and Archives

"Abbie Mitchell Goes to Perpetual Summertime." *The New York Amsterdam News*, 23 March 1960. Mercer Cook Papers, Moorland Spingarn Research Center, Howard University.

"Abbie Mitchell in a Song Program." Mercer Cook Oversize Moorland-Spingarn Center, Howard University.

Abyssinia Program 1906. Helen Armstead-Johnson Miscellaneous Theater Collection. Rare Books and Manuscripts Division, The Schomburg Center for Research in Black Culture.

Armstrong, General Samuel Chapman. *Hampton Institute 1868–1885. Its Work for the Two Races*. Hampton: Hampton Virginia Normal School Press Print 1885. Hampton University Archives.

Armstrong, Mrs. M. F., and Helen W. Ludlow. *Hampton and Its Students by Two of Its Teachers*. New York: Putnam's Sons, 1874. Hampton University Archives.

Armstrong, Mrs. M. F., and Helen W. Ludlow. *Ten Years Work for Indians at the Hampton Normal and Agricultural Institute, at Hampton Virginia.* Hampton: Virginia Normal School Press Print, 1888.

Anonymous. [1876]. "Indian Hunter Shooting Arrow at Elk." Ledger Art, The United States Department of the Interior. National Park Service. Fort Caroline National Memorial, Timucuan Ecological and Historic Preserve. Jacksonville, Florida.

Anonymous. [1876]. "Mounted Kiowa Warrior going on War Path." Ledger Art, The United States Department of the Interior. National Park Service. Fort Caroline National Memorial, Timucuan Ecological and Historic Preserve. Jacksonville, Florida.

Anonymous. 1876. "Mounted Kiowa Warrior in Action." Ledger Art, The United States Department of the Interior. National Park Service. Fort Caroline National Memorial, Timucuan Ecological and Historic Preserve. Jacksonville, Florida.

ASCAP. N.d. "J. Rosamond Johnson's Obituary." The Billy Rose Collection. Lincoln Center for the Performing Arts, New York City.

ASCAP. N.d. "Biography of J. Rosamond Johnson." The Billy Rose Collection. Lincoln Center for the Performing Arts, New York City.

"Atlanta University Edition of Lift Every Voice and Sing." J.W.J. Collection, box 2, folder 28, James Weldon Johnson Collection, Special Collections Department, Robert W. Woodruff Library, Emory University.

"Auto Speed Costs Jack Johnson $20." N.d. Jack Johnson Scrapbook SCM90–87 box 1. Manuscripts, Archives, and Rare Books Division. The Schomburg Center for Research in Black Culture.

Black Patti's Troubadours Program Announcement. Thirteenth California Tour Season 1908–1909, Black Patti's Troubadours. Jesse Shipp, Gross Collection. Manuscript Department. Moorland Spingarn Research Center. Howard University.

Boston Evening Transcript. February 17, 1917. James Weldon Johnson Papers, JWJ zanj632+zc1 4, 1928 Scrapbook, Yale Collection of American Literature, Beinecke Rare Book and Manuscript Library.

Boston Herald. Jewel Plummer Cobb Collection, Los Angeles, California.

Bowen, Cornelia. "Women's Part in the Uplift of Our Race." *The Colored American* 12, no. 2 (February 1907). Fisk University Archives.

Brown, Sterling. "The Negro on the Stage." In *The Negro in American Culture,* 1940. Vols. 1–2 [Study Guhnar Myrda]: 36. The Schomburg Center for Research in Black Culture, New York.

Brooklyn Eagle, 29 December 1908, The Robinson Locke Collection, Lincoln Center Library for the Performing Art.

The Bulletin of Atlanta University, no. 56 (May 1892): 2. Atlanta University Center, Robert W. Woodruff Library, Clark Atlanta University.

The Bulletin of Atlanta University (June 1892). Atlanta University Center, Robert W. Woodruff Library, Clark Atlanta University, Atlanta, Georgia.

The Bulletin of Atlanta University, no. 51 (December 1893): 8. Atlanta University Center, Robert W. Woodruff Library.

The Bulletin of Atlanta University, no. 38 (June 1894). Atlanta University Center, Robert W. Woodruff Library, Clark Atlanta University.

The Bulletin of Atlanta University, no. 56 (May 1894). Atlanta University Center, Robert W. Woodruff Library, Clark Atlanta University.

The Bulletin of Atlanta University (January 1, 1898). Atlanta University Center, Robert W. Woodruff Library, Clark Atlanta University, Atlanta, Georgia.

The Bulletin of Atlanta University, no. 93 (June 1898). Atlanta University Center, Robert W. Woodruff Library. Clark Atlanta University.

The Bulletin of Atlanta University, no. 140: 5. "Musical Compositions by Negroes." 3 November 1903. Atlanta University Center, Robert W. Woodruff Library, Clark Atlanta University.

The Bulletin of Atlanta University, no. 38 (June 1892): 2. Atlanta University Center, Robert W. Woodruff Library, Clark Atlanta University.

The Bulletin of Atlanta University, no. 48 (July 1893). Atlanta University Center, Robert W. Woodruff Library, Clark Atlanta University.

The Bulletin of Atlanta University, no. 51 (December 1893): 8. Atlanta University Center, Robert W. Woodruff Library, Clark Atlanta University.

The Bulletin of Atlanta University, no. 56 (May 1894): 2–4. Atlanta University Center, Robert W. Woodruff Library, Clark Atlanta University.

The Bulletin of Atlanta University, no. 57 (June 1894). Atlanta University Center, Robert W. Woodruff Library, Clark Atlanta University.

The Bulletin of Atlanta University, no. 90 (March 1898): 1. Atlanta University Center, Robert W. Woodruff Library, Clark Atlanta University.

The Bulletin of Atlanta University, no. 94 (October 1898): 1. Atlanta University Center, Robert W. Woodruff Library, Clark Atlanta University.

The Bulletin of Atlanta University, no. 120 (June 1901): 301. Atlanta University Center, Robert W. Woodruff Library, Clark Atlanta University.

The Bulletin of Atlanta University, 1903. Atlanta University Center, Robert W. Woodruff Library, Atlanta, Georgia.

The Bulletin of Atlanta University [scrapbook], 1903, James Weldon Johnson Papers, Yale Collection of American Literature. Beinecke Rare Books and Manuscripts Library, Yale University.

The Bulletin of Atlanta University, no. 163 (April 1906). Atlanta University Center, Robert W. Woodruff Library, Clark Atlanta University.

The Bulletin of Atlanta University, no. 165 (June 1906). Atlanta University Center, Robert W. Woodruff Library, Clark Atlanta University.

The Bulletin of Atlanta University (June 1907). Atlanta University Center, Robert W. Woodruff Library, Clark Atlanta University, Atlanta, Georgia.

Carney, Sergeant. "Sergeant Carney." *The Colored American* 7, no. 10 (October 1904). Special Collections, Fisk University Library, Nashville Tennessee.

Cashin, Herschel V., Charles Alexander, William T. Anderson, Arthur M. Brown, and Horace W. Bivens. *Under Fire with The Tenth U.S. Cavalry.* London, New York, and Chicago: F. Tennyson Neely, 1899. Manuscripts, Archives and Rare Books Division, The Schomburg Center for Research in Black Culture.

"Certificate of Incorporation of the White Rose Mission and Industrial Association, 1899, White Rose Mission and Industrial Association Collection, SCMS 565 Manuscripts, Archives, and Rare Books Collections. The Schomburg Center for Research in Black Culture.

"Class of 1876. J.C. Robbins." *Twenty-Two Years Work of the Hampton Normal and Agricultural Institute at Hampton Virginia.* Hampton, VA: Hampton Normal School

Press, 1893. Hampton University Archives.

"Class of 1879. Amelia Perry." *Twenty-Two Years Work of the Hampton Normal and Agricultural Institute at Hampton Virginia.* Hampton, VA: Hampton Normal School Press, 1893. Hampton University Archives.

Jewell Plummer Cobb. *The Journal,* 1 March 1896.

Jewell Plummer Cobb. Newspaper clipping [scrapbook]. N.d. Jewel Plummer Cobb Collection, Los Angeles, California.

Jewell Plummer Cobb. *The World,* August 8, 1895.Jewell Plummer Cobb Collection, Los Angeles, California.

Jewell Plummer Cobb. Bob Cole Scrapbook. Jewel Plummer Cobb Collection, Los Angeles, California.

Cole, Bob. *Boston Herald.* Jewell Plummer Cobb Collection.

Cole, Bob. *Florida Times.* Jewell Plummer Cobb Collection.

Cole, Bob. Bob Cole Manuscript Department. Moorland-Spingarn Research Center, Howard University.

Cole, Bob. Bob Cole's Memorial Service Program. Jewell Plummer Cobb Collection, Los Angeles, California.

Cole, Bob. Letter from Bob Cole to Grace Nail Johnson. J. W. Johnson Collection, box number 1, folder number 3, James Weldon Johnson Collection, Special Collections Department, Robert W. Woodruff Library, Emory University.

Cole, Bob. Bob Cole Scrapbook. Jewell Plummer Cobb Collection, Los Angeles, California.

Cole, Bob. Bob Cole Scrapbook. Illustration of The Ethiopians' Defeat of the Italians, Illustration of Menelek. Jewel Plummer Cobb Collection, Los Angeles, California.

Cole, Bob. OG 605. Bob Cole Manuscript Department. Moorland-Spingarn Research Center, Howard University.

Cole, Bob. "Only Negro Officer in the Army" and the philosopher Bishop Abraham Grant. *The World* 1896. Dr. Jewel Plummer Cobb Collection, Los Angeles, California.

Cole, Bob. Robert Allen Cole Theatre Directions for *Red Moon.* N.d. [1908–1910]. OG 248 0G248. Moorland-Spingarn Research Center, Howard University.

Cole, Bob. *The Herald,* June 8, 1895. Dr. Jewel Plummer Cobb Collection, Los Angeles, California.

Cole, Bob. *Kansas City Star,* 1895. Jewell Plummer Cobb Collection.

Cole, Bob. *New Orleans Times Democrat.* Jewell Plummer Cobb Collection.

Cole, Bob. *The New York Recorder,* August 10, 1895. Jewell Plummer Cobb Collection, Los Angeles, California.

Cole, Bob. "On The Road to Monterey." James Weldon Johnson Papers, Yale Collection of American Literature, JWJV3J633. Beinecke Rare Book and Manuscript Library, Yale University.

Cole, Bob. *The Press,* August 7, 1895. Dr. Jewel Plummer Cobb Collection, Los Angeles, California.

Cole, Bob. *The Telegraph,* June 8, 1895. Dr. Jewel Plummer Cobb Collection, Los Angeles, California.

Cole, Bob. *The World,* August 8, 1895. Dr. Jewel Plummer Cobb Collection, Los Angeles, California.

Cole, Bob. *The World,* Sunday, November 13, 1898. Bob Cole Scrapbook. Jewel Plummer Cobb Collection, Los Angeles, California.

Cole, Bob, James Weldon Johnson, and J. Rosamond Johnson. "The Old Flag Never Touched the Ground, MCMI. Cole and Johnson Archives. The Schomburg Center for Research in Black Culture.

The Colored American. N.d. James Weldon Johnson Papers, Yale Collection of American Literature. The Beinecke Rare Books and Manuscript Library, Yale University.

The Colored American. June 1901, vol. III. Fisk University, Special Collections, Nashville, Tennessee.

The Colored American. August 1909. Fisk University, Special Collections, Nashville, Tennessee.

The Colored American. May 1902. Fisk University, Special Collections, Nashville, Tennessee.

"Comanche Peyote Man." Ledger Art, The United States Department of the Interior. National Park Service, Fort Caroline National Memorial, Timucuan Ecological and Historic Preserve. Jacksonville, Florida.

Cook, Mercer. Mercer Cook Papers. Box no. 157–7, folder no. 24. Moorland-Spingarn Research Center, Howard University.

Mercer Cook Papers. Box no. 157–7, folder no. 27. Moorland-Spingarn Research Center, Howard University.

Mercer Cook Papers. Box no. 157–7, folder no. 17. Moorland-Spingarn Research Center, Howard University.

Mercer Cook Papers. Box no. 157–7, folder no. 18. Moorland-Spingarn Research Center, Howard University.

Mercer Cook Papers, National Council of Negro Women, Award to Abbie Mitchell from the National Council of Negro Women. Box 157–8, Folder, 8, Moorland- Spingarn Research Center, Howard University.

Cook, Mercer. "From Clorindy to 'The Red Moon' and Beyond." Paper presented 26 October 1978. Mercer Cook Papers. Box no. 157–4. Moorland-Spingarn Research Center, Howard University.

Mercer Cook Papers. Box no. 157–9, folder no. 39. Moorland-Spingarn Center, Howard University.

Mercer Cook Papers, box 157–4, Moorland Spingarn Research Center, Howard University.

Mercer Cook Papers, 157–9, folder 39. Moorland Spingarn Research Center, Howard University.

Cook, Will Marion. Newspaper clipping. N. d. Stella Wiley Scrapbook. The Negro in the Theatre: XI Scrapbook. James Weldon Johnson Collection. Beinecke Library, Yale University.

Cook, Will Marion. Mercer Cook Papers. Box no. 1, folder no. 3. Moorland-Spingarn Research Center, Howard University.

Cook, Will Marion. Mercer Cook Papers. Box no. 1, folder no. 4. Moorland-Spingarn Research Center, Howard University.

Cook, Will Marion. Mercer Cook Papers. Box no. 1, folder no. 3. Moorland-Spingarn Research Center, Howard University.

Cook, Will Marion. "Autobiographical Notes." Mercer Cook Papers. Box no. 4, folder no. 6. Moorland-Spingarn Research Center, Howard University.

Cook, Will Marion. Letter addressed to the Teachers Association (Carter). 23 November 1934. Jewel Plummer Cobb Collection, Los Angeles, California.

Cowan, Wood. "Them Were the Days Episode No. 2 by Wood Cowan," Jack Johnson Scrapbook SCM90–87 box 1, box 2. Manuscripts, Archives, and Rare Books Division. The Schomburg Center for Research in Black Culture.

The Crisis. J. W. Johnson Collection. Scrapbook BV 6 *The Crisis,* March 1977. James Weldon Johnson Collection. Special Collections Department. Robert Woodruff Library, Emory University.

Crouse, Russel. "One of Gershwin's Actors Has Some Tunes to His Credit Too." *New York Herald Tribune,* 22 December 1935. Box no. 7, pg. 21. Scrapbook 1930s miscellaneous Scrapbook 1936, James Weldon Johnson Papers, JWJ zanj632+zc2. Yale Collection of American Literature, Beinecke Rare Book and Manuscript Library, Yale University.

Cullen/Jackman Collection: box 36, folder 14. "Mercy Hospital Benefit Ada Overton Walker in Vaudeville." Program, 26 May [1889/1898]. Atlanta University Center, Robert W. Woodruff Library, Clark Atlanta University.

Cullen/Jackman Collection: box 36, folder 14. "Souvenir Programme Ada Overton Walker's Benefit for White Rose Industrial Home for Colored Working Girls," Grande Central Palace, 3 June 1908. Atlanta University Center, Robert W. Woodruff Library, Clark Atlanta University.

Cullen/Jackman Collection: box 36, folder 14. "Souvenir Program the Charity Bees Benefit for Mercy Hospital and the Home for the Protection of Colored Women." Atlanta University Center, Robert W. Woodruff Library, Clark Atlanta University. Atlanta University Center, Robert W. Woodruff Library, Clark Atlanta University.

Dayton Journal. March 19, 1907. Bob Cole, Manuscript Department. Moorland-Spingarn Research Center, Howard University.

Department of State. J. W. Johnson Collection, box number 1, folder number 2, James Weldon Johnson Collection, Special Collections Department, Robert W. Woodruff Library, Emory University.

"Dinner in Honor of Dr. W.E. Burghardt Du Bois, April 13, 1924." W. E. B. Du Bois Papers, Folder 8, Rare Books and Manuscript Collection, The Schomburg Center for Research in Black Culture.

Doanmoe. R. H. Pratt Papers, box 2, folder 67, WA MSS S-1174. Pratt Incoming Letters. The Western Americana Collection, Beinecke Rare Book and Manuscript Library, Yale University.

Doughterty, Romeo L. "Aida Overton Walker In Memoriam. A Star among Stars Lies Dead," from "Rambling 'Round," Leigh Whipper Papers, mss 47, Writings and Typescripts, other artists. Rare Books and Manuscript Collection, The Schomburg Center for Research in Black Culture.

Du Bois, W. E. B., Letter from W. E. B. Du Bois to Arturo Schomburg. Correspondence 1911–1957, Letter 20 November 1931, Du Bois MG 109 Box 1- , Schomburg Center for Research in Black Culture.

Eastman, Elaine Goodale. *The Voice of Eve.* Chicago: Bookfellows, 1930, Hampton University Archives.

Edwards, A. M., Cole and Johnson. Music contract with A. M. Edwards. J. W. Johnson Collection, Box number 6 Folder number 1, James Weldon Johnson Collection, Special Collections Department, Robert W. Woodruff Library, Emory University.

Europe, James Reese, Cole, Bob. *Indianapolis Freeman*. Robinson Locke Collection. *Indianapolis Freeman:* 1908, James Reese Europe, Bob Cole, 1905. Lincoln Center Library for the Performing Arts, New York City.

Europe, James Reese, Cole, Bob. "On The Gay Luneta." Sheet music from *Shoo Fly Regiment,* 1905. Cole and Johnson Collection. The Schomburg Center for Research in Black Culture, New York Public Library.

The Evening Telegram. August 2, 1898. Jewel Plummer Cobb Collection, Los Angeles, California.

Florida Times Union. Jewel Plummer Cobb Collection, Los Angeles, California.

Folsom, Cora. "Indian Days at Hampton." Unpublished Manuscript, May 1918. Hampton University Archives.

Folsom, Cora. *Friends Intelligencer* (Vol. 38, 1881–1882). Hampton University Archives.

"Former Champ in Paris." Jack Johnson Scrapbook, box 3, Manuscripts, Archives, and Rare Books Division. The Schomburg Center for Research in Black Culture.

"Former Champ in Paris." N.d. probably 1933. Jack Johnson Scrapbook, box 3, Manuscripts, Archives, and Rare Books Division. The Schomburg Center for Research in Black Culture.

Photo of Johnson and his "beautiful" wife. Jack Johnson Scrapbook, box 3, Manuscripts, Archives, and Rare Books Division. The Schomburg Center for Research in Black Culture.

Fortune, T. Thomas. "Afro-Americans Not Cowards," *Sun,* August 1898. T. Thomas Fortune Scrapbook, Manuscripts, Archives and Rare Books Division, The Schomburg Center for Research in Black Culture.

Fortune, T. Thomas. "Afro American Notes," *The Sun,* 1898, T. Thomas Fortune Scrapbook, Manuscripts, Archives and Rare Books Division, The Schomburg Center for Research in Black Culture, Rare Books and Manuscripts Collection.

Fortune, T. Thomas. "Race War in Alabama, Riot and Bloodshed in the Town of Blossburg." *The Sun,* Wednesday, 28 June 1899. T. Thomas Fortune Scrapbook, Manuscripts, Archives and Rare Books Division, The Schomburg Center for Research in Black Culture.

Foster, William. "Pioneers of the Stage." *The Official Theatrical World of Colored Artists 'National Directory and Guide* 1, no. 1 (April 1928): 1–97. Black Culture Collection Contents by Reel, UCSD Geisel Library.

Frissell, H. B. "Georgia Washington." *Hampton Graduates, 1871–1899.* Hampton University Archives.

Garrison, Frances J. Letter to Washington from Frances J. Garrison, December 3, 1906, Booker T. Washington Collection MG 182 box 1(1), The Schomburg Center for Research in Black Culture.

Gibson, C. D. *Drawings by C. D. Gibson.* New York: R.H. Russell & Son, 1894. Special Collections, Virginia Tech.

Goodale, Elaine Eastman. *The Voice at Eve.* Chicago: The Bookfellows, 1930. Hampton University Archives.

Goode, William T. *The Eighth Illinois.* Chicago, The Blakely Printing Company, 1899. Manuscripts, Archives and Rare Books Division, The Schomburg Center for Research in Black Culture.

Gould Fletcher, John, *John Smith—Also Pocahontas*. New York: Brentano's Publisher, 1928, 124, 259–61. (F229S7174), Special Collections University Libraries, Virginia Tech.

Gregg, James E. *The Southern Workman* 51 (August 1922). Hampton University Archives.

Guthrie, Chaplin Jas. M. *Camp-Fires of the Afro- American: or, The Colored Man as a Patriot, Soldier, Sailor, and Hero, in the Cause of Free America: Displayed in Colonial Struggle, in the Revolution, the War of 1812, and in Later Wars, Particularly the Great Civil War—1861–5, And the Spanish-American War—1898: Concluding with The Filipinos—1899*. Philadelphia, PA, Afro-American Pub Co., 1899, 692 Manuscripts, Archives, and Rare Books Division, The Schomburg Center for Research in Black Culture.

Hampton Graduates, 1871–1899, box 42, Peoples Village School Correspondence 1917–1988. Hampton University Archives.

Hampton Questionnaire, 16 January 1928. Hampton University Archives.

Harpers Weekly, May 11, 1878. The United States Department of the Interior. National Park Service. Fort Caroline National Memorial, Timucuan Ecological and Historic Preserve. Jacksonville, Florida.

"Heifetz and Abbie Mitchell Heard in Recitals. *The New York Evening Journal,* n.d, Mercer Cook Oversize Moorland-Spingarn Center, Howard University.

"Here and There." *The Colored American,* January 3, 1903. Fisk University Archives.

"The History of Florida Normal and Industrial Institute." *Florida Normal and Industrial Bulletin 50th Anniversary Catalog* (1941–1942). Florida Memorial College Archives.

Howling Wolf. R. H. Pratt Papers WAMSS S-1174, Pratt incoming letters, box 4. The Western Americana Collection, Beinecke Rare Book and Manuscript Library, Yale University.

Hyde, Mary Kendall, and Mrs. S.E. Wilkerson, Treasurer. "White Rose Home Its Work and Need," probably 1898–1899, White Rose Mission and Industrial Association Collection, SCMS 565 Manuscripts, Archives, and Rare Books Collections.

"Igerje meg, hogy, ezt" nem Irja meg" (Budapest, 1933). Jack Johnson Scrapbook, box 3. Manuscripts, Archives, and Rare Books Division. The Schomburg Center for Research in Black Culture.

Isaacs, Edith J. R. "The Middle Distance: 1890–1917." *Theatre Arts, The Negro in the American Theatre,* August, 1942, 527. Lester A. Walton Papers, The Schomburg Center for Research in Black Culture.

"It Was A Dark Day in Australia." *The Evening World,* Saturday December 26, 1908. The Jack Johnson Scrapbook, box 3. Manuscripts, Archives, and Rare Books Division. The Schomburg Center for Research in Black Culture.

Johnson, Grace Nail. J. W Johnson Collection, box number 1, James Weldon Johnson Collection, Special Collections Department, Robert W. Woodruff Library, Emory University.

Johnson, Grace Nail. J. W. Johnson Collection. Box no. 1. James Weldon Johnson Collection. Special Collections Department. Robert W. Woodruff Library, Emory University.

Johnson, Helen Armstead. "Some Late Information on Some Early People." *Encore American and World Wide News*, 23 June 1975, 48–55. The Schomburg Center for Research in Black Culture.

"Jack Johnson L'ancien Champion Du Monde De Boxe Arrive Ce Soir A Paris" (1913). Jack Johnson Scrapbook, box 3. Jack Johnson Scrapbook SCM90–87 box 1. Manuscripts, Archives, and Rare Books Division. The Schomburg Center for Research in Black Culture.

"Jack Johnson is fined $25 for Speeding." Jack Johnson Scrapbook SCM90–87 box 1. Manuscripts, Archives and Rare Books Division. The Schomburg Center for Research in Black Culture.

"Jack Johnson with the Carnival" by James R. Scott of the Review Staff. N.d. [1940s]. box 2, Manuscripts, Archives, and Rare Books Division. The Schomburg Center for Research in Black Culture.

"Jack Johnson Revealed in New Light to Harsh Critics." N.d. (probably 1929). *New York Evening Graphic*. The Jack Johnson Scrapbook, box 2, Manuscripts, Archives, and Rare Books Division. The Schomburg Center for Research in Black Culture.

"James W. Johnson, Consul." *The Colored American* 10, no. 3 (March 1904). Special Collections. Fisk University Library, Nashville, Tennessee.

James Weldon Johnson Collection, Fisk University Special Collections, Nashville, Tennessee.

James Weldon Johnson, George A. Towns Papers, box 2 folder 12, December 30 1896, Special Collections. Atlanta University Center, Robert W. Woodruff Library.

James Weldon Johnson, George A. Towns Papers, box 2, folder 12, May 14, 1914, Special Collections, Atlanta University Center, Robert W. Woodruff Library.

James Weldon Johnson Biography. James Weldon Johnson Collection, Fisk University Special Collections, Nashville, Tennessee.

James Weldon Johnson Papers. Yale Collection of American Literature. JWJV3J335a, folder 44. Beinecke Rare Book and Manuscript Library, Yale University.

James Weldon Johnson Papers. Yale Collection of American Literature. JWJ zanj632+zc2,box no. 2, scrapbook 1. Yale Collection of American Literature, Beinecke Rare Book and Manuscript Library, Yale University.

James Weldon Johnson Papers. Yale Collection of American Literature. JWJMSS Johnson box 41, folder 12, Beinecke Rare Book and Manuscript Library, Yale University.

James Weldon Johnson Papers. Yale Collection of American Literature. JWJMSS Johnson Box 41, folder 21, Beinecke Rare Book and Manuscript Library, Yale University.

James Weldon Johnson Papers. Yale Collection of American Literature. JWJMSS Johnson box 41, folder 5, Beinecke Rare Book and Manuscript Library, Yale University.

James Weldon Johnson Papers. Yale Collection of American Literature. JWJMSS Johnson box 41, folder 6, Beinecke Rare Book and Manuscript Library, Yale University.

J. W. Johnson Collection, box 1, folder 3, Special Collections Department, Robert W. Woodruff Library, Emory University.

J. W. Johnson collection, box 6, folder 1, James Weldon Johnson Collection, Special Collections Department, Robert W. Woodruff Library, Emory University.

James Weldon Johnson Papers, box 6, folder 3, Special Collections Department, Robert W. Woodruff Library, Emory University.

James Weldon Johnson Papers. Yale Collection of American Literature. JWJV3J633B49,

Yale University James Weldon Johnson Papers, Beinecke Rare Book and Manuscript Library, Yale University.

Johnson, James Weldon. "American Democracy and the Negro." Cullen Jackman Memorial Collection, box 20, folder 4. Atlanta University Center, Robert W. Woodruff Library.

Johnson, James Weldon. James Weldon Johnson to George A. Towns engagement announcement. George A. Towns Papers. Box no. 2, folder no. 12, 1909. Special Collections. Atlanta University Center, Robert W. Woodruff Library.

"Johnson Best Defensive Boxer." N.d. Jack Johnson Scrapbook, box 3, Jack Johnson Scrapbook, box 1. Manuscripts, Archives, and Rare Books Division, The Schomburg Center for Research in Black Culture.

Johnson, John Rosamond. *New York Amsterdam News,* 28 January 1938. Box 8, Irving S. Gilmore Music Library at Yale University.

Johnson, John Rosamond. John Rosamond Johnson Papers: 1905–06 B, Irving S. Gilmore Music Library, Yale University.

Johnson, John Rosamond. John Rosamond Papers, Irving S. Gilmore Music Library at Yale University box 6, folder 14.

Johnson, John Rosamond. John Rosamond Papers, Irving S. Gilmore Music Library at Yale University Box 6, folder 15.

Johnson, John Rosamond. Irving S. Gilmore Music Library at Yale University, box 8.

Johnson, John Rosamond. Photograph of John Rosamond Johnson. J. Rosamond Johnson Papers, Irving S. Gilmore Music Library at Yale University.

Johnson, John Rosamond. J. Rosamond Johnson Papers, Irving S. Gilmore Music Library at Yale University.

John Rosamond Johnson Papers, box 6, folder 15. Irving S. Gilmore Music Library, Yale University.

Johnson, John Rosamond. Paris Photo Album Photographs of Cole and Johnson European Tour. Box 3. John Rosamond Johnson Papers, MSS 21, Irving S. Gilmore Music Library, Yale University.

Johnson, J. Rosamond. J. Rosamond Johnson Papers. Irving S. Gilmore Music Library, Yale University.

A: "Teddy (A Republican Campaign Song)." MCMIV. Box no. 6, folder no. 17.

B: Libretto *Shoo Fly Regiment* 1905–1906 (J. Rosamond Johnson Papers, box 6, folder 15.

Johnson, J. Rosamond. John Rosamond Johnson Papers, MSS 21, 24–27, 1989. Box no. 6, folder no. 14. Irving S. Gilmore Music Library, Yale University.

Johnson, James Weldon. George A. Papers. Box no. 2, folder no. 12, December 30, 1896. Special Collections, Atlanta University Center, Clark Atlanta University.

Johnson, John Rosamond. 1921 photograph of John Rosamond Johnson. J. Rosamond Johnson Papers, Irving S. Gilmore Music Library at Yale University.

Johnson, James Weldon. "American Democracy and the Negro," Cullen Jackman Memorial Collection, box 20 folder 4, Atlanta University Center, Robert W. Woodruff Library.

Johnson, James Weldon. George A. Towns Papers. Box no. 2, folder no. 12, April 26, 1911. Special Collections. Atlanta University Center, Robert W. Woodruff Library.

Johnson, James Weldon. George A. Towns Papers. Box no. 2, folder no. 12, September

27, 1913. Special Collections, Atlanta University Center, Clark Atlanta University.

Johnson, James Weldon. George A. Towns Papers. Box no. 2, folder no. 12, May 14, 1914. Special Collections, Atlanta University Center, Clark Atlanta University.

Johnson, James Weldon. George A. Towns Papers. Box no. 2, folder no. 12. Special Collections. Atlanta University Center, Robert W. Woodruff Library.

Johnson, James Weldon. George A. Towns Papers. Box no. 2, folder no. 13. Special Collections. Atlanta University Center, Robert W. Woodruff Library.

Johnson, James Weldon. George A. Towns Papers. Box no. 2, folder no. 13. Special Collections. Atlanta University Center, Robert W. Woodruff Library.

Johnson, James Weldon. "What Atlanta University Has Done for Me." *The Bulletin of Atlanta University*, no. 64 (April 1895). Atlanta University Center, Robert W. Woodruff Library, Emory University.

Johnson, James Weldon. Letter to J. Rosamond Johnson. J. W. Johnson Collection. Box no. 1, folder no. 3. Special Collections Department. Robert Woodruff Library, Emory University.

Johnson, James Weldon, Johnson, J. Rosamond. J. W. Johnson Collection, box number 1, folder number 3. May 13, 1913. James Weldon Johnson Collection, Special Collections Department, Robert W. Woodruff Library, Emory University.

Johnson, James Weldon, Johnson, J. Rosamond. J. W. Johnson Collection, box number 2, folder number 12. 1916. James Weldon Johnson Collection, Special Collections Department, Robert W. Woodruff Library, Emory University.

Johnson, James Weldon, Johnson, J. Rosamond. J. W. Johnson Collection, box number 1. James Weldon Johnson correspondence to J. Rosamond Johnson, March 2, 1928. James Weldon Johnson Collection, Special Collections Department, Robert W. Woodruff Library, Emory University.

Johnson, James Weldon. J. W. Johnson Collection. "NAACP Farewell Speech," 1931, box number 2, folder number 34, James Weldon Johnson Collection, Special Collections Department, Robert W. Woodruff Library, Emory University.

Johnson, James Weldon. J. W. Johnson Collection, box 1, Special Collections Department, Robert W. Woodruff Library, Emory University.

Johnson, James Weldon. J. W. Johnson Collection, box 1, folder 3. Correspondence from James Weldon Johnson to J. Rosamond Johnson, December 15, 1913. Special Collections Department, Robert W. Woodruff Library, Emory University.

Johnson, James Weldon. "James Weldon Johnson Biography." James Weldon Johnson Collection, Fisk University Special Collections, Nashville, Tennessee.

Johnson, James Weldon. James Weldon Johnson Papers, Yale Collection of American Literature. GNK James Weldon Johnson to Series No. III Folder No. 21, Beinecke Rare Book and Manuscript Library, Yale University.

J. W. Johnson Collection. "Atlanta University Edition of Lift Every Voice and Sing." Box no. 2, folder no. 28. James Weldon Johnson Collection. Special Collections Department. Robert W. Woodruff Library, Emory University.

Johnson, James Weldon. James Weldon Johnson Collection. Beinecke Rare Book and Manuscript Library, Yale University.

A: "Lynch Laws in the South." *Lutheran Courier*. James Weldon Johnson's oldest scrapbook letter to the editor of a Lutheran periodical.

B: *The Daily American Newspaper*. J. W. Johnson, Editor and Manager. James Weldon

Johnson collection oldest scrapbook.

James Weldon Johnson Papers, JWJ zanj632+zc2, box no. 2, scrapbook 1. Yale Collection of American Literature, Beinecke Rare Book and Manuscript Library, Yale University.

C: *Lutheran Courier.* N.d. (James Weldon Johnson oldest scrapbook). James Weldon Johnson Collection. Beinecke Rare Book and Manuscript Library, Yale University. Johnson, James Weldon. "The Negro in the Theatre." XI., ZANJ632+Zc2 1: 1–3. Stella Wiley Scrapbook. James Weldon Johnson Collection. Beinecke Rare Book and Manuscript Library, Yale University.

D: Cook, Will Marion. "Black Patti Troubadours: the Best Colored Company on the Road Notes and Comments." Newspaper article about Cole and Johnson by Will Marion Cook. N.d.

E: "Seized Black Patti Music." Newspaper article about Bob Cole's financial disagreement with the Black Patti Troubadours. N.d.

F: "From Sunday School to Stage." Newspaper article about Cole and Johnson and their musical writing practices. N.d.

G: Earle, Victoria. *The Colored American Magazine.* Washington, D.C. N.d.

H: Jacksonville newspaper, which announced James Weldon Johnson's resignation from the Stanton School. N.d.

I: *The New York Age.* N.d.

J: *The New York Age.* N.d. Article about Cole and Johnson as athletes and musicians.

K: Cartoon dated 1903 with the copyright of the Judge Company of New York. References to "Under the Bamboo Tree" and Theodore Roosevelt and the Panama Canal appear.

L: "Flowers for Another Caused Trouble between a Husband and Wife." Newspaper clipping. N.d.

M: "The Theaters/Another Visit of the Octoroons Other Plays." Syracuse newspaper. N.d.

N. "The Matinee Girl." *The New York Dramatic Mirror.* N.d.

O: *(Cleveland) Plain Dealer.* 16 August 1903. Stella Wiley Scrapbook. The Negro in the Theatre: XI Scrapbook James Weldon Johnson Collection. Beinecke Rare Book and Manuscript Library, Yale University.

P: "Prima Donnas of African Blood: A Recent Development in the Musical World. Some Sing Negro Songs written by Negro Poets and set to music by Negro Composer-Appreciated by White Audiences as well as by People of their Own Race. *The Sun,* 13 November 1904. Stella Wiley Scrapbook. James Weldon Johnson Collection. Beinecke Library, Yale University. The Negro in the Theatre: XI Scrapbook

Q: Simmons, Conkling Roscoe. "Afro American in the Musical World." *The New York Age.* N.d. Stella Wiley Scrapbook. James Weldon Johnson Collection, Beinecke Rare Book and Manuscript Library, Yale University.

J. W. Johnson Collection. James Weldon Johnson and Grace Nail's Wedding Announcement. Box no. 2, folder no. 12. James Weldon Johnson Collection. Special Collections Department. Robert W. Woodruff Library, Emory University.

J. W. Johnson Collection. Scrapbook BV 6 *New York Amsterdam News,* 6 November 1976. James Weldon Johnson Collection. Special Collections Department. Robert W. Woodruff Library, Emory University.

J. W. Johnson Collection. Scrapbook BV 6 *The Crisis,* March 1977. James Weldon Johnson Collection. Special Collections Department. Robert W. Woodruff Library, Emory University.

J. W. Johnson Collection, box 1, James Weldon Johnson Collection, Special Collections Department, Robert W. Woodruff Library, Emory University.

J. W. Johnson Collection, box no. 2, folder 28. James Weldon Johnson Collection, Special Collections Department, Robert W. Woodruff Library, Emory University

J. W. Johnson Collection, box no. 2, folder no. 34. James Weldon Johnson Collection. Special Collections Department. Robert W. Woodruff Library, Emory University.

J. W. Johnson Collection, box no. 6, folder no. 1. James Weldon Johnson Collection. Special Collections Department. Robert W. Woodruff Library, Emory University.

Kansas City Star, 1895. Jewel Plummer Cobb Collection, Los Angeles, California.

Lemus, Rienzi B. Company K, Twenty-fifth Infantry. "The Enlisted Man in Action or, The Colored American Soldier in the Philippines." *The Colored American* 5 (May 1902). Special Collections. Fisk University Library, Nashville, Tennessee.

Lemus, Rienzi B. Company K, Twenty-fifth Infantry. "The Negro and the Philippines." *The Colored American* 6, no. 4 (February 1903). Special Collections. Fisk University Library, Nashville, Tennessee.

L'Engle, John C. Letter to J. W. Johnson, 1 April 1913. J. W. Johnson Collection. Box no. 1, folder no. 3. Special Collections Department. Robert W. Woodruff Library, Emory University.

Les Sports Illustrés, France (1933). Jack Johnson Scrapbook SCM90–87, box 3. Manuscripts, Archives, and Rare Books Division. The Schomburg Center for Research in Black Culture.

"Li'l Artha Panics Bears and Bulls on 'Change Visit.'" Jack Johnson Scrapbook, Manuscripts, Archives, and Rare Books Division. The Schomburg Center for Research in Black Culture.

"Life Looks Back, 28 Years Ago to the Johnson-Jeffries Fight in Reno" (1938). The Jack Johnson Scrapbook, box 3, Manuscripts, Archives, and Rare Books Division, The Schomburg Center for Research in Black Culture.

Ludlow, Helen. "An Indian Raid on Hampton Institute." *Southern Workman,* May 1878. Hampton University Archives.

Ludlow, Helen. "Hampton Indian Students at Home." *Hampton Institute 1868 to 1885: Its Work for Two Races.* Hampton: Virginia Normal School Press Print, 1885. Hampton University Archives.

Ludlow, Helen. "Incidents of Indian Life at Hampton." *The Southern Workman* 8, no. 7 (July 1879). Hampton University Archives.

Ludlow, Helen. *Southern Workman,* December 1878. Hampton University Archives.

Ludlow, Helen. *Hampton Institute 1868–1885: Its Work for the Two Races.* Hampton Virginia Normal School Press Print, 1885. Hampton University Archives.

Lynk, Miles V., M.D., *The Black Troopers or The Daring Heroism of the Negro Soldiers in the Spanish American War.* Jackson, TN: M. V. Lynk Publishing House, 1899. Manuscripts, Archives, and Rare Books Division. The Schomburg Center for Research in Black Culture.

"Majestic–Abyssinia." *The New York Dramatic Mirror,* 20 February 1906. Helen Armstead-Johnson Miscellaneous Theater Collection. Rare Books and Manuscripts Division, The Schomburg Center for Research in Black Culture.

Mamba's Daughter. J. Rosamond Johnson Actors Equity Deputy document. MSS 21 Series No. VII Folder No. 8 John Rosamond Johnson Papers, MSS 21, Irving S. Gilmore Music Library, Yale University.

Mamba's Daughter Program (1941). Box 3, series no. II folder no. 3. John Rosamond Johnson Papers, MSS 21, Irving S. Gilmore Music Library, Yale University, Yale University.

"The Man They All Dodge." N.d. Jack Johnson Scrapbook, box 3. Manuscripts, Archives, and Rare Books Division. The Schomburg Center for Research in Black Culture.

Marks, Max. Letter from Max Marks to Carriebel Plummer, July 23, 1942. Jewel Plummer Cobb Collection, Los Angeles, California.

Mayo, Lovey. "Class of 1880." Lovey A. Mayo, *Twenty-Two Year Work of the Hampton Normal and Agricultural Institute at Hampton Virginia.* Hampton Normal School Press, 1893. Hampton University Archives.

McGrath, Jim. "Old Timers Scrapbook by Jim McGrath," Los Angeles, 1942, newspaper clipping. Jack Johnson Scrapbook SCM90–87 box 1, box 2. Manuscripts, Archives, and Rare Books Division. The Schomburg Center for Research in Black Culture.

Mitchell, Abbie. "Autobiographical Notes." Mercer Cook Papers. Box no. 157–7, folder no. 29. Moorland- Spingarn Research Center, Howard University.

Mitchell, Abbie. Mercer Cook Papers. Box no. 157–7, folder no. 24, pg. 2–3. Moorland-Spingarn Research Center, Howard University.

Mitchell, Abbie. Mercer Cook Papers. Box no. 157–7, folder no. 27, pg. 1. Moorland-Spingarn Research Center, Howard University.

Mitchell, Abbie. Mercer Cook Papers, box 157–7, folder 29, pg. 2 Moorland-Spingarn Center, Howard University.

Mitchell, Abbie. Mercer Cook Papers. Box no. 157–9, folder no. 39. Moorland-Spingarn Center. Howard University.

Mitchell, Abbie. Mercer Cook Papers. Box no. 157–7, folder no. 17, pg. 9, pg. 11. Moorland-Spingarn Collection. Howard University.

Mitchell, Abbie. Mercer Cook Papers. Box no. 157–7, folder no. 17, folder 29, pg. 2 Moorland-Spingarn Research Center, Howard University.

Moore, Fred B. Letter to Booker T. Washington from Fred B. Moore, March 23, 1910, Booker T. Washington Collection MG 182 Box 1(1). The Schomburg Center for Research in Black Culture Rare Books and Manuscripts Collection.

Mortgage, White Rose Mission and Industrial Association (1930). White Rose Mission and Industrial Association Collection, SCMS 565 Manuscripts, Archives, and Rare Books Collections. The Schomburg Center for Research in Black Culture.

"Musical Compositions by Negroes." *The Bulletin of Atlanta University,* no. 140 (November 1903).

Music Settlement School Programs (1918). Box 2 Scrapbook 1, Box 1, folder II, John Rosamond Johnson Papers, MSS 21 Irving S. Gilmore Music Library, Yale University.

Music Settlement School photographs. Box 4, folder 8A, John Rosamond Johnson Papers, MSS 21 Irving S. Gilmore Music Library, Yale University.

"The Musical Courier Says." "Heifetz and Abbie Mitchell Heard in Recitals." *The New*

York Evening Journal. N.d. Mercer Cook Oversize Moorland-Spingarn Center, Howard University.

Nail, Grace, J. W. J. Collection, box 1, James Weldon Johnson Collection, Special Collections Department, Robert W. Woodruff Library, Emory University.

Nail, John. J. W. J. Johnson Collection. Wedding Announcement for Grace Nail. Box no. 2, folder no. 13. James Weldon Johnson Collection. Special Collections Department. Robert W. Woodruff Library, Emory University.

"The National Association of Colored Women's Clubs." *The Colored American* 14, no. 8 (September 1908): 498–508. Fisk University Archives.

"Negro and Filipino." *The Colored American* 1, no. 5 (1901): 334. Special Collections. Fisk University Library, Nashville, Tennessee.

Negro Actors Guild of America Booklet, 1946–1961. Lester A. Walton Papers, Entertainment Career, Coordinating Council for Negro Performers, box 6, MG 183, folder 8, Rare Books and Manuscript Division, The Schomburg Center for Research in Black Culture.

New Orleans Picayune. Jewel Plummer Cobb Collection, Los Angeles, California.

New Orleans Times Democrat. Jewel Plummer Cobb Collection, Los Angeles, California.

The New York Age, June 6, 1907. W.C. Cawley Collection, Lincoln Center Library for the Performing Arts.

The New York Dramatic Mirror, 20 February 1906. Helen Armstead-Johnson Miscellaneous Theater Collection, Rare Books and Manuscript Division, The Schomburg Center for Research in Black Culture.

New York Evening Graphic, n.d. [probably 1929]. The Jack Johnson Scrapbook, box 2, Rare Books and Manuscript Collection, The Schomburg Center for Research in Black Culture.

New York Evening Journal, 1893. Jewel Plummer Collection, Los Angeles, California.

The New Yorker, 30 September 1933. Fisk University Archives.

"News of the Theater *In Dahomey: A* Musical Comedy in Two Acts." Helen Armstead-Johnson Miscellaneous Theater Collection. Rare Books and Manuscripts Division, The Schomburg Center for Research in Black Culture.

Newspaper clipping. N.d. Bob Cole Scrapbook. Jewel Plummer Cobb Collection, Los Angeles, California.

New York Amsterdam News. J. W. Johnson Collection. Scrapbook BV 6. James Weldon Johnson Papers, Yale Collection of American Literature. The Beinecke Rare Books and Manuscript Library, Yale University.

New York Amsterdam News, January 29, 1938. J. Rosamond Johnson Papers, Irving S. Gilmore Music Library at Yale University.

New York Amsterdam News, 6 November 1976. James Weldon Johnson Collection. Special Collections Department. Robert Woodruff Library, Emory University.

The New York Dramatic Mirror. "The Matinee Girl." N.d. Lincoln Center Library for the Performing Arts.

New York Recorder, August 10, 1895. Jewell Plummer Cobb Collection, Los Angeles, California.

New York Times. "J. R. Johnson, 81, Composer, Dead." 12 November 1954. Lincoln Center Library for the Performing Arts.

"New York and the Fighting Tenth." *The Colored American* 16, no. 2 (August 1909): 123–27. Special Collections. Fisk University Library, Nashville, Tennessee.

"On the Road to Monterey." James Weldon Johnson Papers. Yale Collection of American Literature. JWJV 3J633. Beinecke Rare Book and Manuscript Library, Yale University.

"Our Appeal." White Rose Mission and Industrial Association Collection, SCMS 565 Manuscripts, Archives, and Rare Books Collections. The Schomburg Center for Research in Black Culture.

"The White Rose Home Gypsy Tea," 26 October 1952, White Rose Mission and Industrial Association Collection, SCMS 565 Manuscripts, Archives, and Rare Books Collections.

"White Rose Home Its Work and Need." N.d. White Rose Mission and Industrial Association Collection, SCMS 565 Manuscripts, Archives, and Rare Books Collections. The Schomburg Center for Research in Black Culture.

Outgrowths of Hampton Peoples Village School, Georgia Washington Box 45 G. Washington Papers *Southern Workman* folder March 1916 *Southern Workman* March 1916, pg. 199. Hampton University Archives.

Perry-Pride, Amelia. "Incidents of Indian Life at Hampton." February 1880, pg. 19. Hampton University Archives.

Perry-Pride, Amelia. Letter addressed to Dr. Frissell, President of Hampton (1901), Amelia Perry Pride Papers, Hampton University Archives.

Perry-Pride, Amelia. Letter addressed to Mrs. Cleveland, December 1892, Amelia Perry Pride Papers, Hampton University Archives.

Perry-Pride, Amelia. Letter from Amelia Perry Pride to General Armstrong dated 12 November 1888, Hampton University Archives.

Perry-Pride, Amelia. "Report on the Committee on Domestic Economy, by A.E. Pride," Amelia Perry Pride Papers, Hampton University Archives.

Photograph. Indians at Fort Marion (probably 1876). The United States Department of the Interior. National Park Service. Fort Caroline National Memorial, Timucuan Ecological and Historic Preserve. Jacksonville, Florida.

"Pioneer Teacher Ends Busy Life: Amelia Perry Pride Teacher in Negro Schools for 33 Years Dies Today." Hampton University Archives.

Plain Dealer. 1903. James Weldon Johnson Papers, Yale Collection of American Literature. Beinecke Rare Book and Manuscript Library, Yale University. Scrapbook.

Plummer, Carriebel C. "Under the Bamboo Tree: The Bob Cole Story." N.d. Jewell Plummer Cobb Collection, Los Angeles, California.

Plummer, Carriebel. Biographical Sketch, n.d. Jewell Plummer Cobb Collection, Los Angeles, California.

Plummer, Carriebel. Letter to Leigh Whipper from Carriebel Plummer, 20 February 1944, Leigh Whipper Papers, MSS 47, box 1, Manuscripts and Rare Books Collection, The Schomburg Center for Research in Black Culture.

Plummer, Carriebel C. July 21, 1942. Jewell Plummer Cobb Collection, Los Angeles, California.

Plummer, Carriebel Cole. "What's in a Song: Highlights of a Songwriter's Career as Told by His Sister." 1938. The Leigh Whipper Papers, MSS 47, Box 1, Rare books and Manuscript Collection. The Schomburg Center for Research in Black Culture.

Porgy and Bess Program (1936). Box Series No. II folder no. 4 John Rosamond Johnson Papers, MSS 21, Irving S. Gilmore Music Library, Yale University.

Pratt, R. H. R. H. Pratt Papers Series no. 1, box no. 10, folder no. 342. Outgoing letters. WAMSS S-1174 in the Western Americana Collection. Beinecke Rare Book and Manuscript Library, Yale University.

Pratt, R. H. R. H. Pratt Papers WAMSS S-1174 Series I, Box no. 10, folder 342. Outgoing letters. The Western Americana Collection, Beinecke Rare Book and Manuscript Library, Yale University.

Pratt, R. H. R. H. Pratt Papers, Pratt Incoming letters, WA MSS S-1174 Series I, Box 7, folder 235. The Western Americana Collection, Beinecke Rare Book and Manuscript Library, Yale University.

Pratt, R. H. R. H. Pratt Papers. Pratt Incoming Letters, WA MSS S-1174 Box 8, folder 296. The Western Americana Collection, Beinecke Rare Book and Manuscript Library, Yale University.

The Press, 7 August 1895. The Jewell Plummer Cobb Collection, Los Angeles, California.

R. H. Pratt Papers. Pratt WA MSS S-1174 Letter Press Bound Volume #3 1877 November 1878. The Western Americana Collection, Beinecke Rare Book and Manuscript Library, Yale University.

The Red Moon Program. The Majestic Theater, 3 May 1909. Cole and Johnson Collection. Museum of the City of New York.

Red Moon Review. W. C. Cawley Collection. Lincoln Center Library for the Performing Arts.

Rental Agreement between Abraham C. Quackenbush and The White Rose Industrial Association (1908). White Rose Mission and Industrial Association Collection, SCMS 565 Manuscripts, Archives, and Rare Books Collections. The Schomburg Center for Research in Black Culture.

"Report of the White Rose Home for the Summer of 1906." White Rose Mission and Industrial Association Collection, SCMS 565 Manuscripts, Archives, and Rare Books Collections. The Schomburg Center for Research in Black Culture.

Review of *Shoo Fly Regiment. Indianapolis Freeman,* 14 January 1908. Lincoln Center Library for the Performing Arts, New York City.

Rickard, Tex. "Tex Rickard Tells How Ring Champions Are Made." Copyright, 1925 North American Newspaper Alliance. Jack Johnson Scrapbook SCM90–87 box 2. Manuscripts, Archives, and Rare Books Division. The Schomburg Center for Research in Black Culture.

Riis, Thomas Laurence. "Black Musical Theatre in New York, 1890–1915." Ph.D. diss., University of Michigan, 1981.

Robertson, Wyndham, *Pocahontas alias Matoaka and Her Descendants through the Marriage at Jamestown, Virginia in April 1614 with John Rolfe, Gentleman.* Richmond, VA: J. W. Randolph & English Publishers and Booksellers, 1887 (CS 71 R747). Special Collections University Libraries, Virginia Tech.

Robeson, Paul. Nude photograph of Paul Robeson. Paula Marie Seniors Collection.

Robinson Locke Collection. *Indianapolis Freeman,* 1908, Europe, Cole: 1905, Lincoln Center Library for the Performing Arts, New York City.

Robinson Locke Collection. Lincoln Center Library for the Performing Arts, New York.

Roosevelt, Theodore. Letter to Washington from Theodore Roosevelt, November 5, 1906. Booker T. Washington Collection MG 182 box 1(1), The Schomburg Center for Research in Black Culture.

Roosevelt, Theodore. Letter from President Theodore Roosevelt to Booker T. Washington, November 5, 1906. Booker T. Washington Collection MG 182, box 1, Manuscripts, Archives, and Rare Books Division. The Schomburg Center for Research in Black Culture.

Rudwick, Elliott M. "Booker T. Washington's Relations with the National Association for the Advancement of Colored People." *The Journal of Negro Education* 29, no. 2 (Spring 1960). James Weldon Johnson Collection, Special Collections Department, Robert W. Woodruff Library, Emory University.

St. Joseph Radical, in Lynk, Miles V., *The Black Troopers or the Daring Heroism of the Negro Soldiers in the Spanish American War.* Jackson, TN: M.V. Lynk Publishing House, 1899, Manuscripts, Archives, and Rare books Division, The Schomburg Center for Research in Black Culture.

A: *Shoo Fly Regiment* Program, 1906.

B: *Shoo Fly Regiment* Program, 1906.

C: *Shoo Fly Regiment* Program, 1906.

D: Review of *Shoo Fly Regiment,* 27 January 1908. Ser. 33339.

E: *Shoo Fly Regiment* Program, 1906.

F: *Shoo Fly Regiment* Program, 1906.

G: *Shoo Fly Regiment* Program, 1906.

"Shoo Fly Regiment Review." *Indianapolis Freeman,* Robinson Locke Collection, The Lincoln Center Library for the Performing Arts.

"Shoo Fly Regiment Review." *Indianapolis Freeman,* January 14, 1908.

"Shoo Fly Regiment" Program. Robinson Locke Collection, The Lincoln Center Library for the Performing Arts.

Schomburg, Arturo. Letter to W. E. B. Du Bois from Arturo Schomburg, 18 November 1931. W. E. B. Du Bois Correspondence 1911–1957, MG 109 box 1, Rare Books and Manuscript Collection, Schomburg Center for Research in Black Culture.

"Shoofly Regiment Review," January 27, 1908. Robinson Locke Collection, Lincoln Center Library for the Performing Art, New York [n.pag., uncited clipping].

Sissle, Noble (president of the Negro's Actor's Guild of America, Inc.). "Highlights of the Negro's Contribution in the Development of Music and Theatre in the American Scene," 3–4. Leigh Whipper Papers, MS 47, box 1, The Schomburg Center for Research in Black Culture.

Smith, Hudsey. "Partial History of White Rose Mission and Industrial Association," SCMS 565 Manuscripts, Archives, and Rare Books Collections. The Schomburg Center for Research in Black Culture.

The Southern Workman 7, no. 5 (May 1878). Hampton University Archives.

The Southern Workman, October 1880. Hampton University Archives.

The Southern Workman, December 1882. Hampton University Archives.

The Southern Workman 21, no. 7 (July 1892). Hampton University Archives.

The Southern Workman. "William Jones Obituary." May 1909. Hampton University Archives.

The Southern Workman, March 1916. Hampton University Archives.

The Sun. 1904, Stella Wiley Scrapbook.

State Department, February 26, 1906. J. W. Johnson Collection, box 1, folder number 2. Special Collections Department, Robert W. Woodruff Library, Emory University.

St. Louis Dispatch Post, March 25, 1907. Lincoln Center Library for the Performing Arts, New York.

Talks and Thoughts. October [1895]. Hampton University Archives.

Talks and Thoughts 3, no. 6 (November 1888): 1895. Hampton University Archives.

Talks and Thoughts of the Indian Students. Editors: Sam Defond, Rebecca Mazakute, Richard Powless; Manager: Thomas Sloan. Vol. 3, no. 5 (September 1888): 2. Hampton University Archives

Talks and Thoughts 18, no. 7 (January 1904), no. 7 (January 1904). Hampton University Archives.

Theater Magazine "*Shoo Fly Regiment,*" September 1907. Billy Rose Collection. Lincoln Center Library for the Performing Arts, New York.

Tingsey, Joseph Willard. "Indians and Blacks Together: An Experiment in BiRacial Education at Hampton Institute (1878–1923)." Ph.D. diss., Teachers College, Columbia University, 1978. Hampton University Archives.

Toledo Blade. Review of *Shoo Fly Regiment,* 11 December 1906. Robinson Locke Collection. The Lincoln Center Library for the Performing Arts, New York City.

Toledo Blade, 14 December 1908. Robinson Locke Collection. The Lincoln Center Library for the Performing Arts, New York City.

Toun ke uh. R. H. Pratt Papers, Pratt Incoming letters, WA MSS S-1174 box 8, folder 296. The Western Americana Collection, Beinecke Rare Book and Manuscript Library, Yale University.

Towns, George A. George A. Towns Papers. Box no. 2, folder no. 12, December 30, 1896. Special Collections, Atlanta University Center, Clark Atlanta University.

Towns, George A. George A. Towns Papers. Box no. 2, folder no. 12, April 26, 1911. Special Collections, Atlanta University Center, Clark Atlanta University.

"*A Trip to Coontown*" Program, The Grand Opera House, 1898. Theater Collection, the Museum of the City of New York.

True, George. "In the Women's Behalf," *The Colored American* 9, no. 19 (10 August 1901). Fisk University Archives.

The Tuskegee Student, 18 April 1903. Mercer Cook Papers, Box 157–7, Mercer Cook Oversize Moorland-Spingarn Center, Howard University.

Variety. 1937. Lincoln Center Library for the Performing Arts, New York.

Walker, Sarah. Fort Berthold, Dakota" (Hidasta) Sarah Walker. "Incidents of Indian Life at Hampton." February 1880. Hampton University Archives.

Walker, Ada Overton. "Colored Men and Women on the Stage." *The Colored American* 9, no 4 (June 1905): 571. Special Collections, Fisk University Library, Nashville Tennessee.

True, George. "In the Women's Behalf," *The Colored American* 9, no. 19 (10 August 1901). Fisk University Archives.

Walton, Lester. "The Death of Bob Cole." *The New York Age,* 10 August 1911. Stella Wiley Scrapbook. James Weldon Johnson Collection. The Negro in the Theatre: XI Scrapbook. Beinecke Rare Book and Manuscript Library, Yale University.

Walton, Lester A. "Music and the Stage." *The Colored American* 14, no. 7 (June 1908).

Fisk University Special Collections.

Walton, Lester A. "Music and the Stage." *The Colored American* 14, no. 8 (September 1908). Fisk University Special Collections.

Washington, Booker T. Letter to William E. Curtis from Booker T. Washington, January 24, 1905, Booker T. Washington Collection MG 182, box 1, Manuscripts, Archives, and Rare Books Division. The Schomburg Center for Research in Black Culture.

Washington, Booker T. Letter to Francis J. Garrison from Booker T. Washington, February 27, 1900. Booker T. Washington Collection MG 182, box 1, Manuscripts, Archives, and Rare Books Division. The Schomburg Center for Research in Black Culture.

Washington, Booker T. Letter to Emily Howland from Booker T. Washington, October 15, 1900. Booker T. Washington Collection MG 182, box 1, Manuscripts, Archives, and Rare Books Division. The Schomburg Center for Research in Black Culture.

Washington, Booker T. Letter to Francis J. Garrison from Booker T. Washington, August 31, 1903. Booker T. Washington Collection MG 182, box 1, Manuscripts, Archives, and Rare Books Division. The Schomburg Center for Research in Black Culture.

Washington, Booker T. Letter to Francis J. Garrison from Booker T. Washington, November 25, 1905. Booker T. Washington Collection MG 182, box 1(1), Correspondence 1905–1913. Rare Books and Manuscript Collection. The Schomburg Center for Research in Black Culture.

Washington, Booker T. Letter to Francis J. Garrison from Booker T. Washington, October 2, 1906. Booker T. Washington Collection MG 182, box 1, Manuscripts, Archives, and Rare Books Division. The Schomburg Center for Research in Black Culture.

Washington, Booker T. Letter to Francis Garrison from Booker T. Washington, December 3, 1906. Booker T. Washington Collection MG 182, box 1, Manuscripts, Archives, and Rare Books Division. The Schomburg Center for Research in Black Culture.

Washington, Booker T. Letter to Francis Garrison, from Booker T. Washington, January 10, 1906. Booker T. Washington Collection MG 182, box 1, Manuscripts, Archives, and Rare Books Division. The Schomburg Center for Research in Black Culture.

Washington, Booker T. "Magnanimity of the Negro toward The Indian." *The Southern Workman* , October 1880. Hampton, Virginia. Hampton University Archives.

Washington, Booker T. "From Mr. Washington's Jubilee Address." *The Bulletin of Atlanta University,* January 1898. Atlanta University Center, Robert W. Woodruff Library, Clark Atlanta University.

Washington, Georgiana. Georgiana Washington's School Records. Hampton University Archives.

Washington, Georgiana. "A Resident Graduate's Fifteen Years at Hampton" by Georgiana Washington, Class of '82." *Southern Workman* 21, no. 7 (July 1892): 116–17. (Essay read at the Hampton Anniversary, May 19, 1892) Hampton University Archives.

Washington, Mrs. Booker T. (Margaret James Murray). "Practical Help Leaflet No. 1. Hampton University Archives.

Whipper, Leigh. "The Negro Actor's Guild Scoreboard." Leigh Whipper Papers. Box no.114–5, folder no.125, pg. 71. Moorland-Spingarn Research Center, Howard University. Leigh Whipper Papers, Moorland Spingarn Center, Howard University.

"The White Rose Home Gypsy Tea Program," 26 October 1952, White Rose Mission and Industrial Association Collection, SCMS 565 Manuscripts, Archives and Rare

Books Collection. The Schomburg Center for Research in Black Culture.

White Rose Industrial Association. "An Appeal to Our Friends," April 6, 1910. White Rose Mission and Industrial Association Collection, SCMS 565 Manuscripts, Archives, and Rare Books Collections. The Schomburg Center for Research in Black Culture.

"White Rose Home: Its Work and Need," probably 1898–1899, White Rose Mission and Industrial Association Collection, SCMS 565 Manuscripts, Archives and Rare Books Collection. The Schomburg Center for Research in Black Culture.

"The White Rose Mission and Industrial Association, Inc. aka "The White Rose Home." White Rose Mission and Industrial Association Collection, SCMS 565 Manuscripts, Archives, and Rare Books Collection. The Schomburg Center for Research in Black Culture.

White, Walter. "James Weldon Johnson: A Biographical Sketch by Walter White, Exec Secy., NAACP." Box no. 1, file no. 1, Special Collections, Fisk University Library, Nashville, Tennessee.

Wiley, Stella. N.d. A. Stella Wiley Scrapbook. James Weldon Johnson Papers, Yale Collection of American Literature, Beinecke Rare Book and Manuscript Library, Yale University. The Negro in the Theatre: XI Scrapbook.

Wiley, Stella. N.d. B. Stella Wiley Scrapbook. James Weldon Johnson Papers, Yale Collection of American Literature, Beinecke Rare Book and Manuscript Library, Yale University. The Negro in the Theatre: XI Scrapbook.

Wiley, Stella. N.d. C. Stella Wiley Scrapbook. James Weldon Johnson Papers, Yale Collection of American Literature, Beinecke Rare Book and Manuscript Library, Yale University. The Negro in the Theatre: XI Scrapbook.

Wiley, Stella. N.d. C. Stella Wiley Scrapbook. James Weldon Johnson Papers, Yale Collection of American Literature, Beinecke Rare Book and Manuscript Library, Yale University. The Negro in the Theatre: XI Scrapbook.

Wiley, Stella. N.d. E. Stella Wiley Scrapbook. James Weldon Johnson Papers, Yale Collection of American Literature, Beinecke Rare Book and Manuscript Library, Yale University. The Negro in the Theatre: XI Scrapbook.

Wiley, Stella. N.d. E. Crouse: 1935, pg. 21, Box 7 Scrapbook 1930s miscellaneous Scrapbook 1936, James Weldon Johnson Papers, JWJ zanj632+zc2, Yale Collection of American Literature, Beinecke Rare Book and Manuscript Library. Box 2, Scrapbook 1 The Stage 1905–1910 JWJ zanj632+zc2, Yale Collection of American Literature, Beinecke Rare Book and Manuscript Library, Yale University.

Wiley, Stella. N.d. F. *The World.* Stella Wiley Scrapbook. James Weldon Johnson Papers, Yale Collection of American Literature, Beinecke Rare Book and Manuscript Library, Yale University. The Negro in the Theatre: XI Scrapbook.

Wiley, Stella. N.d. G. *The World.* Stella Wiley Scrapbook. James Weldon Johnson Papers, Yale Collection of American Literature, Beinecke Rare Book and Manuscript Library, Yale University. The Negro in the Theatre: XI Scrapbook.

Wiley, Stella. 1903. H. *The World.* Stella Wiley Scrapbook. James Weldon Johnson Papers, Yale Collection of American Literature, Beinecke Rare Book and Manuscript Library, Yale University. The Negro in the Theatre: XI Scrapbook.

"William Jones Obituary." *Southern Workman,* May 1909. Hampton University Archives.

Wilson, George Quizzes. "Johnson Resigns from Azores as Wilson Protest." *The New York Age,* 9 October 1913. James Weldon Johnson Collection. Beinecke Rare Book and Manuscript Library, Yale University.

The World, September 8, 1895. Jewel Plummer Cobb Collection, Los Angeles, California.

The World, 1896. Jewel Plummer Cobb Collection, Los Angeles, California.

The World, n.d. James Weldon Johnson Papers, Yale Collection of American Literature. Beinecke Rare Book and Manuscript Library, Yale University. Scrapbook.

The Young Americans Program (1946). Series II box no. 3, folder no. 5 John Rosamond Johnson Papers, MSS 21, Irving S. Gilmore Music Library, Yale University.

Journals, Periodicals, and Magazines

"Abbie Mitchell, Actress, Is Dead; Singer was Widow of Composer." *The New York Times,* 20 March 1960. Mercer Cook Papers, Moorland-Spingarn Research Center, Howard University.

"Abbie Mitchell Goes to Perpetual Summertime." *New York Amsterdam News,* 23 March 1960. Mercer Cook Papers, Moorland-Spingarn Research Center, Howard University.

"Ada Overton Walker as Salome." *The New York Times,* 24 May 1908.

"Ada Overton Walker in Salome Dance." *The New York Times,* 29 June 1912.

Anderson, Michael. "How a Landmark Lesson in Being Black Made its Way to Broadway." *The New York Times,* 7 March 1999.

Brome, George O. "Geraldine? She Isn't So Flip." *The New York Times,* 3 September 1972.

"Burns and Johnson Ready for Battle." *New York Times,* 21 December 1908.

"Burns Favorite over Negro Fighter. *New York Times,* 25 December 1908.

"Business Man Urges Jeffries." *New York Times,* 31 January 1909.

Cole, Bob. "Mr. Cole's Letter and Thanks," under Walton's Music and Stage, *The New York Age,* 25 June 1908.

The Colored American 8, no. 4 (29 December 1900): 10.

"Dahomey on Broadway," *The New York Times,* 19 February 1903.

"Danger to Nation in Race Prejudice: Speakers at Republican Club Luncheon Point Out Evils of Such a Feeling." *The New York Times,* 5 May 1911.

"The Draft, Cassius vs. Army." *New York Times,* 30 April 1967, 190.

Du Bois, W. E. B. "Industrial Education—Will It Solve the Negro Problem. Answered Each Month by the Greatest Thinkers of the Black Race. VII." *The Colored American* 7, no. 5 (May) 1904.

Du Bois, W. E. B. "The Training of Negroes For Social Power." *The Colored American Magazine* 7, no. 5 (May 1904).

Durbin, William. *Yale Daily News,* 20 February 1999.

Eisenberg, Bernard. "Only for the Bourgeois? James Weldon Johnson and the NAACP, 1916–1930." *Phylon* 43, no. 2 (2nd Quarter, 1982): 110–24.

Ellinghaus, Katherine. "Assimilation by Marriage: White Women and Native American Men at Hampton Institute, 1878–1923." *The Virginia Magazine of History and Biography* 108, no. 3 (2000): 55–77.

Entertainment Weekly. May 20, 2002.

Europe, James Reese. "The Clef Club Orchestra at Manhattan Casino." *The New York*

Age, 11 August 1910.

"Few Novelties in the Waning Theatrical Season." *The New York Times*, 2 May 1909.

Fraden, Rena. "A National Theater that Never Was." *American Visions: A History of African American Theater Production, Performance, and Drama in the United States* 9, no. 5 (October–November 1994): 26.

Gibson, C.D. "A New York Day," *Scribners Magazine*, July–December 1898.

Gibson, C.D. "Evening." *Scribners Magazine*, July–December 1898.

"G.O.P. The First Annual Souvenir Liberty Ball of the Colored Republican Club of the City of New York will be given at Tammany Hall . . . " *The New York Age*, February 22, 1906.

Guardian [London], 15 September 2007. "On this day: September 15 1927: Scarf Strangles Dancer Isadora Duncan in Car."

Holloway, Lynette. "Media; Lil' Kim Surprises Critics as CD Catches On." *New York Times*, March 17, 2003.

"Hon. Charles W. Anderson Elaborately Banqueted." *The New York Age*, February 6, 1908.

Hopkins, Pauline. "Famous Men of the Negro Race. Booker T. Washington." *The Colored American* 3, no. 6 (October 1901).

Hultgren, Mary Lou, and Paulette Fairbanks Molin. *To Lead and to Serve: American Indian Education at Hampton Institute 1878–1923*. The Virginia Foundation for the Humanities, 1989. Hampton University Archives.

"I Outclassed Him, Johnson Declares." *New York Times*, 5 July 1910.

"Jeffries to Sell Ranch: Then He Will Go Into Vaudeville—May Fight Again." *New York Times*, 31 January 1909.

"Jes Like White Folks–A Negro Operetta." *The New York Times*, 24 June 1900.

Johnson, James Weldon. "Attacks Harvard on the Negro Question: J. Weldon Johnson Denounces the Exclusion of Negroes from its Dormitories. The Historical New York Times," January 13, 1923.

"Johnson's Victory Caused No Surprise: New Champion Never Doubted This Issue from the Beginning." *New York Times*, 27 December 1908.

"Johnson Wins; Police Stop Fight." *New York Times*, 26 December 1908.

The Journal, March 1, 1896. Jewel Plummer Cobb Collection, Los Angeles, California.

Martin, John. "Isadora Duncan Danced Like a 'Puritanical Pagan.'" *New York Times* 8 January 1928. ProQuest Historical Newspapers The New York Times (1851–2004).

Millner, Denene. "Minorities Are Landing Fewer Stage Roles: Awards Are Nice, But Blacks Still Wait in Wings." *New York Daily News*, October 25, 2000.

Mitchell, Elvis. "How Out of It Can You Be? Here's Going All the Way. Review of *Bringing Down the House*." *The New York Times*. March 7, 2003.

Morrison, Toni. "What the Black Woman Thinks about Women's Lib." *The New York Times*, August 22, 1971, SM 14.

"Negro Company Has Season at Majestic" [*His Honor the Barber*]. *The New York Times*, 9 May 1911.

The New York Times, 26 December 1908.

Perry, Warren R. "Archeology as Community Service: The African Burial Ground Project," in New York City, 1999, 3. http://www.stpt.usf.edu-jsokolov/burialgr.htm.

"Racial Integrity or 'Race Suicide': Virginia's Eugenic Movement, W. E. B. Du Bois and the Work of Walter A. Plecker." *Negro History Bulletin*, April–September 1999.

"'Red Moon' Uninteresting." *The New York Times,* 4 May 1909.

"Remnants of a Racist Past." *Miami Times,* 17 September 1998.

"Review of *Shoo Fly Regiment.*" *Indianapolis Freeman,* 23 March 1907.

Review of *Bringing Down the House. New York Times* 7 March 2003.

"Robert Cole A Suicide." *The New York Times,* 3 August 1911.

"Robert L. Hargous Dead." *The New York Times,* 26 November 1905.

Roosevelt, Theodore, "Calvary at Santiago," *Scribners Magazine,* 25 (April 1899).

Roosevelt, Theodore. "The Rough Riders." *Scribners Magazine* 25 (January–June 1899).

"Roosevelt to Colored Men." *The New York Times,* October 15, 1898.

Saneh, Kelefa. "Fashion Tip in Rap for Brooklyn Girls." *The New York Times,* May 23, 2003.

"A Royal Coon." *The New York Age,* 13 April 1911.

Scarponi, Diane. *South Coast Today,* 19 November 2000.

"The Smart Set." *The New York Age,* 4 May 1911.

"Study Says White Families' Wealth Advantage Has Grown." *The New York Times,* Monday, 18 October 2004.

Sullivan, John L. "Johnson wins in 15 Rounds; Jeffries Weak." *New York Times,* 5 July 1910.

"Sullivan Offers $75,000." *New York Times,* 21 January 1909."Theodore Drury's Grand Opera Company at 14th Street Theater." *The New York Age,* 12 March 1908.

"Theodore Drury's Grand Opera Company at 14th Street Theater." *TheNew York Age,* 12 March 1908.

"Theodore Drury's Grand Opera Company at 14th Street Theater." *TheNew York Age,* 5 April 1906.

True, George. "In the Woman's Behalf. "*The Colored American* 9, no. 19, 10 (August 1901).

"Two More Challenge Johnson." *The New York Times,* December 30, 1908.

"Tuskegee Institute: Report of the Seventeenth Annual Session of the Tuskegee Negro Conference." *The New York Age,* Thursday, March 5, 1908.

"What is Doing in Society." *The New York Times,* 3 May 1903.

"Williams and Walker *Bandanna Land,* Ada Overton Walker as SALOME." *The New York Times,* 24 August 1908.

"Will Mercer Cook." *The New York Times,* 7 October 1987.

Wiznia, Mark. *Yale Daily News,* 17 November 2000.

Journals

Adams, David Wallace. "Education in Hues: Red and Black at Hampton Institute, 1878–1893." *South Atlantic Quarterly* 76 (Winter 1977).

Bourke, John G. *Journal of American Folk-lore* 7, no. 25 (April–June, 1894).

The Crisis, no 1 (November 1910).

Du Bois, W. E. B. "The Criteria of Negro Art." *The Crisis* 32, no. 6 (October 1920).

Du Bois, W. E. B. "The Drama among Black Folk." *The Crisis* 12, no. 4 (August 1916).

Forbes, Camille F. "Dancing with Racial Feet: Bert Williams and the Performance of Blackness." *Theater Journal* 56, no. 4 (December 2004).

Krasner, David. "The Mirror up to Nature: Modernist Aesthetics and Racial Authenticity in African American Theatre, 1895–1900." *Theatre History Studies* 16 (June 1996):

117–41.

Lemons, Stanley J. "Black Stereotypes as Reflected in Popular Culture, 1880–1920." *American Quarterly* 29, no. 1 (Spring 1977): 102–16.

Newman, Richard. "'The Brightest Star': Aida Overton Walker in the Age of Ragtime and Cakewalk." *Prospects: An Annual of American Cultural Studies,* vol. 18 (New York University Press, 1993).

"Racial Integrity or 'Race Suicide': Virginia's Eugenic Movement, W. E. B. Du Bois and the Work of Walter A. Plecker." *Negro History Bulletin,* April–September 1999.

Roberts, Hilda. *Journal of American Folklore* 40, no. 156 (April–June1927).

Robinson, Edward A. "The Pekin: The Genesis of American Black Theater." *Black American Literature Forum* 16, no. 4, Black Theatre Issue (Winter 1982).

Robinson, Michael, and Frank Schubert. "David Fagen: An Afro American Rebel in the Philippines, 1899–1901." *Pacific Historical Review* (1975): 70.

Rothman, Joshua D. "'Notorious in the Neighborhood': An Interracial Family in Early National and Antebellum Virginia." *Journal of Southern History* 67, no. 1 (February 2001).

Seniors, Paula Marie. "Ada Overton Walker, Abbie Mitchell and the Gibson Girl: Reconstructing African American Womanhood." *The International Journal of Africana Studies* 13, issue 2 (Fall 2007): 38–67.

Seniors, Paula Marie. "Cole and Johnson's *The Red Moon* (1908–1910): Reimagining African American and Native American Female Education at Hampton Institute." *The Journal of African American History* 93, no. 1 (Winter 2008): 21–35.

Solard, Alain. "Myth and Narrative Fiction in *Cane: 'Blood Burning Moon.'* *Callaou,* no. 25, Recent Essays from Europe: A Special Issue (Autumn 1985).

Storey, Moorefield. "Athens and Brownsville." *Crisis* 1, no. 1 (November 1910).

Webb, Barbara L. "The Black Dandyism of George Walker: A Case Study in Genealogical Method." *The Drama Review* 45, no. 4 (Winter 2001): 9.

Microfilm

"Along The Color Line." The *Crisis* 1, no. 1 (10 November 1910).

Cole, Bob. "Mr. Cole's Letter and Thanks," under Walton's "Music and the Stage." *The New York Age,* 25 June 1908.

Cole and Johnson in 'The Red Moon.'" *The New York Age,* 26 August 1909.

Cole and Johnson. *The New York Age,* December 24, 1908.

Cole and Johnson. *The New York Age,* December 24, 1910.

Coleridge, S. Taylor. "The Negro Problem in America." *New York Age* 21, no. 49 (September 3, 1908).

"Drury Grand Opera Co. The Secret and Benevolent Organization of Greater New York." *New York Age,* March 29, 1906.

"Drury Grand Opera Company Week beginning May 28 1906." *The New York Age,* 29 March 1906.

Freeman, 22 May 1909.

Howard, J. D. *Indianapolis Freeman,* 1909–1910.

Hunter, Charles A. "Music and the Stage," edited by Lester A. Walton. *The New York Age,* September 10, 1908.

Hunter, Charles A. "Rays from 'The Red Moon,'" from "Music and the Stage," edited by Lester A. Walton. *The New Age,* 14 January 1909.

Hunter, Charles A. "Red Moon Rays," from "Music and the Stage," edited by Lester A. Walton. *The New Age,* 21 January 1909.

C. A. H. [Charles A. Hunter]. *The New York Age,* 1 April 1909.

Hunter, Charles A. *New York Age,* 10 February 1910, 6.

Hunter, Charles A. "Rays from 'The Red Moon,'" from "Music and the Stage," edited by Lester A. Walton. *The New York Age,* 18 February 1909.

Hunter, Charles A. "Rays from 'The Red Moon,'" from "Music and the Stage," edited by Lester A. Walton. *The New York Age,* 18 March 1909.

Hunter, Charles A. "Red Moon Rays," from "Music and the Stage," edited by Lester A. Walton. *The New York Age,* 25 March 1909.

Hunter, Charles A. "Rays from 'The Red Moon,'" from "Music and the Stage," edited by Lester A. Walton. *The New York Age,* 21 October 1909.

Hunter, Charles A. "Music and the Stage," edited by Lester A. Walton. *The New Age,* 28 January 1910.

"Johnson Resigns from Consular Service." *The New York Age,* 25 September 1913.

The New York Age. Thursday, 18 May 1905.

"Music and the Stage." *The New York Age,* 5 April 1906.

The New York Age, 18 May 1905.

The New York Age, 5 April 6 1906.

The New York Age, 1 June 1906.

The New York Age, 26 July 1906.

The New York Age, 18 October 1906.

The New York Age, 4 May 1911.

"Shoo Fly Regiment." *The New York Age,* 6 June 1907.

The New York Age, May 1907. The Schomburg Center for Research in Black Culture, New York City.

The New York Age, 6 June 1907. The Schomburg Center for Research in Black Culture, New York City.

The New York Age, 24 December 1908.

The New York Age, "Special Announcement: Benefit. Ada Overton Walker on Behalf of White Rose Industrial Association Home for Colored Working Girls," 7 May 1908.

The New York Age, "St. Philip's Parish Home Given by Ada Overton Walker at Grand Central Palace." *The New York Age,* 8 April 1909.

"Notes From the *Shoo Fly Regiment.*" *The New York Age,* 12 March 1908.

Pankey, Theodore. "How to Make Good." *The New York Age,* 18 March 1909.

Pankey, Theodore. "The Need of Negro Theatre." *The New York Age,* 5 May 1910.

The Red Moon Advertisement. "Presenting Real Negro Plays of Real Negro Life." *The New York Age,* December 1910.

The New York Age, "Their Newest Hit: Young Authors Produce Another Musical Comedy," 26 July 1906.

"Review of *Shoo Fly Regiment.*" *The New York Age,* 23 August 1906. The Schomburg Center for Research in Black Culture, New York City.

"Review of *Shoo Fly Regiment.*" Walton, Lester A. "Music and the Stage." *The New York Age,* 10 January 1908.

Russell, Sylvester. "Cole Gives Private Lecture." *The Indianapolis Freeman,* 7 October 1905.

"St. Philip's Parish Home Given by Ada Overton Walker at Grand Central Palace." *The New York Age,* 8 April 1909.

"The Sixth Bi-ennial Convention Held in Brooklyn Ends with Great Enthusiasm." *New York Age* 21, no. 49 (3 September 1908).

"Special Announcement: Benefit Ada Overton Walker on Behalf of White Rose Industrial Home for Colored Working Girls." *The New York Age,* 7 May 1908.

"Their Newest Hit Young Authors Produce Another Musical Comedy." *The New York Age,* 26 July 1906.

Walker, George. "Bert and Me and Them." *The New York Age* 22, no. 13.

Walton, Lester A. "Abyssinia's Star Actress." *The Indianapolis Freeman,* 6 October 1906.

Walton, Lester A. "Art Knows No Color Line, Says the Brooklyn Eagle." *The New York Age,* 30 April 1908.

Walton, Lester A. "Music and the Stage." *The New York Age,* 12 March 1908.

Walton, Lester A. "Bandanna Land." *New York Age,* 6 February 1908.

Walton, Lester A. "The Benefit." *The New York Age,* 8 June 1908.

Walton, Lester A., "The Benefit." *The New York Age,* 11 June 1908.

Walton, Lester A. "Music and the Stage." *The New York Age,* 6 August 1908.

Walton, Lester A. "Music and the Stage." *The New York Age,* 18 March 1908.

Walton, Lester A. "Music and the Stage." *The New York Age,* 7 May 1908.

Walton, Lester A. "Music and the Stage." *The New York Age,* 14 May 1908.

Walton, Lester A. "Music and the Stage." *The New York Age,* 19 May 1908.

Walton, Lester A. "Music and the Stage." *The New York Age,* 21 May 1908.

Walton, Lester A. "Music and the Stage." *The New York Age,* 28 May 1908.

Walton, Lester A. "Music and the Stage." *The New York Age,* 4 June 1908.

Walton, Lester A. "Music and the Stage." *The New York Age,* 11 June 1908.

Walton, Lester A. "Music and the Stage." *The New York Age,* 30 July 1908.

Walton, Lester A. "Music and the Stage." *The New York Age,* 20 August 1908.

Walton, Lester A. "Music and the Stage." *The New York Age,* 26 August 1908.

Walton, Lester A. "Music and the Stage." *The New York Age,* 27 August 1908.

Walton, Lester A. "Music and the Stage." *The New York Age,* 3 September 1908.

Walton, Lester A. "Music and the Stage." *The New York Age,* 10 September 1908

Walton, Lester A. "Music and the Stage," *The New York Age,* 14 January 1909.

Walton, Lester A. "Music and the Stage." *The New York Age,* 28 January 1909.

Walton, Lester A. "Music and the Stage." *The New York Age,* 14 June 1909.

Walton, Lester A. "Music and the Stage." *The New York Age,* 26 August 1909.

Walton, Lester A. "Music and the Stage." *The New York Age,* 10 January 1910.

Walton, Lester A. "Music and the Stage." *The New York Age,* 10 February 1910.

Walton, Lester A. "Music and the Stage." *The New York Age,* 17 February 1910.

Walton, Lester A. "Music and the Stage." *The New York Age,* 31 March 1910.

Walton, Lester A. "Music and the Stage." *The New York Age,* 12 May 1910.

Walton, Lester A. "Music and the Stage." *The New York Age,* 19 May 1910.

Walton, Lester A. "Music and the Stage." *The New York Age,* 26 May 1910.

Walton, Lester A. "Music and the Stage." *The New York Age,* 14 July 1910.

Walton, Lester A. "Music and the Stage." *The New York Age,* 3 August 1911.

Walton, Lester A. "Music and the Stage." *The New York Age,* 10 August 1911.

Walton, Lester A. *The New York Age,* 6 August 1908.

Walton, Lester A. *The New York Age,* 28 January 1909.

Walton, Lester A. "Red Moon Improves with Age." *The New York Age,* 2 September 1909.

White, Charles Cameron. "The Negro in Musical Europe." *The New York Age,* 24 December 1908.

Lectures, Interviews, and Art Exhibits

Beauchamp-Byrd, Mora, Curator. "Body and Soul: Paul Robeson Race and Representation." The Robert and Sallie Brown Gallery and Museum, The Sonja Haynes Stone Center for Black Culture and History, University of North Carolina, Chapel Hill.

Cobb, Jewell Plummer. Jewell Plummer Cobb Interviews. 2003.

Cobb, Jewell Plummer. Jewell Plummer Cobb Interview, 24 April 2003, Los Angeles, California.

Franklin, John Hope. John Hope Franklin Plenary Session, The Association for the Study of African American Life and History, Atlanta, Georgia, Fall 2006.

Gutierrez, Ramon. "Graduate Seminar." A lecture at the University of California San Diego, Fall 1998.

Internet Sources

gibsongirls.com

"James Weldon Johnson Honored." *New York Times,* May 15, 1931. ProQuest Historical Newspapers, New York Times.

"Negro Poet Gets Prize." *New York Times,* December 28, 1933, 17. ProQuest Historical Newspapers, New York Times.

Theatre.com:11/25/00.

Recordings

Litefoot. "The Life and Times." *Litefoot Redvolution.* Seattle, WA: Limited Release, Collectors Edition, 2005.

Litefoot, "Seein' Red." *Litefoot Redvolution.* Seattle, WA: Limited Release, Collectors Edition, 2005.

Litefoot. "Tribal Boogie." *Litefoot Redvolution.* Seattle, WA: Limited Release, Collectors Edition, 2005.

Litefoot, "Stereotipik." *The Messenger.* Seattle, WA: Red Vinyl Records, 2002.

Films

John Waters, Leslie Dixon, Mark O'Donnell, and Thomas Meehan. *Hairspray,* 2007.

Jerry Lewis, Bill Richmond, David Sheffield, Barry W. Blaustein, Tom Shadyac, and Steve Oederkerk. *The Nutty Professor,* 1996.

Warner Brothers. *Whoopee,* 1931.

INDEX

Aaron, Hank, African American masculinity-African American hypermasculine übermensch, 50

Abyssinia (1906), 74, 179

Abolition Democracy. *See* Radical Reconstruction

Abyssinia (Williams and Walker), 74; Ada Overton Walker, 179, 232 n68

Ada Girls, 114

"Ada My Sweet Potato," 114

Adams, David Wallace, Hampton students and, 108; on Native American boarding school experience, 108

African Americans: African American wealth accumulation, 92, 100; African American Club Women, 21, 31; *The Red Moon* and 162, 167, 168, 174; African American female uplift, 68, 75, 159–73; African American soldiers, Civil War, Sergeant William Carney, 63; Tenth Regiment 101; Indian Wars, 53; Spanish-American War, 5, 44, 50, 51–57, 59, 90, 187; Battle of San Juan Hill, 52, 53, 55, 63, 208 n139; Siboney heroism of black soldiers, 54; Ninth Calvary, 53; Tenth Regiment 101; Tenth Calvary, 51, 53, 57, 63, 208 n138; Twenty-Fourth Infantry, 54–55; African American Soldiers and Haitian Revolutionary Soldiers, 55, 69, 90; Afro-Cuban Commissioned Officers; 55–56; fight for Black commissioned officers, 56; Roosevelt negative image of Black soldiers, 54, 56; Black soldiers and Jim Crow racism, 57, 68–69

African Burial Ground: discovery of, 84; and the reality of the Pickanninny, 84; web site for, 211n65

"Afro-American Notes" (Fortune), 167

Akron, Ohio, 68

Alexie, Sherman, 132; *Reservation Blues* (1995) and, 132

Alhambra Theater, 93

Ali, Muhammad, 187; black masculinity and, 50, 187; image of African American masculinity, 50

Allen, Robert, creation of bourgeoisie self, 81

All Stock Theatre Company, formation of, 14, 16, 178

"All's Well That Ends Well" (Gibson), Gibson Girls and, 170

All Stock Theatre Company, formation of, 14, 16

Along This Way, Johnson autobiographical work, 230n38

"American Democracy and the Negro" (Johnson), 59

American Gangster (2007), hyper-

Overton Walker and, 178; African American culture in plays, 34; African American masculinity and, 45; Americanization program and, 103; buying of *New York Age,* 228 n17; castigation of Roosevelt and, 58–59; daughter's education and, 230 n40; effects of discarding one's culture and, 110–111; Hampton students and, 109–110; ideology of black economic nationalism and, 16, 69; Jack Johnson and, 47; letter to Francis Garrison from, 197 n94; progressive approach to gender equality, 42; *"The Red Moon Rays"* and, 161–62; reelection of Roosevelt and, 60; reversals of Abolition Democracy and, 30; song for, 23; teaching methods and, 104; uplift ideology and, 51, 104, 114, 127, 170, 186

Washington, George, 34; on being attacked, 57

Washington, Georgiana, black Hampton teacher of Native American girls: club woman, 167; death of, 217 n77; education, 104, 105; familial relations with Native American students, 112; Georgiana Washington High School, 218 n77; Hampton teacher and, 107–108, 113–114, 167; People's Village School, 113; teaching Native American girls domestic science, 107–108, 110

Washington Post, saving of Rough Riders and, 53

Webb, Margo: description of pickaninny dancing and, 128; stage "Picks" and, 84

Weldon, Isabella Thomas, 11

West, Nancy, interracial marriages and, 151

"What's in a Song," Cole autobiography, 13

The Wheeling Daily News, review of *Shoo Fly Regiment,* 41

Whipper, Leigh: attitudes toward female stage performers, 83; Creole shows and, 81

Whipple, Henry, Native American reform advocate, 102

White, Allon: black female stereotypes and, 27; burlesque during the early 1900s and, 81

White, Clarence Cameron; review of Arthur Talbot and, 139

white masculinity, 52, 53, 57; rewrite history of Spanish-American War, 52, 89; negative image of Black soldiers, 54, 56, 59; fear of black, Filipino, Native American and Cuban insurrection, 68; Booker T. Washington on, 44; connect Spanish-American War with Indian Wars, 57; strenuous life discourse, 58; Roosevelt on Filipinos, Chinese, and Puerto Ricans, 205 n71

White Rose Home, 73; anti-Semitism and, 225 n234; Victoria Earle Matthews and, 226 n237

White Rose Industrial Home for Colored Girls (also White Rose Mission and the Travelers Aid Society): African and African American history course taught at, 73; *Intimate Apparel* and 152; charity work of Abbie Mitchell and Ada Overton Walker for, 167, 181, 184, 227 n254; protection of Black women from Jewish men/anti-semitism, 226 n234; and Great Migration and safe affordable housing, 226 n237

White Rose Mission and the Travelers Aid Society, 167

white supremacy: threat of lynching and, 7; withdrawal of federal troops from the South and, 58

Whitman, Mabel, stage "Picks" and, 84

Whitman sisters: Gibson Girls and, 161; performances of, 74–75

Whoopee, film production of, 144

Wilder, C. B., 100

Wiley, Stella, 6, 13; marriage and, 163; tobacco advertisement and, 179